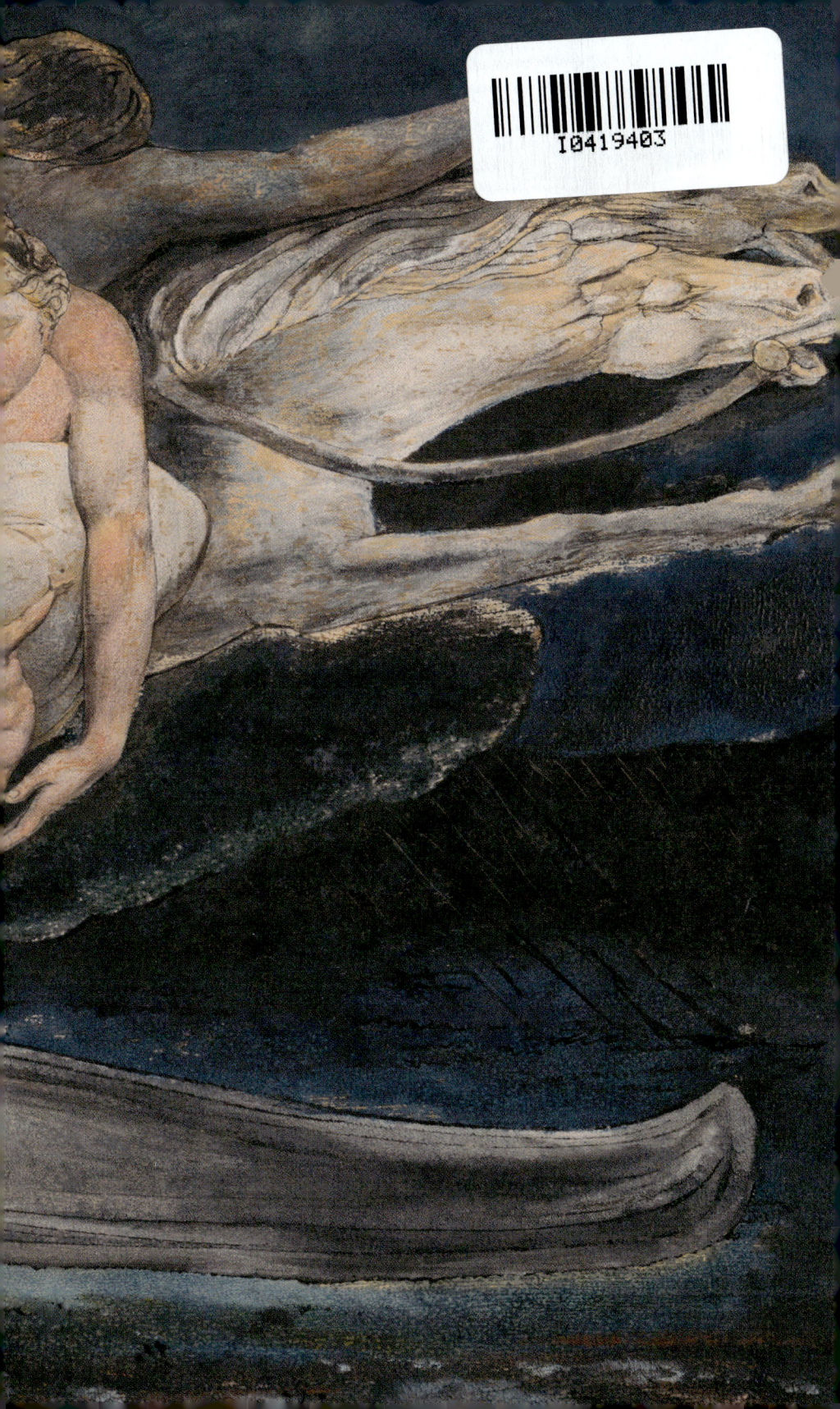

WILLIAM BLAKE
AND THE SEA MONSTERS
OF LOVE

WILLIAM BLAKE AND THE SEA MONSTERS OF LOVE

PHILIP HOARE

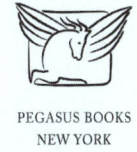

PEGASUS BOOKS
NEW YORK

WILLIAM BLAKE AND THE SEA MONSTERS OF LOVE

Pegasus Books, Ltd.
148 West 37th Street, 13th Floor
New York, NY 10018

First Pegasus Books cloth edition April 2025

ISBN: 978-1-63936-847-1

10 9 8 7 6 5 4 3 2 1

Printed in the United States of America
Distributed by Simon & Schuster
www.pegasusbooks.com

For Christina and Katherine

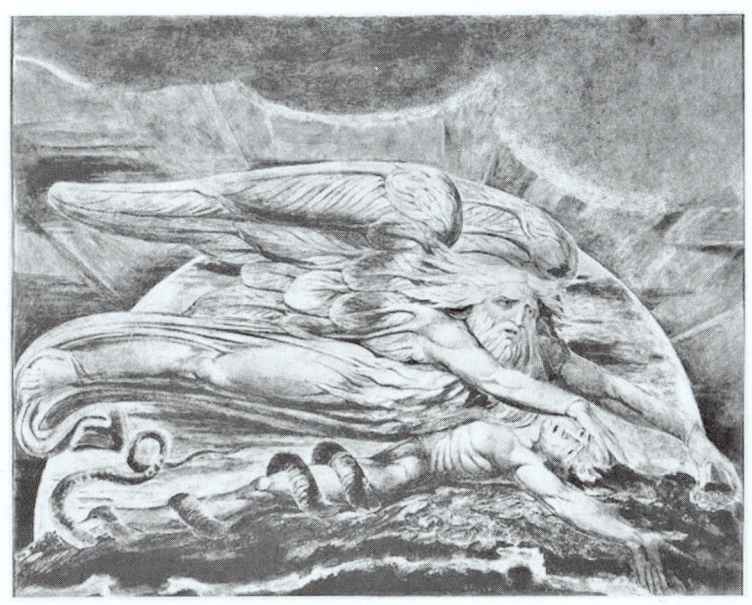

Adam lies sprawled on the shore. The rocks are washed green by the sea. His new-born body is spreadeagled, arms outstretched. He doesn't know what he's for. There's a serpent already wrapped round his legs. The pain of creation is on his face. You can see it in the whites of his eyes.

God flies over the abyss, bestowing the sentence of humanity, his holy hand held over Adam's fiery head. After all the storms and the planets and the seas, all the whales and the birds and the trees, he decided to make this beautiful creature out of earth and water to hold dominion over them all.

God's wings—who made them? who took the picture?— sprout out of his shoulders like a cape. He's a swan or a dove. The new dawn is fading, there are dark clouds in the rosy sky. God knows what he has done. The anguish is in his face. It's too late. There's no escape. Adam is already abandoned. Stranded, on the rocks.

Something the tide left behind.

5.15 am, winter dark. A bright white light moves across the sky as I swim out to sea. Low down but high up, it slides steadily from Jupiter in the west towards Orion in the east. Over the distant refinery, with all its towers and silos.

Ahead of it is a smaller light, like a companion star, travelling at the same speed. In between them is a scrap of white cloud, an abstract ice-cream swirl. It is lit by the bright light which shines on it with the intensity of a stadium at night.

I watch it for a little while. Everything takes place in silence, except for the sound of me in the sea. Slowly, steadily, the starry entourage moves across the sky, then sinks into a low bank of cloud. It doesn't come out the other side.

It wasn't a plane or a helicopter or a drone; it glowed from inside and made no noise. Too low for a satellite, too slow for a meteorite. I am used to seeing all these things. Fireballs and airliners carrying everyone and all their dreams. Some days I see more stars than I see people.

I felt sad when it had gone. I wondered if I should have seen it at all. It was like standing in a crowd but being the only one to notice the dead queen being carried past your eyes. The parade passed me by. I wanted it to stop for me.

But I also wanted to be left alone.

Maybe it's the sea that's done this to me, spoilt me for the ordinariness of life. Maybe it was a mistake to give myself up to it, to the exclusion of everything else. It was a deliberate experiment that I undertook, willingly. To be unmoored by the sea, leaving me attached to no one and nothing else. Forever unsure of myself, the way you feel when you see yourself in the mirror in the hall and wonder who you are.

I pull up to the junction on my bike. Music from vehicles leaks out. The dual carriageway runs either side of me, a race that no one ever wins. On the corner is an abandoned petrol station, its forecourt empty. Under the asphalt is the house where I was born, bulldozed to make room for this road so that I could ride by. Its ghost lingers in the only things I can remember: its strange name, Akaba, and the bedroom where I came out, cracked open to the sky.

The lights change and I ride over the bridge where they once hung a shark upside down. The river runs down to the sea, past rubbish dumps and back gardens. No one notices me. I'm a secret agent of myself, the way dogs keep themselves to themselves with barely a hint of melancholy, only a furrowed brow or the lift of an eye.

I race to get back to the sea in the dark. It's still there. So still I could slide across it. So black it becomes like the sky. It's my faith. I place all my trust in it. If only we knew what God looked like, we'd know what to expect. It makes time stop, or even go into reverse. The sea is the perfectible me, my bones out of a cuttlefish. It turns me inside out. There's no alternative. Either you're in or you're out. The refinery spouts tongues of fire, roaring, something loosed from below. I've been all over the world.

This is the most exciting place I know.

————

A long time ago I was with a good friend driving south in his car. For some reason we started talking about William Blake. We were having an argument about something else.

You don't know anything about him, my friend said, quite fiercely and randomly.

I remember looking up at the green hills that had been cut open, slashed to bare chalk to create a bypass so that we could drive by.

The silence stretched on. I wondered if I should tell him to stop the car and let me get out.

But then I thought, inside, how remarkable it was, that we should be arguing about a man who had died two hundred years ago. I knew, secretly, that my friend was right. I didn't know anything about Blake.

So I started to write this book.

In the summer of 1971, Marc Balet, a young student from the Rhode Island School of Design, came to England in search of diversion and, perhaps, a job. Someone told him Derek Jarman was the Andy Warhol of London.

That sounded good to me, Balet said. So he rang the number he'd been given, and Derek Jarman picked up.

The artist was living in a derelict warehouse on the south bank of the Thames. A decaying part of the city where huge buildings lay empty, their blank windows eyes open to the sky. At night he slept in a greenhouse he'd put up in the cavernous space as if it might rain indoors. He sipped his tea by an open door three floors up, looking down on the river below as it gathered speed on its way to the sea. I distrust all figures of authority, including the artist, he said.

In those days you could walk into those places and live in them. The city was still porous, unpatrolled, unCCTV'd. You could move through it unseen. Parts of it were still blackened, still wrecked by history. Glamorous, dead or alive. Dark corners where something used to be, made wild by destruction. Rising and falling with the river that wound through them like a big fat snake.

5

Black timbers in the mud. The rot of the city, the flow of the river, what it left in its wake. The way we knew things would always be and secretly hoped they would not.

Marc Balet came armed with a Super 8 cine camera. It was a magical invention from America: part roving eye, part ray gun. He lent it to Jarman, who began collecting glittering glimpses of his friends, fabulous figures seen among the ruins on the decayed riverside. People I wanted to be, people who would soon fade away. He was filming the future from his past. His promised land. Something sensational and strange. Unnatural and natural, the way that he was.

The following summer, our handsome young American from Connecticut joined Jarman and his friends on a trip to the Isle of Purbeck in Dorset on the far coast of England. There was the artist Andrew Logan; Bente and Ernst Lohse, two architect students from Denmark; and a young man named Ian whom they may have picked up in a club, no one knows. They drove down in an old car, intending to spend the night together in a cave overlooking the sea, ready to make their film the next day.

I remember the rocks and sea, Andrew Logan told me, and the excitement of making a movie. He'd brought along a wind-up gramophone and one record to play on it: Land of Hope and Glory.

It was a big adventure and they were ready for it. It was fifty years ago and things were different then. People looked different, behaved differently. Even the sky looked different. We were an earlier edition, a different shape, a different species. There were fewer things to wear, to use, abuse and destroy, but just as much to worry about. Always waiting for what would happen next. We had no choice.

That year the miners and dockers went on strike, one million people were unemployed and two states of emergency were declared, one after the other. It seemed like the aftershock of something yet to happen.

Everything was unresolved, beyond our control. Power was cut off for nine hours a day. We ate and read by flickering candlelight, as if we'd gone underground, like miners ourselves. Life was rationed, work a three-day week. We were living through a play for today. It played out on our screens, like the video films we saw.

Fourteen British citizens shot by British troops in a British city, devices exploding in the Tower of London and Aldershot and a Birmingham pub. In Dublin, the British embassy was set on fire. An alien in a telephone box told us we had five years left and my father went to work in the factory, clocking in and clocking out. On Saturdays we went to the seaside and the sun shone as we climbed out of our shiny blue second-hand car. The sea, so dark and so bright.

That January a blueprint for survival had been published in a magazine. Its authors hoped it would lead to the dawn of a new age in which Man will learn to live with the rest of Nature rather than against it.

An examination of the relevant information available has impressed upon us the extreme gravity of the global situation today, they told us. For, if current trends are allowed to persist, the breakdown of society and the irreversible disruption of the life-support systems on this planet, possibly by the end of the century, certainly within the lifetimes of our children, are inevitable.

Governments, and ours is no exception, are either refusing to face the relevant facts, or are briefing their scientists in such a way that their seriousness is played down. Whatever the reasons, no corrective measures of any consequence are being undertaken.

When the manifesto appeared as a book later that year, it sold three-quarters of a million copies and no one took any notice.

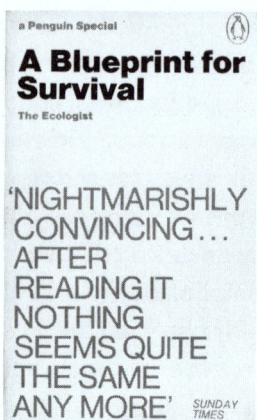

Jarman and his crew stumble down the hill to the shore and install themselves in a cave for the night, a deep slit left behind by an abandoned quarry, like a landing strip set high on the cliff. In the nineteen-thirties, the artist Paul Nash had seen this rocky shore as an iron wall of grey-black blocks. The seas are vicious here, he said, and there is no more bitter war between land and water than is fought along Winspit Cliff and Dancing Ledge, where the waves can be seen leaping in eccentric frenzy.

Even to stand there is an effort. The world seems upside down. There could be anything hiding in those caves, anything washed in on the waves below. It all seems so exciting, as far from London as it is possible to be.

They're not terribly well prepared. Their communal bed is a foam mattress laid on the rocks. They eat fish and chips by candlelight. The mist closes in and the waves send plumes of spray in the air. Darkness falls and it feels like the cave is gradually closing in on them.

It's not working out the way they planned.

At one am Balet hands out a ritual dose of sleeping pills; his mother sends them every month from Connecticut. The drug swoons and soothes them and they fall into a fitful sleep. Their rocky bed doesn't seem so cold and hard after all.

They emerge the next morning at dawn, only to find that the sea has gone. They wanted to make a film, about a drowned sailor lying in a rock pool, a siren sitting by him, floating her silver-paper boats. No sound, no script, just lovely bodies on rocks washed green by the sea as a masked god looked on.

But the fog has rolled in and the seagulls are crying. They have been defeated by the elements that had lured them to this elemental place.

Their film will have to wait till the stormy weather has blown over and the skies have cleared.

Derek Jarman was thirty years old. A dark and handsome man with a posh voice, shyer than you might suppose, given all the films he would make, hiding behind his camera. He'd spent his boyhood in Dorset in the years just after the war. His father served there as an air force officer before they were posted abroad. He remembered the sixpence offered for the first one to see Corfe Castle as they drove down to Swanage Bay; the way he would remember his family through the home movies his father had made. His mother, a dark-haired, beautiful woman, moving like a film star against a background of barracks and rose-filled gardens, from southern England to Rome and Karachi.

Growing up on military bases and in boarding schools, Jarman felt extremely isolated, he said. It was a world of men and machines. But he also remembered riding pillion on a motorbike with his hands dug deep in the pockets of a handsome rider as they sped through the countryside, like the peculiar man his father talked about meeting in the air force before the war, who lived nearby in a strange forester's cottage and rode his own motorbike down the same lanes. And he remembered being ordered into the sea off Dancing Ledge as a schoolboy, as though the water were a punishment rather than something to be enjoyed.

In the autumn of 1963, Jarman went up to London to the Slade School of Art. It sounded like a quarry itself, which wasn't surprising, since it was made of Dorset stone and had ammonites embedded in its porticoes and steps. At the Slade he painted scenes of strange spores and pyramids and chimneys floating on the horizon. They were sets for an imagined opera or a picnic on the beach, and he gave them titles that deliberately echoed those used by Paul Nash, who had been at the Slade fifty years before.

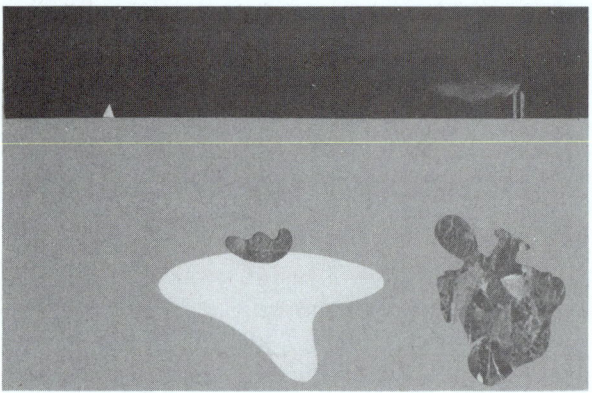

He was painting the last of England and he took it all very seriously. Art was an ordination, not a pastime to him. The chief means of communication with the dead, as Auden said. England was still a twilight place, Jarman said. He was quoting Nash, and thinking of the way that the future leaked out of the past.

In the late nineteen-thirties, when he was investigating southern England as if he were a foreign explorer in a land yet to be civilised, Nash came upon a pair of monsters in a field masquerading as dead trees.

They could only have one equivalent, he decided. In his mind's eye their whitened, upended stumps and limbs turned into The sightlesse Couriers of the Ayre in William Blake's haunting colour print Pity, created in 1795, an extraordinary image that acted more like a film or a photograph, beyond anything else of its time. Even now we're not quite sure how it was made. But it spoke to Nash as though Blake was standing by his side.

A pair of horses career blindly through the stormy night bearing angels on their backs. Hair and manes merge in the wind, as if streaming in an ocean current. They glow in the dark; you can hear them whinny and roar. Below, on a mossy bed, a young woman lies supine as her baby leaps into the arms of the pale riders above. It's a terrifying scene: the outstretched whiteness of the wild horses set against the vulnerability of the mother and the doll-like child. The picture was Blake's response to a quote from Macbeth. No one else would think that an occasion for a picture, said Robbie Ross.

Endpaper

> And pity, like a naked new-born babe,
> Striding the blast, or heaven's cherubin, hors'd
> Upon the sightless couriers of the air,
> Shall blow the horrid deed in every eye

Perhaps it was an echo of a later episode in the play in which we are told, in a casual aside, that the king's horses, beauteous and swift, have turned wild and are eating each other.

Whatever was going on in Blake's head, it made a big impression on Nash. Blind and 'blake', he said, playing with words—blake meaning both black and white—felled by the storm, the horses had crashed to earth. Now they lay splayed out on their backs in the grass, their five or six legs jerked out with epileptic force.

Both trees were bleached to a ghastly pallor wherever the bark had broken and fallen away, he said. They had been struck by lightning and violently pulled out of the earth. Now they were alive with a new power, it seemed to him, existing on another plane, not made visible by the complicated machinery of spiritualism, but so much with us, he said, that they had to be photographed in full sunlight. There was an urgency to this encounter, and the artist felt sure that it would not be wise to stay in the field after a certain hour.

Not that he had any choice. As his companion walked towards him, her steel-blue hair and white face and red lips somehow animating the scene like a movie, a farmer's boy appeared behind her, telling them off for spreading foot-and-mouth disease.

What if the field itself became infected, Nash thought; what if its monsters might rise up in madness and stampede? He saw their whitened stumps as jawbones or scars, as holes that opened up in the earth and clouds that cluttered the sky. That the landscape itself could be fearful, the way that the shells had burst over his head in the flooded wastes of the Western Front.

As he and his companion left, the grass seemed to undulate like a river and the field had no beginning or end. Land and sea and sky were filled with foreboding: he believed that people or places or objects could have a mysterious charge which could not be analysed. But just as his friend, the sculptor Barbara Hepworth, declared there was no landscape without a human figure, so all this shuffling around of things and ideas was as much about the artist's own body as it was a search for a lost Eden or a mission to the stars.

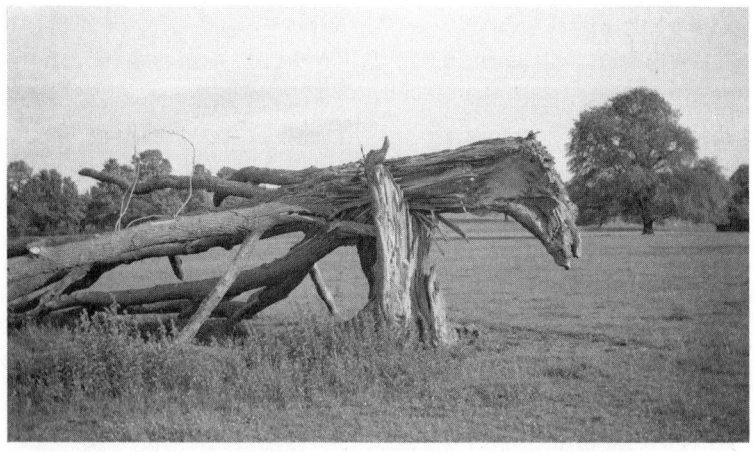

Nash was obsessed with the sense of places and the power they could imply. Five years before, in the summer of 1933, he had visited Avebury and its standing stones for the first time; they had been waiting for him. They had mass and power, like those nightmare horse-trees; they hardly seemed to stand still for all the four thousand years they'd spent stuck in the ground. Spotted with black and orange lichen, some were upright, others fallen in the grass.

At first, he could only stare at them. Who made them? What were they for? He was in an excitable mood. He had just founded UNIT I which he described, in a letter to *The Times*, as a method of concentrating certain individual forces as a hard defence, a compact wall against the tide. It was a new movement, bright and modern, like sans-serif lettering on a whitewashed wall, and Nash's roll call of collaborators—Barbara Hepworth, Ben Nicholson, Edward Burra, Edward Wadsworth and Henry Moore among them—constituted an advance guard of the avant garde.

Unit One may be said to stand for the expression of a truly contemporary spirit, for that thing which is recognised as peculiarly *of to-day*, he told *The Times*. He hastened to add that this was just an update of the Pre-Raphaelite Brotherhood, making his apologies in an English manner, the way American friends tell me I always qualify my statements as if only suggesting that we might agree, the way I murmur, mmm, mmm, when other people speak.

But Nash was not meek or mild. He was determined, calling for decisive action in difficult times. To some his new gang sounded a bit too Soviet, too collective. Yet the readers who harrumphed over their morning paper and the way the world was going might have been surprised to discover that, shortly after issuing his declaration of modestly revolutionary intent, the artist was standing in a field in southern England, communing with one of the oldest expressions of human culture in the land.

Embedded at Avebury, Nash found a vast site of spectacular installations, sprawling for acres like some long-lost festival still going on, only all the people had gone. The place was filled with megaliths and mounds; deep ditches and ramparts surrounded the village, stitched with stones like knots in a wound. Avenues led to the horizon and dark clumps of trees on distant hills. Anything could happen there, in the stillness of summer with the larks rising. The stones gave you a choice: you could analyse them scientifically, or take them as romantic emblems of a past that only existed in your head.

Avebury, a buried prayer. A defiant place, difficult to negotiate or understand. There are no vantage points from which it may be seen completely, said Nikolaus Pevsner's rigorous twentieth-century guidebook; the broken stones and rugged forms suggest a work of nature rather than the hand of man.

This field was stripped back, exposed, carved out like the bombsite it nearly became: not long after Nash's visit the air force identified it as a possible practice site, its stones as unexploded ordnance. In the distance, a green pyramid cast its gigantic shadow. At his feet, a white convolvulus flower spiralled up to the sun. The land was so old it became modern, like a digital watch on an ancient wrist. An exotic place, older than England, barely English at all.

Transported, Nash took out his new Kodak and, using it as an extension of his eye, he framed the stones against the sky, combining two images in one by not winding the film on. It was as if he had blinked, not believing what he saw the first time. New shapes emerged, rolling aright, rocks as ghosts as leviathans.

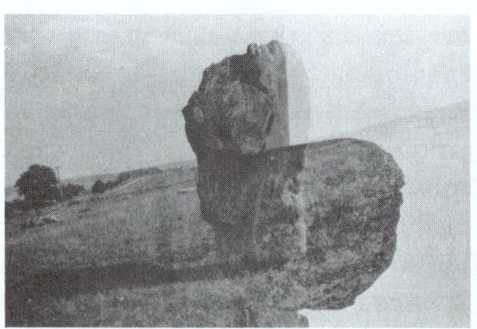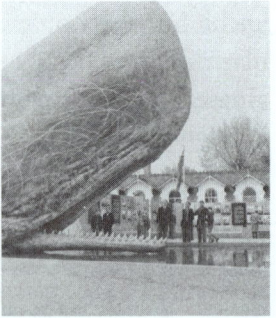

Forty years later, in the summer of 1973, Jarman stood in the same field, filming through a yellow filter as if he were visiting another planet. You can almost hear him breathe. The heat peels away a veneer. No fog or seagulls here. The sky turns sulphur with neolithic sunlight and the stones radiate an ancient heat. Or maybe their glow was more nuclear and Jarman's journey to Avebury was a protest march.

His fingers fall over the lens like an errant cameraman catching the microphone in the shot. We feel the view in his hands, juddering with power. He could hardly keep still himself. He'd ring his friends at three am to tell them his latest idea. He talked quickly all the time. He had a teenage energy, like a light going on and off. That's why he made films: they were art that didn't stop. They could rewind or fast-forward time: pictures stilled, then started again.

Trees and roads go nowhere and a lorry drives past as if lost. A row of children sit on a wall, dangling their feet, like the children in a TV series filmed here during the drought of 1976 when the earth began to crack. The stones emit an energy to the touch and a teenage boy jokes about his crashed bike becoming a display in the Tate, a wry reference to Carl Andre's one hundred and twenty bricks laid in a grid on the gallery floor.

Nash had painted the stones as icebergs, floating on a polar sea; Jarman turned them into flint-like dorsal fins. The stones resisted interpretation, impassively, declining to tell their stories. They were modern works of art, four thousand years old. I'm sure lots of people complained at the time. PI II

Jarman walks through the circles as if he might come out somewhere completely different on the other side. Cattle stand about in fields, livestock already dead by the time he screens his film. He sees the stones the way Blake saw them, even though he never came here. Blake had only seen them in books, but to him they were as real as anything else. He had read William Stukeley's account of 1743, which suggested that Avebury's avenues represented a snake transmitted through its circles, brooding there like Ovid's fables of serpents of extravagant bulk sowing their teeth.

It was a grand conceit of monstrous molars pushing up through the turf or a pagan cathedral stuck at the bottom of the sea. Even as Stukeley pointed at the stones with his stick, the villagers were pulling them down or burying them as the devil's work; they boasted of being stone-killers and even burned them, using the rubble to build their own homes.

But Blake had another explanation for these indefinite Druid rocks, as he called them. To him, Avebury and nearby Stonehenge were the building blocks of a new Jerusalem; Solomon's temple as rebuilt by ancient Britons in the form of a curling serpent and Plac'd in the order of the stars, and he drew them like a cartoon next to his verse in which he imagined those feet in ancient time walking upon England's mountains green. He sent Stukeley's prancing horse and scampering dog through an arched portal, past a teetering stone, while a crescent moon hung in the starry sky like a tattoo on an angel's thigh. All things would begin and end here, he declared. These stones were not dead but living emblems of his imaginary Albion, a place free of tyranny, slavery, and hate.

Pl II

As a boy I felt those same stones and trees around me. I was the last of four brothers and all the mannish genes had run out by the time they got to me. I was small and bony; I could fit into places they couldn't. In my school-grey shorts and green jumper, I rolled down grassy embankments of defunct forts.

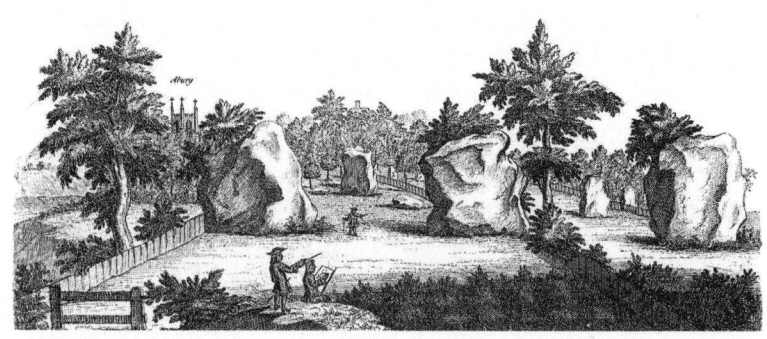

I put my arms round shiny beech trees and stuck my face in emerald moss.

I didn't care what anyone thought. I felt that the trees and the stones owned me, that I was inside them and they were inside me. I knew they were alive and alone, like me. I felt their bulging trunks and weathered bulks as if they might burst open, the way I felt the sea, thrashing about, beyond me, fearful and out of reach.

I knew that nothing was necessarily true, and I was afraid of everything and everyone, including my family and especially myself. I was a foreign body, waiting for something or somewhere else.

My family were not well off, and London was a foreign place. We'd driven there once or twice. It seemed like an impossible journey, even though it was only seventy miles away. We felt our father's anxiety. He couldn't wait to get out again. It might have been another country where anything could go wrong and probably would. As if once we were in its grasp, we'd never escape. Soon I would take the train there, crossing the river at night, its black waters swirling below. I was being pulled into its orbit. The dark city, made darker by its endless suburbs reaching into the night. I knew I'd have to wade through them in an emergency.

But it was a good place to hide, too. No one could see you there.

The Isle of Purbeck is not an island at all, but it acts like one, a bulging peninsula held out to sea, made of limestone and chalk, layers of rocks rucked up like fossilised waves. Manor houses and Stone Age barrows compete with maggoty sheep and tanks roaring over the plains. Hares quiver in the fields, staring straight ahead, declining to meet your eyes. The land is colonised and abandoned at the same time, caught between military occupation and second homes where the bins are never put out. To get here you must pass the broken stumps of Corfe Castle sticking out of a huge mound, standing guard over the shores beyond.

The whole place is a wreck. A geological map redrawn by a wayward child. Purbeck was once connected to the distant Isle of Wight before the river Solent became a new sea, circa 5000 BC, and washed away all the wolves and the bears. Now only the chalk stacks of the Needles and Old Harry Rocks remain either side of the sea as silent witnesses to the flood. They peer across the water, the way the captains of the two island ferries that shuttle to and fro cast lovelorn glances at one another from their wheelhouses, but never meet.

All of this might be romantic if it weren't for the violence. It's amazing people come here at all. Purbeck ends abruptly at the sea, unannounced by cliffs three hundred feet high, so huge you'd think they'd shout. The land just stops, then drops away. It's too far to fall, and there's no one to catch you if you did. There are no friendly sandy beaches, no signs to say you're welcome or to warn you that this is where England runs out. No ice cream parlours. But there's a stone chapel where they said prayers for the souls of sailors lost at sea seven centuries ago. Down below, a solitary seal swims in the cove.

There's not another soul to be seen: apart from a watcher in the coastguard station, scanning the sea hour after hour, as if hypnotised. Peter says he'd do that job, any day. He comes from Ireland; he likes the emptiness ahead. It's easy to forget how many people lived and worked here. That this was one big factory of workers and martyrs and thieves.

Walking through the field, we find bits of stuff thrown up by the plough. Peter picks up a green-glazed shard of medieval tile; Clara finds a chip from a flint tool. She shows me how it contained the blade inside, like a flick knife. My prize doesn't require her archaeologist's eyes. It is a military button, stamped FIRMIN LONDON on the back. I imagine it popping off a soldier's flies.

There's a sudden burst of rock music from a dip in the

downs. In a hidden quarry they're still grinding out the stone; we might have passed by if it weren't for Van Halen. London was stolen from here. Purbeck paved its streets; Portland supplied its great offices of state. It's a wonder Dorset didn't tip into the sea.

Purbeck: such a perfect name, like tern, or gown, or wrack. It sounds like an empty place to contend with, a blank space on the map. Like its rocks, its people too were dug up and taken away. To the west, Portland dangles out to sea. A port land, a peninsula of a peninsula, a tied island, only tentatively connected to the mainland by its endless shingle beach and its own brutal history.

In the seventeenth century, Portland's stone was a monarchical monopoly; daylight robbery by royal decree. The quarries were managed by Inigo Jones, surveyor to James I and architect of his dreams. His job description: flattery on a monumental scale. For *The Masque of Blackness*, written by bricklayer-turned-dramatist Ben Jonson and performed in the Banqueting Hall on Twelfth Night, 1605, Jones created an entire ocean in Whitehall, as if the river were under royal orders to rise up and flood the place.

For one night only, Jones built a forty-foot-square stage raised four feet off the floor; the space below concealed machines and the men operating them. The opening scene was stupendous. An artificiall sea was seene to shoote forth, as if it flowed to the land, raysed with waves, which seemed to move. The scene was filled with tritons, mermaids, sea horses and six huge sea monsters, all caught in dazzling light the like of which the audience had never seen in their lives.

It was a glorious delusion, of course. The power of the masque was its disguise, a theatre of complicity. For *The Masque of Blackness*, Anne of Denmark, James's queen, demanded that the cast (with herself as its star) should impersonate Africans, like the Black servants she kept as a mark of her exotic taste. The radiance of the king, so these daughters of Niger were promised, would turn their darkness white, like their palace. The queen's retainers looked on from the wings, watching white people impersonating themselves.

It was hardly an orderly affair anyway. They were all amateurs, members of the royal family or the aristocracy mumbling their lines and missing their cues, wanting only to look good for their lovers or further their petitions to the king. At the end there was an unseemly rush for the refreshments, sending the tables sprawling. Meanwhile Francis Bacon, the cleverest and queerest man in all England, got on with marvelling at Inigo Jones's colours: white, carnation and a kind of sea-water green, Bacon wrote, dipping his quill in sepia ink; and ouches or spangs, as they are of no great cost, so they are of most glory, he said.

And all of this spangled glory, all this pantomime, all that money vanishing in a flash, was set against the theatrical backdrop of Whitehall, named after its white stone. When *The Tempest* was first performed there, in 1611, Shakespeare's watery play became a mirror and a parody of transience. And when the old Banqueting Hall burned down, another rose in its place, for which an entire new pier was built at Portland, to export the stone to London. Out of stone came sly deceptions, like toads. When James I asked Jones to explain Stonehenge, the architect went and camped at the site and reported back that the Romans, not the Druids, were responsible for it. It was another attempt to appease his monarch's imperial delusions.

From Portland's cliffs and Purbeck's ledges, the royal thievery gathered pace, through fire and plague and war. Portland stone was seen fit for the new empire; it was no coincidence that it was white. They'd even call one quarry Albion, as though all England had been dug out of there. Portland and Purbeck furnished the charter'd streets of London, by the charter'd Thames, where, in his *Visions of the Daughters of Albion*, Blake would hear

> . . . like waves on a desart shore
> The voice of slaves beneath the sun,
> and children bought with money

as if the city might sink under its stony sins. A prison was built on Portland and its inmates set to work the stone to make more cells for themselves. The colonial project replicated itself everywhere like a bacterium. Portland as Dorset's Van Diemen's Land; an isle of strange noises where they put all the devils. The convicts wore masks: not to perform in or to protect them from the dust that could turn their lungs to stone, but to save the state from its shame.

It was complete control; no one left to blame. By the time Paul Nash arrived a century later, the inmates had built a whole new gaol for themselves. Behind the cliffs, with their cloven rock and massive platforms, as Nash wrote in 1936, the derricks of the quarry seemed to stride against the sky. The earth yawned and gave up gigantic white blocks. In his eyes, they were as strange as Avebury's megaliths or the electric pylons that were just beginning to march over the land.

Portland is still a frightening place, fit to drag you into the sea. It looked like the end of the world to me. It was there that I saw my first cetaceans: a pod of dolphins passing by, framed in my father's military-scale binoculars, which he kept in a leather case slung over his shoulder; he always wore shorts on holiday.

As I held the lumpy lenses to my eyes, I saw the grey fins like discs of rolling light. Indeliable, remote, they had nothing to do with me. They made me tremendously sad, as if I knew this would be my first and last sight of such creatures. They would soon be gone for ever, leaving me alone; the way that I lay in bed at night and wondered what it would be like when my mother was dead.

God lived in a box on the altar, dinosaurs walked out of library books. I saw ghosts and the future. A bus to the other side of town scared me. When you're young you always feel you are being stared at, as if nobody had anything better to do. Early one Saturday morning we arrived in Swanage and I realised I was still wearing my bedroom slippers. They dared me to step outside.

No one will notice, my mother told me, but I knew they would.

In his unfinished memoir, which he called *Genius Loci*, Paul Nash would write about a place he had discovered when he was a boy. It was somewhere in Kensington Gardens and it was strangely beautiful and excitingly unsafe, he said.

He couldn't define this unsafe space—it had no boundaries—but he felt it. It was more like the sea, he said, whose tides determine its confines, now encroaching, now receding on its shores. It was between trees, in some grass, he remembered, on the other side of the broad road that divided the park from the Serpentine.

We all had places like that, even if it was just a den under the table or a cupboard under the stairs or under the stars. In-between spaces, the way stairs and halls and stars are, away from the adult world. Nash's place, in the middle of London yet in a wilderness, seemed to quiver through a timeless, filmy haze.

It was where he started to think about how inanimate things might have an inner life. The way he would draw trees in dark clumps on top of a hill, or willowy beings swaying over a pond. The way he would draw the wind itself, in parallel lines like a speeding car in a cartoon, while swifts carved arcs out of the sky and the little pool below stayed still despite being filled with medieval fishes.

He might have been waiting for a boy to emerge from the water into another mysterious world.

In those days I knew nothing of the sea, Nash said, or the magical implication of aerial perspective across miles of shore where waves alternately devour and restore the land.

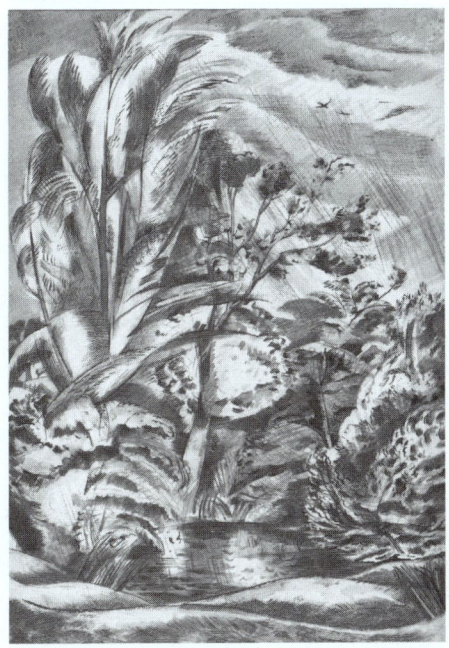

If anyone had asked Digory,
Where did you come from,
he would probably have said,
I've always been here.

Writing this years later, he saw these scenes spread before him as if he had left his body behind. He was seeking transformation and escape and, as a teenager, he would find it in the shape of a man who died a long, long time ago but still seemed close enough almost to touch.

Someone you might pass on the stairs or in a busy street, not quite sure but almost certain that you had seen them somewhere before. Someone full of mystery and grace, someone from another time and another place.

In the summer of 1906, Paul Nash left school. He was sixteen years old and feeling bemused. He didn't want to follow in the family tradition and join the navy, and no one was taking him seriously about his desire to be an artist. So he took the train up to London.

He often did so, because the city was a scary and exciting place. Over in Paris that summer there were anarchist bombings. In imperial London, things seemed more secure. But within an hour of leaving his comfortable home in Buckinghamshire, the teenager could be strolling down Piccadilly, following in Oscar Wilde's steps, to a new sort of space. It was a secret street, Nash said, and the Carfax was the most distinguished and exclusive gallery in London.

It was always afternoon there, someone said, and there were always tall, vague, well-dressed men talking about unknown poets. It had the air of a forbidden place, like a nightclub, not least because it was managed by Robert Ross, Wilde's devoted friend. So devoted that when Oscar's surprisingly unrotten corpse, his hair and his beard having continued to grow after death like a saint, was exhumed in Paris to be taken to Père-Lachaise, a better address to be seen dead in, Ross stopped the sextons lifting it with their spades and stepped into the grave to raise up his long-dead lover in his own arms.

Wilde had hardly died in 1901. He lived on like an impeccably dressed wraith, still disturbing the course of society with his wit and wilfulness. Ross's acquisition of the Carfax was financed by his loyal mother, Augusta Elizabeth Ross, who, when Wilde was arrested, had paid £500 towards the cost of his defence on the condition that her son left the country to avoid arrest himself. He never went. Wildean people lingered from the nineties, when nobody was very old, as another of Oscar's lovers said. They hung around as a faint scent, waiting for what came next.

Ross lived just across Piccadilly from the Carfax, at 40 Half Moon Street, another hidden address. It was there in 1918, the last year of his life, that he would play host to the young war poets Siegfried Sassoon and Wilfred Owen, both of whom took rooms in that establishment for single gentlemen of a certain kind. Ross had his salon painted gold in protest against the conflict; like Owen, he kept photographs of mutilated soldiers in his pocket to show to anyone who supported the war, like some terrible tarot card. That same year, Nash met Ross socially; perhaps he was entertained in that golden room with its Turkish cigarettes and sugared almonds. But he was certainly a visitor to the Carfax long before that.

In June 1906 the gallery held a great exhibition of work by William Blake, who, as Ross told the readers of the *Burlington Magazine*, constituted no link in English painting. Unlike other important artists such as Turner or Constable, Blake did not change the character of art, and for this reason he has been overlooked.

With delicious Wildean ambiguity, drawing on his Turkish cigarette, Ross declared Blake to be an exquisite accident.

But this was no accident. None of it was. There were good reasons for the cult that had grown up around Blake. The co-founder of the Carfax, the artist William Rothenstein, another friend of Wilde, had a particular connection to Blake via Dante Gabriel Rossetti and the Pre-Raphaelites, who had seen in the wildness of Blake's work the seeds of their own brotherhood. Yet for all their efforts—or perhaps, because of them—Blake remained an outsider, a freak; and now, to mark his strangeness, accidental or otherwise, the Carfax assembled the most extensive and comprehensive exhibition of his work to date, as Ross boasted.

It was a sensation, a freak show, and if Paul Nash was waiting for someone or something to transform him, nothing could fit the bill better than the announcement slipped almost surreptitiously into the pages of The Times. It was enough to make you hold your breath. The circus had come to town.

WILLIAM BLAKE EXHIBITION of PAINTINGS and WATER-COLOURS, the largest ever brought together in England, at CARFAX GALLERY, 24, Bury-street, St. James's, 10 till 6. Admission One Shilling.

Not everyone was convinced; that was the point. The paper's critic was distinctly equivocal. Blake was too weird, too little sane, to excite a very deep interest, he declared. But he also acknowledged that while the wild, imaginative remoteness and the formlessness of Blake's work could disconcert, he was the only artist of his time who could paint spiritual visions (angels and the like) without making them ridiculous. Another reviewer of these angels and devils called the pictures performances, as if they were works in progress, still going on. Which they were, of course; that was the point too. A third reviewer insisted that to call the artist important would be absurd, but had to admit that there was now a persistent and insistent cult of Blake which could not be denied.

A crack in the sky opened up and a hand reached down. It was a great connection for a young artist to make: from Blake's obscurity to a new age that claimed him as one of their own. Blake's stars aligned in a way they had never done while he was alive. It was all down to fate. That his works survived at all owed much to his loyal patron, Thomas Butts, who had bought pictures almost weekly from Blake and whose descendants had miraculously preserved them in their private gallery. And it was there that they were rediscovered by another young man who would become the instrument of Blake's resurrection, installing him as a kind of prophet for modern art.

In the summer of 1894, John Singer Sargent stood in his studio in Chelsea, its huge window looking down to the river at the end of the street. Inscribed in terracotta plaques over Sargent's doorway were two quotations: To Thine Own Self Be True and The Only Thing We Have to Fear is Fear Itself.

Oscar Wilde, who lived at the other end of the street, had only to peer over his balcony to see what was going on. Who was coming and who was going. It was all a performance. Inside Sargent's studio, one of the great set pieces of the period was under way: a picture that would become something more than merely the portrait of a wealthy young man. Something mysterious and grand.

W. Graham Robertson was already renowned as the first of Wilde's favourites to wear a green carnation. Now, in the heat of summer, Sargent was painting him as a very thin boy in a very tight coat, as the model himself would recall. He posed there for hours, the light falling on his face; his jade-topped cane in one hand, the other on his hip; his boon companion, Mouton, a lamb-like poodle from Biarritz, lay at his feet. At the beginning of every sitting, Mouton bit the painter. He has bitten me now, Sargent said, so we can go ahead.

For the artist, the whole composition revolved round the garment and its black velvet collar. So he made Robertson take off most of his clothes underneath; not so much as to keep him cool as to make him look even thinner, all the more like the immortal aesthete they were creating; all the more like a relic of the future past.

Sargent knew his power. His portraits swirl with glamour and poise; his evocation of children lighting lanterns in the violet twilight, Carnation, Lily, Lily, Rose, painted between games of tennis, makes even time look like a theatre set. All of his paintings were events. They drew a select crowd. His friend and fellow American, Henry James, came in to see Robertson's portrait, several times; perhaps he was taking notes. Sarah Bernhardt peered at it on tiptoe, her head thrown back. The whole thing might have been a drama written by Wilde over the road. Everyone hiding in plain sight. Life imitating art. The alluring young man, an artist himself, ready to play his part.

When Sargent asked him why he hadn't painted a self-portrait, Robertson replied, Because I am not my style.

What do you allow your friends to call you? Wilde asked him. W? or Graham? I like my friends to call me Oscar.

Their friendship flourished in words and gestures. Oscar thanked him for his dancing and told him not to read his *Picture of Dorian Gray*. You can see why: the book opens with an artist painting the portrait of a young man who is doomed by his extraordinary personal beauty. But did Robertson obey? He had the look of a faun in Mayfair; those might be goat's legs under his West End coat.

You are made for olive-groves, Wilde told him, and for meadows starred with white narcissi. I tried to invent a fairy tale for you to illustrate. I kept looking at the moon.

And when Robertson sent his drawings, Wilde replied, The star-child is lovely: it is clear you have seen him.

But there's already a sadness in Robertson's eyes. He had shared Mouton with Walter Hiley, his first friend. They'd been at school together. Hiley had joined the army. On leave, he came to stay with the Robertsons in Mayfair, suddenly took ill and died, aged twenty-one.

A year later Robertson met Oscar and everything changed again. He tried to forget his first friend and the promises they

Pl II

made. Sargent's picture was a portrait in a mourning coat. It was also a dangerous image. The artist in Wilde's book never tells his friends' names to anyone. It is like surrendering a part of them, he says. After Wilde was imprisoned as convict c.3.3., as though they'd tried to destroy his identity, he wrote to Alfred Douglas from Reading Gaol in an extended letter that became known as *De Profundis* and which would address his sense of betrayal. In the text, which he entrusted to Ross for publication, Wilde resorted, in his despair, to quoting William Blake.

Where others, says Blake, see but the Dawn coming over the hill, I see the sons of God shouting for joy.

But Oscar knew it was a forlorn hope, as he acknowledged in the next line:

What lies before me is my past.

It is hard now to comprehend the hatred Wilde faced, dead or alive. The news travelled as far as Nebraska, where Willa Cather declared, Civilisation shudders at his name. My mother, born in 1921, understood he was a wicked man, but no one would tell her why. Even Robertson's own friend, Kerrison Preston, writing in 1953, spoke of the sinister evil inherent in Wilde as the older man in the relationship. Passers-by in this drive-by shooting casually described Wilde after the fact (we knew it all along, but were too well bred to say) as a plump, pasty, flabby, round-faced, preposterously-garbed man at their family wedding, delivering an outrageously flattering speech which produced a slight feeling of nausea. They were so afraid. They had no name for what he was.

When we see people in old photographs we wonder where in time they were. Robertson was immortal in Wildean guises, changing shape. Dancing in white tights and flipperty-flopperty hat; in velvet jacket, waistcoat and breeches, doubly exposed, in two places at once like Jekyll and Hyde or a little ghost.

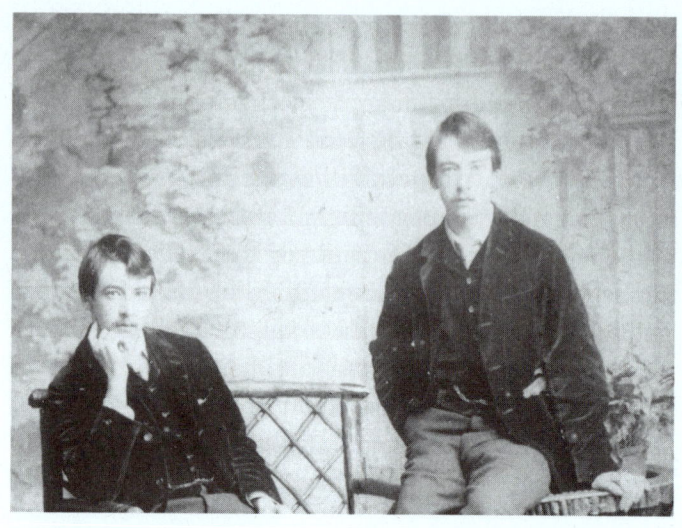

Even then, no one was quite sure. Mouton sat still at his master's feet, saying nothing. Robertson was wrapped up in wealth as well as that long coat, and as he moved through his life, a lover of things being not quite what they seemed, he could afford to encourage other artists with his patronage, especially his new friend, Algernon Blackwood, a noted author of tales of the uncanny.

In Blackwood's book *Pan's Garden*, published in 1912, Robertson appears as an artist, The Man Whom the Trees Loved of the opening story. Sanderson is a dandy, a magical creature, able to intuit the spirit of the forest, and he painted trees (as Robertson did) as by some special divining instinct of their essential qualities, we are told. He understood them, Blackwood wrote. The story, as slippery as Wilde's novel or Sargent's picture, draws on a collective spirit of ambiguity.

Blackwood was born in Kent of upper-class parents; his mother was a dowager duchesss. As a boy he would climb out of his bedroom window and into the garden to practise incantations to ghosts and faeries in a boat on the pond. As a strong and athletic young man, Blackwood went to work in Canada with John Kay, a delightful comrade with a happy light in his frank blue eyes, and a good heavyweight boxer too, Blackwood recalled. There the two men became aware of the sometimes hostile power of Nature and the primeval woods, and the way they wove in and out of Native American myths. These wild tales made us almost feel supermen, Blackwood said; he was evoking a Jack London existence, living in lonely and untrodden beauty where he believed some Pan-like deity looked after them. It was a stark contrast to their later adventures in downtown Manhattan where they ended up taking drugs, including cannabis and morphine.

Algernon Blackwood: as a binomial, his name was evocative. Wilde's most famous play, The Importance of Being Earnest, in which the word earnest is itself a code, opens in Algernon Moncrieff's flat in Half Moon Street. It is a heady address, where Ross's golden room was host to Charles Scott Moncrieff, the translator of Proust, bringing with him his young friends Wilfred Owen and Noël Coward. And if Half Moon Street, a half place, was one of those secret spaces, then Blackwood's stories were full of the dark woods in which you might be lost.

In a sly underworld of assignations and assumptions, art allowed unsayable things. Blackwood asked Robertson to illustrate Pan's Garden, part of which was written at Robertson's house on the Surrey heath. And just as blake meant black or perhaps white, so Robertson's pen-and-ink drawings in lush black and white aspired to a Blakean transcendence. Robertson even described his images of trees as a grim, hooded yew and an oak which was a Blake old man. Nature and bodies blur. Sanderson-slash-Robertson is a duality, well met by moonlight. Like Sargent's painting of Robertson, as if he were a tree in the forest, these were dangerous things to turn a young person's head, and Robertson's youthful dalliance with Wilde gave Pan's Garden an added mortal allure. To those in the know and even those who weren't, it was a conspiracy: a game of hide-and-seek in the black wood, a portrait in an attic or a Chelsea studio.

In the story, David Bittacy lives on the verge of the New Forest in Dorset, where he has asked Sanderson to paint a portrait of a cedar tree that stands alone on his lawn like a silent sentinel. Bittacy's wife worries that he loves trees more than her. Perhaps she suspects that they are a guise for other desires. Into this scene comes the disruptive spirit of Sanderson, an artist who is able to portray the effects of wind in foliage, as Bittacy says, admiringly.

It was quite arresting, this way Sanderson had of making a tree look almost like a being—alive. It approached the uncanny.

Queer, Bittacy says

—Blackwood uses the word thirty-six times in his book; it already has another meaning: the Marquess of Queensberry, Oscar's arch-enemy, had referred to Wilde and his friends as snob queers—

awfully queer, Bittacy goes on, that trees should bring me such a sense of dim, vast living!

The uncanny and the queer are synonymous; half something, half something else. That's why they all love the idea of Pan: neither animal nor man, the beauty in the beast. He was everywhere. Kenneth Grahame, one of Robertson's closest friends, asked him to draw the frontispiece for his *Wind in the Willows*, in which Pan appears as A Piper at the Gates of Dawn. They share the same territory, these ideas: the same ambiguity, secrets told in dreamtime. In his book, Blackwood describes a gathering addressed by an artist. Being a group of normal Englishmen, they disliked mystery, he says; it made them feel uncomfortable.

Nature rises like sap. Senses heighten, nerves twitch. That kind of elemental terror, Blackwood says, can be guarded by culture, but never wholly concealed.

They are things which are uncommonly—er—queer, another character says.

The hesitancy is all, Algy Moncrieff might reply.

Not to give anything away: least of all, one's true self, deep down.

There's nothing anywhere—unnatural, says Blackwood.

What's natural or unnatural, anyway? A thrill of unaccustomed life runs through David Bittacy. Some writing fellow tells him trees were once moving things, animal organisms of some sort, which had stood so long feeding, sleeping, dreaming, or something, in the same place, that they had lost the power to get away. Old as he is, Bittacy has not given up on the idea that we could be something other than we are, that he could get away. And when he reads in *The Times* an address by Francis Darwin, son of Charles, who suggests that there exists in trees a faint copy of what we know as consciousness within ourselves, he is convinced. The edge of the forest, like the shoreline of a sea, looks like some slumbering monster to him. He is more than ready for young Sanderson, who arrives for the weekend with no evening clothes in his suitcase but wearing very low collars with big balloon ties like a Frenchman.

He has also let his hair grow longer than Mrs Bittacy thinks nice.

Sanderson is an excitable man, she says, more than a person in his thirties should be, when most men of that age have become blasé.

It is a portrait of Robertson in disguise. With his arrival, the forest starts to stir. It had been waiting for this visionary off the 9.35 from Waterloo. In everything that grows, has life, that is, there's mystery past all finding out, he says.

Every thing that lives is Holy, Blake says.

Even in decay there's life, says Sanderson. Even a stone is crammed with heat and weight and potencies of all sorts; even that apparently inert object may be a mode of life.

My copy of *Pan's Garden* is falling apart, a former library book so well thumbed that in 1915, after three years' circulation, the librarian ordered it to be rebound. There's something initiate, complicit, about its decay of lies. Books can be haunted, falling open as if turned by mysterious hands, studied for clues the way you'd pore over an album cover. You could find yourself in there. Blackwood's subtitle announces A Volume of Nature Studies as if it were a guide to growing your roses. But facing its title page is a sheet of thin tissue lying coyly, like Salome's veil, over Robertson's orgasmic frontispiece.

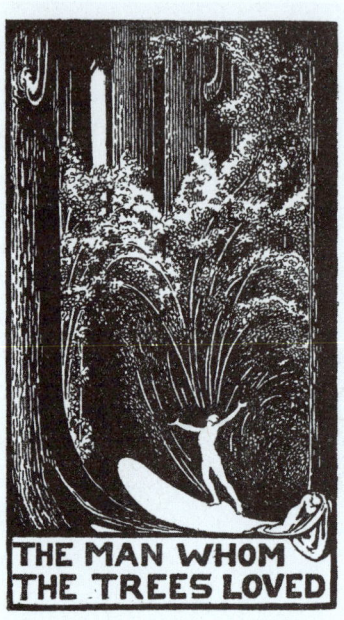

It's quite an introduction. A superhero figure (my friend Ed says it looks like the Silver Surfer out of a Marvel Comic) throws their arms up into the trees, shooting sprays of ectoplasmic energy into the foaming leaves. The image is directly inspired by Blake's white-line prints; it is also an echo of Blackwood's time in the Canadian woods. The trees are totemic, the air occult. The queerness of the other world could encompass all these desires. Blackwood and Robertson were members of the Order of the Golden Dawn, as were W.B. Yeats and Algernon Swinburne; Constance Wilde infiltrated the secret society like a greenery-yallery spy to supply Oscar with details for his *Dorian Gray*. Living in an oppressive material world, they were all drawn to the psychical, these artists, in their radical, darkened rooms in Bloomsbury and Chelsea, just as Blake himself had been drawn to Emanuel Swedenborg, scientist turned mystic, who saw and believed in his own visions, too.

The spirits were eternal, and they were everywhere.

All these tendrils seek and find each other like fungi, like tree roots talking to themselves through the earth. Sanderson's sensitiveness, perhaps, was morbid, Blackwood admits. No wonder Paul Nash found all of this so exciting. I quite believe in Pan, he said, and he called Blackwood's stories mystical and almost insanely imaginative.

The Sea Fit, another story in *Pan's Garden*, was written by Blackwood at the Haven Hotel on Sandbanks beach in Dorset in 1909. He got the idea from his friends at nearby Rempstone Hall, part of a vast estate which took in half of Purbeck, from Studland Bay all the way down to Winspit's quarry. Nine Barrow Down, where the house stood, was studded with earthworks; next door there was a stone circle where magical rituals were conducted by the wickedest man in the world. It is possible that Blackwood himself was present at such rites.

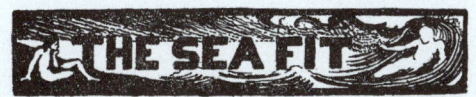

Under an Easter moon, three men gather in a beach house at Studland. It is low-roofed, ramshackle and made of timbers, more like a ship's cabin, as Blackwood says it, a mere sea-shell on the beach. Its owner is Captain Erricson, a great blond-haired man of the sea; a Viking reincarnated if ever there was one, that type of primitive man in whom burns an inborn love and passion for the sea that amounts to positive worship—devouring tide, a lust and fever in the soul.

It's an opening worthy of Melville or Conrad. We're never at our best away from salt water, never quite right, Erricson says.

He has invited his friends to his shack, with its store of curious reading gathered in long, becalmed days at the ends of the world; heart and mind, that is, carried a queer cargo, we are told.

The summer and its visitors are far away; the men have the sandy dunes to themselves. They're relishing the keen joys of roughing it. Sinbad, Erricson's dog-faithful servant, attends to his master's every need. He knows when the captain has one of his queer sea fits on; that something uncommon was astir.

Just outside their door is the loneliness of the sand-spit and that melancholy singing of the sea, Sinbad says. As the night wears on and the tide rises ever higher, he warns one of the guests in a stage whisper, Full moon, sir, please, and he's better without too much! These high spring tides get him all caught off his feet sometimes—clean sea-crazy.

Erricson is talking wildly about pagan deities, of queer things he had seen in queerer places; of rituals in which the devout worshipper should go to his death singing, as to a wedding—the wedding of his soul with the particular deity he has loved and served all his life. It's playing the whole game, I always think, man-fashion, the Viking says.

That secret lust in his heart is born of the old water Powers— the Sea Gods. No dying in bed or fading out from old age for him, but to plunge full-blooded and alive into the great Body of the god who has deigned to descend and fetch you—

It doesn't take much to imagine how all this will end. There was something coming, coming from the sand-dunes or the sea, as Blackwood writes. And it is invited, or welcomed at any rate. Erricson's nephew has been summoned to his uncle's aid. He is a Jesuit priest, who cycles, Father Brown-like, from some point beyond Corfe Castle, racing along the hard Studland sand in the moonlight. But neither he nor his faith can do anything to stop what happens next. The sea has been summoned, like a spirit, and it will have its way.

Outside, the massed and awful impetus of whole driven oceans is gathering, says Blackwood. The wind enters the shack itself, with the waves about to follow. Then Erricson, like a madman, leaps out of the window and makes for the sea, watched by the eyeless dunes with the white and silent moon overhead.

Blackwood, standing back, in his psychic eye, imagines that one day, when a later Science shall have learned to develop the photographs that Nature takes incessantly upon her secret plates, the complete record of what happened next would be revealed.

Erricson is stripped of his clothes, his rough tweed torn to ribbons, his figure somehow turned dark like strips of tide-sucked seaweed.

He stood for one instant upright, his hair wild in the moonshine, towering, with arms outstretched. And then he was gone. In fluid form, wave-like, his being slipped away into the Being of the Sea.

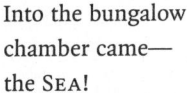

Into the bungalow chamber came— the SEA!

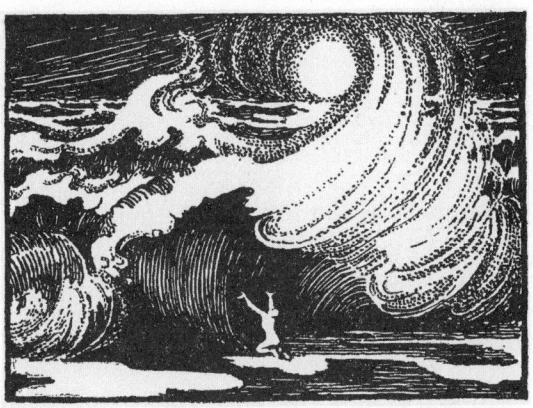

This transition on a Dorset beach catches up everything— magic, mystery and the weather; a sexy Viking in the sea; art as a refuge for the childless, the childlike. Erricson goes to his singular death, as to a wedding, singing, and well content. It was the same way that Blake approached his own ending: singing, immortal, inevitable, explosive, willing himself on.

He had nothing to hide, as history was about to prove.

———

In February 1906, shortly before the Blake exhibition opened at the Carfax, Graham Robertson had his own first show at the gallery. Reviewers thought his work to be in a Velázquez-Whistler tradition; but they also noted his intriguing Experiments in search of the lost method of William Blake—an attempt to reproduce Blake's mysterious colour prints.

A psychic communion with the dead. Robertson had been fascinated by Blake ever since the age of seventeen, when he had discovered a copy of Alexander Gilchrist's lavishly illustrated, two-volume biography in Gilbert's bookshop in Southampton, a dark place with bow windows and dusty stacks and a man who watched you carefully as you moved about. Robertson read Gilchrist's book at a lick. It was published in 1863 to revive Blake's reputation, but his work was still so obscure that forty years later Robertson was able to acquire the artist's Ghost of a Flea for twelve pounds. That eerie half-insect, half-human, lurking like a red-eyed clawed creature in a story by Blackwood or M.R. James, appealed to Robertson for precisely those reasons. It sparked the start of a lifelong mission financed by the vast fortune he inherited at the age of eighteen when his father, a Scottish shipping magnate, died in 1884.

Pl II

By April 1906, Robertson had bought all the remaining Blakes still owned by the Butts family, having made many trips to their home in Dorset, set on the same haunted shore of Blackwood's story. There, in the rambling old mansion with its thirteen grandfather clocks chiming, and its extension specially built to house the collection, Robertson recalled wrestling for the pictures with the elderly Captain Butts, an eccentric in his own right who was usually in bed and very cross and said no to everything, as his own son, Anthony, would recall. But it was well worth the tussle: Robertson's haul included the astonishing images of Newton, Nebuchadnezzar and Pity and sixty-six other magical works, all knocked down for nine thousand pounds. A bargain for the good of humankind.

Set against his reputation, W. Graham Robertson's name

sounded deceptively ordinary, like a bank manager or solictor. He had been christened Graham Walford Robertson, but turned his names around because he was tired of having the initials of the Great Western Railway. Some might have seen this scion of an industrious family as a dilettante, an effete aesthete busy spending profits he had not earned. In fact, his efforts on behalf of his hero were a far greater investment so far as our souls were concerned. Over the succeeding years, Robertson became the man who saved Blake for the nation by acquiring one hundred and forty of his paintings and drawings and prints which he would lend out for exhibition or reproduction without charging any fees. He rescued them like the dogs to whom he devoted the final chapter of his memoirs, published in 1931.

The book, *Time Was*, was full of tales of Wilde and Sarah Bernhardt and W.B. Yeats, who told Robertson how he sent his Spirit to France when he needed to remotely investigate a case of the stigmata in a village priest; and of William Morris, who resembled a burly sea captain with a deep voice and brusque manner, complaining that a dreadful woman has been asking him what was his message to the people of Hackney Wick. Most vividly of all, he portrayed the decadent poet, Robert de Montesquiou, inspiration to Proust and J.K. Huysmans and a most kind friend to Robertson, who was not long out of Eton when he came under the Comte's spell in the glamour of Paris, where their mutual friend Sargent roamed, looking for boys.

Robertson repeatedly visited Montesquiou's extraordinary rooms on the Quai d'Orsay, a vague dream of the Arabian Nights translated into japonaiserie, with a series of chambers successively decorated in red, rose, pink and finally fading to grey (the poet would search Paris for grey flowers to match). In his bedroom, a black dragon with glassy, rolling eyes carried the bed on its back and the pillow in the coil of its tail; the bathroom was filled with fishes painted in filmy gauzes, giving it the feel of green gloom that might have been full fathom five under the waves so far as Robertson was concerned; it was all queer, disturbing, baroque, he said. It is a scene worthy of Huysmans's *A Rebours*, whose Comte des Esseintes is forever planning to travel, but remains content in Paris with his tortoise whose carapace has been studded with precious gems.

All these stories, against nature as they may seem, give way to Robertson's last chapter devoted to his greatest loves: My Most Notable Acquaintances, each boasting a section of their own: Bob, Portly, Ben and Richard, as distinctly drawn as any aristocrat or actor and only nominally sheepdogs in their owner's eyes. Mouton, his first dog, is described as terribly self-conscious and conceited, with a genuine dramatic gift and a former career with a fisherman fishing for sardines, and later a reputation as a sly thief, stealing, and eating, artists' sticks of charcoal. Portly's most deftly practised joke, said his owner, was to pluck people off their bicycles. Richard's extreme beauty was such that it stopped people in their tracks when he was walked down Kensington High Street; a friend said he'd seen nothing like it since the early days of Mrs Langtry. Robertson tells tales of other dogs, too, such as Fussie, companion to Ellen Terry and Henry Irving, who, as the theatre company embarked at Southampton docks for New York, somehow became left behind, only to appear a few days later back at the Lyceum in London, having walked all the way along the train line to Waterloo. It was a good lesson to learn for a dog: Fussie was lost again on a second tour when he strayed at the station in New York, to be found just in time, having already begun plodding steadily along the tracks to California.

Yet in all this canine devotion there is no mention of Robertson's first friend, Mouton's joint master, Walter Hiley, by whose side the poodle had sat, and on whose shoulder Robertson's hand had rested for the photograph. It was too painful to remember, too soon to forget. Robertson only added a note bemoaning his own survival into the modern world, to which I do not belong, he said, and which I do not understand.

And having accidentally slopped over into it, he said,

perhaps the best thing we can do is to hold our tongues and efface ourselves.

By now Robertson was spending most of his time at Sandhills, his rustic retreat in the Home Counties where he lived without gas or electricity or running water or even a bathroom as if Surrey were a remote colony—albeit with a substantial staff to heat the water for bathtubs in guests' rooms and order taxis to the station. Robertson's wealth allowed the house to stick in the eighteen-sixties. Henry James complained of having to proceed candle-stuck to bed, and when Wilde came to stay, he had to deploy his desire to tell his host a story in order to sit down halfway through a country walk. Robertson continued to work as an artist and designer and author of a celebrated play, *Pinkie and the Fairies*. His portrait of his strange and fantastic friend, Mabel Beardsley, showed her dressed as a man and renamed Philip, a private code used by her brother Aubrey, who was also drawn to cross-dressing.

Gradually, professionally, Robertson receded from public life, backing into the shadows. Now my gallery of Blakes, he concluded wryly, is felt to represent one of my few excuses for existence. The wanting, the longing, the being left behind. Yet this ageing Peter Pan had salvaged Blake's art from its slumber by the sea, bringing it back to the city where it belonged; just as if it hadn't been for that bookshop in Southampton, where the sea light poured up the high street, those artworks may never have been brought together and I wouldn't have been able to write this.

Even now I find it incredible: the idea of walking into that Mayfair gallery and finding all these things crammed into one room. The colour prints of Newton, Nebuchadnezzar and Pity; twelve illustrations of Milton's *Paradise Lost*; The Ghost of a Flea and dozens and dozens of other rescued works. All there, reverberating on the wall. But not for sale.

That autumn, 1906, Paul Nash became an art student in Chelsea. He was already tuned into what he would call the disintegrating charm of the Pre-Raphaelites. Their indiscreet visions of beauty infected him, prompting him to paint a haunting woman's face hanging in the night sky like a moon, her hair as the clouds. Now Blake's works summoned up even stranger things for Nash. It was like seeing the god behind the machine. He felt chosen, picked upon. And when he began to read Blake's poems, he found one which completely arrested his thought. It was written to Thomas Butts, Blake's devoted friend, to whom he sent

> My first Vision of Light,
> On the yellow sands sitting.

It was Blake's epiphany on the shores of Sussex, although it might have been on the moon. Reading it, Nash felt the same sensation, of being taken out of himself. Blake was holding up a screen, like a romantic remote-viewing a landscape reflected in a black Claude glass or an iPad, seeing all of nature, where

> Mountain, hill, earth, & sea,
> Cloud, Meteor & Star,
> Are Men Seen Afar.

That was an instant of recognition for Nash. The strange and the familiar, the natural and the supernatural combined. Blake appeared to him a spirit of place, a genius loci, surrounded by rays from a diamond-star halo. Suddenly the whole world opened up. Albion was a potential reality, not just a future dream; the plan Blake was charged to carry out: as an artist, as a poet, as a man.

There have been many prophets, before and since, but Blake was an entirely practical kind of visionary. That is part of his appeal. An ordinary person who bore witness to miracles in the trees and in the streets and recorded them for us in the physical practice of his art. But in his exultant optimism for humanity, Blake also saw the consequences of that dark reflection. What if we followed Satan instead? After all, the devil was real, and he meant what he said.

Satan is merely the stranger, Blake said, turning biblical verse round to suit his purposes. Satan was science and rationalism; the demon Reason who curbed all Desire. Anyone like Nash would recognise this language. I grew up with it, too, all its cadences and its repetitions, all beaten into you from the moment they pour the water over your head. But Blake took it up, that dread vocabulary, and turned it on its head too, filling the skies with angels and falling stars, the land with snarling beasts and blasted trees, and the sea with carnivorous fishes and dragons of the deep.

Most of all, he remade us in imaginary form. He did it to embody his fantastical ideas. He gave voice to spirits waiting to be released from a tree or a cave. Fertile, sensual, tactile, tortured exalted bodies, unabashed by their disinclination to wear anything other than their own skin. They become entire continents, universes, micro-macrocosms, uttering outrageous messages in speech bubbles edited for the beginning or ending of time. In his prophetic books, Blake issued sequences of words and images that could be barely understood in his own age let alone ours. But like lyrics you never learn, they still mean the same; you feel them, in your bones. Blake's was a priestly mission, a vocation, and he would never leave it till his work was done.

For Nash, at a sensitive age, Blake's words, as much as his art, revealed impossibilities. Memory, reason, imagination. A disturbance in the ether, like vision on sound. The possibilities that lay ahead, at the back of his head like a distant beat. He discovered them in the heady opening years of the twentieth century, just as they were written at the beginning of the poet's slumber on the banks of the ocean in 1800.

Blake chose to spend those first years of his new century by the sea. He was full of its sense of promise. His calendar was empty: reset at two zeroes, before it filled up with dates and regrets and woes. With the millennium at hand, he was waiting for revelation across the dark fields of night, from the roaring sea at the land's end. The end of England, the beginning of the rest of time.

He was a deeply romantic man. He chose his moments well. They chose him. I think he's the god I expected. At least, he knew what God looked like and could give us a clue. He makes this book worth the price you paid for it.

He is its admission, and he gives me permission for what I am about to tell you.

In the autumn of 1800, as the swallows were flying past his window bound for Africa, Blake was preparing for a new career in a new town. He was forty-three years old and in need of a change. So he set off south himself, sixty miles to the sweet Heaven of Sussex, leaving the terrible desart of London behind.

With him was his beloved Catherine, his heroine, Kate. She was like a flame of many colours of precious jewels whenever she heard their destination named, he said. They travelled light, with sixteen boxes of belongings, as if embarking on a voyage to the ends of the earth. Inside were all their worldly possessions and many unworldly ones too: all the prints Blake had been unable to sell (that is, most of them), together with the engine of anarchy that gave them birth—his printing press.

William Blake is a perfect name, most excellent. Plain and no-nonsense. Like his tradesman's clothes, the best disguise for a man with such a wild mind. You might imagine a purveyor of hardware, or of socks, as indeed his father was. Unlike other people in this story, he did not come from a wealthy family. He had to advertise himself. 'William Blake' starts like the wind, rises to a pitch and ends in an ache. It suits its owner's own true heart: his one pure being of hope, of whirling prophecies for life here on earth. It could almost have been anyone standing there that night in Soho when the star of inspiration fell out of the sky. Blake just happened to be in the right place at the right time, ready to take the call.

He had the air of innocence and experience, a faerie child or a candle flame. A subtle, gentle smile that seemed somehow interior and knowing. Huge pale blue eyes that saw into the far distance but looked right into you, too. Red hair that stuck up like a cockscomb in his youth. An aura of quiet power within. But no one could have expected this stubby Londoner, barely five foot five, to arrive in this sleepy seaside village, bringing with him intimations of revolution and wild desire.

When the Blakes appeared in Felpham, it was a shock for the villagers, like discovering new-age hippies had moved in overnight. It was a shock for William too: the invitation, arranged by his friend, the artist John Flaxman, had come from the renowned but not entirely inspired poet and biographer of John Milton, William Hayley, who wanted Blake to illustrate his work. Hayley lived in The Turret, a villa topped with a grandiose tower almost as high as the church. He called it his little marine hermitage, complete with a warm sea-bath. He had bought the field between the villa and the shore to ensure his view of the sea. It spoke of his lordly demeanour, and did not augur well for Blake.

Felpham may have been a dozy place of barely two dozen homes, but already Londoners were arriving in their droves, taking summer cottages to escape the city's smoke and noise. That was why the Blakes' landlord, Mr Grinder, the Dickensian owner of the Fox Inn across the street, could charge them twenty pounds per annum for his Rose Cottage. Any old place with a lick of paint demanded a premium from the carriage trade.

It was the sea that drew them here; the same sea that had only recently begun its transformation from a place of terror to a site of nature worship. Salt-water bathing hit as a fever, as it had up and down the coast as hydrophilia took hold. A body to receive other bodies, the union of flesh and seawater could cure anything from an upset stomach to a rent in the fabric of your soul. The sea-as-therapy also subverted Albion's defensive shores. Its beaches faced not the French and their monkeys and their Antichrist, but an invasion of home-grown bathers, announced twice daily with the tides. War stopped all frivolous travel. You couldn't get any further than this. It's why Blake never left England. And it was why the sea leapt from fearful element to frivolous entertainment. It was the new dispensation and people came here for the cure, as they still do.

If you half-closed your eyes on Felpham's genteel shore, you could just about ignore Bognor, not yet Regis, next door. It was not yet Piccadilly-by-the-sea, as Constable saw Brighton, nor Byron's Venice, his Sea-Sodom. Nor ugly and repulsive, either, as Blake's admirer Dante Gabriel Rossetti complained when he moved to Bognor in the eighteen-seventies. But things were changing fast. Rather than a new Jerusalem, Sir Richard Hotham built an hotel with its own warm sea bath and a trio of Georgian mansions with a tea room under a golden dome. It wasn't quite Kubla Khan, more hot tub and cocktails. The facilities were designed to lure people of quality: the Prince of Wales duly arrived to visit his mistress, Lady Jersey, but they didn't spend the night together.

Felpham dozed through all this furore. It had its own bathing machines, admittedly, from which bathers might be launched naked into the sea. But as Bognor, like Brighton, Southampton and Weymouth, turned into a site of watery outrage, a decadent resort for gouty bodies and youths in fearfully made garb, the village held out against those marine villas busy rising in Regency allure. Rose Cottage, set at right angles to a sandy lane, had a thatched roof that sloped steeply at the back; it clamped the house down to the land like a limpet, and provided a summer home for swallows. There were just four and a half rooms, two up, two down, with a kitchen extension for that sort of thing. The Blakes weren't interested in domesticity.

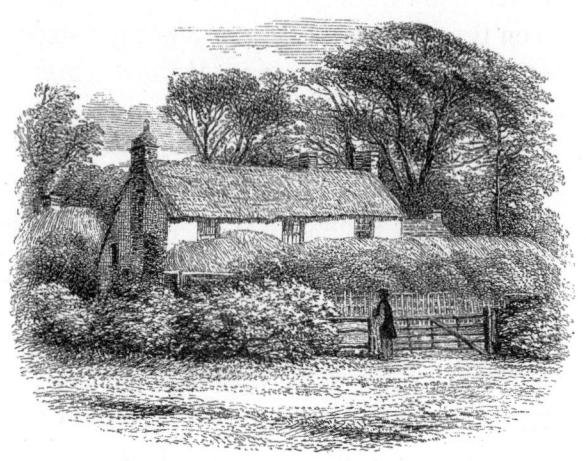

BLAKE'S COTTAGE AT FELPHAM.

Tucked up in their cosy nest, they preferred to peer out from under the eaves, over the fields of corn and down to the sea. It was the first time Blake had seen it with his own eyes. He'd imagined it endlessly in his art, in his head; now it was at the end of his lane. He could walk down there in his dressing gown and slippers, if he so desired. The sea hung there like a perpetually unfolding panorama, an unignorable flicker in the corner of his eye. Always different, always the same. The sea had no limits and neither did he. It promised everything. So did he.

The Blakes' cottage rivalled any Palace of Magnificence, William announced. Nothing can be more Grand than its Simplicity & Usefulness. It was the Spontaneous Effusion of Humanity, he said.

For a visionary, Blake could often sound like Mr Micawber. The sweet air & the voices of the winds make this a dwelling for immortals, he told Thomas Butts, his Dear Friend of the Angels whose wealth lay in the business of coal and who used it to buy Blake's works so often he might have had a weekly subscription. Whenever poverty overwhelmed the Blakes,

48

Butts had fuel delivered to their door; pictures for coal. No one had seen the sea before Blake. He got the sixpence. But what would his spirits say as he set up home in his own marine hermitage?

Heaven opens here on all sides her Golden Gates, he enthused, as if reading out the particulars from an ethereal estate agent; her windows are not obstructed by vapours; voices of Celestial inhabitants are more distinctly heard, & their forms more distinctly seen. The Cottage was a Shadow of their heavenly houses, he said, for all that it was rented from the landlord of the local pub.

He called the cottage their mundane shell, as if his skull echoed with the sound of the sea, and even as he wrote, Kate and his sister Catherine were down on the shore, courting Neptune for an Embrace. The sea's terrors that morning had made them afraid, he told Butts, but the ocean's mildness was often Equal to his terrors. The Blakes had arrived at the autumn equinox, and in the softness of September, when the English sea is finally starting to get warm, the two women took advantage of the spirit of the age to dip in. I don't know whether William joined them as their bodies were borne up in the swell, but as Hayley recommended it as a great reviver of health, I doubt William would have got away without Hayley getting him in.

Blake left no note of that; he left almost no letters, considering his long life, which was either careless or very careful of him. But his poem *Milton*, which was born out of this place as though borne on the tide, would be filled with seaweedy lovers and divers diving down its margins and Blake himself, strolling in his seaside Eden as if bound for the beach, apparently naked save for his hat and unaware of an angel in the trees like a blown-in plastic bag. You can hear the crows protest. She is the Virgin of Providence, Milton's feminine aspect, and she came in on the breeze like a siren, all fluttering drapes and streaming hair.   Pl V

The gates of Heaven did indeed open up for Blake here; they'd been waiting for him all along, and it would have been rude to decline. By day he walked the shore, communing with his spirits. At night he wandered into the countryside, where the crescent moon hung ominous and bright and alive. The blighted wheat lay felled in the field, a blasted oak bends in the storm. Back on the beach, the sails of two windmills spun round, grinding the corn. To Blake they were factories worked by slave labour, grinding out the whole of the world.

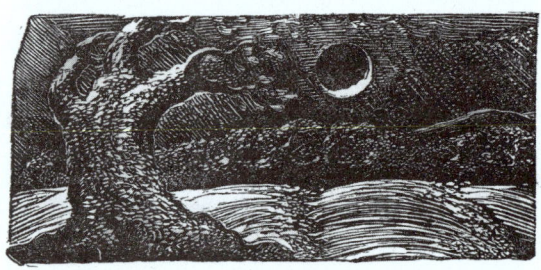

Everyone mentioned his big wide eyes, open wide to everything. Here they opened up to a new infinity: the sea and a horizon beyond the city's no exit. It was existential. His gaze was suddenly released, the way your eyes loosen when you get on a train after too much time in town. You can feel his pupils dilate

> My Eyes more & more
> Like a Sea without shore
> Continuc Expanding,

and there, on the sand, were Moses, Homer, Dante and Milton, no less, strolling with their trousers rolled up, Blake at their side, talking to his spiritual companions as they paced the sands of time. They looked like men, he said, only taller, and composed of grey but luminous shadows. The sea as a ghost, now rising up to take new forms, now lying down low.

Filled with this spirit, how he would grow! Blake was forty-three years old and the sea re-energised him in his midlife crisis. He plugged into it like a battery. In the words that would inspire Paul Nash a century later, he emanated his vision of light to Butts, in staccato lines; he'd have sent them by text if he could. Away from all care, he wrote, in this signal of delight, as in particles bright, in each grain of sand, he looked on,

> Astonish'd, Amazed;
> For each was a Man
> Human-form'd. Swift I ran,
> For they beckon'd to me,
> Remote by the Sea.

His visions were sea-borne, electric; those grains might have been bioluminescent zooplankton or asteroids spinning in outer space. I hope he'll forgive my crude interruptions and allusions, grinding him up for this book. His childlike reaction to the sea was cause and effect, somewhere so animate and alive that it could even predict itself, as he told Butts in a handy PS: A Piece of Sea Weed serves for a Barometer, it gets wet & dry as the weather gets so.

The sea had always been there, of course. An everywhere-nowhere place, hovering in the periphery of his art. Now it became part of his life, the angel-hair trail he blazed. Nothing can withstand the fury of my Course among the Stars of God, he boasted to Butts. My fingers Emit sparks of fire with Expectation of my future labours, he informed Hayley, like a comet.

Blake, in rapture, became the moon, became the stars. He was in England, sure enough, but in his head he was a world away, careering across the sky. That's why his visions stay long after they've gone, after-images on our collective retinas like dark stars, all the gods on the stairs and the angels in the trees, and a man carrying a glowing sun through a doorway as if he were holding a bowling ball or an atomic bomb. The way that, as a boy, Isaac Newton invented a kite laden with a candle-lit paper lantern which he flew in the dark. Hanging in the night sky, it wonderfully affrighted the neighbours, as Newton's antiquarian friend William Stukeley wrote. It was an omen of his discoverys, he said. Later Newton came to believe that comets fed the sun like coals in a fire, thundering into its nuclear core, sparking the solar god back into life.

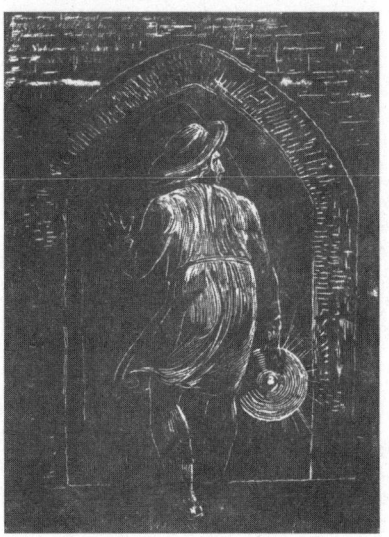

Blake, like other artists of his time, feared Newton's dissection of our dreams, the ominous consequences of his discoverys. Science was taking the natural world apart. Samuel Taylor Coleridge said it would take the souls of five hundred Newtons to make a Shakespeare or a Milton; Charles Lamb and John Keats, over an immortal dinner at Christmas, 1817, blamed him for destroying all the poetry of the rainbow by reducing it to the prismatic colours.

Science was no gift to humanity in their eyes; but it was impossible to resist, so they drank a toast to Newton's health and the confusion of mathematics. Perhaps they'd heard the rumours that, in secret, Newton practised alchemy and meta-physics, rewrote the book of Revelations and, as Jacob Bronowski the twentieth-century philosopher said, only understood the movements of stars as ships in the sea, riding through space; the way that the planets are on an endless spiral into the sun, or the way that matter itself might become sentient, evolving like organic life. Name something once and it's doomed for ever. Nations, states of mind, storms, animals, ideas, diseases. Like Adam in Paradise, science gave names to things that had no name. Industry then exploited them, again and again. They lined up for their new names, all the same.

In 1937, Humphrey Jennings, the writer and film-maker who had helped arrange the International Surrealist Exhibition the year before and who had just founded Mass Observation, a kind of art-inflected gathering of social information, began to apply the same techniques to a decade-long literary project. Jennings called it Pandæmonium, a term invented by Milton for the Palace of Satan: a place where all devils would be found, as opposed to the Pantheon of all gods.

Like Nash's Unit One or NASA's mission to Mars, Jennings's book was another impossible task, never to be finished in his lifetime. Bronowski, his college friend and collaborator, said Jennings's mind was too subtle and nimble to get everything down on the page that he wanted to say. Pandæmonium was designed as an anthology of terrible wonder; a collage of texts or images, as Jennings called it, which would reveal the real cost of the Industrial Revolution to humanity. His nineteen-thirties-search-engine sorted eyewitness accounts from the seventeenth, eighteenth and nineteenth centuries to present a series of snapshots of how we got to here from where we had been.

Combining the rage of Blake with the random energy of surrealism, Jennings relayed reports of machines able to carve sculptures and newspaper presses whose system of machinery were declared to be almost organic by *The Times* in 1814; devised and arranged, the newspaper said, to relieve the human frame of its most laborious efforts in printing and in so doing far exceed all human powers in rapidity and dispatch. It was artificial intelligence: the word frame itself was an image of the industrial leviathan to which workers were enslaved, humans as future robots, and the new metropolis a man-machine.

It was all happening too fast for anyone to keep up. In 1791, Jeremy Bentham devised an all-seeing panopticon in which prisoners might be kept under permanent surveillance; by 1824, the *Glasgow Mechanics' Magazine* was suggesting that a camera obscura might be usefully employed on the city's streets to locate criminals, sending the reports straight to the police station by telegraph.

By then Charles Babbage was already at work on his difference engine, a calculating computer which astonished even its own inventor, who told friends that he did not profess to know all the powers of his machine. In 1812 Byron had declared to Parliament that his sympathies lay with workers suffering the most unparalleled distress: By the Lord! he told the frame-breakers in 1816, if there's a row, but I'll be among ye! Thirty years later his own daughter, Ada Lovelace, would devise the first algorithms for Babbage's computer.

Science suborned art. When the French inventor Nicéphore Niépce brought his first photograph to England in 1826, William Blake was still alive; had he perfected his invention a little earlier, we might have seen Blake in the flesh; imagine what Julia Margaret Cameron might have made of those eyes. Six years later, in 1834, when Henry Fox Talbot created his device, using it to make images of his grand country house, Lacock, he declared that the building was the first that was ever known *to have drawn its own picture*.

All this panorama of invention and fear was a world Blake recognised and diagnosed. An artist felt like a stranger in a strange land where parts of England had come to resemble battlefields in an industrial war, eaten up in enclosures, with farmhouses left ruined and deserted as collateral damage. Clumps of dead trees stood like skeletons while the new manufactories rumbled and roared. Servile workers ran as attendants to serve the beasts amidst flames as in a pandemonium, the engineer and philosopher James Nasmyth wrote; to him it seemed the earth had been turned inside out, its entrails strewn about; and above, in a night sky which was no longer sacrosanct, even the stars were made pale and feeble by the cindered and blasted scenes below.

Satan was gaining sway in this lost paradise. Milton describes Pandemonium with the kind of matter-of-fact detail Thomas More applied to his island of Utopia and its fifty-four cities. Milton's devilish settlement is a high Capitol suddenly built out of the Deep. It is a stronghold born of darkness, of belched fire and rolling smoke and sulphur, like the chemosynthetic life conceived on the deep ocean floor, the same profound we now plumb for rare-earth minerals to power our own revolution. Mammon, another of Satan's angels, says Hell will be bettered by mining for such minerals, and he sets his crew to work as they

> Ransacked the center, and with impious hands
> Rifled the bowels of their mother earth
> For treasures better hid.

Who would ever have imagined such resources might be finite? Who knew?

Well, quite a lot of people, actually. Thomas Carlyle saw the mines and furnaces of the north as worked by half-naked demons, black as ravens, their bodies besmeared with soot. He knew it could not go on in this way. In Manchester, the artist and reformer Benjamin Haydon felt physically sick at the sight of hideous mill-prisons for children. New demagogues rose to voice opposition to these conditions, exhorting workers to turn against their tyrannical masters. In Bradford, Richard Oastler roused the crowd to tell their oppressors, Go back to your dens and there feed on the blood of your own cruelty.

The whole of London, with its own chimneys and manufactories, seemed surmounted by a black vapour, a permanent cloud hanging over Holborn, like fluid ink, Carlyle said, while its flood of humanity and animals toiled to run the capital, as if it were one huge machine itself. The black rain of flakes of soot Dickens saw fall from the sky in *Bleak House* had gone into mourning for the death of the sun.

The idyllic Albion that Blake had hymned, populated with ancient Britons painted with woad, was now filled with mill children whose faces were permanently stained blue from the dyes to which they were exposed.

What did all this mean for the soul? Who asked questions about the wisdom of progress and its stealth? Jennings thought the use by capital of science had repressed the imaginative vision in ordinary folk. He saw industrial Britain as a colony, its people as savages to be exploited; its wealth the property of the conquerors, and its preachers the missionaries to dope and convert the natives. There is no wealth but life, as John Ruskin said, always sure of himself, telling the good people of Tunbridge Wells that they were cannibals and hypocrites for dealing in stealing and speculation by buying cheap goods and investing in shares. Over in New England, Henry David Thoreau would be obliged to resist the endless march with his own body.

Let your life be a counter friction to stop the machine, he said. As men were enslaved to industry, Blake and his fellow artists felt they were about to be replaced. When he was shown a copy of the *Mechanic's Magazine* which celebrated the rise of the machine, Blake said,

Ah, sir, these things we artists HATE!

And all the Arts of Life they chang'd into the Arts of Death in Albion.

A Machine is not a Man nor a Work of Art; it is destructive of Humanity & of Art.

And when he read, in one of those magazines, of a surgeon who had, with the Cold fury of Robespierre, caused the police to arrest and imprison an astrologer, Blake wrote a letter of protest defending this Man who could Read the Stars, against the Newtonian who is opressed by his own Reasonings & Experiments.

As if the state could outlaw ghosts. Blake's inner universe was one long-running dream. He read the stars in a persistent, insistent series of episodes, played out in idealised places where his spirit would resist, like the faeries he saw in his cottage garden by the sea, carrying a funeral cortège. They were grey and green, he said, the colour of grasshoppers—which is probably what they were—but Blake had faith in their existence as surely as Gerard Manley Hopkins believed in the piskies of Dartmoor and W.B. Yeats, the water-horses of Galway.

The Industrial Revolution was the English revolution, Jacob Bronowski told his television audience, as all the lights went dark in 1973. Bronowski (Bruno to his friends) was speaking in his European accent with precision and grace, wearing a bright brown suit and a sky-blue tie (Ruskin used the same ploy to make his blue eyes seem bluer). It was a revolution with reverberations far in excess of what had happened in America and France, Bronowski said. At the start of the nineteenth century, when the country's population was being sucked into those dark cities, when families were being deformed to the demands of industry, and when the ticking clock came to dominate all effort and exclude all leisure and time to think; when Orlando saw a small cloud over St Paul's suddenly turn black and grow until it covered the whole of the sky at the stroke of midnight as the eighteenth became the nineteenth century; so it was then that Blake left the great wen of London for the freedom of the sea.

It was as though he had been given a secret key. All the things you wish had never happened? AI and satellites playing pinball among the stars? All the ways we went wrong? Blake offered a remedy. He needed no opium, no drink or drugs or kites to attain such a suspension of doubt; he was there already, physically intoxicated by the incalculable hardship and the glorious possibilities of life here on earth. He saw and felt this in his own body, incarnate in his flesh; in the planet spinning round the sun, the sea being tugged by the moon. He was an astro-priest launched into the unknown, ready to leave the shell of himself in the alien dust as the sun turned black and his spirit hurtled on.

It was the ultimate release, a little death. It's why he was inclined to the unreformed past, when churches were as gaudy as his designs; where everyone prayed for their own death every day, and when mystics like Teresa of Ávila said that Christ has no body now on earth but yours, no hands, no feet but your own, they were believed. It is why his last, unfinished designs, of Dante's *Divine Comedy* (he learned Italian to read it in the original), depicted devils and angels in such bright colours that they might have been discovered hidden under Victorian white-wash, painted over to censor their tormented souls.

Blake preferred a faith that preached forgiveness. One in which the goddess had not been forgotten, replaced by the rational patriarchy of industrialism and enlightenment that permitted all the isms to come. He did not set up any such obstacles to the holiness of life. And if I sat in my room all afternoon, I think, he might just come and see me, stepping in through my bedroom door.

Everything had a story in his art. He was a literary artist, as Geoffrey Keynes said. He's always illustrating something, showing us the way. His big idea, drawing us in. His Prophecies were issued via his holy ministry. Blake's industry was his revolution, and his machine was the printing press, purring like a tyger in the corner of the room. A potent engine waiting to start up its radical business with a roar, sending out news to the rich and the poor, the way Ruskin would hurl his *Fors Clavigera*, his monthly newsletter to the working classes, alerting them to the latest outrages inflicted by the relentless engine of economy; the way Jacob Bronowski would issue instructions through the cathode ray tube, telling us in his *Ascent of Man* that the origin of all art and mathematics is summed up in one simple graph: the division of the line of gravity by the horizon:

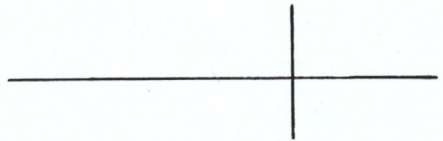

They never told us about that at school. We cower from the clouds and retreat in fear from the sea, trying to work out their power and if we can run faster than them. So Blake's art too would overcome us, ironically, through his science; the same way that Dürer played God by perfecting perspective, as Bronowski said, as a way of not so much recording a place as marking a moment in time. Blake reached back to the past to show what the future could do, and Samuel Palmer, his devoted acolyte, said no man more admired Albert Dürer than Blake.

Dürer, the Renaissance modernist, relied on printing to promote his art, despite Martin Luther's warning that installing such software would steal men's souls. The press was a time machine: you could programme it to go fast-forward or into reverse. Warhol would do the same, screen-printing reality, again and again. Blake became absolutely modern in his own medium, his message, his name, which said it all. As Wilde said, to make a great impression you had to have just five letters to your name.

A revolt in style. Blake is his art, personified. The fancy of this statement, as I put words in his mouth, is justified by his practicality. He may have despised rationality, but he was a technician, a designer as well. Blake and Dürer and Warhol all trained as commercial artists. Their sense of the graphic distilled everything; made reality more exciting, gave it life. It concentrated their visions and made them real, contained within what Blake called the bounding line. Like Botticelli, he drew firm and determinate outlines around his figures. He despised the modelling of later artists. The volume and weight of western art, as Kathleen Raine wrote, with all its naturalism, could not express mental space for Blake. It was stifling, all that chiaroscuro and muddy oil. Blake's aesthetic was closer to Byzantine, Buddhist or Chinese art, Raine said.

His characters parade in an array, bounded by his black lines, like animated cartoons or stained-glass windows. He records the eternal fantastical by rejecting everyday realism. Men think they can Copy Nature as Correctly as I copy Imagination, he said. This they will find Impossible. You can't copy nature, so why try? It is why he was such an influence on Aubrey Beardsley, himself a kind of enervated Blake at the decayed end of the century, picking up where Blake left off, with his red hair and pale hatchet face, all that stark fantasy in inky black and white. Beardsley's consumptive creatures crawling around the room could not have existed without Blake's sacred monsters and hermaphrodites; he foresaw the flow and fluidity of Beardsley's queer bodies.

Blake's bounding line was dynamic and direct; it was about making your mark, the way we draw the width of a circle because things go round. It was not about containment: like a giant loop, his line had no limits, no hierachy, no end. Like a cell it could expand to take in the universe or contract to the size of a flea. Blake needed no microscope or telescope to zoom in or out of the picture, to examine an atom or a planet spinning in infinity. After all, when told the moon was thousands of miles away, he said that was nonsense, he could go outside and touch the sky with his stick. He wanted to throw himself into it.

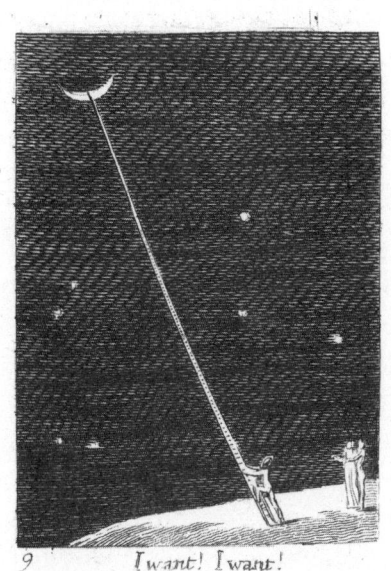

9   I want! I want!

Pub by WBlake 17 May 1793

He was nothing if not contradictory. He couldn't get any higher. They all came within his compass, these things, caught in his fearless gaze, the beam of his headlights. At Felpham, Blake was commissioned to paint miniature portraits of selected customers such as Thomas Butts, stippling their likenesses onto slices of luminous ivory, another stolen commodity. He was taught the technique by Hayley—flattery the size of a playing card, the classic new romantic look, all big eyes and big hair and big collars, caught in photo-booth snaps. The reduced scale of these images, made in the lee of the immensity of the sea, pleased Blake.

For a while, at least. He was, at any rate, accustomed to working with precious components, fitting as much as he could into a small frame for reasons of economy as much as for style. Copper was expensive, so were paper and ink; and so like Dürer, Blake pushed every image to the edge, all the while cutting in deeper to find what he was looking for, like a miner at the rock face. His process of printing came upon him as a necessity. It was waiting for him. As an apprentice he had learned all the tricks of the trade. Now he invented his own. It was entirely practical. How could he be his own publisher except by creating a new way to bring images and text together, at the same time obviating the need for a typesetter and any interfering outsider's eye?

He began, always with Catherine's help, by preparing a shiny sheet of copper plate, all glinting in the daylight, coating it with a mixture of virgin wax and Burgundy pitch. Then he smoked it under a candle flame to give it a thin layer of soot, subduing the sheen. Next, he took up his brush and, dipping it in stopping-out varnish, wrote his text in reverse by looking in a mirror as he worked. He was a spy creating a secret message, covering his work with his arm to stop anyone copying him at school. Only this covert technique, like an anarchist preparing a samizdat text (was that a bomb in his hands, or a black hole?), could enable this purity of transfer, this physical realisation of his visionary ideas.

Once the varnish had dried to a resistant sheen, they allowed a bath of acid—aqua fortis diluted with common water—to bite away around the unvarnished areas. Blake bit his nails. This baptism could take six to eight hours to complete. It left his designs standing proud like archipelagos. Blake would then perfect the images and words with a sharp tool before delicately daubing and pressing ink onto the raised design with a pillowy leather pad, another slow process that could take half an hour to ensure coverage and mop up drips. Meanwhile Catherine prepared the fine paper (they were proud of its quality), dampening it to receive the images. She then held it over the press, taking care not to let it sag onto the precious impregnated plate. And so the whole assembly was sent under the rollers of his press.

It was a marriage of paper and ink, of William and Kate.

In the studio with his students, rolling up his sleeves (in fact he's wearing a black T-shirt), Martin shows me how it worked. After all the inking and wiping, the care not to get our fingers inky too, he turns the great star wheel round like a ship's helmsman, sending the components in one side and out the other. As I take my turn at the wheel, I feel the sensation of pressure as the paper, cushioned under layers of wool felt, makes its transfer.

It is a very satisfying sensation. Everyone in the room is excited by its possibilities. Under pressure, Blake's drawings and words came together in one creation; launched out, newly made, as he peeled back the receiving paper to reveal the image like a holy shroud. No wonder his bodies looked so saintly, so sensual. This was miraculous art, capable of recreating itself. It was a triumphant trick; today he'd be doing it on YouTube.

As with Dürer's engraved plates, Blake's copper tablets took on the very shape of his vision, brought down from the mountain top. He bypassed censors, cynics and critics by publishing himself. He had to: declaring that God was a tyrant crown'd could have landed him in gaol. No editor or publisher nor arm of the state could stop him now. He evaded them as a thief in the night. He could be true to his words and the spirits on his stairs and dead poets on the beach. He'd harnessed the means of production in an industrial age, subverting the process by producing angels out of ink and Satan out of his Printing house in Hell.

A rose is a rose is a rose. His writing is his art on his sleeve. The one becomes the other, the perfect marriage of image and ideas, far more modern than anything else being done in his time or ours. His impulse becomes compulsion: he's an outsider artist, outside his society, telling the truth as the enemy within. The printed sheets emerge as outlines, butterflies to be coloured in by William and Kate using pigments ground by themselves: bone black, Prussian blue, red madder, yellow ochre, lead white; precious ores and organic residues; their cottage industry; a manufactory producing goods for the good of the world, hanging them up to dry.

After all, William's family were shopkeepers; friends remarked on his workaday clothes, his plain black suit and broad-brimmed, but not Quakerish, hat. He never wore trousers, only knee breeches with buckles and black worsted stockings. He was no Beau Brummell, having to send his shirts to the countryside of Islington to be laundered white; but he appeared pristine. Mr Blake's skin don't dirt, Kate said. Under it all he was a magician, a dandy in the underworld, and his Illuminated Books, as he called them—illuminated, not illustrated, since their images glowed with the meaning of his words—looked as though they had been switched on. They were electric magic, the eternal spark of his art.

The pictures that he produced were small for reasons of economy but their intention was vast. For an artist with a deep fear of failure and high expectation of success, printing permitted multiple choices in repeated runs at the same idea: each one the same, each one unique too. Why make something once when you could make it again? His prints could explore the original idea in new colour ways, adjusting to the climate and temperature of the time. They reacted like the sea or the sky to reflect the day; they echoed the mood of the artist and the time.

Did his customers deserve it? Who would decide? Blake selected them carefully. He didn't just drag them in from outside (although he tried). There were only sixty-one of them in his lifetime; but he knew his power. His source material may have been heavenly, but his undertaking was practical and it gave us reasons to be cheerful:

1. It conserved resources by bringing words and pictures all together on one page. So: Blake's was a reasonable œconomy, a personal paradise.
2. It avoided interference from meddlesome folk with limited horizons. Therefore: he could do what he wanted and to hell with the rest.
3. The process was immortal: it could carry on. Kate continued to colour in the sheets from the stockpile long after William had gone.

And so his art would outlive him. It was the ultimate satisfaction: each spread-out sheet became a legacy, a prayer, a thousand mysteries, all rolled into one as it rolled off the press. Blake as a cycle, continually recycling himself.

In Felpham his spirit soared away. Blake breathed in new inspiration with the sea air. He was like a horse let loose in soft grass, standing still and striking a pose. I labour incessantly, he told Thomas Butts on 11 September 1801. He could hardly keep up with himself.

I accomplish not one half of what I intend, because my abstract folly hurries me often away while I am at work, carrying me over mountains and valleys, which are not real, into a land of abstraction where spectres of the dead wander. This I endeavour to prevent.

I, with my whole might, chain my feet to the world of duty and reality. But in vain! the faster I bind, the better is the ballast; for I, so far from being bound down, take the world with me in my flights, and often it seems lighter than a ball of wool rolled by the wind. Bacon and Newton would prescribe ways of making the world heavier to me, and Pitt would prescribe distress for a medicinal potion.

Away with the physics and physicians! Blake never let gravity or melancholy pin him down. Of course, his freedom created its own problems; the most important part of art is what you leave out or what you take away. The cardinal labour of composition, which is excision, as Orlando learned.

But he wasn't alone. This was a two-person operation, conducted by himself and Kate. And they offered a pure distillation, not to be taken lightly. You weren't just buying a text or a picture or even a tincture, but an emanation of everything that was in Blake's head. Such was the completeness of his vision that it was not necessary to comprehend its meaning, any more than it was necessary to understand the stars. It was a bold mission, and had been ever since Blake had set off on his fantastic voyage to strange new worlds, using his new technology to record an astounding series of prophecies.

When Blake published his account of The Marriage of Heaven and Hell in 1793, it opened up his art. He created a multi-media work which never makes up its mind where or what it might be, precisely because its creator is forever open to endless possibilities. In it Blake launches himself into infinity and beyond, ecstatically snatching at words, the way he sang his own poems aloud, making up his own tunes as he went along. You can still hear his voice in his lines, as good a recording as we'll ever get, full of urgent and contrary epigrams that swing between paradise and the other place, paradoxical riffs that pre-empt Oscar's stagey asides, or the lyrics of a finely tuned pop song or a country-and-western ballad where anything can go wrong if you don't attend to the parables:

> The road of excess leads to the palace of wisdom.
> Eternity is in love with the productions of time.
> Enough! or Too much.

There's quite a lot of Johnny Cash and Dolly Parton to William Blake. He's folkloric, not far from the spiritual, how sweet the sound. His Songs of Innocence and Experience had set the tone with their titles and their tiny illustrations. The Little Black Boy, The Chimney Sweeper, The Garden of Love. How sick the rose. They were sentimental-harsh narratives like flowers of romance, testing the boundaries of what we see and hear.

Gravity, horizon.

Now, in The Marriage of Heaven and Hell, he took it all much further, pushing at the boundaries of acceptability. Part prose, part poem, part drama, he puts everything in there. Everything is beautiful, Blake declares, outrageously; even, and especially,

66

Satan. Leave all your troubles outside. Heaven represents reason. Hell is the energy, the necessary corollary, of fire and light. Without this balance we are lost and human wholeness impossible. We must be open to everything.

How do you know but ev'ry Bird that cuts the airy way,

Satan suggests, since the devil has all the best lines,

Is an immense world of delight, clos'd by your senses five?

Blake's art is air itself. It came out of nowhere and everywhere like a wild yeast. Objectivity meant nothing to him. That was a trick of what they would call enlightenment which was not enlightening at all; it had the reverse effect. From the apparent innocence of his songs to the sheer wildness of his prophecies, it is why his art remains so powerful. Even now, after being displayed, his pictures must rest for fifteen years, lying fallow in the darkness like cicadas, lest they disturb our inexorable progress and perturb our illusory selves. They become more powerful the less they are seen; the way he may fade away like their paint and ink, till all that will be left will be the legend he made. That's the danger. That's the allure, that possibility of loss.

Blake is the great director, the high auteur; dramatist of his own art, dictator of his own fate. Like Shakespeare, its onlie begetter. Everything follows on from that. His Iluminated Books are as much playscripts as poems or prophecies; cinematic renderings of things that happened before and after time began. He is a new wave of his own.

Where did it all come from, this new way of seeing and being, all this energy, all this darkness reigning in light, this new kind of man?

I, William Blake, a Mental Prince, I know my Execution is not like Any Body Else.

His earthly influences are fugitive but you can trace them in the art of his friends. In the muscular bodies painted by James Barry, RA, a visionary from Cork who would end up as a recluse in his ramshackle house off Oxford Street, his windowpanes pelted with stones by boys; or in the sensations of Henry Fuseli, RA, a foul-mouthed Swiss-born purveyor of erotic nightmares. But Blake stepped beyond them, beyond his own bounding line, into worlds which proved to his peers that he was clearly insane. He knew very well what they said, as he wrote in his notebook

> Who cries, 'all art is a fraud & Genius a trick,
> 'And Blake is an unfortunate Lunatic'?

Blake's art seemed one step from Bedlam, which was precisely where they thought he had ended up in his obscurity, his destiny, chained up along with his angelic anatomy and crazy cosmologies. Rumours were rife that he spent three years in the madhouse, if not the rest of his life. Ruskin, in the hours before he lost his sanity in his villa over Coniston Water, believing the devil was coming for him, looked at the Blakes on his walls and recalled the Auguries of Innocence: And when gold and gems adorn the plough. Oh—you dear Blake—and so mad too.

Ruskin may be forgiven his presumption. Blake didn't exactly cover his tracks; he glorifies in his lack of restraint and never holds back. As *The Marriage of Heaven and Hell* gathers pace, our hero finds himself in the Printing house in Hell, a cavern where the doors of perception will be opened and the truth will be revealed to us. We're intrepid tourists, quaking by his side. He enters the cave warily, like Beowulf, proceeding through a series of chambers containing Dragon-men and folded Vipers and an Eagle with feathers of air who causes the cave to become infinite.

This is fiction before and after science. Bird-men build

immense palaces in cliffs while lions of flaming fire rage around, melting metals into living fluids, and unnam'd forms cast metal into books arranged in libraries, the strange ones in the dome. In his Memorable Fancies, we are taken by the hand like Doktor Faustus; only, in lieu of Mephistopheles or the devil in disguise, our guide is an angel leading us through the disc of Earth to emerge into outer space, where the roots of twisted trees dangle down into the infinite Abyss, and the admonishing Angel—with whom Blake conducts a running debate about Newtonian Analytics—becomes suspended in a fungus, hanging head downward into the nothingness like the prey of an alien while shapes swim in the infinite deep like extraterrestrial whales in watery atmospheres awaiting the airy taxonomies of modern astrobiologists.

They continue on, poet and angel, on their odyssey into the void, surrounded by black-and-white spiders, passing the moon and Mars. The sun turns black and the deep returns.

Then, suddenly, not many stones' throw from them, appear'd and sunk again the scaly fold of a monstrous serpent. A fiery crest rises above the waves, like a ridge of golden rocks, from which the sea fled away in clouds of smoke.

And through the smoke, we see it: the dreaded Leviathan.

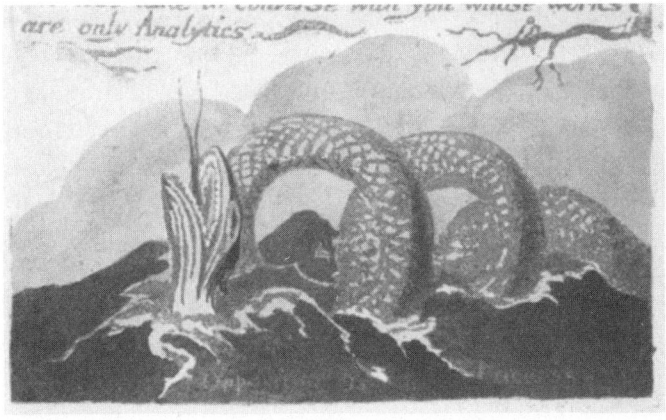

Oh horror! Oh terrible thing! A sight to strike terror into the hearts of Ishmael or Ahab; enough to loosen the bowels of Stephen Dedalus or threaten the sanity of Charles Arrowby. Something impossible to report back to ground control as the satellite link crackles.

His forehead was divided into streaks of green & purple like those on a tyger's forehead, rubbing it in, soon we saw his mouth & red gills hang just above the raging foam, tinging the black deep with beams of blood, advancing toward us with all the fury of a spiritual existence.

This sea-beast is a super-compendium, the ultimate chimera of all there is to be feared. One of the dragons that lurk at the edge of things. Blake's world is forever coursed with sea creatures in strange and terrible ways: in his *Visions of the Daughters of Albion*, jealous dolphins sport around a lovely maid and he asks,

Does the whale worship at thy footsteps as the hungry dog?
Or does he scent the mountain prey, because his nostrils wide
Draw in the ocean? does his eye discern the flying cloud
As the raven's eye?

He can't leave these visions alone. They won't leave him alone. In his next, transatlantic prophecy, *America*, he returns to the whale in its most vivid shape-shifting form: as the alter-ego of Orc, spirit of energy, born in the Atlantic deeps: a terrible boy, so full of elemental power that his consort, the Shadowy Female, stands in fear of his ability to transform himself into an eagle, a lion or a whale. Blake's metamorphoses outdo all Ovid and Kafka and the werewolf of London, evolving through many forms of fish, bird, & beast as Orc does.

Orc: the American Revolution, the trickster, sexy sea-beast of our dreams

the Antichrist, hater of Dignities,
Lover of wild rebellion, and transgressor of God's Law.

Orc: naked spirit of youth, burning so bright with radical energy that he produces his own flames; surrounded by but not consumed by them, fuelled by his own ecstasy; an incandescent superhero, a devilish jumping jack, a lightning flash born in a hurricane. A twenty-first-century gamer in a T-shirt would have a better hold on this rollercoaster ride of shifting identities.

Orc: running amok, flinging flaming fire round earth's rolling circles of space, defying the rational, the surrogate spirit of his creator Blake, an anti-Blake.

And all this turmoil and furore is happening now and in another dimension, across the ocean or just over the river.

Orc: nude and handsome as any Leonardo diagram, drags his torments into St James's Park via the gate in Great George Street, part dragon, part beautiful man. It's why he inspires dark angels in *Blade Runner* and *Alien*, and it is how he achieves his Outrageous form here.

His eyes behold the secrets of infinite mountains and his locks are like the forests of wild beasts. His bosom is like starry heaven expanded, where all the stars sing round; his loins are interwoven with silken fire, while his knees are rocks of adamant & rubie & emerald. Crossing continents and oceans, he rages in the European darkness like a fiery serpent of flame!

Part zoology, part nuclear fission.

Such is the Demon, says Blake, such his terror in the nether deep. Pl XI

And such is despair. It doesn't end there, it never does. In all of Blake's sprawling prophecies, with their interchangeable, confusing cast, Orc remains a constant, constantly reiterated but clearly identifiable by his one-syllable name. He fits so many guises into those three letters. Easy to say and to imagine, he's a byword for chaos, deeply glamorous, the way the forbidden will always be.

Orc: born from his mother's heart—Enormous Demons howl at the time—which is why William Michael Rossetti said his name was an anagram of cor. But its blunt beauty also evokes a Celtic-Nordic air; a bit Beowulf, or Balder the sun god.

Then, in this dark parlour game of attribution carried on over centuries, Samuel Foster Damon, a poet working in Rhode Island in the nineteen-twenties, decides that Orc's alter ego is Orca. *Orcinus orca, Orca gladiator,* god of the underworld.

Orc: ferocious sea monster from hell. The killer whale.

As a New Englander, Foster Damon knew what he was doing when he invoked this cetacean. Not yet a SeaWorld performer nor an emoji, but a swift and sentient assassin, capable of sudden violence, the mechanism of their own culture which enabled them to flourish for six millennia, evolving even now, as I speak, into different species perfectly adapted to their environment. An animal so graphic as to be almost animatronic, ready to rise up from the deep; a black-and-white emblem of revenge, memory and grief. Living for a hundred years or more, always there but somehow not, there could be no better disguise for Orc: a non-human being sharing our piteous sense of self, rehearsing their alien interactions in our elemental world. It might even look like a campaign.

But I digress. Whales do that to you. Once you've met them, in a theme park or the open ocean, they forever exert their power over you. For the purposes of this story, however, it is clear that Blake first came upon this fierce impersonation—the whale as fallen angel as Satan—in a poem which had more influence over his art than any other, and in which the devil took animal form so vividly that it is hard to know what to call him, or what to say when he introduces himself.

I'd never read the poem before. Like *Moby-Dick* or *Ulysses* or *The Magic Mountain* or a great grey whale, it hovered there, huge and unapproachable. Not a set text but an intimidation, a barrier to be overcome. But I knew I had to try.

One morning, as I was leaving the hospital—they'd been sticking their tubes in me again—I saw a pile of books outside a consultant's room. They were being given away. On top lay a new edition of *Paradise Lost*; not yellowing and forbidding like the ones I'd seen in charity shops, but printed on bright thin pages, more like a manual or a prescription for the soul. I stashed it in my knapsack and ran down all six flights of stairs in case anyone wanted it back.

Safely home, I opened it up like a box of delights; a light went on as I did. Arranged in twelve books over two hundred and thirty pages and ten thousand, five hundred and sixty-five lines, the poem was happening in real time: extravagant, disturbing, exciting. As a Puritan, Milton wore only black and white; this was a Technicolor endeavour and it was impossible to believe it was born of one man's mind. It might even blow yours. And as I read it, I realised how much Blake stole from Milton. Yet far from resenting the theft, Milton became a kind of posthumous godfather to him.

Milton lov'd me in childhood & shew'd me his face, he said.

He might have been the God whom Blake saw in the window as a boy, peering in on his four-year-old soul. And although Blake was by no means unsceptical—he criticised the poet for being too far governed by Reason, too bound by the physical world that separated the human from the divine—Milton kept on appearing to William, despite having died eight decades ago. They almost passed on the stairs, as

>   trembling I stood
> Exceedingly with fear & terror, standing in the Vale
> Of Lambeth; but he kissed me, and wish'd me health.

It was all you could ask of a hero, really.

And just as all of Blake's art is one long continuum, so Milton, who was known as The Lady at Cambridge on account of his feminine beauty, spent most of his life writing an outrageous account of the beginning of time. It was the founding myth out of which Blake's art would arise.

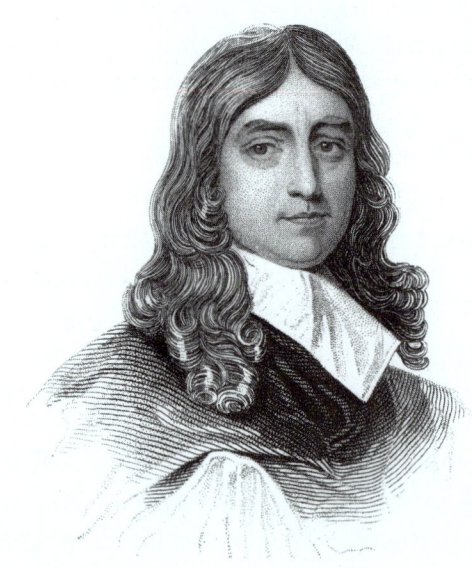

Milton's story was, quite frankly, almost blasphemous, a bare-faced act of appropriation. God could have claimed infringement of copyright. But, like Job, the biblical prophet who suffered so many trials and tribulations, the poet had to live through a lot of history to write his poem: the execution of the king, which he saw as a necessary evil; the personal bereavement of losing two wives, a son and a daughter; becoming a wanted man; losing his sight. Being blind made things worse; it meant he was forced to remember everything he had seen.

Milton: his name sounds mild and ordinary, almost mundane. He signed himself, John Milton, Englishman, the way Blake called himself the English William Blake. Their names were convenient guises: they were both wild and revolutionary, and, as Blake reinvented art, so Milton reinvented poetry. As an arrogant and beautiful young man, he promised the nation a great English epic; thirty years later he delivered *Paradise Lost*, completed after apocalyptic war, regicide, interregnum, plague and fire had turned the world upside down.

How to deal with that sense of an ending but write the backstory? As the spectacular prequel to Genesis, *Paradise Lost* hovers between medieval and modern, between science and faith, full of doubt and betrayal and shocking evil. It is happening now and before time, reliving events that shaped the earth even as Milton's own world teetered at the edge of darkness. His poem might as well be non-fiction; not least since Milton believed in the truth of the Bible and wrote his story like a war reporter, a foreign correspondent.

The story is as classic as any sci-fi origin myth rolling out over the opening shots. Satan and his bad angels have been flung out of heaven for defying God. It's a hard rain for their leader, aka Lucifer: bright star of the morning, now become the Prince of Darkness. He and his cohorts have been thrown over the crystal battlements, as though through the plate-glass window of a

Manhattan apartment. Vulcan, future architect of Pandemonium, takes a whole day to fall,

> Dropped from the zenith like a falling star

This box set comes complete with sound effects. It's an audible book, a poetic symphony composed in endless time, conceived in heaven, where only the unfallen can hear the music of the spheres, while the deselected descend to the new hell, a seething abysm where the disgruntled renegades gather to make war on God. It is there, in the sea, the vast and boundless deep, as Milton sees it, that we are thrown into the story halfway through—in medias res, the great screenwriter's trick. We meet Satan at full pelt, naked in his fiery skin. His name means adversary, and we come upon him rolling in the billowing sea

> talking to his nearest mate
> With head uplift above the wave, and eyes
> That sparkling blazed, his other parts besides
> Prone on the flood, extended long and large
> Lay floating many a rood, in bulk as huge
> As whom the fables name of monstrous size.

Only five pages in and Satan has already changed shape. The whale is the first animal to appear in Milton's poem; that is how important it is to his conceit. From the start, the poet associates the devil with the leviathan; an enemy of God but also an emblem of his will. We know where all this is going and it's not going to end well; that's what makes it so thrilling. Rearing up out of the deep, we see

> that sea-beast
> Leviathan, which God of all his works
> Created hugest that swim th' ocean stream:
> Him haply slumb'ring on the Norway foam.

The scene comes straight out of Milton's imagination, yet it may also be something he remembered, too. In June 1658, the year the poet began writing *Paradise Lost*, a leviathan arrived in the Thames during a storm. The whale had been deceived into turning from the North Sea into the river. It was a dead end. Caught as if in a trap, thrashing and roaring, they were slaughtered for their sins, not with Satan's spear, but with a sailor's harping iron on the muddy shore.

The fatality at Deptford was recorded by Milton's contemporary, the diarist John Evelyn; it was his land that the whale had arrived on. Evelyn had a penchant for cetaceans and their bones—he often remarked on their remains when he found them on his journeys from Coventry to Leyden. He reported that this whale was fifty-eight feet long, with skin like black coach leather and a mouth so wide divers men might have stood upright in it. He also noted those jaws were filled with strange plates in lieu of teeth, the which he found nothing more wonderful than that an animal of so great a bulk should be nourished only by slime strained through those grates. So accurate is Evelyn's description that we can be sure this was a right whale who had made the wrong choice.

Right whales are huge animals; they look more like houses when stranded on a beach. John Milton, blinded by glaucoma, could not have seen but must have known of the whale. He may even have joined the Infinite Concourse of people who came to hear the animal's dying groans. He would certainly have noted the later claim that the monster's demise was an augury of the death of Oliver Cromwell that year. The Lord Protector: a monster to some; protector to Milton, who now found himself on the wrong side. That same year, Milton suffered the death of both his wife and his daughter and, soon after, had to go into hiding, rightly fearful of the returning royalists and their retribution: he was arrested and imprisoned for three months.

Milton may or may not have regarded the whale, real or imagined, as an omen of his own fate; but there are enough sea beasts strewn through his poem to establish his debt to another fantastical chronicle: Olaus Magnus's sensational account of the Arctic seas, where, at the edge of the world, an abundance of monsters was to be found. Bishop Magnus had them engraved to prove it.

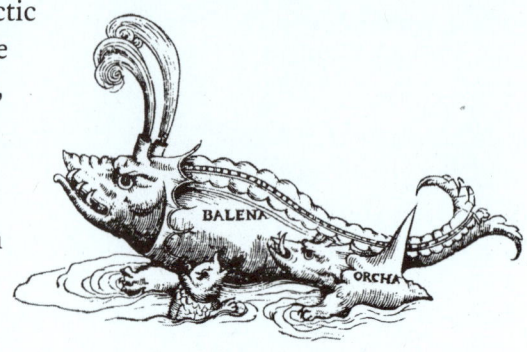

I've met these beasts before, but they still astound me. How much more so for a poet. Milton must have seen them before too, before he lost his sight, in order to be able to describe them. Yet, ironically, Magnus hadn't seen the animals himself. The whole thing was a deceit, designed to extend dominion over the wilderness. The great extraction was under way. It was all recorded in ledgers, bureacratically. In 1588, the Swiss doctor Conrad Gesner reluctantly—perhaps even sarcastically—gave space to Magnus's engravings in his otherwise accurate encyclopedia, *Historiae animalium*, which is where Milton probably saw them.

But they also appear vividly in a poem Milton knew very well: Edmund Spenser's reckless epic, *The Faerie Queene*, which Spenser presented to Elizabeth in 1589, just as evidence for the same half-real animals was arriving in the shape of spiralling narwhal tusks brought back by her Arctic explorer, Martin Frobisher; he had been searching, fruitlessly, for gold ore; his harvest of ivory spikes was worth more than their weight in gold (or, indeed, than the Inuk arrow he'd received in his buttocks).

So powerful were these strange animals that the Virgin Queen had them embroidered on her lavish gown, its silk petticoat teeming with spouting whales, seals and sea horses as emblems of her own imperial sway. After all, every time the queen entered her palace of Whitehall, she passed a monstrous whale bone hung in its courtyard; while in 1602 William Percy wrote a marine masque for her to be performed there. Entitled *The Aphrodysial, or, Sea-Feast*, it was designed to take place entirely underwater, with its star turn, a Leviathan roaring lyke Thirty Barril of gunpowder, a Monstrous Horrendum, huge as an Ork, who also possesses the art of philosophy and prophesy, is able to dance the Canarys, and speaks in Latin, Hebrew, Greeke, Italian, French, Spanish, German, Dutch and Welch.

They might have been spies, these scary creatures, draped in threads and dreams like elaborate jewels or baroque frogs. Scintillating like giant plankton on petticoats, appearing in fables and masques, they blur boundaries the way that Hamlet saw whales in clouds or that Orlando, lying in the long grass in the lee of an enormous house down whose corridors dolphins swam, waiting for the queen to arrive, wondered how one should speak to a poet who does not see you, who sees ogres, satyrs, perhaps the depths of the sea instead? as Virginia Woolf would write. After all, if a prince could be a dauphin, then why not her lover a porpoise on a marble fishmonger's slab in Tunbridge Wells, or a dolphin in Caithness introducing herself to a pod of porpoises by using their clicks rather than those of her own species, thereby identifying as a porpoise herself?

In the sea, nothing is as certain as it seems, and Edmund Spenser got particularly excited about its possibilities in his darke conceit, his embroidered allegory,

All dreadfull pourtraicts of deformitee:
Spring-headed Hydraes, and sea-shouldring Whales,
Great whirlpooles, which all fishes make to flee,
Bright Scolopendraes, arm'd with silver scales,
Mighty Monoceroses, with immeasured tayles . . .
Huge Ziffius, whom Mariners eschew
No lesse then rockes, (as travellers informe)
And greedy Rosmarines with visages deforme.

All this uproar seemed like alchemy, yet these were portraits of real animals: right whales, narwhals, beaked whales and walruses, far more extraordinary than their poetic alter egos. The sea and its denizens were shorthand for the strangeness of the undiscovered world. Dwarfing dominions, princedoms, virtues, and powers, the sea defied all earthly intentions; it might be full of ghosts or a training ground for fallen angels bent on revenge. And like Percy's horrendous whale, it proved capable of any kind of philosophy. In 1651, Milton's contemporary Thomas Hobbes created his own Leviathan to straddle the chaos of civil war, a colossus composed of other bodies like maggots: a squirming, towering construction; Godzilla wielding a crozier and a sword.

As a young man Hobbes had been secretary to Francis Bacon, taking notes from the scientist-philosopher for his catalogue of the known world. Now Hobbes had turned to his own writing, dealing in metaphysics that read more like contemporary art criticism or a mechanical manual that a sermon. He described life as but a motion of Limbs, and asked why may we not say, that all *Automata* (Engines that move themselves by springs and wheeles as doth a watch) have an artificiall life? For what is the *Heart* but a *Spring*; and the *Nerves* but so many *Strings*; and the *Joynts* but so many *Wheeles*, giving motion to the whole Body, such as was intended by the Artificer?

In Hobbes's eyes art imitates that Rationall and most

excellent work of nature, *Man*. For by Art is created that great LEVIATHAN called a COMMON-WEALTH or STATE, he said, which is but an Artificiall Man. All the while his giant loomed over the brow of a hill like a Goya nightmare, a robo-regicide; sermonising, monolithic, quoting the Book of Job at you, as if you didn't know that

There is no power on earth to be compared with him.

Job 41.24

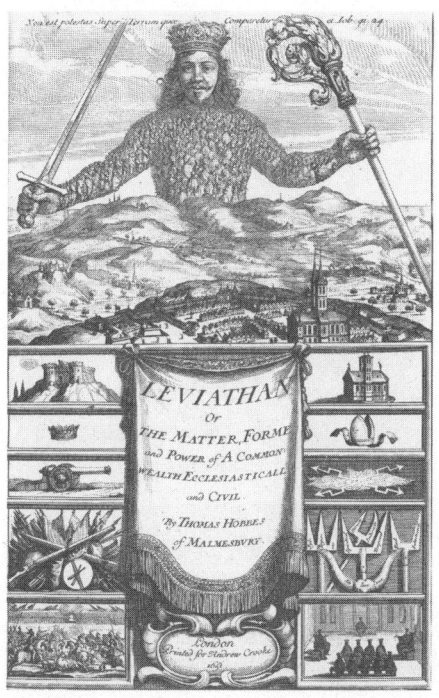

Hobbes saw our lives as solitary, poor, nasty, brutish and short. He reduced us to biological organisms of sensation and matter, and argued that marriage was a mutual agreement for two people to share the use of their genitalia. He never married and all of his close relationships, including his five years with Bacon, were with men. In *Paradise Lost*, Milton took it all a step further; he turned the act of creation into a cosmic emission.

God thought it was a good idea at the time. The beginning of time, that is. The all-powerful deity has set the clock ticking, starting the stopwatch. The spirit of God spreads his wings over the vast abyss and makes it pregnant. Inseminated by the deity, the spinning planet becomes its own foetus, with the ocean as its caul, one giant sea covering the entirety of the globe. Milton anticipates James Lovelock's vision of Gaia, of earth's living, watery veil. A thousand thousand stars shine and the waters generate,

> And God created the great whales, and each
> Soul living . . .

and the whale becomes everything, before or since. His rival is the first human who comes into being on a flow'ry herb bed in one of the most evocative scenes in the poem. Milton describes Adam's body as steaming in the new dawn, drying in the sun like a butterfly out of their chrysalis or a newly unfolded leaf. It's a sensual evocation of the first sexual act.

And when Adam complains about being lonely, God says, What about me? He's lonely too. But God is perfect and needs no such solace, unlike Man, says Milton. It is why Adam gets the animals for company; they are paraded before him, one by one (except the creatures of the sea, since they cannot thrive out of their wat'ry residence in the thinner air). Adam names them all, and so brings them under the dominion granted to him by God. In Blake's illumination of the scene, Adam gestures to heaven like a priest and strokes the serpent who will bring about his own downfall. Blake even gives Adam his own face: idealised, almond-eyed, naked; the Adam he wanted to be. Pl IV

Blake, a collector of funky devils and angels in old books and prints, is sure to have seen Magnus's pictures of sea monsters; they were reproduced whenever anyone wanted to evoke the dread and awe of the sea. They are its vocabulary: roiling, hornèd, spouting promoters of their own myths. Milton shamelessly recycles persistent reports of mariners like Brendan landing on an island unaware that, with fixèd anchor in his scaly rind, they've moored to a leviathan, only discovering their mistake when he dives. What a sensational hell: on Magnus's little map of horrors, gigantic sea serpents wrap their coils round unsuspecting galleons, snatching out sailors like ravens raiding a nest.

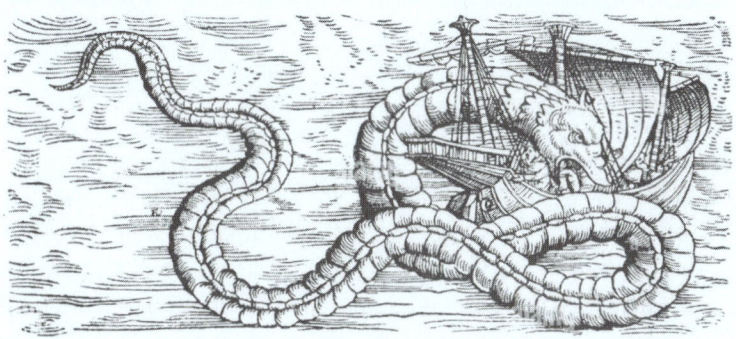

Personally I believe sea serpents existed. When and how I couldn't say, though I knew a scientist whose colleague saw one, in a remote ocean, far away. Of course, whales, sinuous and whiskery as they can be, could stand in for serpents when seen by unsuspecting civilians on a deceptive sea. A fin whale underwater looks decidedly serpentine, more like a giant eel, taking for ever to pass by. Milton himself confused the whale with the sea serpent when describing them as hairy maned and brazen-eyed beasts. A century later, when Oliver Goldsmith published his *History of the Earth and Animated Nature* in 1774, he correctly diagnosed whales as mammals like us, but adds that greater animals, who might not be obliged to show themselves in order to take a breath, might have been increasing in magnitude for centuries. To believe all that has been said of the sea-serpent, or the Kraken, he said, would be credulity, but to reject the possibility of their existence would be presumptuous.

As a boy growing up in London, Blake read Milton's saga in excitement and trepidation, in thrall to its Satan rising, stretched out huge in length on the deep as he becomes his own monstrous attribute, a whale. Then, morphing into a dragon, he unfolds his wings and flies up into the night sky, wreathed in flames. Milton's Satan, as much as Adam, is the almost perfected self (if you exclude his corrupted soul). He's alive to his own fantasies and deceits, rejoicing in the terror he choreographs, down there, in

> his dark pavilion spread
> Wide on the wasteful deep . . .

where he finds Orcus, the God of Hell, whom he enlists in his vengeful war. Milton's ocean is a thrilling foment of evil and anarchy; a place of banishment, an anti-region of the abyss as opposed to the empyrean Heaven where God and his swan-like angels dwell in their reign of ambrosial fragrance.

You have to admit Milton's devil is far more exciting than his heaven with its airy seraphim and Paradise's flow'ry vales. Adam and Eve are too good to be believed, living in Eden, their immaculate garden on a hill. They're stupid and naked and innocent as they prune their bushes although, as Blake will insist, they enjoy guilt-free sex before the Fall. No wonder the Lord kicked them out of the Garden, said D.H. Lawrence; dirty hypocrites. We itch for Satan to appear, a pantomime demon, disrupting God's golden kingdom. He is all too human, an anti-hero like Hamlet, obsessed with his own complexes

> Of what he was, what is, and what must be

a devil deserving our sympathy as he suffers the PTSD of exile, determined to raise hell on earth in revenge for his banishment. He might as well be in analysis with his crisis of identity. Intimately self-aware, he's forever casting to change his proper shape. Scheming, slyly seeking knowledge of where this new race of mankind might be found, Satan boldly assumes the figure of a stripling Cherub, a trainee angel with a deceptive smile on his face. In this guise, the imposter solicits directions from the Archangel Uriel, one of the seven who guard God's throne. Where may the First Man be found? he asks.

Down there,

he is told by unsuspecting Uriel,

That spot to which I point is Paradise,
Adam's abode . . .

the duped angel says, giving the game away. At that, Satan,

throwing his steep flight in many an airy wheel,

does a reverse turn and heads for the unsuspecting earth.

So Satan arrives on our planet as a spore, ready to seed Eden with doubt and furore—all those things that give the devil a bad name. At one point he's perched on the highest tree like a cormorant, the next he grows four legs and turns into a lion, rampant, sinking his claws into a deer. Before we know it he has slipped into the mouth of a serpent, telling Eve the words she's longing to hear: bite into the fruit of the Tree of Knowledge and become a mortal human, he says—and wreck God's plan. He's only one slither from pointing out that, having been fashioned from his rib, Eve's relationship with Adam is virtually incestuous. God promptly casts them out of Eden on account of their sin; a sin for which we are all still being punished on the day we are born, which, as Blake would point out, is rather tough on us since God is guilty of setting up the whole thing in the first place and should surely shoulder the blame.

All this, as exhausting as it sounds, took a lifetime to write, as you may imagine. There was a lot to fit in. Unlike Blake,

Milton, this handsome, hard-faced, college-educated man had been to France and Switzerland and Italy. He'd met Galileo, the perfector of the telescope, now blind and under house arrest, imprisoned for his beliefs, as Milton himself would be. He had seen Dürer's Melencolia; it inspired his own melancholy poetry. He had lost his young college friend, Edward King, drowned in the Irish Sea. He had lost two wives and his family. He had fallen so far he could only rise again, resurgam, to write his poem in episodes dictated to his son every morning as the poet woke up and recounted his dreams of leviathan.

He sets the scene like a framing device for a film, filling the sea with fishes and their fins and shining scales striped and flecked with gold, gliding under the green waves, grazing on seaweed and coral groves, or at ease in their pearly shells. At the calm surface, seals and bended dolphins play, stirring up the ocean, while down below, lingering for maximum impact, returning for their starring role

there leviathan
Hugest of living creatures, on the deep
Stretched like a promontory sleeps or swims,
And seems a moving land, and at his gills
Draws in, and at his trunk spouts out a sea.

Milton knew what he was doing. Whales always make a great entrance; they overwhelm everything else. They are inarguable. Milton's whale is an ocean: an elemental, apprehensible being beyond allegory, caught between natural and unnatural history. Everything follows on from them. Having filled the sea, God's earth opens her fertile womb and out come teeming, numerous living creatures, perfect forms. The elephant, the Behemoth, biggest born of earth, upheaves his vastness; the swift stag rears up from underground, bearing his branching head as from a rose garden; and ambiguous between sea and land, the river-horse and the scaly crocodile are to be found.

All these will fill Blake's mind too, from his boyhood on. Yet none rival the whale: both good and evil, the whale is set apart: an unknowable philosophical quandary to challenge humans who already believe that they rule uniquely. When Raphael the archangel appears to the newly made Adam, who's still rubbing his eyes in surprise, he tells him there are astronomical truths he cannot reveal: that there are other universes and other suns and other planets and other lives out there

> As when by night the glass
> Of Galileo, less assured, observes
> Imagined lands and regions in the moon

more things than our philosophies. Raphael advises Adam to

> Leave them to God above . . .
> Dream not of other worlds, what creatures there
> Live, in what state, condition, or degree.

The archangel is clearly admitting to the existence of extraterrestrials. He is also echoing Miranda's remark in *The Tempest* when she sees her first man: O brave new world that has such beautiful creatures in it. Like Shakespeare, Milton returns to the sea again and again as an image of loss and despair but rebirth too, as if it might be the remaking of us. At the end of the poem, the archangel Michael shows Adam a vision of the future in which the storm fills the thickened sky like a dark ceiling and all the world is underwater

> sea covered sea,
> Sea without shore; and in their palaces
> Where luxury late reigned, sea monsters whelped
> And stabled.

Sea covered sea. What an image that is! How jealous Melville would be. They might be plesiosaurs down there, twirling their terrible necks in Inigo Jones's inundated banqueting hall, twining their tails round its bone-hung pillars. The Ark sails on, with its chosen species, riding the hornèd flood, past islands salt and bare, the haunt of seales and orcs, where sea-mews clang.

No one ever wonders what happened to them. How did they live? What did they eat? Were they cast out for defying the Flood? In *Moby-Dick*, the biblical anti-hero Ishmael declares that the whales will not become extinct as a result of man's efforts, but would spout their frothed defiance over a newly drowned world when humans had been wiped out. In Milton's story, the world is ruined before it began. In Blake's version, God realises his great mistake.

Blake could never shake Milton's influence; the same shapes of spirits and animals lodged in his head. All these scenes of beasts and angels are only a step away from his *Marriage of Heaven and Hell*, where the Leviathan lies beyond the edge of the world, loitering in the nether deep that rolls with a terrible noise in a black tempest. And yet Blake went one step further: he turned the whole story, the whole allegory, into a new allegory of itself. Blake believed in the Bible too, but he also knew his visions were fantasies, woven from his dreams. You can see where he got his big ideas.

Milton's Orcus is the product of one age of revolution; Blake's Orc is the child of another, born even more slippery, peeling off one skin only to reveal another beneath. Sometimes his Orc is red and hairy, clad in furr'd robes & false locks which adhered and grew one with his flesh, and nerves & veins shot through them. He might be hollow. Sometimes he is the One mighty Polypus. And sometimes he incessantly howls like a wolf, burning in the fires of his Eternal Youth. Orc keeps on going robotically, Ariel crossed with Caliban and Hobbes's Leviathan, shewn to Dr

Faustus on a hand-held screen. He is modern and he is fearful, Frankensteinian, even stranger and more gothic than anything in Milton's blind ambition.

Orc stalks the future ruins of London and New York like an apocalyptic diamond dog, crossing Boston Common as a coyote, stealing into the marble halls of the library, only to be told to hush. He's an alluring leading player luring you on, a heartless lover, bound to betray you, ready to drag you down. Later we will see him change at lightning speed, from an inseminal serpent to a lion, an eagle, and finally, a whale in the South-sea.

My God, what have I done? Like Orc, the myth of the whale changed according to human need. Blake's own neighbourhood in Lambeth was home to two manufactories busily refining spermaceti oil brought back by British whale ships sent to the South Seas with their harping irons.

Deconstructed and processed into the rapacious economy of the late eighteenth and early nineteenth centuries—the exact point at which British and American whaling was at its swaggering height—the whale, real or supposed, would remain elusive to Blake. He wasn't particularly bothered about portraying any creature accurately; yet all his animals possess souls of their own. We know, for instance, that he'd been held by a raven's eye, probably in the Tower of London. Let the Priests of the Raven of dawn, no longer in deadly black, with hoarse note curse the sons of joy, he wrote in The Marriage of Heaven and Hell. For every thing that lives is Holy.

But to look a whale in the eye? In Blake's lifetime, countless whales appeared in the city as if posing for their portraits. Whole or in bits, they arrived in the vast Greenland Dock in Rotherhithe, ships tying up to bollards made of whales' jawbones, laying out great lumps of whale on the quayside, to be reduced to oil and decanted into barrels. Blake's career coincided with the peak of the metropolis as a whaling port. The same ships doubled up as slavers. Whales and people in containers. Blood for sugar or oil. The shareholders rubbed their hands.

The whale fisheries promised great wealth to oil barons and great death to whales. In just three years, from 1785 to 1788, the number of vessels trebled to more than three hundred ships. In July 1788, *The Times* declared the whale fishery had never been so fortunate. The whales were less impressed. You can't say they weren't warned.

It is not only upon land that man has exerted his power of destroying the larger tribes of Animated Nature, Goldsmith reported in 1774; he has extended his efforts even into the midst of the ocean, and has cut off numbers of those enormous animals that had, perhaps, existed for ages.

We now no longer hear of whales two hundred, and two hundred and fifty feet long, which we are certain were often seen about two centuries ago, he said. They have all been destroyed by the skill of mankind, and the species is now dwindled into a race of diminutive animals, from thirty to about eighty feet long.

Goldsmith's claims sound wild, but the cull of great whales did indeed reduce their size. By the twentieth century, sperm whales had shrunk by an average of four metres in length. At the same time we would discover that bowhead whales being hunted in the Arctic could live for up to three hundred years. Whales swimming in those waters while Blake was a boy could still be alive now. It was another kind of revenge. Goldsmith said he was quite sure that of all the enemies of these enormous fishes, man is the greatest. His book, which included accurate engravings of the cetaceous fishes, was familiar to Blake. One day, Goldsmith walked into the print shop on Great Queen Street where William lived and worked as an apprentice; he admired the shape of the Irishman's head as if he were a whale himself.

No one took any notice of Goldsmith's warnings. Hiding their dread behind expressionless smiles, the whale tribes sent their delegates up the river like desperate diplomats determined to press their case:

1. 1762. William is four years old. A sperm whale strands at Hope Point without hope, one of a dozen that had appeared in and around the Thames, and is exhibited in the Greenland Dock. Blake may or may not have remembered it, but plenty more arrive to make him consider what whales may or may not mean.

2. 1783. William is twenty-five. A bottlenose whale is captured by London Bridge and is promptly acquired by Alderman Pugh for his soap-boiling business.

3. 1788. William is thirty. Seventeen sperm whales founder at the mouth of the river as petitions are being laid before Parliament. No one apologises.

HOUSE OF COM'MONS.

WEDNESDAY, MARCH 19.

SLAVE TRADE.

Sir *Charles Bamfield* prefented a petition from the inhabitants of Exeter againſt the Slave Trade. Ordered to lie on the table.

SOUTHERN WHALE FISHERY.

Mr. *Grenvil'e* brought up the report of the Committee of yeſterday on the Southern Whale Fiſhery. From the refolutions that were reported, Mr. Grenville moved for leave to bring in a bill to explain and amend the 26th of his preſent Majeſty, regulating the bounties to be given to thofe who engage in the Southern Whale Fiſhery.

Granted.

4. 1791. William is thirty-three. A killer whale appears off
   Greenwich. Orc in a Georgian port, harpooned by sailors
   rowing out from the hospital, bent on a bit of adrenalin.

In this cut-price, cut-throat world where whales are weighed by
the pound, cetaceans take their chances. Some make it out alive.
Others end up skewered on pikes like enormous kebabs. In his
laboratory, the surgeon-scientist John Hunter—caricatured by
Blake as Jack Tearguts—is busy collecting and dissecting whales
the way he collects and dissects humans: i.e. dispassionately.
He has his trophies illustrated for the Royal Society.

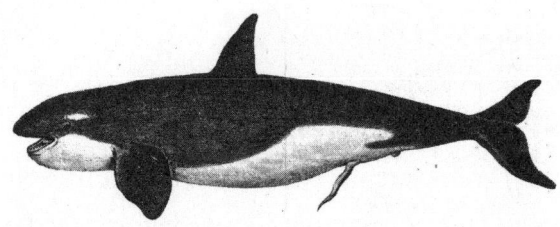

5. (cont.) March 1809. William is fifty-one. Shortly before his
   first and last exhibition opens over his brother's sock shop
   in Soho, a fin whale is slain at Sea Reach, beyond Gravesend.

The second largest animal in the world had taken a wrong
turning up the river and was shot by a passing pilot, John Barnes.
After four hours of death throes, the whale was carried cere-
moniously on a barge and shackled to the quayside, just below
Derek Jarman's window.

A WHALE.

Yesterday the curious were gratified by the exhibition
of an enormous fish of this species, in a barge on the
South side of the river, between Blackfriars and London
bridges. A spectacle so unusual in this latitude attracted, for many hours, some thousand spectators, who
crowded round the barge in boats, and furnished a brisk
and most productive trade as well to the exhibitors as to
the watermen, who conveyed them to behold this stupendous monster of the deep.

The carcase, seventy-six feet and six inches long, was far beyond the capabilities of the butchers of nearby Smithfield Market. The barge, bearing the whale like a queen, could barely contain all that decaying splendour; the flukes flopped for four yards over the stern and there were fears the rotting flesh would infect citizens with a deadly miasma. Like Milton, Blake could hardly ignore such a sensation; it was just a mile up the road. A whale on his doorstep like a dead salmon. When his exhibition opened that May (admission one shilling, or half a crown with the catalogue included), the first image to greet visitors, item No. 1 on the wall, was

The spiritual form of Nelson guiding Leviathan, in whose wreathings are infolded the Nations of the Earth   Pl IV

the imperial idol as a golden-haired god, whose own body had also been carried up the river on a barge before being lowered into the crypt of St Paul's. The funeral had cost £14,000, but it was a waste of money, since Blake had resurrected the hero and set him, stark naked, perched on a sea monster's coils.

A tumult of bodies tumble, caught in those scaly lengths, while at the admiral's feet lies a manacled figure: a Black person. Draw your own conclusions. Blake knew what he was about. In 1792, he had engraved images for John Gabriel Stedman's book on Surinam showing enslaved people in tortures too appalling to reproduce here. Don't expect me to educate you, he says. His painting is a poster for a perverted circus act or a tragedy of revenge.

We peer over the shoulder of the sole visitor to the gallery that morning, having been shown up the rickety stairs by Blake's brother James. The viewer, bemused, reads the catalogue essay (price half a crown, included admission, no free badges). In sixty-six pages of bombast and semi-apology, Blake announces his intention to recreate his works as giant versions in bright frescoes of pure and permanent colour, bright as precious stones. He is sure to secure an official commission for this task, he says, as something suitable to the grandeur of the nation. Like Milton, he is promising a national epic. Nelson, his intended angel, would be one hundred foot high, as tall as the leviathan was long. It would stand as a monumental signpost to the millennium, cynosure of all eyes driving down the dual carriageway.

Welcome to Albion. Art will show you the way. When Ruskin wrote about Turner's Harbours of England in 1856, the Athenaeum said it had not seen, since Byron's Address to the Ocean, a prose poem more worthy of a nation at whose throne the seas, like captive monsters, are chained and bound. It is worthy of the nation of Blake and Nelson, the magazine claimed, and true island hearts will beat quicker as they read. A few years later, Ruskin declared Turner the greatest man of England, but that he could only make manifest the dragon, not slay him, sea-serpent as he is. The fairy English Queen was once thought to command the waves, Ruskin added, but it is now the sea-dragon who commands her valleys.

Ruskin's crazy allusion saw industrial England as a rampaging monster, a new leviathan, and the land defiled by it, its harbours and mouths and chains and dominions and even its emperor queen overruled by a sea-dragon. Sinners and heroes and monsters and slaves were necessary, seen but not seen, appearing in the city as marine apparitions, both living and dead. The pavements Blake walked were lit so brightly with whale oil that a visiting German prince thought they had been illuminated purely on account of his arrival. And when the king rode out in his glass carriage, his royal corpulence was suspended by whalebone shock absorbers lest it be shaken by stones on the ground or the jeers of protestors as he passed by. When the Blakes moved to South Molton Street, they lived over a fashionable shop selling corsets stiff with whalebone, as worn by the Prince of Whales.

It was the greatest possible analogy of luxury and greed. Huge as they were, whales were both divisible and invisible. Turner was busy mixing his pigments with spermaceti dragged out of the depths, the same supposedly seminal oil being refined by his patron, whaleship owner Elhanan Bicknell, in order that

Turner could turn them back into pictures of sea monsters and dying slaves thrown into the water to be eaten by them. Bicknell had established his manufactory at Newington Butts, near Lambeth, where his colleague Thomas Sturge, Quaker and reformer, whose son Thomas would make incessant efforts to liberate the Negro from the condition of the slave, also established a spermaceti refinery. There was nothing refined about these enterprises, conjoined in darkness over the ocean depths, ending in premises no more than a stroll from Blake's Lambeth studio where he had created images of Black bodies dangling from trees like Billie Holiday's strange fruit.

Sadly, predictably, but also magnificently, hardly anyone came to see Blake's vision of Nelson wresting with Leviathan. Along with the rest of his art hanging in that upper room in Soho, the painting drew far fewer visitors than the real thing dangling off the riverside. Albion groans By the time the exhibition closed, not a single work had been sold.

From that moment on Blake gave up making such paintings. His super-sized Leviathan never got commissioned, never rose over the river to hold the gaze of amazed citizens. And yet, in his Prophecy for America, something mysterious appears as a physical rather than a spiritual presence, hiding in plain sight.

Not haply slumbering, but lurking in wait for us.

Taking his cue from Milton, Blake's *America* presents us with a whale on its first page. Orc is shackled like a slave in his dark abode, yet he fiercely embraces the strange Shadowy Female as black clouds shew their lightings to the silent deep.

Dark Virgin, said the hairy youth, thy father stern, abhorr'd,
Rivets my tenfold chains while still on high my spirit soars;
Sometimes an eagle screaming in the sky, sometimes a lion
Stalking upon the mountains, & sometimes a whale, I lash
The raging, fathomless abyss . . .

It is a Shakespearean scene, a brave new world, terrified. Ariel imprisoned by Sycorax; Caliban enslaved by Prospero. As soon as she sees Orc, the terrible boy, the virgin cries:

On my American plains I feel the struggling afflictions
Endur'd by roots that writhe their arms into the nether deep:
I see a serpent in Canada, who courts me to his love;
In Mexico an Eagle, and a Lion in Peru;
I see a Whale in the South-sea, drinking my soul away.

Like a ship in the harbour, the coming of Red Orc changes everything. He is an American phenomenon. The sky is dark and inky. The colour of polished whalebone, Woolf would say. Angry. It drips with discord.

Albion is sick. America faints!

You can hear the lightning crack and the thunder roar. Some terrible beast is about to be born, a beautiful Creature. Solemn heave the Atlantic waves between the gloomy nations, and as Orc rises over the sea,

Intense! Naked! A Human fire fierce glowing

a dragon drags along the sky and turns into Albion's prince diving down the side of the page, armed with a harpoon, like an angel aiming poisoned arrows at Amsterdam.

All the while, far below, under the yellow and magenta clouds, a strange grey mass lies sprawled on the shore. In Blake's first version of the page, it looks like the root of a tree. But in the final print it acquires flipper-like appendages and a tail. The King of England looking westward trembles. As well he might. This is no tea party. The form lies there as folded blubber, something splayed on a quayside, slumped like a slave. There's a new air of abuse to this picture. The sprawl of the beast, the way the body lies there, the fact that Blake coloured it in grey in the finished copy he sold to his close friend, John Linnell, suggests that he saw the real thing, something once alive.

Pl V

I thought I was imagining it; I see whales everywhere, as you can tell. But in 1954 the distinguished Blakean David V. Erdman identified the king on Albion's shore as looking at a beached sea monster, a revolutionary whale, Orcus as a Hell reaper of kings. In 1793, Blake had shown Urizen standing on the same giant carcase, a vast Spine that writh'd in torment. In 1979, Allen Ginsberg would see it as the Leviathan of Revolution, that big blunk on the seashore.

Everything will rot away. Everyone is agitated. Blake removes references to George III breathing with flames for fear of the state. Death closes the circle of darkness. The sullen thud of the waves, the chained beast on the beach, as Woolf says in *The Waves*; the canopy of civilisation is burnt out. All is lost in the raging storm. It is no coincidence that Blake's page echoes the first illustration of *The Tempest*, published in 1709.

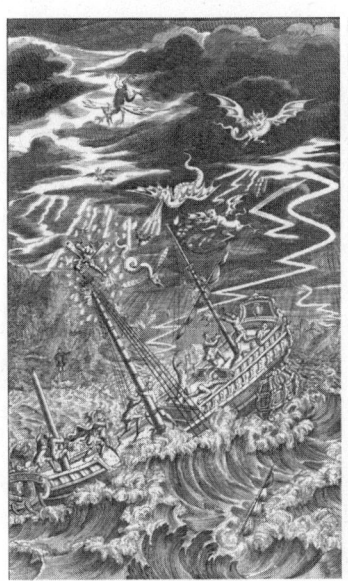
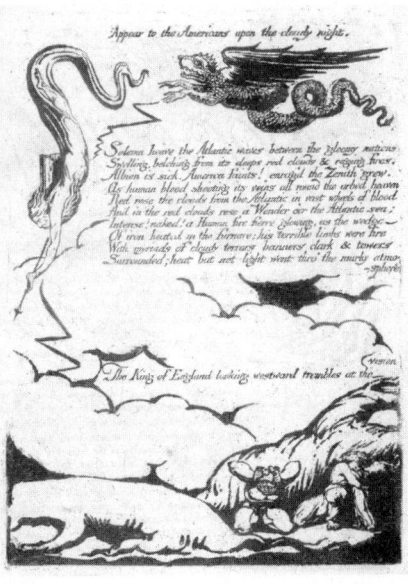

No wonder Blake's books came in loose sheets. How could you bind infinity? His art was a climate and an atmosphere of its own, said Kathleen Raine. Like Shakespeare and Dürer, Blake created an other, entirely comprehensive, if not quite comprehendible, world, she said.

That's what leads us on. There is nothing between Blake's work and himself. The two become one, unified in his hand-writing, joined in his marriage of heaven and hell; the way that his figures become characters of his words, hieroglyphically blurring into one long dream. His art is the language of bodies; ideas in idealised flesh. They embody his meaning. We're all naked in his world. Intimate with the elements and everything around them, his players swim in the air and in fire too. They are his AI avatars; from alpha to omega and back again. No space is left unfilled, no body unentwined or untempted. If you've ever felt a snake curl round your arm, lovingly tightening their embrace, scaly skin glowing with interior heat, forked tongue tasting the air around you, you'll know what he means.

Every image reaches to the edge of its frame. Nothing is left unembroidered. Tendrils and insects and weird beings creep in between the cracks, falling into the gutters. Someone once told me it was the sign of an unhinged mind, filling a page like that. But Blake was cranked up high and unconfined. His pictures are words, realised. In his commercial life he once designed printed plates for toy theatres, to be cut out of paper and card and coloured in; they were advertisements for contemporary melodramas, but they could have been acting out Blake's prophecies, where all of his characters are performing all of the time.

You get more for your money with Blake. He's the Willy Wonka of art, your golden ticket to other worlds. He takes you there by the hand. His generosity is magical and without limits. Blake in fire, in iron, in paint; in ink, in the flesh, in the stars. Like the sea, you can't be for or against him; he doesn't give you that choice and he never, ever gives way. In his certainty is his ambiguity. He's a cloud floating over the ocean, a layer of unknowingness through which new worlds arise. The stars rearrange themselves before your eyes.

The Nature of Visionary Fancy, or Imagination, as he says.

An amorous camera, recording everything he ever saw. He applies the sublime not to the landscape but to the human body itself, as Raine says. They call him a Romantic artist. If so, he was the first and the last.

In *The Marriage of Heaven and Hell*, Blake and the Angel throw themselves into the sun, and career on their space odyssey into the void between Saturn and the stars. The sun turns black and is surrounded by spiders while Mars whirls about. At the nadir of their journey the two look on, horrified, as a group of apes rape then eat their weakest members, tearing their limbs off one by one till they are mere trunks. It's a glimpse of the dawn before humanity; they might as well throw their bones in the air. We see the simian assailants grinning and kissing their victims, before they resort to eating their own tails, the way Ishmael will watch wounded sharks eating their own guts.

No worse, there is none. Art eats itself. We leave only our bones behind. Nothing ends, it always does. Blake's dream machine spews out images from a medieval maw like a desktop printer. He's the modern world, its consummation.

He sees it all.

That's his power, and our downfall.

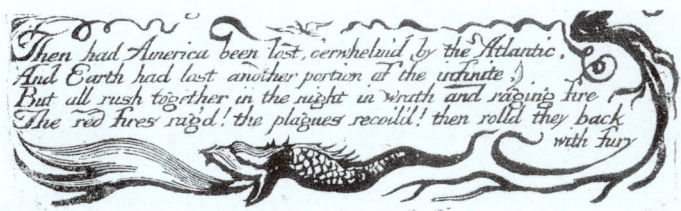

By the summer of 1803, Felpham had become an unsettling place. The sea that lulled Blake into a visionary state now terrified him. Far from slumbering, he was sleep-deprived. The ocean became his fate: to be stranded here, forced to count every grain of sand, every bit of shingle rattling on the beach.

He hadn't counted on playing Sisyphus for the rest of his life. What had the sea done to him? Its wild expanse was a trap, not an escape. A dead end. A place where the sinful were chained in a sea cave, back to back, while the waves roll'd around and the black jealous waters are their prison walls. The Blakes' pleasure turned to pain. What fresh hell is this? Their idyllic cottage was damp and the salt air got into their lungs and into their bones. Their uncellar'd floor seemed to allow the sea in, as if the tide itself might rise up through their rooms.

For a while it went swimmingly. Kate made money from the engraving plates she was printing for Hayley; William was writing wildly, without Premeditation & even against my Will, he reported, receiving Dictation from the dead. His deadline. As he walked the lanes he saw his father and his mother and his two brothers, one good, one evil, before him on the path. A thistle turned into an old man telling him not to return to

London. Words poured into his head. Like Melville writing his epic in Western Massachusetts, far from the sea, Blake's sojourn on the coast, away from the city, had given birth to a leviathanic text. He confessed to Thomas Butts the true reason of his being brought down here.

I have in these three years composed an immense number of verses on One Grand Theme, Similar to Homer's *Iliad* or Milton's *Paradise Lost*, the Persons & Machinery intirely new to the Inhabitants of Earth.

I consider it, he told Butts breathlessly, with no hint of immodesty, as the Grandest Poem that this World Contains.

I may praise it, he hastened to add, since I dare not pretend to be any other than the Secretary; the Authors are in Eternity. He would sing forth the Lord's Praises, that the Dragons of the Deep may praise him, he said, & that those who dwell in darkness & in the Sea coasts may be gather'd into his Kingdom.

Others had resort to the shore for recreation and the physical cure; Blake came here as an emissary to the leviathan and the polypus. He might as well emit sonar clicks from his great square head. The words spill onto the page. Twelve or twenty or thirty lines at a time, he said, as if the act of writing were entirely separate from him, spooling out from some infernal desk. The spirit was upon him. A sea fit. An immense Poem Exists which seems to be the Labour of a long Life, he said, as if it had appeared almost without his intervention at all; all produc'd without Labour or Study, he declared.

The nature of this new epic, almost automatically written, was not to be revealed all at once, nor was it accessible to the future, despite being squashed into the little tower of books by my bed. Instead, it shifts and forms and coalesces like a cloud too big to fill the sky, part of one overarching saga, all the instalments of his illustrated books to date and those yet to come, coming together in a total work of art that seemed barely comprehensible at the time and even less so now.

In his biography of Blake, Gilchrist sees these books as

allegory beyond allegory; most readers will give up trying to understand them after the first page or two, he says. It is true enough: we hear them like a song: not necessarily knowing its meaning, but sensing it all the same; the way A.E. Housman said Blake's meaning was unimportant or virtually non-existent, so we can listen with all our hearing to his celestial tune and appreciate its ravishing beauty, greater even than Shakespeare in his opinion. Meaning, Housman added, is a poor foolish disappointing thing in comparison with the verses themselves; in the same way that Eliot would later declare that genuine poetry communicates before it is understood. The Tyger growls and snarls but we can't translate them any more than we could a lion or a whale, and we wouldn't want to know what they meant to say anyway.

Blake sang his verse. His tunes, described as singularly beautiful, were noted down by musical professors, and promptly lost to us. I never became who I should have been, the starman said. O why was I born with a different face? said Blake. No one understands, they moan, like Job. In the rhetorical twists of chance and fate, pain produces great art, and not one, not two, but three epics emerged from Blake's disturbing sea interlude, viz:

1. *Vala, or The Four Zoas*, a gothic riot of explicit sensuality, full of crocodiles and orgies, drawn to meandering conclusion here at the coast, never to be published; 2. *Milton*, in which Blake imagined John Milton returned from Heaven to consider the errors he had made on earth, rendered in forty-five plates; and, striding over one hundred pages,

3. 𝕵erusalem the 𝕰manation of the 𝕲iant 𝕬lbion

After my three years' slumber on the banks of the Ocean, I again display my Giant forms to the Public, Blake declared in his needy foreword to *Jerusalem*. Reader, <u>forgive</u> what you do not approve, & <u>love</u> me for this energetic exertion of my talent.

We do love him, and forgive him, too. He makes evangelists of us all, through the power and insistence and obscurity and light of his art. He demands our loyalty, not our pity. We have no choice. He's our here and now, here, and now. Happening in his future, not our past. Albion is his own body, like London, a place where Jerusalem's ancient pillars stood and where Boys would bathe in delight in the ponds and where all that has existed in the space of six thousand years was not lost.

And all of this justified Blake's golden years by the sea. This was no sabbatical, no respite, but a foment: an act of involuntary recollection and prediction, like the future receding year by year or the great shroud of the sea rolling in. Just as Dürer's year by the sea in search of a leviathan appeared to end in disaster, but in fact impelled him to ever greater works, so the sea empowered Blake's vision in a remote-viewing episode, a suspended state. Yet, as it demonstrated only too clearly, it could also withdraw its patronage, cruelly, like the tide, leaving the artist high and dry with nowhere to hide. I was brought here, he said,

> that in three years I might write all these Visions
> To display Nature's cruel holiness . . .

Expecting the Millennium, disconcerted when the sense of an ending did not transpire, Blake was overwhelmed. The Visions were angry with me at Felpham, he said. He'd lost control. He was too far from the great movements of the city, from Albion, from the forces that shaped him. He admitted to missing the influences of other artists and the opportunities of seeing fine Pictures in galleries. He needed the desart of London to reassure him; its dense streets meant salvation and freedom. No one would stare at him there; he could carry on his conversations with his friends in Eternity, unannoy'd, unobserv'd.

He described that time later in the form of allegory, as if trying to deal with the trauma that way. In one of the most fantastical scenes in his *Milton*—his most fantastical work, part folk horror, part chart of the deep unknown—he tells us how

Satan stirs:

And he appear'd the Wicker Man of Scandinavia, in whom
Jerusalem's children consume in flames among the Stars

while

In Palestine Dagon, Sea Monster, worship'd o'er the Sea

and out of the Head and the Heart, the Loins and the Seminal
Vessels, the Stomach & the Intestines, a dreadful body forms
like a prolapse,

the Ulro: a vast Polypus
Of living fibres down into the Sea of Time & Space growing,
A self-devouring monstrous Human Death Twenty-seven fold

an image which would resurface in H.P. Lovecraft's 1917 story
of Dagon, the Fish-God, seen in the Pacific by the shipwrecked
survivor of a German attack who is driven insane by the gigantic
tentacled deity, who is worshipped by aquatic beings, likewise
half-human, half-piscine. And just as Dagon also appears in
Paradise Lost as upward man/downward fish, so in Blake's poem
Milton himself arrives out of the sky, down a path paved with
precious stones, as if stepping off an astral escalator,

into my Cottage
Garden, clothed in black, scvcrc & silent he descended.

It was a matter of life and death. No sooner had Milton
arrived—a more welcome garden visitor than a drunken gren-
adier—than did the most stupendous spectacle appear: nothing
less than the Spectre of Satan,

trembling & shudd'ring

He stood upon the waves, a Twenty-seven-fold mighty Demon
Gorgeous & beautiful; loud roll his thunders against Milton.

No Nelson in coils, this, but the real thing, a colossus in sonic
waves. Like Byron, who implored, Roll on, thou deep and dark
blue Ocean—roll!, Blake's

Loud Satan thunder'd, loud & dark upon mild Felpham shore
Not daring to touch one fibre he howl'd round upon the Sea.

Tidal, pulsating, rising out of the English Channel. Nothing to
give. Everything collides,

Where Orc incessant howls, burning in fires of Eternal Youth,
Within the vegetated mortal Nerves; for every Man born is joined
Within into One mighty Polypus, and this Polypus is Orc.

All sea beasts and queer creatures conjoin, snakes and anem-
ones and slimy things under suspicion for lacking the usual
number of limbs. Satan and Leviathan roar and Felpham
becomes the epicentre of a new Revelation. Everything is
thrown into chaos by the terror and Milton beholds his own
Shadow in transition, like a mollusc changing sex:

A mournful form double, hermaphroditic, male & female
In one wonderful body.

And all this, all this palaver and fuss, all this tumult of words
and pictures and fluidity which he could only complete after
he returned to the city, merely goes to show how the ocean
stayed with him as an idea and now a reality, and how Blake
would weather it all like a piece of seaweed, raw and justified;
determined, with his sweet Shadow of Delight, his Kate trembling by his side, that they would return to London, to hear
the Cry of the Poor Man. It is there that his great sea-of-

subconsciousness closes over and concludes with a portentous scene in which terrific Lions & Tygers sport & play and All Animals upon the Earth are prepar'd in all their strength, as if the whole poem had been merely the prelude to something even more wild and majestic.

Milton, the poem, begins with the enduring words of Blake's Jerusalem, his clarion call to action; it ends in the legacy of *Paradise Lost* and its filled-to-bursting sea. It is pure Blake: his victory and his defeat. More pragmaticially, Blake's great escape from Felpham's tentacles would free him of the demands of the now-hated Hayley, his poet-patron whom he now cast as Satan himself, setting impossible tasks, asking William to illustrate his mediocre verse which stood in such a contrast to the thermodynamic blast of Blake's work.

Both my good Blakes have been confined to their beds by a severe fever, Hayley said blithely, complacently, as if they were his live-in butler and housekeeper, living so close by as they did. Their tedious employer was entirely unaware, for all his lordly generosity, of the power of the Lamb turned Leviathan. Blake's art fed on chaos; he felt he was prostituting his talent for cash. Those miniatures, which Hayley taught him to paint, made him feel claustrophobic, like the low roof of the cottage itself. They darkened his horizon and compressed the light of his visions.

He couldn't think with the roar of the sea in his head. The shore was a full stop, and the weekenders having fun were treating him like some seaside artist offering to do your portrait on the prom. His friends had made him go to Felpham for rehabilitation, for the good of his soul. They thought commercial viability would divert him from his troublesome visions. He should have said no. It was like sending him to America to get his teeth fixed. Blake now knew it was a mistake. He was not Hayley's pet.

The truth is, As a Poet he is frighten'd at me; he thinks to turn me into a Portrait Painter, but this he nor all the devils in hell will never do. I am determin'd to be no longer Pester'd with his Genteel Ignorance & Polite Disapprobation, he declared. Twenty-seven Heavens and all their Hells.

Blake needed a city vibe to concentrate his thoughts and entice his visions, not this parochial backwater. Also, Hayley had declined to give him a rise.

William rose above it all. Money meant nothing: his pale face turned even paler when it was offered to him. He left it to Kate to settle the accounts and got on with being a great artist of whom almost nobody had heard.

It was no surprise that in his engravings for Hayley's self-published *Ballads, Founded On Anecdotes Relating To Animals*, Blake's gallery turned gothic. To illustrate his patron's doggerel, he drew a spectral horse emerging out of a Dürer forest via a Fuseli nightmare. A giant eagle with hooked beak hovers over a human baby installed in their nest on a vertiginous ledge. Most terrifying of all, a swimmer casts his clothes aside to take a fearless dip—Bold in a flood he lov'd to leap, as Hayley did—only to stall in horror, hands upthrown, as his brave and beloved Fido falls headlong into open jaws.

Hayley imagined a crocodile; Blake gave him Leviathan, coils curling unseen under the waves. Kathleen Raine thought this image unintentionally funny. She should have known better, writing in 1968. It might have been another beast: the state, come snapping for Blake.

It was a brutal new world. The revolutions in America and France that seemed so attractive to Blake and his love of the disruption of the status quo were horrifying to the authorities, desperate to suppress any dissent. During the anti-Catholic Gordon Riots of the summer of 1780—when wild and savage insurrection quitted the woods and prowled about our streets in the name of reform, as Edmund Burke reported from the frontline—Blake had been caught up in the mob and found

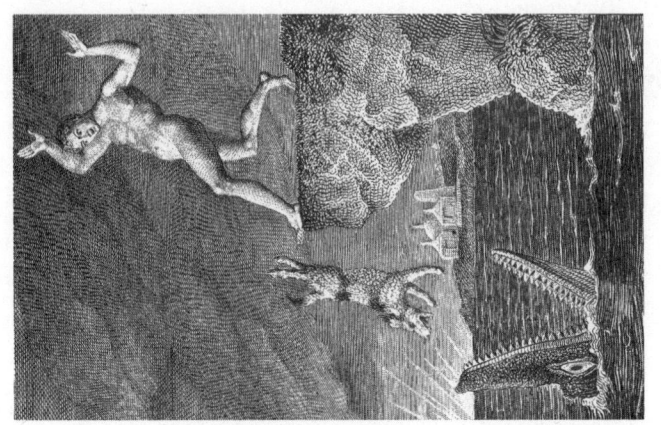

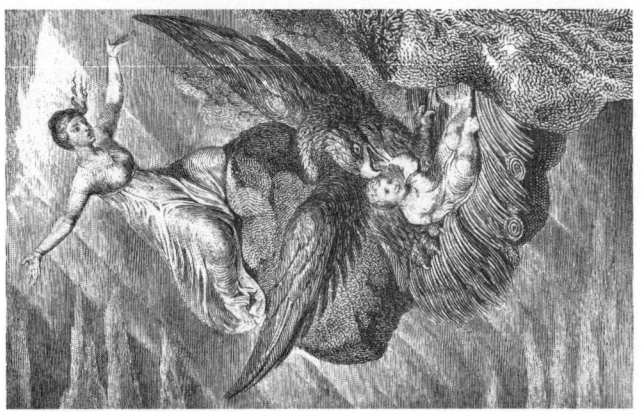

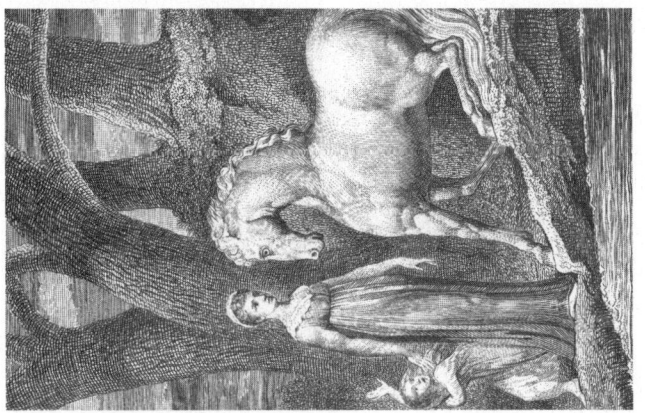

himself carried along. It was the nearest Britain came to revolution, and he witnessed it at first hand.

Private houses and Popish chapels were burning down; people chalked No Popery on their walls, whether they believed it or not; even Jewish people wrote, This House True Protestant, to defend them from the hordes. As the week-long riot reached Newgate, Blake was at the front of the crowd, watching as the prison was stormed and three hundred convicts were set free. The Houses of Parliament were assailed. Outraged newspapers reported that the duke of Northumberland's pocket was picked, the wheels were taken off the bishop of Lincoln's carriage, and the Lord Mansfield was daringly abused and traduced to his face. When the Bank of England was attacked, it seemed total anarchy was at hand.

A ferocious energy was released along with those prisoners. Martial law was declared, fifteen thousand troops were called out and up to three hundred rioters were shot dead. The formal retribution, when it came, was vicious. Strings of boys under fourteen were hanged in a row like gamekeepers' birds. I never saw boys cry so! said one witness. They were silenced, like deserters, crying for their mothers before they were shot against a wall.

Any kind of anarchy might prevail in such feverish times. In 1795, as George III was being driven to Parliament in a glass-enclosed coach, as though he were made of glass himself, crowds shouted and hissed at him, No George, No War! and threw sticks and stones at the coach. One of them, Kyd Wake, a wondrously punkish name for a revolutionary, albeit a bookbinder from Gosport, was sentenced to five years' imprisonment for using such seditious words. Uncertainty bred any number of conspiracies; sometimes to extravagant extremes which now sound like the wildest prophecies dreamed up by Blake.

In the summer of 1796, Robert Thomas Crossfield, who had served as a surgeon on a South Sea whaler, the *Pomona*, where he was praised by the sailors whom he treated for his humane care, but who was also a member of the radical London Corresponding Society, was arraigned at the Old Bailey on a charge of high treason. Crossfield stood accused of plotting to assassinate the king on his way to the theatre using an airgun of the surgeon's own invention, designed to kill a man silently at a distance of forty yards by firing a poison arrow into the corpus of His Majesty and thereby causing him to expire in the greatest agonies.

The dart, as the boatsteerer of the *Pomona* told the court, was like one of our harpoons which we kill whales with.

There was a fearful sense of farce to this allegation—not least because contemporary cartoons satirised the king's own son as the corpulent Prince of Whales. But the state was right to be afraid. The London Corresponding Society, whose subscribers included Olaudah Equiano, former slave turned activist, was gaining substantial support, with public meetings of tens of thousands of people on St George's Fields, which the Blakes could see through their rear window in Lambeth. All the while the Society was being spied upon by the government, which was also receiving reports of a militant group calling itself the Lambeth Loyal Association holding secret meetings in the upper rooms of taverns, where they performed military drill in training for armed insurrection. That they were establishing links with the United Irishmen attempting to free their land from British control was even more worrying. With their unpowdered cropped hair and loose simplified clothing, these radicals were visible and they were dangerous, and the authorities had their own devious means of subverting such seditionairies. In that light, the arrest of Crossfield and other conspirators on such an extraordinary charge seems suspicious, to say the least.

In scenes retold in the Old Bailey, having been played out in prison hulks and the confines of ships in Portsmouth and Brest—men in places made open to mutiny by their proximity to the sea—one witness said that Crossfield had told him his name was Tom Paine and had laughed heartily, declaring that Paine's works were the best in the world, and revealing that they planned to shoot Pitt, the prime minister, too. Then he sang a seditious song and exclaimed, Damnation to the King of England! All this anarchy could have come from Melville's *Billy Budd*, set in the summer of 1797, after mutineers in the Solent and the Thames had flown the red flag and blockaded the city; Billy Budd, the Handsome Sailor, is press-ganged from a ship named the *Rights-of-Man* after Paine's book, only to be hanged as the innocent victim of a treasonous plot.

Crossfield's ship had set sail from Portsmouth, but was captured off Falmouth by a French corvette and set adrift. Crossfield, already a wanted man, was arrested in Fowey and sent to Bodmin Gaol; on the way he attempted to bribe his captors and escape, but failed to convince them of the price he offered to pay, and ended up in the Tower instead.

The case, which Blake would have read about in *The Times*, was dismissed for lack of evidence (the court also heard, tellingly, that Crossfield was accustomed to taking large quantities of opium). But such scenes would have worried Blake, like anyone else who questioned the status quo. The state was not to be challenged, as the deaths of 25,000 people killed in the suppression of the Irish Rebellion of the death of 1798 proved. Blake had known Tom Paine and was said to have warned him of his imminent arrest, encouraging him to flee London. He knew he might already be under suspicion: after all, his art itself was insurrectional and defiant, sending inflammatory words and revolutionary images rolling out of his printing press.

In the summer of 1803, as the Blakes were making plans to leave Felpham, William discovered a soldier in their garden. He was probably drunk, but what began as a minor dispute escalated into a serious situation as Blake asked the trespasser to leave. He did not know that Private John Schofield, a demoted sergeant in the Dragoons, had been asked to cut the grass by Blake's gardener, William, who also worked as an ostler in the nearby Fox Inn. When challenged, Schofield refused to go, threatening & swearing, as Blake told Thomas Butts.

I, perhaps foolishly & perhaps not, putting aside his blows, took him again by the Elbows, &, keeping his back to me, pushed him forwards down the road.

Having been frogmarched back to the inn, Schofield was ordered by the landlord, Mr Grinder, to return to his quarters— the stable, which he was sharing with his comrade, Private Cock. It was there, Blake said, that they planned their Method of Revenge.

Schofield, outraged at having been so manhandled, took advantage of the artist's suspicious reputation to invent a story about Blake, claiming that he had uttered Seditious words & said D— the K—. It was noted, when the case came to court, that no one else had heard those words; although the neighbours, who disliked the billeted troops as much as Blake did, may have been keen to defend him, for all, or even because of, his eccentricity. But Schofield's cock-and-bull story had serious implications that threatened not just William, but Kate too.

Schofield claimed that Mrs Blake had not only agreed with what her husband had said, but came up & said that the King of England wd run himself so far into the Fire that he might not get himself out again & altho' she was but a Woman she wd fight as long as she had a Drop of Blood in her—to which Blake replied; my Dear you wd not fight against France—she replied, no, I wd fight for Buonaparte as long as I am able. As the writer Norah Owens suggests, Kate was excitable, and she may indeed have said such things. Was William protecting his wife by taking the blame upon himself?

The quotes appeared over the courtroom like captions for a Gillray cartoon; the cast and the situation were straight out of James Joyce or Joe Orton. Indeed, the bitter mixture of farce and threat was recycled in Joyce's *Ulysses*, in which his anti-hero, Stephen Dedalus, encounters two British soldiers, Privates Carr and Compton, who accuse him of insulting their monarch,

I'll wring the neck of any bugger says a word against my fucking king.

In return, Dedalus repurposes a quote from Blake's Auguries of Innocence to hurl at them like a grenade,

> The harlot's cry from street to street
> Shall weave old Ireland's windingsheet

while Joyce went on to reprise the scenario in *Finnegans Wake*, in which a pair of British soldiers are portrayed as buggers ready to drop their pantaloons for one another.

Privates and cocks were great ways to undermine the state. But for Blake the clear and present danger went beyond wild words spat out by drunken dragoons. When the civil court declined to take the matter further, the military authorities forced a prosecution with a charge of sedition and assault. Things became much more serious, and Blake was forced to find bail from Hayley, his patron, until the case could be heard at the quarter sessions in Chichester. He faced possible imprisonment, with the prospect of hard labour which, like Wilde's, could have killed him.

Blake, always oppositional, suspected it was a set-up. He thought the government, knowing of his association with radical figures such as Paine and Mary Wollstonecraft, had sent the soldier to entrap him. Artists were dangerous: a few years later, Percy Shelley believed he was being followed by agents of the state, along with the foul fiend. It was a jittery time, of war and espionage and insurrection, and Felpham was not far from the French coast, which was why Schofield and his regiment were stationed there. Blake's arrival had coincided with this sense of the vulnerabililty of England's underbelly, its southern coast. In other times, an artist of Blake's ambition might have launched themselves across the Channel, to expand their horizons in Europe and beyond. But now the coast was not only a barrier, but a danger zone.

That year, 1803, hostilities between Britain and France had recommenced after an uneasy peace. Bonaparte prepared to invade. Three hundred thousand Britons were enlisted in the militia. In Sussex, soldiers were being trained to fight waist-deep in the sea like commandos. Blake's beach had become a front line, and every loyal citizen was ready to scent out spies. As men were being hanged in Ireland on trivial charges, Schofield and Cock were boasting around Felpham that they would have Blake hanged too.

In such a heightened atmosphere of invasion and fear, of espionage and treason and surgical assassins planning to spear the king like a whale, the *Sussex Advertiser*'s report of Blake's trial was not encouraging; still less so for someone known to be associated with such sentiments and who possessed an explosive weapon, a printing press, and a dangerous attitude; resistance in a time of war. Like his hero Milton, Blake stood accused of sedition and his fate was held in the balance of Chichester's parochial guildhall. It was the worst time of his life.

William Blake, an engraver at Felpham, the *Advertiser* reported, was tried on a charge exhibited against him by two soldiers for having uttered seditious and treasonable expressions, such as D—n the King, d—n all his subjects, d—n his soldiers, they are all slaves; when Bonaparte comes, it will be cut-throat for cut-throat, and the weakest must go to the wall; I will help him; &c. &c.

In court, Blake had shouted out, False!, every time the accusations were repeated. But the spirits, like the locals, were on his side, and William Hayley redeemed himself by vouching for the artist's innocence and thus clearing his name. The *Advertiser* reported that Blake's acquittal so gratified his supporters that the court was, in defiance of all decency, thrown into an uproar by their noisy exultations. But Blake blamed his own name for the affair, intensely self-aware as he was: of his art and his reputation, and most of all, his strangeness, forever wracked with uncertainty. When I speak, I offend, he told Butts in a verse. Then I'm silent & passive, and lose every Friend . . . I am either too low or too highly priz'd. When Elate I am Envy'd, When Meek I'm despis'd. But then, he added, this too is just a picture of my present state.

By the time the case was resolved, the Blakes were back in town. They had courted the embraces of Neptune, but now they sought refuge from the sea. It chased them away, its waves lapping at their heels. The sea of time & space roaring and following swiftly, he who keeps not right onwards is lost, Blake said.

He had felt the water rising, about to engulf him, leaving him floundering in the waves. People often appear drowning in his works, the way I feel out of my depth when I discuss them. London was safe in comparison to this place where the land ran out and even the stars seemed to go wild. The Blakes were now safely housed in South Molton Street, in a two-room, first-floor apartment. It was tiny compared to Lambeth or Felpham, but at least they felt secure there, above sea level. They would never go back there again, not in a hurry, oh no.

I run up the hill, afraid of falling down. The stones stand in a circle on the moor. No one knows what they're for. It's nearly midsummer's day, cold and grey. The sea is on the far horizon to the south, a glitter of sound. A herd of ponies stand in the middle, as if coralled, observing some invisible electrical fence. They're all brown, but one is ghostly white. Crouching in front of a flipper-shaped stone, I try to draw it in my notebook. The rain spatters the ink. Down in the valley, the river rushes up out of the earth. I clamber through ferns and rowans and purple spires of foxgloves. A giant boulder, a huge hag stone, is held over a little pool. I take off my clothes and slide through it, its hole worn smooth by water and humans. Then I climb back up and do it again and again. Three times to heal me, inside and out.

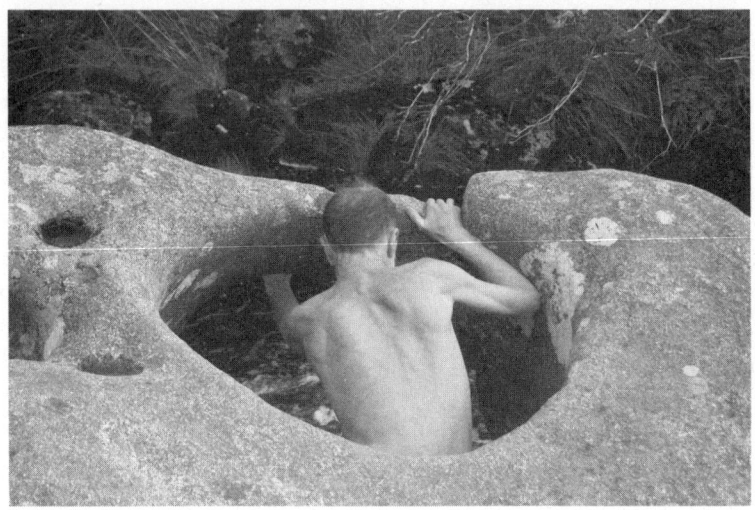

Dip him in the river who loves water, Blake says. They say all rivers were once fallen trees, says Alice Oswald. That night we dance in the terraced cottage, two dozen bodies squeezed into one small room, led by our great god Pan, a portable speaker on his shoulder and a flask of poitín in his hand. His legs might be furred. A boy kisses everyone, then falls over the sofa upside down. Another wears a pearl earring and two golden hoops. Out in the garden we watch the stars fall over the moor, three of us seeing our own different versions of the same thing, convergent but apart in our separate worlds.

Every Eye Sees differently As the Eye, says Blake.

He could touch the moon with his stick, after all. His bodies tumble and fall, hands open up like flowers. Humans turn into mountains and trees, eagles become whales and stars. And dogs. Blake loved dogs. All dogs are visionaries, they're not here to remind us of ourselves. Immortal, eternally renewed, they howl for our souls. They bear witness to our despair; Blake is angry on their behalf and ours:

> A dog starvd at his Masters Gate
> Predicts the ruin of the State.

There were as many animals as humans in London at that time: horses and dogs and pigs, cats and rats and sheep, cows and birds and mice, living meat, loving pets. Blake's parents in Soho owned a cow which their maid milked. Imagine all that non-human life, all that shit. Blake sketched a handsome wolfhound from the life, an Irish sort of Rover. Peter Ackroyd says Blake preferred cats to dogs, but I've seen a dozen images of dogs by Blake and not a single cat.*

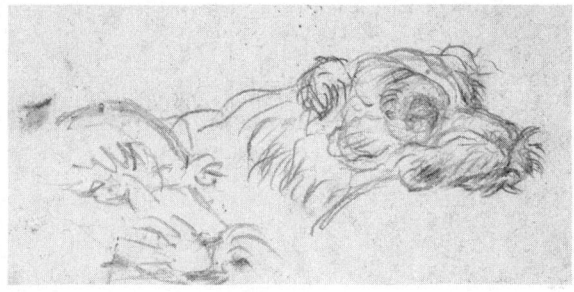

In October 1941, Ruthven Todd, a close friend of Jennings and Raine, finished his wartime edition of Gilchrist's book on Blake, squeezing it into one little Everyman like a charm against destruction, a hand-held device, incendiary in its own way. In his preface Todd extended his thanks to Geoffrey Keynes, Robin Ironside and W. Graham Robertson, who told a friend that he appreciated visits from this enthusiastic and very attractive young man.

* Mr Ackroyd, a splendid writer, got me very drunk once. He wouldn't remember, but I do. At least, I think I do.

It was a good time to revive Blake, who had become an inspiration to a new generation of neo-romantic artists like Graham Sutherland, John Craxton, Keith Vaughan, John Minton, Cecil Collins and Denton Welch. Their twisted roots and thorns, haunted half-moons, dark tunnels and weird blooms grew out of Blake's melding of plant and animal and human, rendered in fiery, acid colours like the weeds already sprouting from bomb-sites, projecting Blake out of his past and into their apocalypse. Blake had released something for them, two hundred years on, fomenting new action Sutherland said his blasted landscapes were a deliberate appropriation of Blake; Welch wrote in his Kentish journal, as the bombs fell: When I read about William Blake, I know what I am for; and Ruthven Todd was deeply jealous when Craxton bought Blake's colour print of Satan Exulting Over Eve in a Marylebone bookshop for fifteen pounds.

All of these friends aided Todd in his task, at a time, as he said, when so many more immediate problems present themselves for solution. In his detective work he discovered that Blake's Nebuchadnezzar was inspired by Dürer's engraving of the penance of St John Chrysostom; he did not add that the saint looked more like he was crawling out of a bunker. Todd thought it better, in the aftermath of the Blitz, not to update Gilchrist's descriptions of Blake's London, considering the changes that were now taking place in the structure of the city. As if not even Blake could have imagined that disaster.

In the same wrecked city, Todd's friend Jacob Bronowski would soon be working by day on formulae to increase the effectiveness of Allied bombing raids on Germany while his relatives were being sent to concentration camps. By night, he was reading Blake, he said, when it seemed likely that England would be invaded and as a Jew, he did not expect to survive. He wanted to assert his Englishness in a personal act of resistance, writing his own book on Blake, with whom he felt a deep and particular affinity, on account of their shared opposition to the disasters of war, empire, violence and oppression.

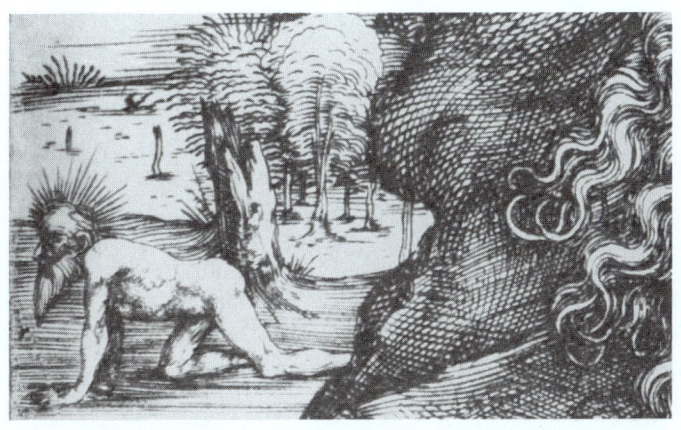

As John Craxton took his copy of Blake's poems to his army medical as a talisman against the war and the world descended into barbarism and people partied at the Ritz, Bronowski saw Blake as an imaginative force for good. It was through art that opposition could be expressed, Bronowski said, for the generation of Belsen. Yet he too was suspected of radical beliefs, and even as he wrote his book, in which he discussed Blake's trial for sedition, Bronowski was himself placed under the surveillance of the British state.

Blake's barbaric art presented an alternative defence in his liberation of body and mind. His utopian visions really are the work of a subversive spy, the enemy within. Bodies lock like clockwork, like cogs on a wheel, and he sees himself in heavenly perfection, his stumpy legs, his big head, his bird eyes turning into new forms. Strangely androgynous, his characters flex pecs and knuckles under their skin. Articulate and articulated, endlessly poseable, they inhabit the glorious future foretold. Swimmers dive in unfolding clouds, long-limbed gymnasts vault the skies; dancers slide on rainbows, clad in heavenly neoprene, sleek as dolphins, part of a gigantic organic machine.

O Young Men of the New Age!

he calls in his preface from *Milton*: a lucid vision, a persistent memory, a waking dream.

In the summer of 1969 the same text appears on the back page of the *International Times*, along with Stonehenge and a UFO on the front cover and Mick Jagger inside talking about Black Power, shortly before his performance in a dress; a strapline from Jesus about making the male and the female into one single one; the Plastic Ono Band giving peace a chance; William Burroughs in dark glasses and trilby recently arrived to sort this planet out; Sun Ra and his Space Arkestra and adverts for free love and gay young men.

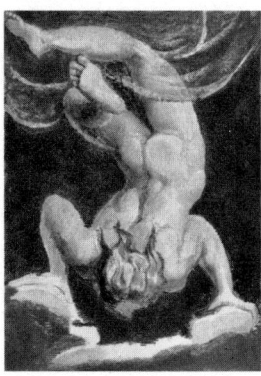

Art degraded, Imagination Denied, War Governs the Nations! Rouse Up, O Young Men of the New Age! Set your Foreheads Against the Ignorant Hirelings! For we have Hirelings in the Camp & in the Court & in the University who Would, if they Could Forever Depress Mental and Prolong Corporeal War!

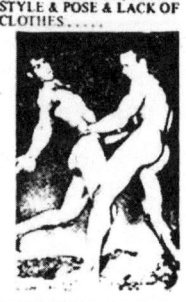

GAY YOUNG MEN, WITH STYLE & POSE & LACK OF CLOTHES.....

16 SUPERB, BRAND NEW PHOTOS OF GAY YOUNG MEN.

Around the same time, living wild in their Brooklyn dive, Patti Smith and Robert Mapplethorpe's most prized books are by Blake; she reads them aloud before they go to sleep. They admire the image of Robert Blake with a star at his feet in colours that seem to generate light. When she was young, Smith thought he must be American, so wild was his voice.

Working in a Manhattan bookstore, Mapplethorpe steals an original print from Blake's *America*, rolls it up and sticks it down his trousers, only to lose his nerve before leaving the shop, shredding it and flushing it down the toilet. Smith imagines his horror and triumph as bits of Blake swirl into the sewers, as if they might infect the whole of New York.

Blake convenes his radical crew. They're not classical casts from the Academy, but outcasts, revolutionaries, pretty things. They might be giants or young Americans. They unfurl as he carves them out of copper plate. Ink swills through their veins and there they are: indisputably alive and throbbing as you open the page, quivering with energy and rage, stepping out of their clothes to touch the face of God. Art can never exist without Naked Beauty displayed, he said.

Pl V

Even now they retain their power, their eternal summer of love, free as they are from venal decency. In Blake's *Milton*, men appear to be fellated by men. They're only one step away from his private sketchbooks in which, as Ackroyd notes, females with impossibly huge erect penises vie with young and old men in erotic embraces. Like photographs by Mapplethorpe. Gender evaporates in space beyond time; hermaphrodites become sea gods. Shame has no part in this creed. No one ever called a dog naked. How bizarre Blake would think it, that people should have labels. What are called the vices in the natural world are the highest sublimities in the spiritual world, he said. The first Adam was a union of sexes, he said. Neither one nor the other but both all together in one.

You can't synthesise Blake. He's not a set text. He doesn't belong to any academy we have yet devised. He showed what we could be like beneath the skin. He sought to understand existence within his own physical self, through his visionary eye, better than any sawguts cutting up stolen bodies still warm from the cemetery. He is open to things we cannot see as he makes everything new. It is the secret of his rare and wondrous success, says Gilchrist; ravished by devotion, he does everything as if for the first time. Bronowski noted, with characteristic insight, that Blake sometimes spoke as if no one had thought of the things he had thought about. I guess he may not have been a particularly good listener, especially when launched in full flow.

But what do we know? One thing: in an age of great pretenders, Blake was the real thing. His innocence inspired loyalty; it still does. After all, we're all making it up as we go along. Blake made up people out of ideas, like Mary Shelley's beautiful Creature. In his other, commercial life, like an adman on Shaftesbury Avenue, Blake drew designs for Shelley's mother, Mary Wollstonecraft; there were hints that he had designs on her too. Her daughter's book, *Frankenstein*, with its sense of doubt and its epigraph from *Paradise Lost*,

> Did I request thee, Maker, from my clay
> To mould me man? Did I solicit thee
> From darkness to promote me?

would echo Blake's sense of the gothic, as demonstrated by the sensational art of his friend Fuseli, who certainly did conduct an affair with Wollstonecraft.

Blake: before and after science, delved in his boxes of body parts, the arms and legs and heads in his sketchbooks, ready for assembly. With no offspring of his own, he generated life in his art. His star-children hang over the abyss, suspended in amniotic sacs; semaphore beings ready to spring out, lithe and pulsating, torsos networked with visible veins. Supple and sappy, flushed in perpetual arousal, their paradoxical rebirth.

Contraries are Positives, said Blake. A Negation is not a Contrary.

I'm glad I found him after all this time. He was worth waiting for. No wonder he saw angels spangling the trees of Peckham Rye as vividly as he saw human beings walking along Piccadilly. They were one and the same to him. Isn't that what's great about Blake? We're all angels in his eyes. Am I reading the right book? you may ask. It's a bit late now; we're a third of the way through and there's a lot more of this to come.

In Blake, in visions, in actuality, in outer and inner space. His puppets represent all our desires, so powerful they were still frightening T.S. Eliot a century later. As the voice of authority high in his Bloomsbury room, the austere modernist found Blake peculiarly honest, and peculiarly terrifying, he had to confess. Blake was naked and saw man naked, and from the centre of his own crystal, Eliot said. All those acres of unadorned flesh were enough to perturb a puritan in a pinstripe suit. But it was what was wrapped round them that was truly scary: unbridled futurity, made manifest.

Eliot was right to be scared. It wasn't that long ago and Blake fucked with the fabric of time. He was the revelation that lay beyond the wasted land, the dark fields at the edge of night. Everything laid bare, nowhere left to hide. The energies he released still reverberate and he's still not respectable, for all that we see him in museums and hear him in an anthem whose words we misconstrue. His bodies rise like lions, idealised editions of scrawny Londoners who never saw the sun. Ackroyd writes movingly of Blake's empathy for chimney-sweep boys, their short-lived, scarred bodies engrained with soot, allowed into the light on one day of the year like pit ponies, cruelly turned into princes for twenty-four hours. In Blake's song of innocence they become evolutionary water babies,

> And wash in a river and shine in the Sun.
> Then naked & white, all their bags left behind,
> They rise upon clouds, and sport in the wind.

Blake's folk art feeds on London, a pagan place for all its bishops and spires. He's printing new myths for a new dispensation, responding to glorious uprisings in France and America. Everything is in an uproar, raw power. He fills the margins of his prophecies with flying crawling things and rude human bodies like doodles made by bored monks in illuminated manuscripts. Big fishes eat little fishes. Men sprout bats' wings. Women are cocooned, wrapped about in serpents and vines. Blake creates micro-dramas of metamorphoses, blending animals, rocks and humans into one. Muscles become branches, trees become seas. Miniature people occupy vast spaces like the extravagant spectacles staged by Blake's contemporary Philip de Loutherbourg, a latter-day Inigo Jones who devised secret techniques to achieve his effects, hanging strips of coloured silk in front of lamps burning whale oil to give the impression of depth and atmosphere, using painted glass slides to project images of Satan and his Palace of Pandemonium rising out of a fiery lake.

Deeply theatrical, Blakeworld™ is a terrifying Christmas pantomime, a furious ghost-train ride. Deploying his print technology in what only appeared to be two dimensions, he created one long river of images and words. Evoking Milton, anticipating Joyce and Woolf, he is the fountainhead of the stream of consciousness, the voice of modernity before it began.

And like the modernists looking to their inner child, Blake is always running back to the beginning again. It's why children loved him and how he remained excited and so exciting. People tell me I get over-excited, as if excitement were rationed. Well, bollocks to that. There isn't a lot of time left, and we're all in this chaos together like strangers on a train. The world is ordered in Blake's mind, following his instructions. Bring me my bow of burning gold, bring me my arrows of desire, he demands, in his male-female body, leaving us far behind as he races his chariot of fire down the Strand, Kate's tresses flying as she stands beside him, her Enitharmon of time to his Los of space.

This is a collaborative effort, after all. Kate shared in William's visions. She printed his books and coloured them in. She made her own drawings and engravings, in between making clothes, singing delightfully, and abusing the king. Their lives in art were all-encompassing. Nowadays we would see them as one artist; co-creators, a single aesthetic entity. They might have sung underneath the arches together, their faces painted gold.

What happens when our visions forsake us, Mrs Blake?
William asked.

We kneel down and pray, Kate said.

People who pay attention to their dreams are the most practical of all. The reaction is deep suspicion. Kate's part in this process, still mysterious and veiled, was purposefully ignored by their contemporaries. How could the illiterate daughter of a market gardener from Battersea have anything to offer? Blake had married beneath himself, and this maidservant ought to have stuck to mending her husband's clothes. Still less should she have opinions on politics or art, or that any credence should be given to her own visions, such as the procession of figures she saw one morning wending their way along the Thames in broad daylight, only to give her a start when they disappeared into the river.

Later Kate painted faces she saw in the fire as if she and William had merged in the flames; some kind of a morphic chaos, an automatic image, strange as any psychedelic work. In an even darker painting which she gave to her friend Elizabeth Butts, wife of Thomas, she portrayed Agnes, the sixteen-year-old heroine of Matthew Lewis's gothic novel, The Monk. In the book, Agnes is forced into a convent-dungeon, where she herself becomes an artist, making drawings of grotesque figures and the ghost of a bleeding nun. Kate's painting, so much more tender than Lewis's shock-horror, may tell its own story. The picture shows Agnes cradling a sad little bundle: the infant to whom she gave birth while imprisoned, and who had died in her arms. Was Blake's gothic image of Pity, with its babe being carried away, as my friend Angela suggests, a memory of their own still-born child?

Elizabeth Butts, known as Betsy, ran her own school in South Molton Street, where she and Thomas had lived. Blake loved her: he designed hares and birds for her to embroider. She was the only one of his friends with whom Kate had a close and loving friendship, a confidante in whatever Kate went through in her life with William. Thomas and William shared an interest in the wild teachings of Swedenborg, until his radical ideas on sexual magic came to seem like a cursed folly to Blake. Kate was upset when William suggested adding another lover to their matrimonial bed. He never made that mistake again.

Having never been a mother, as one of Blake's friends assumed, this devoted wife was at once lover, husband, child. She was rigid, punctual, firm and precise, they said. In a sketch William made of her at Felpham, Kate looks down at her work intently, her open face, her curls falling out of her headscarf: a modern woman, to our eyes, as if fresh from her swim in the sea. Her own feelings go unrecorded, but she was far more than a medium or a muse. What we see as Blake's art would never have existed without her. He knew it. He wasn't grateful. It went so much deeper than that.

William and Kate were a revolutionary society of their own. Imagine if they'd had an audience. But after the business in Felpham, he was no longer someone's funny uncle. All it would take was another drunken soldier. He stepped back from open subversion. Another kind of revolution fed his art, as he found new ways to express his rage. He held up no flags, participated in no more protests. He wouldn't get caught by a truncheon at his throat on the Mile End Road. Writing and drawing in acid and fire, biting, incensing, arousing, exhorting, he evoked the end of one age and the beginning of what was possible. He stood on the edge; his soul wasn't for hire. We can't comprehend the effect of his art when the reproduction of images had barely moved on since Dürer's time.

That's why he failed in his time—he was too far ahead of us. A twentieth-century Blake would have made movies. All that constant flow and dissolve and jump-cutting; imagine the trailers, the audience, the noise. The poise. The costumes, or lack of them (that would be a great economy). His art bursts with colour and sound, all the noises you ever heard gathered up in a ball in your head. Trumpets blast, whales lash, winds roar and clouds unfold.

There's nothing provisional or tentative about this stuff, nothing between it and you and me. It doesn't mislead or deceive or leave you undecided, except about what it all means. It doesn't dither or pretend. Blake has no filter and his work is exactly what it seems to be, there on the page. As to how it got there, well, that's a different matter, my friend.

In order to realise his dreams, to get them all out into the world, Blake had to invent another technique, producing large colour prints that became paintings almost magically. And like the act of creation itself, God's hand on Adam's brow, no one could quite work out how or why they were made. It was a secret process and he didn't leave me any instructions. But here I am and I'll give it a go.

It appears that he drew the outlines of his designs on thick card or millboard rather than engraving them on copper plates as he did with his illuminated books. Then, when the paint was still wet, he laid paper on them and passed them through his rolling press. Using pigment mixed with egg yolk or glue, he then painted areas of colour onto the same board, laid the prints back down on them—Kate was on hand to help with the large sheets and the delicate registration—and then sent the assembly back through the press again. The process produced mottled, spongy areas as the paper was pulled away; on some prints you can see where the colour has gone over the edge of the design, slightly misaligned. The prints were finished with ink and watercolour, graphite or chalk, and sometimes scratched for added detail.

You can feel Blake's hand in them. The hand of the Maker, the Inventor; one of the few in any age, as Samuel Palmer said. In one fell swoop Blake democratises art. He erases the grounds for hierarchies in the arts, as the great modern Blakeans Robert N. Essick and Joseph Viscomi unerringly state.

The effects are as unpredictable and exciting as a Polaroid.

It was an intense discovery: he could take two or three impressions of the original work, creating something between a print and a painting; something rare and unique. A new species of art.

They are the single greatest works he ever made.

Why did he do it? To make it new. In a burning flurry of creativity in the mid-seventeen-nineties, Blake achieved something that had never been done before and has never been seen since. He could have just made a painting. Or a print. But he made something in between, something mysterious and open to interpretation. It was almost abstract, this process, built up and scratched out. There was something magical happening, something that transcended the process itself. Also: it was cheap. To have printed such a large image on copper would have been expensive. Using millboard was a reasonable economy.

The results were more like relief maps: textured, contoured, with a congealed, living look. Action paintings, made with gluey, granular pigment. William's hands in the sandpit, making his heavenly visions real. Art as climate or geology; a moment of revelation catching the exact moment of its creation as he peeled back the paper to reveal infinity. Biological, pathological, born in the dark, drying in the light, they were polytypes in modern art terminology, but multi-tentacular creations in Blake's mind

Like as a Polypus that vegetates beneath the deep

dredged up from the ocean depths. Octopodous anemone jellyfish squid studding a fossil bed. Pre-Cambrian before the Fall, falling out of some future strata, still wriggling and writhing in the rocks. Growing on. To feed the Human Vegetable, he said. To feed the enemy. Art as disease as tattoo. Occupying another world. Rising and falling with the tide of his imagination, swelling to fill their space, their paper, the room.

The universe.

And if the sea was the greatest emblem of unknowing in Romantic art, then Blake's grand conception of it is embodied in these colour prints. They express the actual texture and darkness of the abyss. They are the spiritual profound, the way that the ocean is the reservoir of our poetic intent. Crouched on his rock, Newton is drawing at the bottom of the Sea of Time and Space, immersed, as Kathleen Raine said, in the dark and dense medium of water, the traditional esoteric symbol of the material 'world'. We are what the tide left behind, after the Flood. Blake was a material man, but his colour prints leapt over aeons. In his images of the fallen world, he achieved detail that defied scrutiny. It is art by sleight of hand, William and Kate's conjuring double act, and all we can do is to stand and stare.

One evening in January 1863, the brothers Dante Gabriel and William Michael Rossetti called at the Regent's Park home of Captain Butts. The Zoological Society was nearby. The neighbours could hear the lions and tigers roaring in the night. But the Rossettis had come to inspect another menagerie.

A hero of the Crimean War, Butts was accustomed to riding, elegantly uniformed, in the park. Dante Gabriel, who was a friend of his, also knew that he happened to own, courtesy of his grandfather, Thomas, the greatest surviving collection of works by Blake. That they had made it this far was a miracle: other members of his family had stashed Blake's paintings and prints in their attic, where they were eaten by rats.

The Rossettis were astounded at what they found in Regent's Park. It was like coming upon the tomb of an ancient Egyptian king. Reporting back to Anne Gilchrist, who was busy trying to complete the book her husband had begun, William Michael Rossetti recorded the incredulity of Capt. Butts the other night, & even Gabriel sided with him, that certain works are really prints. This is often not at all apparent on the face of the works, he said, as they marvelled at the peculiar quality of execution.

Seaching for some explanation for Blake's technique, Dante Gabriel could only describe the print of Newton as endlessly varied and intricate as a photograph from a piece of seaweed. He was thinking of Anna Atkins's experimental cyanotypes of algae made in the eighteen-forties, blueprints for evolutionary life.

Blake might have been a diving deep down into the ocean, recording the watery details from his Georgian bathysphere, dangling in the abyss as bug-eyed anglerfish swam by, swigging on his jar of ale as he peered through the crystal window into the eerie chemosynthetic light. There were plenty of Coleridge's slimy things crawling down there too, just behind the boulders of Newton's seat. Coleridge told Blake so: when the two poets met, it seemed to an observer that they were like congenial beings of another sphere, breathing for a while on our earth.

Gilchrist's book about Blake, which would so entrance Robertson, appeared just as Darwin's theory of life overturned our past. Dante Gabriel Rossetti tried to assess what he was seeing. Even a presentiment of the most abstract truths of natural science is not only attempted by this new painter, he said, but actually effected by legitimate pictorial ways; and we are somehow shown, Rossetti went on, in figurative yet not wholly unreal shapes and hues, the mingling of organic substances, the gradual development and perpetual transfusion of life.

As the Rossettis looked on, dumbfounded, Blake was transitioning, evolving into something else. It would take a hundred years for anyone to catch up. Precisely because he was almost unknown in his time, far from being history, Blake was *a new kind of man*, as his young followers would say, someone wholly original, and in all things, in the same way that his perhaps lover Mary Wollstonecraft saw herself as the first of a new genus. Like their art, they were another species, newly evolved, still steaming in the bright light of the sun. Art was an infernal facility, the revolutionary means to an eternal end. After all, Blake himself had been taught to make his images by his beloved younger brother and erstwhile pupil, Robert, despite the fact that he had died years before at the age of nineteen.

Taken by consumption, Robert had passed on in William's arms in the house that they shared: Blake watched his soulmate ascend through the ceiling clapping his hands with joy as he made for heaven. He might have grabbed Robert's feet and yanked his brother back from the beyond. But death was nothing more than the going out of one room into another, as William said, and now Robert would be forever nineteen. For the rest of Blake's life he would converse daily with his dead brother, who gave him a new technique, issuing specific instructions about how to print words and pictures on the same page.

Blake fed on his brother's spiritual inspiration for his genius; being genetic, it explained why God had been so generous to him. In an alternative time and collapsing space, the two brothers become twins: a Geminian constellation, only with more muscles and sinews and strength. Art sparks between them, the living and the dead, the way Blake saw the Angel and the Devil in man as Soul and Body, the way that all the nude men he drew came direct from Michelangelo. The two boys knew the order of the stars. They had only to climb out of their bunk beds and up to the roof to see them spread out over their heads, the city stripped back to reveal the dark infinity of the sky.

We're all naked in Blake's pictures, all born to die, ready to fly. Blake always puts us in the picture so as not to confuse us or leave us behind. He is everywhere in majesty; he thought all those thoughts for you and me. Those nightmares from which you wake at three am? They happen to him in real time. He takes us by the hand to show us angels in the trees and faeries in the grass. He fills us with his own spirit—oh, that we would listen to his voice and harden not our hearts!—the way he likes to picture us, heads in heaven, feet on earth, each and every one a potential star, since that was where we came from in the first place.

We are the natural world. We are every thing that is holy. After all, there's nothing else to do, and there's no thing in heaven or on earth which does not also exist in Man and God, Blake said. He would ring you at three am.

At nine o'clock on the evening of 18 August 1783, William and Robert looked up into the sky above Soho and saw a star fall to earth. It was a meteor half the size of the moon, lighting up all of London, turning night into day ❧ Its trail blazed brilliant red and orange and flashed across the faces of the watchers like a lightning bolt and there was a sound like thunder or the coming of God. A prophecy or a siren.

Something foretold.

Hundreds, thousands of other citizens witnessed this event. The Blake brothers were not on their own, peering up into the unsodium-lit sky. It was a summer of portents: the great meteor came in the wake of the Perseids, the shooting stars of August, as a series of violent thunderstorms broke the peace like a riot.

The two brothers saw the same thing differently, transecting it with their art. Robert drew the heavenly body as a sign of the Approach of Doom. In William's eyes it was an intimation of Liberty, a new-born fire thrown into the starry night, coursing over the infinite mountains, now barr'd out by the Atlantic sea; in the same way that, just fifty years later, on the other side of that ocean, Frederick Douglass and Harriet Tubman saw, separately, a stupendous shower of meteorites over the American plains, taking it as a sign of freedom, like the North Star which they would follow in the darkness as they escaped slavery; just as Blake, roused the African! black African! to revolution in his own Song of Liberty, an itemised manifesto:

10. The speary hand burned aloft, unbuckled was the shield,
    forth went the hand of jealousy among the flaming hair,
    and hurl'd the new born wonder thro' the starry night.
11. The fire, the fire is falling!
12. Look up! look up!

In his book Milton, Blake carves himself and his brother out of waxy black, creating ecstatic mirror-images of their naked selves, each with a star falling at their feet as if they'd missed the catch in a fiery cricket match. In fact the star was Milton, a man falling to earth, through Precipitant loud thundering into the Sea of Time & Space ✶✶

Pl VII

> Then first I saw him in the Zenith as a falling star,
> Descending perpendicular, swift as the swallow or swift.

Milton, the beautiful man, blind as he was, came crashing through, neuro-sublime in re-entry, ready to enter the Blake boys via their feet. Ovid and Lou Reed would have approved. Blake reports it all as fact. We go about our daily lives, heedless of the drama happening over our heads or at our own feet.

It's no good waiting for things to happen. You've got to stand up. Blake was optimistic on our behalf. He confidently expected the rebuilding of Albion. In the interests of clarity and clairvoyance and the avoidance of all doubt, he drew it all out so you could see for yourself. Like a Jesuit priest, he saw it as his duty as a Soldier of Christ, he told Thomas Butts.

Spirits are organised men, and they appear every now and again, from heaven, on earth, he said. Of the gift of Vision (and sound, he might have added), all might have it if they would.

I have five years left, he went on, tho' he feared it might only be one. It gives me the greatest of torments. I am not ashamed, afraid, or averse to tell You what Ought to be Told: That I am under the direction of Messengers from Heaven, Daily & Nightly.

He knew you must stay true to the dreams of your youth.

Refuse, & bury your Talent in the Earth, and Every one in Eternity will leave you, aghast at the Man who betray'd their cause.

In an age of great betrayal, of humanity and nature and the soul, Blake never betrayed anyone.

And so in the exploding firmament, in the new nature of this new kind of man, in whom all Creation was valued, from a flea to a human being; all these would return in a poem that in Blake's lifetime was read by almost no one, yet which is now the most beloved of all his works. When I read it at school I had no idea what it was about, but I knew exactly what it meant.

His Tyger's fury turns fiery stripes into tongues of flames, licking the big cat's side as he pads through the forests of the night. His burning eyes turn into meteors and the stars throw down their spears, watering heaven with their tears. It would take a while for poets to catch up with such ferocity: for Shelley's lions to rise out of slumber, for Marianne Moore to turn an octopus into a glacier, for Ted Hughes to form a night fox out of his thoughts, for Allen Ginsberg to howl like a wolf and hallucinate with Blake-light; for Patti Smith to see wild horses as white shining silver studs with their nose in flame. (I once slept in the same bed in Paris that Ginsberg and Burroughs slept in. They weren't there at the time. Ginsberg was reading naked on the quai outside.) We see tigers and stars differently now. To Blake they were revolutionary energy, lights no one could put out. No sin could extinguish them. Other artists were merely earthly to him.

He knew it. So did they.

That's why they saw him as a lunatic, which was also true enough, since he was hopelessly aligned to that watery star, as Shakespeare called it. It was his moon-ark, his great covenant of hope, a crescent-shaped wingèd boat riding the waves, filled with rescued people and animals to restock the new world after the Flood.

After all, he was born in water, in St James's Church, Piccadilly. In the silence, in the noisy city, held over the font for a moment that went on for ever.

In the austere interior of the church, with its box pews and pillars and hush, the font still stands, carved out of marble the colour of the London light. It sprouts up like a fountain out of the floor, as if fed by a holy spring from below. On the front, Adam and Eve stand in Eden, either side of the Tree of Life; the serpent, an apple in its mouth, is entwined around its trunk.

I don't know whether he dribbled his mother's milk down his christening robe, or whether a swan-winged God flew over-head, but my young friends Lilian and Freddie were baptised there, too, and they didn't cry.

On the other side of the bowl, next to St Philip, is the ark: a house on a boat, ploughing through high seas, its bow breaking the waves. Up in the sky, a branch in their beak, the dove of peace brings the good news.

Stop the clock.

The saviour of art has been found.

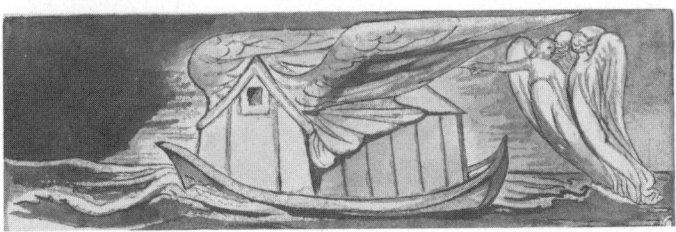

In the autumn of 1790, the Blakes left their dingy rooms in Soho and moved across the river. The skies were bigger over there. They might have rowed there in their moon-ark. You could see the wharves at the end of the road, ships and sails and rigging, full of movement, the ebb and flow of the sea. Lambeth's name came from its role as a harbour or landing place for lambs. It would be here that Blake asked if he who made the Lamb made thee. The artist as tyger or God.

Dogs ran wild and masts rose as high as the roofs. Everything was different this side of the river where cab drivers refused to go. You could encounter, in those thoroughfares nigh the docks, people and animals imported for their rarity.

It was an heroic address, and it would prove lucky for the Blakes. From the back, they looked out over fields where London ran out and lambs grazed. In the distance, the Surrey Hills showed blue in the twilight or red in the dawn. It was in Lambeth's Vale that Jerusalem's foundations began, Blake declared, while the Surrey Hills glowed like the clinkers of the furnace where his tyger was forged.

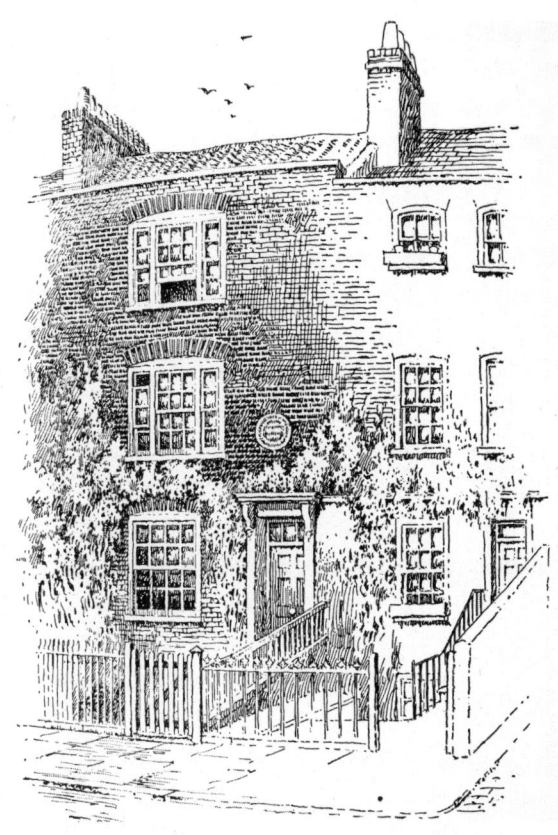

Mr & Mrs Blake, 13 Hercules Buildings

From the front, with no houses directly ahead, the Blakes could see two great estates: the domain of the Archbishop of Canterbury in his Lambeth Palace and his grace behind the high walls; and over the Thames to Westminster and its buildings of state. Neither drew much respect from William or Kate.

The river was quiet in the early morning when Wordsworth saw London from the coach as he crossed Westminster Bridge on the third of September 1802,

> Ships, towers, domes, theatres, and temples lie
> Open unto the fields, and to the sky.

Although that same year, the poet also called for

> Milton! thou shouldst be living at this hour:
> England hath need of thee: she is a fen
> Of stagnant waters.

Wordsworth preferred the great Wye winding romantically past Tintern Abbey, in the days when the river ran so clear and fast you had to clutch at roots for fear of being carried away. But Blake liked the life of the Thames flowing past, for all that he saw it as a charter'd way, filled with the dirt and foetid oppression of the city. The river was uncontained by embankments then, wilder yet far more connected to the city in its own way. Its water reflected the light, lending a looseness to Lambeth's shores. Along its banks, beside boathouses and timber yards fit to deplete the forests of Norway and the Baltic, as Thomas Pennant wrote in 1790, were dozens of riverside taverns and tea gardens. Places with glorious or dubious reputations, depending on your tastes. To enter Cuper's Gardens—the great resort of the profligate of both sexes, as Pennant noted—revellers had to pass under a whale-bone arch. As a portal, it promised some sort of transformation. At night the sky burst with fireworks; below, anything might be going on in the alcoves and bushes.

By the time the Blakes arrived Cuper's Gardens had turned sour, becoming a Vinegar Manufactory, but Lambeth retained its liberated air. It was like going on holiday. A penny for the first to see the river, another for spotting the Chevalier d'Éon and correctly guessing their sex that day. For some, there was a high price to be paid. The Asylum was an orphanage for girls, designed to prevent their prostitution; it was built on the site of the Hercules Inn, from which the Blakes' street took its name.

Lambeth, mythic and free, was where they would feel happiest. Kate was at home there; after all, she was a south London girl from Battersea. There was a sort of thrill to the place, an openness and an edge, as if any variety of being might appear. Their neighbour was Philip Astley, the inventor of the modern circus and tenant of his grand villa, Hercules Hall, just behind their house. An enterprising former sergeant in the Dragoons, Astley was famous for his Amphitheatre and Riding School set next to Westminster Bridge, opposite Noah's Ark Court. There, among other spectacles, the human pyramid act of La Force d'Hercule performed every night, climbing to heaven on each other's shoulders.

Astley, an uneducated, plus sized man of great poise, was as ambitious as a Hollywood director with his re-enactments of the French Revolution—Paris In An Uproar! (with an interval entertainment of Philosophical Fireworks, From Inflammable Air) and battles during whose rehearsal he would shout, Stop! stop! This will never do. It's not half noisy enough; we must get shields! Another of his acts were three Catawba Indian Chiefs from Carolina who exhibited the Exercises and Manners of their Country with so interesting an effect that most of the boxes for their performances sold out. They had been brought to London and Ireland by a gang of white men who defrauded, then abandoned them. On their way back home, two of the Catawbas jumped into the sea out of despair, leaving only the third to return and tell the tale.

Sensation was all for Astley. The great Riding-Master also presided as an investigator of Natural Magic, presenting mysterious Experiments such as the grand Sultan, an Automaton who could answer different Questions, the learned Horse and The Bird Dead returned to Life, and The Rings that jumped and danced about in a Glass. Such sleights of hand and tricks of the eye were so deft and suspicious that Astley was accused of dealing with the devil like some south London Faust. Blake, however, found his neighbour guilty of a far greater evil.

One day, looking out from his window down into Astley's backyard, William saw a boy hobbling about with a log chained to his leg. It was a shocking sight, like seeing a tethered elephant or a convict constrained to stop them from running away. When he asked her why such a thing had been done, Kate replied that it must have been a punishment for some misdemeanour committed by the boy. In a rage, and possibly encouraged by his wife, Blake marched round to tell Astley's staff that they must release the boy at once.

No one, he said, not even a slave, deserved to be treated that way. No sooner had he returned home than Blake was greeted by Astley himself knocking on their door, demanding to know by what authority his neighbours dared intervene in his personal affairs. Blake was not a man to back down when injustice was at hand. His anger rose and the two came near to blows, till reason intervened and they calmed down. By the end, Astley even found himself forced to admit admiration for Blake's outraged sense of right and wrong. Perhaps he gave Wiliam and Kate a free pair of tickets to his show.

If Astley's exotic Amphitheatre resembled Wordsworth's Bartholomew Fair with its Parliament of Monsters, painted Indians, Dwarfs and the Horse of Knowledge, it was nothing compared with the fairground going on in Blake's head. He was an actor-manager, conducting a troupe more exotic than any automata or even the performing monkey, General Jacko, who wore a red coat and rode one of Astley's horses, as conjured up by Joyce in his recording of *Finnegans Wake* in 1927.

What's your trouble? says Joyce in his high, riverrun voice,

Is that the great Finnleader himself in his joakimono on his statue riding the high horse there forehengist? . . . You're thinking of Astley's Amphitheayter where the bobby restrained you making sugarstuck pouts to the ghostwhite horse . . .

Blake, of course, had accomplished his own linguistic feats, having already been to the moon. It was much like your place, only different. In the Moon, he said, in an untitled text that reads more like a masque or a modernist experiment, is a certain Island near by a mighty continent, which small island seems to have some affinity to England. & what is more extraordinary the people are so much alike & their language so much the same that you would think you was among your friends.

With a circus of characters that echoes Swift's satirical travels with Gulliver and pre-empts Thomas Love Peacock's gothic camp, Ruskin's wild newsletter-podcasts, Lewis Carroll's Wonderland, Wilde's flippant scenarios, Firbank's purple ink, Tristan Tzara's Dada cabarets, Joyce's grotesque burlesque, Edward Burra's letters, John Waters' pop-art anarchy, an Alan Bennett monologue or Jarman's queer outrage, Blake's breathless dialogue is punctuated for a crazy cocktail party always going on

with Tilly Lally the Siptippidist who laught like a Cherry clapper, Aradobo, the dean of Morocco, and Inflammable Gass, who was the Glory of France (I have got a bottle of air that would spread a Plague, I have got a camera obscura at home, What was it you was talking about?), along with Gass's wife, Gibble Gabble, and Sir Obtuse Angle, God of Physic, with the beads of every art & science around his neck (Astronomy, Cookery, Chymistry, Tactics, Pathology, Mythology, Osteology, Somatology, &c, &c). Then Mr Inflammable Gass ran & shovd his head into the fire & set his hair all in a flame

into which we are dropped mid-conversation. It's no coincidence that Blake's stream of consciousness reads like Joyce. It was given its title, An Island in the Moon, by Yeats when he published Blake's work in the eighteen-nineties. It was in Yeats's edition that Joyce first read Blake; which is why Blake's lines sound like terse stage directions from Joyce's assistant, Samuel Beckett:

After this they all sat silent for a quarter of an hour.

Then they ended up, as Blake goes on,

their nasty hearts poor devils are eat up with envy—all the Women envy your abilities my dear they hate people who are of higher abilities than their nasty filthy Selves but do you outface them & then Strangers will see you have an opinion—now I think we should do as much good as we can when we are at Mr Femality's do you snap & take me up

Here comes everyone. Mr Femality is the celebrated Chevalier d'Éon, former French diplomat and spy, lately of Lambeth, where they lived as Madame Duval, now an ornament of their own salon in Soho's Golden Square—and therefore a neighbour of the Blakes—where d'Éon gave audiences a decorative Chevalier who declined to be defined by the apparel of either sex that was available at the time, and was promptly caricatured in turn in a half-and-half portrait, an Alternative Miss World in the Vauxhall Tavern guest-starring Orlando:

You're a woman! You're a man!

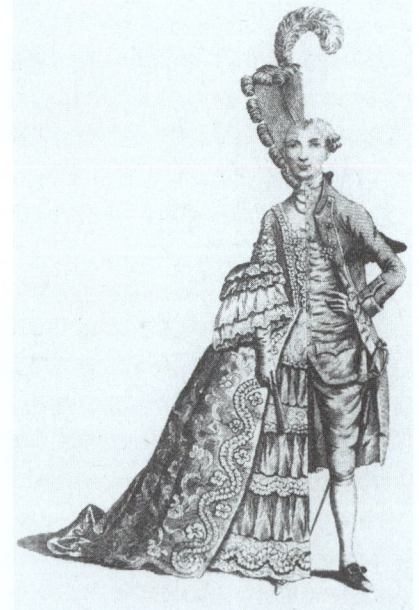

D'Éon: a ship in full sail, dragged up on deck in the ambiguous glory of it all. The state of her. D'Éon of an age, unsayable. A trick pony in the circus. Our modern spirit, as Orlando's biographer says, can almost dispense with language.

It was all gesture from now on. D'Éon, open to inspection. D'Éon, spying on us. To Blake, sex was a mere restriction of time. He believed the advanced human was androgynous, and he took his cue from *Paradise Lost*, whose angels

                                                          those male,
          These Feminine. For Spirits when they please
          Can either Sex assume, or both . . .

a fluidity Blake echoes in his own poem, *Milton*,

                                                 the Female-Males,
          A Male within a Female hid as in an Ark & Curtains

in which he turns the puritan poet into a woman. The Chevalier
demonstrates their fencing skills in uniform or stays and a
becoming black silk dress, performing at the Haymarket (never,
since the death of Garrick, had the house been so full) and in
Vauxhall (till the cops burst in, wearing protective gloves).

In one astounding appearance in the presence of the Prince
of Wales no less, the Chevalier won a brilliant victory over an
English officer. But with their rise comes the fall. In a parabola
of fame and poverty, with wagers being conducted to decide
their true sex, society moves on and D'Éon becomes a tour de
force forced to tour. It all comes to a halt at a final fencing
match, a great *Grand Assault d'Armes* in the Long Rooms on
Southampton's fashionable shore.

26 August 1796. La Chevalière is here, in this smartest of
south-coast resorts, performing in the ballroom with its sea
baths attached. And here they meet their professional end at
the point of an unbuttoned foil—Ah sir, unkind!—although by
now they looked, I must confess, a little more like my grandmother than a grandmaster of the flashing blade.

Their opponent's sword pierces the Chevalier's armpit,
curtailing their career. In the symbolic moment of penetration,
in the great glazed ballroom overlooking the sea, another uncov-
ering is threatened. As a result of their wound, D'Eon is
examined by a physician and two surgeons who were present
at the event and who rushed to their aid. You might suspect
these men hanging about. But they had no doubt of their

patient's sex; viz, being female, as far as they could see (which wasn't very far).

My sex, as Orlando reported, is pronounced indisputably. It is the first decade of the nineteenth century, after all. The Chevalier promptly sent out a press release, complete with a personal statement and the medical report, addressed, from Mademoiselle D'Éon, to the Benevolent Gentry of the Town and Neighbourhood, thanking them for the kind Interest they were so good as to take in the dangerous Wound they received that Day.

After four months' recuperation abed in Southampton, borne with the utmost Fortitude, Patience, and Resignation, the Chevalier moved back to Lambeth with their friend Mrs Mary Coles (widow of a pump-maker to the Royal Navy), staying so close to the Blakes that one might think them attached in their respective destinies, nodding good morning as they pass one another on the street.

The Chevalier lived entirely on charity and the kindness of strangers. Their last move was to the Foundling Hospital Estate in Bloomsbury. There, like a token of an orphan left behind, all their jewels pawned or sold by auction, D'Éon died on 21 May 1810; only to be again inspected in a final anatomical outrage as a plaster cast and a watercolour were made of their lower body, like a whale prepared for Tearguts' collection, and which revealed, to the apparent astonishment of D'Éon's companion, Mrs Coles, that her Chevalier possessed male organs.

The freakishness was on the other side, the male gaze. D'Éon's body was found bound in a gown of red cloth, fiercely stiffened with seven whalebones, sixteen and one half inches deep. Those baleen stays had done the job of armouring the Chevalier all these years but at the last were not enough to fend off those prying eyes.

———

The world was changing faster than we knew, and 13 Hercules Road was set ready for what would unfold in its three storeys plus a cellar. It was Blake's palace, its chambers arranged like a snail. The principal rooms had marble fireplaces; the parlour was wainscoted and the study set up as a studio where art would roll out of his press like laundry from a magical mangle. The machine was the height of a man; you could see it looming through the window, as if the house were a manufactory of subversive dreams.

There was a short front garden and a long narrow garden at the back with a fig tree and a vine that Blake declined to prune; he preferred to let the plant grow wild, forming a shady arbour where he and Kate could spend Sunday afternoons. When handsome Thomas Butts came to call, licking his curls down with his fingers before knocking at the door, he was shown through to be greeted by his hosts in their summer house, where they had dispensed with that which the ordinary world deemed necessary in the way of earthly arrays. It's great set piece.

Come on in, says William, it's only Adam and Eve you know.

He and Kate are sitting naked in their Paradise Lost; hand in hand in a shady bower, as Milton wrote, putting off those troublesome disguises which we wear.

It may have been done for effect; Butts was their best customer, after all. Some people think it didn't happen at all. But south London was a radical site, with Ranters and Quakers who had gone naked for a sign, and even over in genteel Belgravia John Frank Newton, author of The Return to Nature, allowed his children to run naked round the family home, believing clothes to be a burden; his wife Cornelia liked to spend the morning in her bedroom, in the nude.

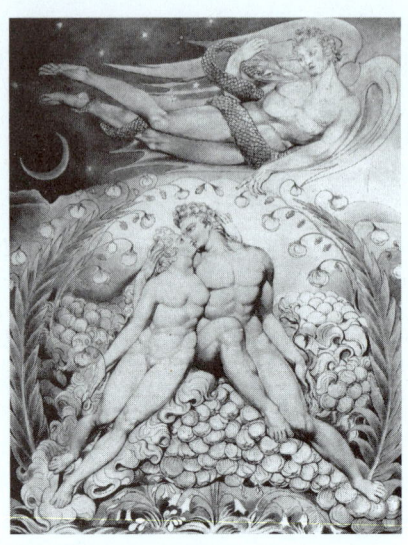

In Paris the diplomat and river-swimmer Benjamin Franklin had been fond of taking air-baths in his garden, surprising his servant when he came to bring him a letter. All these bodies were brave and free in the spirit of Rousseau, who thought we should go wild in the country, rolling naked in the grass under the trees. The moralists couldn't have it both ways. The Chevalier outraged by what they wore; the Blakes outraged by what they didn't. Blake's nakedness is itself forgiveness, a return to a world without sin. A protest against progress which is leaving humans behind. It is difficult to tell lies when you aren't wearing any clothes.

Back to nature, classical too, nude or not in their rented Eden, William and Kate felt happy and free. I had a whole House to range in, Blake said later, wistfully. It helped that, financially, it was his most successful period: the fact that they were burgled says as much. The thieves' haul included forty pounds' worth of clothing and sixty pounds of plate.

Most of all, it was in Lambeth that Blake experienced his most intense visions, leaping out of bed in the middle of the night to write them down. The archangel Gabriel stood in the sun, moving the universe in the middle of the room. Other spirits sat for their portraits; Satan did so, obligingly perched on a chair. Then one day, as Blake stood at his garden door, he looked to the top of the stairs and saw the Ancient of Days hovering in an orb of light over the void; the world as yet unborn, as Milton saw it,

> and in his hand
> He took the golden compasses, prepared
> In God's eternal store, to circumscribe
> This Universe, and all created things; Pl VII
> One foot he center'd, and the other turn'd
> Round through the vast profunditie obscure,

the terrible patriarch measuring out our fates. It was the most powerful vision Blake ever saw, he said, and it would stay with him till the end of his days.

But then, on that same spot, he witnessed something even more terrifying.

The Ghost of a Flea.

It was scaly, speckled, very awful, he said, and he ran out of the house in fear. It was his first and last ghost; his spirits were finer visions, he said, thankfully. To isolate the horror, he would capture it in paint, heightened with gold leaf, on a tiny panel of mahogany, no bigger than this book. And having trapped it like a genie, he hoped never to see its like again.

A hundred years later, as he saw Blake's pictures and read his words, Paul Nash began to believe that, by a process of an inward dilation of the eyes, he could actually increase his vision. As if he might see into the thingness of things.

I seemed to develop a power of interpenetration which disclosed strange phenomena. I persuaded myself I was seeing visions. It was a peculiar thrill, he said.

He had entered an altered state. An out-of-body and beyond-species experience in which he could rise like the kestrel he saw hovering over the wood. We all know that feeling. The way you see the shadows of ghosts in the darkness of summer trees. The way you see things out of the corner of your eye, and when you look back, they are no longer there. The way anything might change; a hawk become a chevalier.

Nash was subsumed into Blake's vision: he felt the quiet corners of the world around him which appeared to escape others' eyes, he said. It was 1912. A year later the Tate would host the first national exhibition of Blake's work, which Nash almost certainly saw. Gerard Manley Hopkins's poetry had yet to be made public (it wasn't widely published until 1918), but Nash seemed to see into that mystical otherworld too; what Hopkins called a sense of inscape and instress in animals, plants, rocks, clouds and waves, between animate and inanimate reality. In his own imagining of the natural world, Nash drew the night air itself, as if he'd acquired the nocturnal vision of an owl or the echo location of a bat. He now had the power, through his interpenetration, as he called it, to convene the seen and the unseen.

This was what he could do in art, he realised. It was one long experiment stretching ahead of him, as it had for Blake. He would move through his allotted time, losing his way in the wild wood or the spectral sea, drawing trees with stars falling through their dark branches and an angel doing battle with a half-human hawk. Then he set a half-moon over a crumbing cliff, as the cold bitter sea and its gnawing waves lay below, as he wrote, while the beam from an unseen lighthouse skimmed over the downs and a shadowy female form fell into view.

It was a window into the eerie, like a scene from M.R. James, whose stories Nash knew well. A desolate beach seen by moonlight, by the stars, by the sea that took on a luminous spirit of its own; the same sea that dogged him. A melancholy shore transformed by the shadow of the twentieth century and what lay ahead, just out of sight, but not quite. Nash was haunted by Blake as he was haunted by the ghostly black dog he saw as a boy, silent and still in the dark corner at the turn of the stairs in his childhood home. It would appear abruptly, unseen by anyone, even at a party.

There it would stand, without snarl or bark, Nash said, with hardly a threatening move, dire only by its presence, but oh, how dire!

The impact of Blake's visions and words, all combined in one filmy verve, became a physical connection for Nash. Not least because he was making his drawings under the encouragement of Sir William Blake Richmond, son of Blake's young friend George Richmond, who had kissed Blake on his deathbed. Here at last was a living person who knew what art was for.

With his wild beard and wide-awake hat and his huge blue eyes, Sir William, who had been taught art by Ruskin and whose godfather was Samuel Palmer, looked like one of Blake's ancients. He had inherited a life mask of Blake; it stood on his shelf as if the poet-prophet might still open his mouth. Richmond's mere presence was a tangible link to the mystical past, enough to give the young artist permission to proceed; even his habit of pronouncing his Rs as Ws seemed like a voice from another age, a Blakean benediction of perfection via a speech defect. (I stumbled over the same sounds as a boy; it made me afraid to speak, but also forced me to choose my words carefully.) It was through Sir William that Nash, like Robertson, received his first exhibition in the prestigious interior of the Carfax (albeit that his work was hung in the hall). He attended his own private view that afternoon wearing a silk top hat, snuff-coloured trousers, a black jacket and white spats, carrying a silver-headed cane.

Blake was a prophecy, waiting for people like Nash or Gilbert & George to come along and worship at his shrine. The problem with being a visionary is that you are operating out of time: your peers don't want to hear what you have to say; they're fearful and jealous, and you never get to hear what you want to hear anyway. You are working in a world of your own.

Blake blended land and sea and time and space to fit his art, some kind of heaven which was a vision but not a dream, a fluid, flexible place, the way I imagine my hands and feet fusing into fins in the swirly blue, steely blue sea; the way that Walt Whitman, crossing from Brooklyn to Broadway, confessed himself in love with himself and everyone he might meet; or the way that Gerard Manley Hopkins was transfixed by the crystalline, snail-like trails on a seminary latrine. Before and after them all, Blake was caught between heaven and hell and the wastes of the ocean where hungry clouds swag on the deep and souls are lost

for Cities
Are Men, fathers of multitudes, and Rivers & Mountains
Are also Men; every thing is Human, mighty! sublime!

Alexander Gilchrist's biography of Blake, published in 1863, established Blake's post-mortal reputation and provided the Pre-Raphaelites with their kick. Within its lavish purple and gilt covers, scattered with singing angels and golden stars, it declared that Blake's art had the look as of coming straight from another world; a shock as of something wholly fresh and new; something almost frightful. When George III was shown Blake's pictures (someone had the mad idea of suggesting that the artist might teach art to the royal family), the king cried, Take them away, take them away! Even Wordsworth, who liked his work, thought Blake insane. So-called friends resorted to ridicule. A Man sitting on the Moon, and drowning the sun out, they said. They called him eccentric for want of anything more imaginative to say, and when he disappeared off their radar, they claimed he'd been admitted to Bedlam.

No one and nothing came close to the newness of what he was trying to do. The whole of his aim is to produce singular shapes and odd combinations; fancy is the end and not a means in his designs, said Fuseli, who admitted to stealing from him. Benjamin West and his friends acknowledge—since they must—the designs of Blake the Engraver, as works of extraordinary genius and imagination. But their praise often sounds like something you'd say about a particularly artistic plumber, not a demigod creating the astonishingly new.

Gilchrist had begun work on his book less than twenty years after Blake had passed on. Both he and his wife Anne were literary figures—their next-door neighbours in Chelsea's Cheyne Row were Thomas and Jane Carlyle—and Gilchrist had been able to speak to people who had known the artist. But having written eight chapters, the author died suddenly of scarlet fever in 1861, leaving his work to be completed by committee: the brothers, Dante Gabriel and William Michael Rossetti, who assisted Gilchrist's wife Anne in assessing Blake's art. She was a writer in her own right, especially on nature and science, who had contributed a lengthy essay on whales for *Chambers's Journal* in 1860, in which she quoted from *Moby-Dick*; both she and the Rossettis were early fans of Melville, that clever Yankee who instructs and befools his reader by turns, as she said; in 1879 Dante Gabriel would recommend to his publisher Melville's distinctly queer follow-up book, *Pierre*, later illustrated by Maurice Sendak, another admirer of Blake and his wild things.

As a supporter of the American Revolution, Blake would have been pleased to find himself in New England, as if it were his Albion made manifest. He was already admired by the Transcendentalists of Concord: Ralph Waldo Emerson read his *Songs of Innocence and Experience* in 1842 and by 1850 Thoreau had written his poem The Little Irish Boy, seeing Blake's The Little Black Boy in the Irish navvies living round

Walden Pond. You might even hear Blake's sayings echoed in Thoreau's voice

As if you could kill time without injuring eternity, he said. To hold Infinity in the palm of your hand, and Eternity in an hour, Blake replied.

But it was Gilchrist's biography that confirmed Blake's presence across the Atlantic. Melville would buy the book in New York in 1870 and set his last work, Billy Budd, in Blake's revolutionary time, with his Handsome Sailor as a song of innocence, an Apollo, Nelson guiding Leviathan. Meanwhile, in another transatlantic twist, Anne Gilchrist had fallen in love with Melville's contemporary Walt Whitman, and decamped to Philadelphia to be closer to him. Your very voice & touch, she wrote, drawing me across the Atlantic close beside you. It was hopeless: Whitman was no woman's man and he only sang of himself. But, being composed of multitudes, he designed his own tomb based on Blake's drawing of Deaths Door from Gilchrist's book.

Back in England, it wasn't exactly what Blake would have wanted, tbh: this erratic editorial team reordering him for posterity, all curly hair and velvet eyes and blue stockings, re-arranging his poems, changing words because they looked better that way. They had their own agenda: Anne Gilchrist was pursuing her literary career and Walt Whitman, while the Rossettis were bent on claiming Blake as a pre-Pre-Raphaelite, making a Blake for their time. Like all artists, they looked to the past to reassure their revolutionary selves; it was only because he was safely dead that they dared take such liberties. If he'd still been around they wouldn't have been able to face the challenge of those disconcerting blue eyes.

As they turned the vivid pages of Blake's America, whose prophecies seemed to predict the works of Thoreau and Melville and Whitman, they agreed that the effect of Blake's illuminated books was like an increase of daylight on the retina, by skies of sapphire, or gold, rayed with hues of sunset. The clouds unfold for them. But the Prophecy is deathly too, ghastly and terrible, they decided, especially in a dramatic scene set in the darkness of the storm in which two people have drowned at sea.

One is a woman, cast up by the purple waves on the rocky shore where an eagle gnaws on her ribs. The other is a young man who has sunk to the seabed; his entrails are about to be devoured by hollow-eyed denizens who gape over his pallid corpse, and snaky loathsome things wrap themselves round his legs. The effect is as of looking through water down into wondrous depths, Gilchrist says—an image that seems to echo his wife's reading of Moby-Dick, as well as Coleridge's ancient mariner adrift over the rotting deep where slimy things did crawl, or Ariel's song of a duke's bones and eyes turning into corals and pearls, full fathom five.

We may forgive Anne Gilchrist and the Rossettis for their headlong ardour. Blake was a one-man utopia, and it is hard not to love such a man, who kept his best time for young people and children and who was himself childlike, with his certain virgin freshness of mind and that piled-up brow, as Samuel Palmer said.

Those eyes take it all in. He's an ageless spirit: hypnotic, irresistible, both there and not there. A divine being, caught in some kind of current or veil, always held just beyond us, beckoning us on to heaven or hell. Angelic and animal: with his fiery red halo of flaming hair and cat-like gaze, looking at us like Prospero, through a filmy gauze, the dark backward and abysm of time Why draw himself so? For posterity, to make sure of himself? Like Dürer's self-portraits, peering unerringly at us, this was an exercise in self-certification. After all, no one was going to buy this picture, or even be interested in it, not until it was too late.

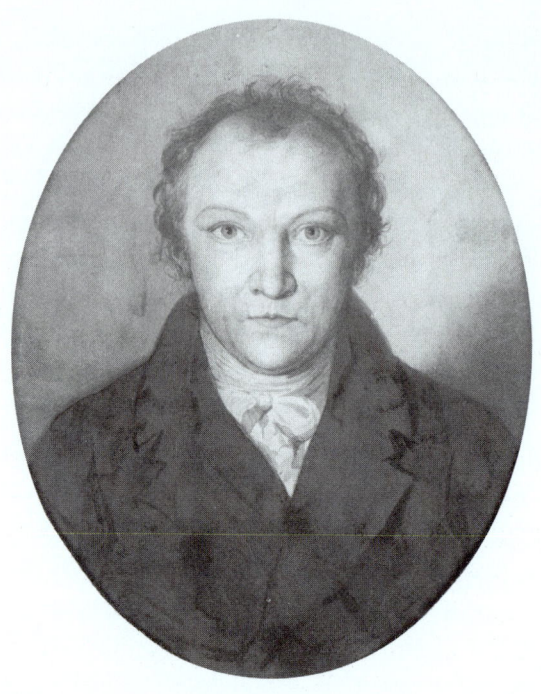

And it is hard, as the Gilchrists and their Pre-Raphaelite board of trade maintain, to describe poems wherein the dramatis personae are giant shadows, gloomy phantoms, set in the realms of space and in time of such corresponding vastness that eighteen hundred years pass as a dream.

I must confess my opinion that they are, taken as a whole, neither readable nor even entirely sane performances, William Michael Rossetti said. To him they were dark and chaotic to the extremest degree; ponderous and turbid; battling and baffling, like the arms of a windmill when the wind blows shiftingly from all quarters. Almost accidentally, as my friend Mark remarks, Rossetti evokes all of Blake's wildness in that one whirling image.

Blake's seven angels had no precedent for this extravagant output. Even the modernists would be hard-pushed to explain it, though they fed on its energy like hawks circling a thermal on outstretched wings. Woolf's Orlando has their model in Blake's goddess dozing her way through the millennia like an actor in a vitrine or Molly Bloom lolling on her rhododendron bed in Howth,

> Enitharmon slept,
> Eighteen hundred years. Man was a Dream!
> The night of Nature and their harps unstrung.
> She slept in middle of her nightly song
> Eighteen hundred years, a female dream.

Unlike the sexed-up Rossettis, I can't turn the pristine pages of Blake's books with their prismatic colours, the iridescence of a bubble or bright sun forced through fine fabric, filtering out white light into its constituent parts. Unlike Ruskin, who cut up one of only two surviving coloured copies of Blake's *Jerusalem* and rearranged the pieces to create a new narrative like Burroughs, busy quoting Blake as he served his guests hard liquor in smeary jam-jars, or the starman slicing his words in dark hotel rooms by the light of a flickering monitor, I can't take my scissors to these things and make my own version of them. It would not be popular with their curators if I did.

Blake fills our minds with colour; it all comes flooding in. He's so impatient, he can't wait for it all to begin. His work is one long cycle, one long scroll, one long newsreel, and all we can do is to view and review it again and again. His art feeds back into his words, and vice versa; the one powers the other. He is his own critic, disdaining all others, the only narrator of his art. Sometimes, as I look at these images, I fear their effect on me. Blake moves among us, in an enactment of something that has already been and is yet to come. You feel him as you walk down the city's streets. He's there, singing behind you, as Jah Wobble says, his angels sparkling in the trees as the trains rattle over your head.

And so, when Joyce writes Circe, the queerest, most phantasmagorical chapter in *Ulysses*, using his own cut-up techniques, he turns to Blake to create a scene set in the chaos of a twentieth-century city. The sequence takes place in a brothel in Nighttown, Dublin's red-light district of sin and despair, and Joyce draws deeply, for the whole gothic swirl of it all, on Blake, whom he greatly admires for having conquered tyranny by imagination, as Richard Ellmann said. And just as Blake didn't imagine things but saw them, so Joyce's characters appear as visions in the nowhere world of Nighttown, singing their lines in speech bubbles, the way Blakean people seem to do.

Joyce, who also made toy theatres as a teenager, manipulates his figures like Blake, whose art and poetry and prose—especially his satirical Island in the Moon—set the tone for Joyce and his masque-like scenario. The result is as uncanny as any ghost story, a pornography of the dead. We see a deafmute idiot with goggle eyes, his shapeless mouth dribbling, jerking past, shaken in Saint Vitus' dance, imprisoned by a chain of children's hands, as Joyce writes. Things move independently, psychically. A form sprawled against a dustbin and muffled by its arm and hat moves, groans, grinding growling teeth, and snores again. The segue from reality to fantasy is subtle and perverse and indeliably Blakean. Leopold Bloom changes sex and species and, in the most extraordinary image in the whole of that big fat book, Stephen Dedalus's dead mother appears before him as a wraith, wrapped in the green slime of the grave, as if reborn out of death.

It is a travesty, and Joyce surveys it all dispassionately, throwing a frame of irony around its decadent rot. Most of all, he sides with Blake against the state. Only a hundred years divide the one artist from the other. When Dedalus, Joyce's alter ego and a fallen angel himself, finds himself beset by vicious British soldiers, his situation is an echo of the most traumatic incident of Blake's life, when he too was threatened by a pair of soldiers, an episode which would confirm his decision to leave the sea behind, in the same way that Joyce himself would flee the shores of Ireland a century later.

Artists require defending wherever they are. They demand it, even, even when they can prove they were born on this earth. There were good reasons for Joyce to connect with Blake, not least because Yeats told him to; and Yeats believed in art as a communication with the dead. Reading Blake's work in a daze of revelation in his college classroom on Stephen's Green or walking under the railway bridge on Westland Row, Joyce enters his own Printing house in Hell. He employs Blake's sensibility; even the manuscripts of *Ulysses* echo Blake with their multi-coloured crayoning and cell-like division into body parts.

Blake's bodies are generally heavenly, Joyce's mostly venal. They meet in between. Both sought to protest against their age in a philosophical, visionary, no-holds-barred rage. Later, in exile in Trieste, by the sea that he feared, Joyce would deliver a lecture on Blake. His text was Yeats's 1893 edition of Blake's poems. And it provided Joyce with a very good reason to empathise with Blake since, according to Yeats, Blake was Irish. It was the only way he could account for Blake's propensity for seeing faeries in the grass or dead poets on the beach. This is the story Yeats told, or was told. I read it in his copy of his own book, in the library on Kildare Street on a dark morning, as he and Joyce walked past.

No one knew where Blake came from—contrary to appearances, he didn't pop out already named and fully formed—and the ambiguity of his background is of a piece with his elusive genius. But in 1893 Yeats created his own Blake by publishing his edition of Blake's poetry, along with a biographical Memoir of Blake, written, with Yeats's approval, by his co-editor, Edwin John Ellis, a Pre-Raphaelite artist and poet who was known to be vague and depressive (his wife had banned Yeats from their house on account of the fact that she suspected he was casting spells on her husband).

In Yeats and Ellis's mystical world, Blake attains a new origin myth, to suit their retrospective story. They claim that, early in the eighteenth century, a certain Dubliner named John O'Neil escaped debt and difficulties by marrying an Ellen Blake, who kept a shebeen in Rathmines; she then lent her name to O'Neil's son by another mistress. It was this son, James Blake, who settled in London, and became the father of William. Their evidence came from Yeats's fellow theosophist, Dr Charles Carter Blake, who claimed to be a relative of Blake's, and who said his family had worked in the wine trade in Malaga, Spain, where another son of Ellen Blake is supposed to have ended up. It is true that a company with Galway roots, Browne & Blake, operated in Malaga in the 1750s; one of them became a famous Spanish general, Joaquín Blake y Joyes, who had red hair and blue eyes like Blake, as well as an Irish mother, Inés Joyes y Brown, herself a writer. Born in 1759, died in 1827, the general was a contemporary of William; his portrait in the Prado displays a certain similarity between the two.

Carter Blake was an anthropologist and palaeontologist, a protégé of Richard Owen and friend of Richard Burton and Swinburne; he was also a member of the Golden Dawn and claimed to be able to astrally project his body. This may have been a good credential for a potential relative of William Blake, but his firm belief in the inferiority of other races was certainly not. Carter Blake lived in Bidborough Street, Bloomsbury, close to Yeats (Paul and Margaret Nash later lived on the same street); he died in penury in 1897, after persuading his thirteen-year-old daughter to write begging letters for him.

Given Carter Blake's background (even Yeats had to admit he was eccentric), you might not place a lot of trust in his story. Yet the notion of Blake's Irishness was persistent, and predates Carter Blake's claims. In 1854 the *Encyclopaedia Britannica* had confidently asserted that the engraver of high but wild genius was born in Ireland. And there was an enduring mystery about Blake's family. His only surviving relative, his sister Catherine, whom we last saw bathing off Felpham beach, and who was said to have fine eyes and to have been decidedly a lady, seems to have sunk, in her latter years, into extreme indigence. Like petitioners in an ancient inheritance, other claims to Blake's genes emerged. In 1893 a biographer of Blake said he had been contacted by two sisters in Southampton who claimed to be Blake's cousins; someone else claimed Blake was related to the English Admiral Blake of the seventeenth century.

Whatever the truth, Yeats and Ellis were convinced of Blake's Irishness. They declared that he was, before all things, an O'Neil with wild O'Neil blood. His descent from a stock who had seldom lacked their attendant banshee, they said, may well have had much to do with his visionary gift. The very manner of Blake's writing has an Irish flavour, they claimed, his lofty extravagance of invention and epithet recalling old Irish epics, while his mythology brought to mind the tumultuous vastness of the ancient tales of god and demon that have come to us from the dawn of mystic tradition in what may be fairly called his fatherland. Their Blake, like everyone else's, including mine, shifts shape according to place and time. A Jungian study of Blake, written by W.P. Witcutt in 1946, went so far as to claim that William ought rightly to have been named Liam O'Neil; a London Irishman given away by his flame-like golden-red hair, standing on end all over his head like a famine victim; physically aware of his erotic body, Witcutt says, quoting Blake's Notebook,

> Abstinence sows sand all over
> The ruddy limbs and flaming hair,
> But Desire Gratified
> Plants fruits of life & beauty there

And so another Blake arose, phoenix-like, Orc-like from the updraught of his own flames, newly revolutionary, to stalk Phoenix Park. William-Liam-O'Neil-Blake takes his place as a hot-tempered, strong-limbed, copper-haired Irish boy, wide-eyed with fiery locks in a punkish sketch drawn by Catherine, a portrait of her lover as a young man. The image may have been imaginary, done after he had passed on, but it is part of his myth: Blake, continually reborn. A young god, unsacrificed his auroral Glad Day, his Dance of Albion, a faerie child, glowing, on the rim of a volcano, all but waving his red cap of revolution on the barricade. It was so natural a covering for the fiery aureole of hair, as Mona Wilson, Blake's biographer, herself a radical writer from the nineteen-twenties, said, that he alone of the Liberty Boys would wear it serenely in the London streets.

A man who watched Newgate Prison burn to the ground. Who read the new demands for Liberty as graffiti chalked on the walls while others burned Tom Paine in effigy. In a fever dream, a woman lies down beside me on a single divan bed and tells me she has definite proof of Blake's Irishness. She looks like a young Iris Murdoch, in a jumper (I assume that it is red or green; I don't dream in colour, so far as I can recall), and proceeds to seduce me, until someone walks in the door. Like tales of sea serpents and krakens, the Irish Blake has the air of legend and myth. And like those stories, I do not necessarily believe it to be untrue.

Whether or not he was Irish didn't matter; Joyce believed, via Yeats, that he was. That was enough. Yeats and Joyce were regenerating a Blake fit for Ireland's revolutionary state; which meant that Blake now lived on in Yeats's prophetic verse, and became a founding fable for Joyce. The most subversive writer of the century found his voice in the subversion of Blake, and in a most personal way, the central dynamic of *Ulysses* took its cue from Blake's own life.

Reading Yeats and Ellis's book, and being highly superstitious and fully aware of all the metaphysical connections, Joyce must have been impressed to discover Blake's grandfather came from the same Dublin district where Joyce himself was born. (He knew, too, that his own father claimed descent from the Joyces of the famed Tribes of Galway, which also included the family of Blakes.) It was as though Blake had walked through the Georgian streets of the Irish capital; Dublin itself meant black pool, just as Joyce played with blake meaning both black and white: With pale blake I write tintingface, he writes. As Leopold Bloom wanders Dublin, through streets that the Easter Rising would raze to the ground, he occupies the city the same way that Blake moved through London after the Gordon Riots. Joyce's oppressive Dublin and Blake's chartered London are both hymned and condemned, venal and innocent; river-strung, sea-dependent cities, open and closed, symbolic and transgressive in the artists' imagining, living as they both were under the tyranny of the same state.

In his lecture on Blake delivered in the port of Trieste in March 1912, just as he was starting to write *Ulysses*, Joyce spoke admiringly of how William would wake first and light the fire and boil the kettle ready for his sleeping Kate; rising from his bed after visionary ecstasy, as Joyce wrote, in his own vision, amazed that Los and Enitharmon and Homer and Milton should have appeared in their poor London room, and no other incense greeted their coming than the smell of East Indian tea and eggs fried in lard.

It was a direct and sensual augury of the scene Joyce would create in his book in which Leopold prepares breakfast for his wife in their Dublin house, cooking offal for his dozing Molly. It was also a vivid echo of his relationship with his own partner from Galway, Nora Barnacle, like Catherine Blake, a siren-like, semi-educated, passionately vital woman. When Joyce evoked William and Kate, he was also evoking himself and Nora.

Isn't this perhaps the first time in the history of the world that the Eternal spoke through the mouth of the humble? Joyce asks his Italian students, who may or may not have been amazed. They could not know what was being rehearsed in front of them. That the recollected image of the Blakes, which

Joyce saw as if they'd just risen, all cosy and post-coital from their marital bed, would translate into another erotically charged scenario in a book filled with erotic bodies and visceral insurrection and the human condition.

The opening and closing pages of Joyce's lecture are lost, so we don't know if he addressed the idea of Blake's Irishness in them. It hardly matters. For Joyce, as for Nash or Robertson or the Rossettis or anyone else, Blake was what he needed at the time, the way we need him now, living under our own tyranny. It was the mark of his immortal power, the degree of his generosity; Blake as a living artist from the future, not a dead white male from the past. Whether or not his fiery genius had its genetic origins in Ireland, it was evident enough to Yeats and Joyce, and it shaped the way they thought of him and the way their art drew on his freedom and his fearlessness.

It allowed them to do what they did.

When Blake called himself English Blake, as he did, it was as if to distinguish himself from this Irish Blake, who takes on a life of his own. He lives on in the way that these two writers reincarnate him, to their own ends. And so it is telling that it was Yeats who gave the name to Blake's proto-modernist monologue, An Island in the Moon, with its own pre-echoes of Ulysses in its cyclical dialogue, heightened caricatures, and the sense of a city in multitudinous operation.

And although Yeats's theory lacked proof, he persisted in maintaining that Ireland took a most important place in Blake's mystical system. So we may almost claim Blake for an Irish poet, he told the literary Jesuit, Father Matthew Russell; who was also Gerard Manley Hopkins's friend, and who had introduced Hopkins to the artist John Yeats and his son William in Yeats's studio on Stephen's Green in 1886.

It's a remarkable set piece. Picture the scene. Yeats, the young upstart poet, with his copycat Wildean long hair and his lofty disdain (he would later affect not to remember having met Hopkins at all); versus Hopkins the hypersensitive, virginal figure from the Catholic university over the road, where even his fellow priests mocked him for wearing little shoes with straps like a girl's and his medieval haircut with a monkish fringe.

Yet Hopkins has already written the most stupendous, proto-modernist epic of pity and disaster and faith in his *Wreck of the Deutschland*, a *Waste Land* in the making, a Catholic *Moby-Dick*, an epic disaster-movie-drama of five German nuns going to their deaths on a ship beached in a storm at the mouth of the Thames. (He sent the only draft to Robert Bridges, his closest friend, by mail; imagine what could have been lost in the post.)

Christ, come quickly! says the mother superior as she pops up through a hatch like a pantomime demon as the sisters await their merciful dispatch—a romantic mortal assertion of faith in the face of death in which Hopkins turned the same seas and rivers in which he loved to swim into a sensual, forbidden yet overt evocation of death and desire. He was haunted by drowning and by lads diving into a moorland river, their ecstatic shouts so far removed from his restricted physicality,

> how the boys
> With dare and with downdolphinry and bellbright bodies
> huddling out,
> Are earthworld, airworld, waterworld thorough hurled, all by
> turn and turn about

and yet the priest dings his own linen and jumper and jumps in. Even Hopkins's titles have a Blakean air; and they too sound ravishing, beyond their meaning. In another poem, That Nature is a Heraclitean Fire and of the Comfort of the Resurrection, he sees, almost feels clouds gloriously as

> heaven-roysterers, in gay-gangs they throng; they glitter in
> marches.

Now, in his Irish exile, faced with Yeats's youthful symbolism and Celtic sensuality, Hopkins is deeply critical.

You Irish, Hopkins said, you drag everything into your net over here.

In the silence of his closeted backroom on Stephen's Green, looking out to the distant Wicklow mountains from central Dublin, he reads young Yeats's poem, The Two Titans, about a young man and a sphinx stranded on a rock in the sea. He found it a strange and unworkable allegory.

How did they get there? What did they eat? he says.

Yeats, as a young man striking a pose with his monocle and floppy bow ties, couldn't care less. He was already referring to Blake as his master and spoke as if his form had appeared to him on a mountain top or in a darkened drawing room. He could not know that he had already been preceded in this radical spiritualist fantasy, in 1877, when a medium named William Lawrence, recently gaoled in Clerkenwell for fraud, claimed to be in communion with Blake, whose spirit issued orders for paint, paper and brushes from a shop near Golden Square which turned out not to exist. Undeterred, Lawrence-as-Blake produced a portrait of Tom Paine-by-Blake, complete with a supernatural halo of light.

Blake's spirit, wanted dead or alive, Irish or not, would haunt Yeats more than any poet: from his Second Coming, with its rough beast slouching like a leviathan, to the terrible beauty born of the Irish uprising as if seen through his eyes (he was in England at the time).

Deploying Blake as a kind of vision, the way Blake did with Milton, Yeats declared that Blake grows always more exciting with every year of his life, as if the pair were walking arm in arm down Molesworth Street. Blake was his fellow traveller from the earthly to the heavenly in the mystic Jewish Cabbala, from Malkuth to Kether, as above, so below, like darts in lovers' eyes. Blake is in perpetual use, in stark black and white. Even at the end of his own life in 1938, as he stood in his Dublin room, Yeats summoned up the vision in his poem, An Acre of Grass, as if in his own defence, of

> William Blake
> Who beat upon the wall
> Till Truth obeyed his call.

Back in his room on Stephen's Green, Fr Hopkins, SJ, was not so sure.

You know what happened to crazy Blake, he said; he fell into a hysterical excitement. Now commonsense forbid we should take on like these unstrung creatures: still it was a proof of the power of the shock.

Hopkins was sceptical because he was writing about himself. Like Blake, his own poems had almost no public audience in his lifetime, no stock: everything was done for the future, an investment in immortality.

The man who never in his mind and thought travelled to heaven is no artist, Blake says. O my chevalier, Hopkins cries to his hovering kestrel. For every thing that lives is Holy, says Blake.

From that same room, Hopkins had written to a friend in 1887, telling him, I have Blake's poems by me. The best are of an exquisite freshness and lyrical inspiration, he said, but there is mingled with the good work a great deal of rubbish, want of sense, and some touches of ribaldry and wickedness. Yet he clearly drew on Blake's Song of Liberty,

> The fire, the fire is falling!
> Look up! look up!

for his poem, The Starlight Night, and its faerie world,

> Look at the stars! look, look up at the skies!
> O look at all the fire-folk sitting in the air!
> The bright boroughs, the circle-citadels there!

Revolutionary in his own sensual augury of modernism, the fire was always falling in Hopkins's Jesuitical mind, a marriage of heaven and hell. Robert Bridges, said that Hopkins's planetary illustration for his youthful poem, A Vision of the Mermaids—full of sirens and deep-sea things—was remarkably Blake-like. In 1929, Paul Nash would design the geometrically patterned cover for its first edition, published forty years after Hopkins's sad decline and lonely death in Dublin at the age of forty-four.

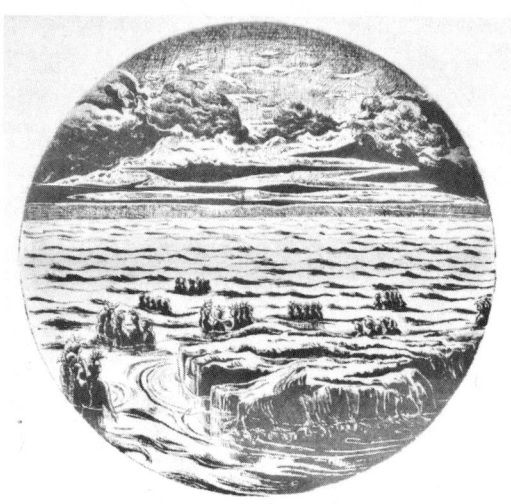

A Vision of the Mermaids.

Things happen to Paul Nash in slow motion. The way his aunt's dog, a large black retriever of a most lovable disposition, as he recalled—the anti-dog to the one that haunted him—would see Nash walking towards him across the field, a joyous moment for me, he said; the moment when, as the boy emerged from the wood, the dog paused and drew himself back in a rather theatrical way, then, with an hysterical bark, bounded forward.

At the same moment, Nash said, I seemed to feel the path quicken under my feet and sweep outward on its course over the field with ever-increasing speed. Thus the path and the dog would meet, he wrote, the path doubling beneath the darting shadow of the dog's curly black belly.

Dog and boy, caught in time. The retriever of memory, an act of retrieval. The unbroken line: of body and memory, of everything speeding up; art as an inventory, an index of futurity.

By now Nash's family were taking their annual summer holidays in Swanage; and the natural world opened itself up to him on the blunt bare chalk cliffs of Ballard Head, sheering away to the sea; an ancient connection with the fractured chalk stacks of the Isle of Wight on the other side of the Solent that was once a river. Nash was creating his own version of inscape;

he was doing in art what Hopkins had done in words. He was born a month before Hopkins died; perhaps some spark had jumped between them. The headland rose in majesty over Swanage Bay, he wrote. It lifted him up, like a raven riding a thermal.

I remembered the curious sense of being alone, he said; the spacious scene beyond emphasising a sense of the power I felt in this isolation.

Soon after this revelation, Nash joined the Slade. He loved London, certain aspects of which he found so joyous, naive and tender, he wrote, in their beauty of grey, white and blue and that miraculous soot-black on Portland stone.

It was a theatre set. So he dressed to match, like an artist of some sort, he said. He wore his hair thick and rather long with slight side whiskers; a fawn hat with a brim as wide as a Stetson; a brown tweed suit checked with a red thread; and a long light-brown Harris tweed cloak with a waistcoat attached (it had flapped pockets). His shirt collar was turned down, fashionably, with long points, white and starched, a special design for him, gathered with a very wide red silk knitted tie in a conventional sailor knot. To complete his ensemble he carried a long ebony stick with a shepherd's crook handle, a cross between a bishop and a dilettante; he might have complained, like Beardsley, that he'd catch cold if he left the tassel off the top of his cane. Sometimes he varied his get-up with sombre black cloth coat and waistcoat, paired with wide oatmeal-coloured trousers, and black patent shoes with cuban heels and white spats. The sort of man to be confined to a secret suite in a decrepit hotel, playing table tennis and drinking neat gin.

Of course, it did occur to him, this Slade dandy with his Spanish features, his raven-black hair contrasting strangely with his alien blue eyes, that his appearance might act as a provocation to the toughs of Tottenham Court Road; but it was well worth the risk for the sake of looking so good. He was in with the in-crowd, and he didn't care what anyone else thought.

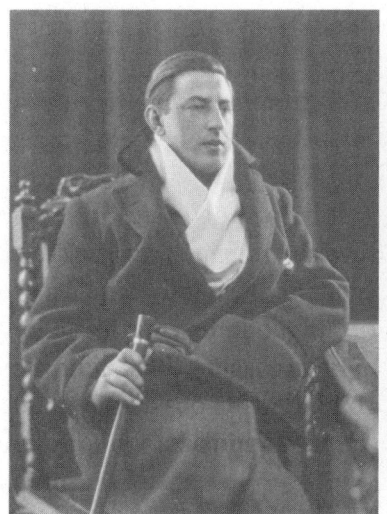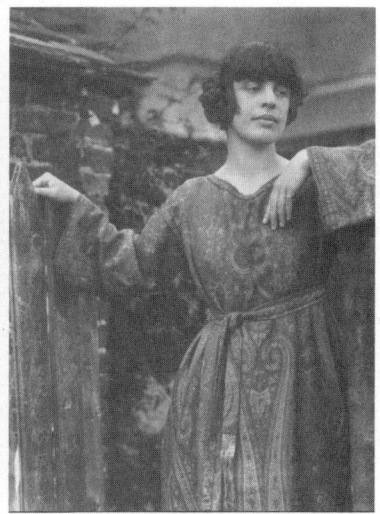

His wife-to-be, Margaret Theodosia Odeh, three years older than him, wasn't taking any nonsense either. She was a new woman. Kate Blake, updated. A fighter for women's suffrage, and her diminutive figure also appeared dressed in brown, head to toe: brown shoes and stockings, brown dress and some sort of knitted coat, but on the soft black cloud of her hair, Nash wrote admiringly, she wore a hard brown hat firmly held to her chin by a brown veil; her hands were covered in very neat gauntlets, and in the right hand, she carried a brown leather dog whip for self-defence. Tough. Odeh had been born in Jerusalem, a subject of the Ottoman Empire; the family had moved to Oxford, where her father, the Reverend Naser Odeh, born in Taiyibeh, Palestine, had taught Arabic to Lawrence of Arabia. Margaret's mother, Mary Anne Dickson, was a strong-headed intellectual from County Dublin. It was a potent mix: half-Arabic, half-Irish, Odeh was said to be clairvoyant, able to intuit things that had yet to happen. She was fierce. Her cheeks were high-coloured and her dark brown eyes had gone almost black with the dark glow of battle, Nash said. He called her his little black rose. With her severely bobbed hair and strong, angular body, she was a new kind of woman, ready for the fray, determined to protest and resist.

And so she did. Odeh became a campaigner for the Tax Resistance League who refused to pay imperial taxes while women went unrepresented in Parliament. In the city, in her suffragette role, Odeh rode on a milk cart like a chariot, having charmed the young driver into steering her through the crowds, pamphlets flying and people parting as they went. When a medical student from University College (they were the worst) leered in her face and said, What you want, sweetheart, is raping, she punched him in the mouth.

I have been thinking a great deal & with intent upon all you have told me about the danger that imperils women day & night in this country, Nash told her, & the revelation you gave me has shocked me, he said. He pledged to do anything in his power to help her fight this devil.

I will emancipate the world for you, he said.

He was amazed when she introduced him to her colleagues at their club. They were busy listening to a handsome, athletic girl striking the table with her fist as she outlined plans outrageous enough to rival Crossfield and his harpoon airgun, in which a suffragette gang would abduct the prime minister, Lloyd George, take him to an island tied up and dressed in his pyjamas and refuse to release him until their demands for the vote were met. Other members carried hammers in bunches of daffodils, ready to smash post office windows; one trained their parrot to utter subversive slogans. Hidden behind a copy of The Times as the pair travelled on the tube, the bird would squawk out, Down with Lloyd George, Down with the Government, George is a damned liar!, only to appear, when revealed, quite nonchalantly chewing their claws.

Nash described such scenes with humour, but he knew this was a civil war. He saw that much of the violence and obscene abuse was being stirred up by Government Men among the crowds. He was radicalised by what he saw. That time seemed like the End of a World to him. Everything was about to change as such dissent was drastically curtailed by the state in pursuit of a war designed, it seemed, to impose order on its own people and their inconvenient ideas.

In September 1914, Nash joined the Artists' Rifles; the same regiment in which, a year later, another young dandy, Wilfred Owen, author of his own poem on the Little Mermaid, would enlist. Transferring to the Hampshire Regiment (in which my own grandfather served at the same time, enlisting in Dorset, before being sent off to India and Arabia), Nash sailed down Southampton Water to fight in France, where the damage done to the landscape and its inscape would leave his body and mind scarred. It was a new epiphany, brought about by industrialised war. Bodies were moulded, mobilised and armoured; then deconstructed, brutalised, ripped up and taken apart, to be put back together again with prosthetic limbs and plastic faces and glass eyes, new sorts of human for a new century.

Blake's delayed apocalypse had arrived, enacted by Edwardian androids in aqualung masks as the land became a foetid sea. Having fallen into a trench and been rendered invalid for service, Nash was reborn as an official war artist; an ambivalent position in itself. He sailed back down Southampton Water to France to record a wasteland that had collapsed into a toxic ocean of mud. A primeval mire laying down future fossils of men and horses and guns.

Sunset and sunrise are blasphemous, Paul told Margaret, whom he had now married for the sake of respectability. They are mockeries to man, he said; only bruised and swollen black clouds of rain were fit atmosphere in such a land. He laid out scenes like projections on a screen; not re-enacted in black and white but in living colour. While moviegoers stood up in the cinema crying, The horror! at the newsreels, Nash reworked the reality back into art. Nature morte. A single shattered tree stood for everything else. Nothing else was left.

The rain drives on, he wrote; the stinking mud becomes-more evilly yellow, the shell holes fill up with green-white water, the roads and tracks are covered in inches of slime, the black dying trees ooze and sweat and the shells never cease.

I am a messenger, he told Margaret, bringing back word from the men who are fighting to those who want the war to go on for ever, he said. It was his equivalent of the photographs in the pockets of Owen and Ross. As if Blake had become a war artist. In a way, he had, in circumstances he would have hated.

In early 1916, Robert Bridges, now the poet laureate, asked Hubert Parry to set Blake's Jerusalem to music to be performed at a Fight for Right Campaign concert at the Queen's Hall, convened to create support for the war. Bridges had included Blake's poem in a patriotic anthology that year, along with six works by Hopkins. Now he asked Parry to add suitable, simple music to Blake's stanzas; music that an audience could take up and join in, he said.

When he realised what had happened to his composition, Parry, appalled by the jingoism of the event, transferred the copyright of his song to the suffragist movement which he and his wife supported. Two years later it was sung at the Royal Albert Hall to celebrate the victory of the Votes for Women campaign, an occasion Margaret Odeh must have attended with pride. She had recently helped found a utopian colony near Newbury, using art and craft to lift women out of prostitution, rescuing many girls from London brothels and from the white slave traffic, as The Times noted.

Yet when the same newspaper reported on the event at the Albert Hall, it was keen to record that the meeting had agreed that the primary duty of women citizens was to defeat pro-Germanism and Bolshevism on the home front, and that the chief cry of Annie Kenney of the Women's Party was, Down with pacifism everywhere. It could hardly have known that Kenney was the lover of Christabel Pankhurst; or that within a few months it would be reporting on a libel case at the Old Bailey brought by the Salome Dancer, Maud Allan, who was accused of leading a lesbian Cult of the Clitoris inspired by Oscar Wilde, himself the posthumous figurehead for a culture of perversion said to be undermining the entire British establishment.

The world was changing even faster than The Times. The same page of that edition reported on a seaplane fight over the North Sea, a tea room in Victoria charging army officers inflated prices for cups of tea and cake served by young women in low-cut dresses who kissed customers on their cheeks; and that dog wool was being collected as a high-class substitute to account for the shortage of the real thing.

Art caught up with war. Nash thought his pictures were feeble and inarticulate, unable to give even a vague idea of the horror; but they had a bitter truth, he admitted to himself. He felt he had failed in his duty as he returned to England and a sort of normality: the old world, reordered: Robbie Ross, the Sitwells, &c, &c. Suddenly, he found himself acclaimed for his images of violence, even as he sought to escape them. In the uneasy peace that followed, he would turn to

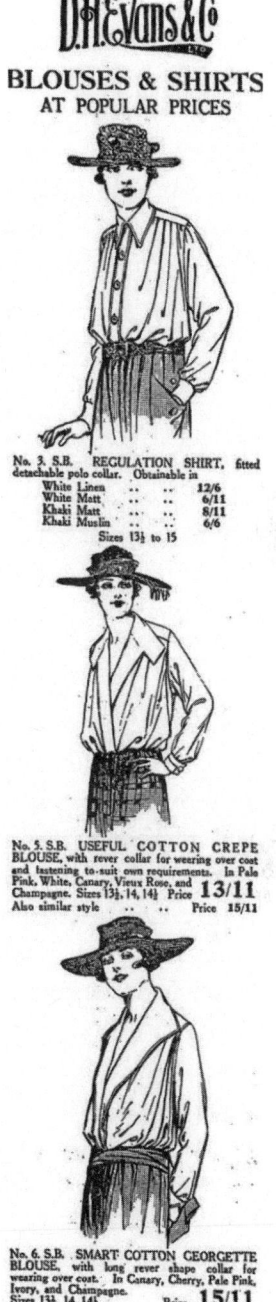

the English landscape in reparation for the damage he had recorded in France, the damage done to himself.

Settling at Dymchurch on the Kentish coast, a hundred miles east of Felpham, where the sea slopes deceptively slowly up from the grey channel, and where the grey concrete wall built to defend the land from it seems to run for a hundred miles, shielding visitors' view of the water till it's too late, Nash painted the sea again and again. In his drawings and paintings from that time, incessant waves meet the slab-like shapes of concrete; the water calm at one point, then churned up like a nightmare.

You can feel him, in his cottage just behind, taking shelter from the rising form, the falling low. Nash's seascapes prefigured the advent of his Unit One: art as a compact wall, a hard defence against the deluge to come. His most famous painting of the war had been his ironically titled We Are Making a New World, as if it were a tourist advertisement for a holiday in hell; a last resort where the imploded terrain of the Western Front had turned to frozen waves of mud. A dark mirror of his boyhood hideaway in Kensington Gardens; a place that was definably strange and decidedly unsafe.

Now, in Kent, where the pandemonium still seemed to reverberate from across the Channel, to be caught in concrete sound mirrors being built on the shore as an early-warning system, Nash echoed the disorder of the new century at the grim edge of Dymchurch, which sounded like a darkened dumb chapel. There he created rhythmical, ritual pictures of the sea, making modernist sense of the primeval disarray. They are depressed images, produced under low pressure, the sky pressing down on the sea. Barometric, the assault continued night and day, and in the twilight of high tide, Nash introduced haunting figures, hooded or cloaked or gesticulating or even floating in the air like Blakean angels or spirits in a Blackwood story; they emerged out of his shell-shocked state, as David Mellor would note. They have the air of revenants or perhaps his own Margaret, his medium and muse.

They soon vanish. Unlike Blake, who filled his art with them, Nash left people out; random objects took their place. His work was as devoid of humans as the dead fields of France. He called himself a war artist without a war.

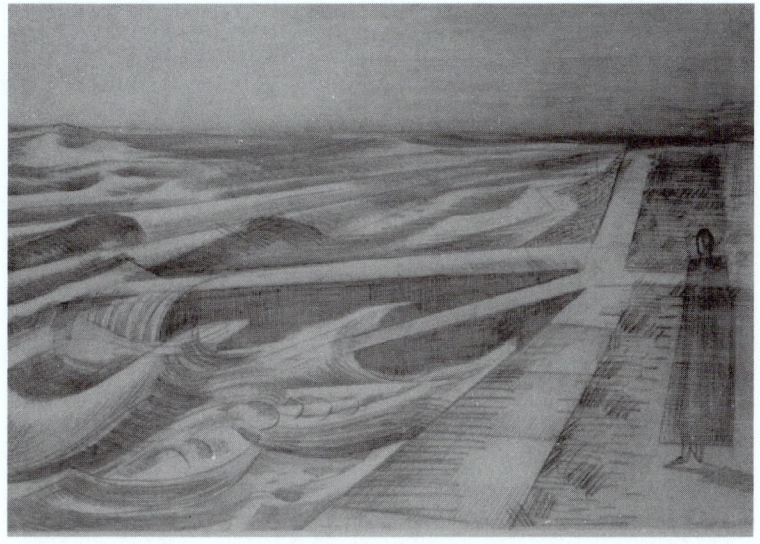

September, 1921. I get up in the night and fall down. Black out. Admitted to the London Hospital for Nervous Diseases, Nash is diagnosed with meningitis; his wife blames his collapse on the suppressed effects of the war and says he slept, as if in a coma, for a week. When he woke from his long slumber like Orlando or Enitharmon, transformed, he was even more aware of his intense sense of the spirit of place and the sense of himself looking on. The only charm, he said, is in seeing something for the first time, for oneself. In his trauma, he knew he had to leave Dymchurch. I shall never work there any more, he announced. He feared its effect on him.

Like Blake, he had been defeated by the sea.

———

In the summer of 1934, as Britain was experiencing unemploy-
ment, riots and failing industries, at the same time that people
were flocking to the beaches and the cinemas, Nash was
suffering from a new condition: asthma, brought on, according
to his physician, by his hypersensitivity. His art was a psycho-
somatic state; and that summer, after spells in Rye and travels
to France and New York, the Nashes moved back to the sea
for respite, seeking to escape the disease which was slowly
depriving Paul of his breath.

Dorset offered the perfect therapy, with its wide-openness
and its mystery, its swelling sea promising an antidote to the
constriction of his lungs, a literal inspiration, breathing in spirit,
for his art. Having seen the stones of Avebury the year before,
he was ready for this place. He saw the Isle of Purbeck as one
gigantic face, a countenance overcast by a noble melancholy. It
reared up in stacks and plunged deep in caves. The past was
entirely subjective; the sea was an emotional state.

Unable to portray people because they were so full of problems, Nash had begun to paint slices of idyllic countryside in
which strange geometrical shapes erupted instead of human
beings. These images, like cross sections of real life, would be
regarded as surreal and modernist, but they too had their
origins in Blake's Druidical rocks and cosmological allegories—
just as Blake had declined to draw from nature and despised
landscapes made for their own sake. Landscapes, like animals
and trees, set on their own, were just too literal: if he used
those elements, they had to have a spiritual intent.

Natural Objects always did & now do weaken, deaden &
obliterate Imagination in Me! said Blake. Nature should be
learned by heart and remembered by the painter, as the poet
remembers language, he declared. He would leave the delusive
Goddess Nature & her Laws behind. He had need of no restraint.
He did not draw from the life; he drew from the life within.

Landscape was literal, non-fiction till Turner came along.
Blake applied the same sense of the sublime to the human form

and turned the land into a spiritual arena. His idealised version of the natural world was an interior narrative—his own and ours, in which he saw himself: in his bodies, his beasts, his rocks, his clouds, his seas, his stars, his trees. They in turn become part of the entire enigma that he, William Blake, represented, and which Paul Nash now took up.

Like for like. These things are happening at the same time. Knowing what we do now, it is impossible to look at Nash's works without seeing the ghosts of Blake's world. Nash had been through a war. So had Blake. Art slides back and forth in the rhythm of cruelty, myth and corruption, a necessary exchange. Blake wore his red bonnet of revolution, Odeh her shiny bowler of suffrage, Nash his helmet in the trenches. Art as a drama, like poetry or prose.

Nash sought to restore the ghosts left behind by the theatre of war. Limbs that were amputated grew back as trees. Landscapes become bodies the way that Blake's characters grow into their appendages and their appendages grow into them; the way that the great Creator's wings weld into his muscles which themselves are part of his gown, like a superhero's costume.

Creation, Blake would say, was an act of mercy. In anarchic slogans tattooed on a cartoon of Laocoön and his sons being crushed by sea serpents like the cover of a fanzine, he said that God had repented that he had made Adam, & it grieved him at his heart. It was like sniffing glue.

It was also the first act of desire and Blake shows us the opposite scene: of destruction, equally sensual, equally astonishing. Against a bursting, spiky-edged sun sinking into a black sea, Satan stretches out his wings as he smites Job with boils. The painting is tiny; it compresses the eye and forces you to feed on the unfolding trauma; even as it seems to recede there on the wall of the Tate on a quiet Saturday afternoon.

It draws me in with a roar. Perversely, set at the dead centre of the picture like a bullseye, is Satan's groin, a green blur, his sex covered by scales. It's a disconcerting sight, to say the least.

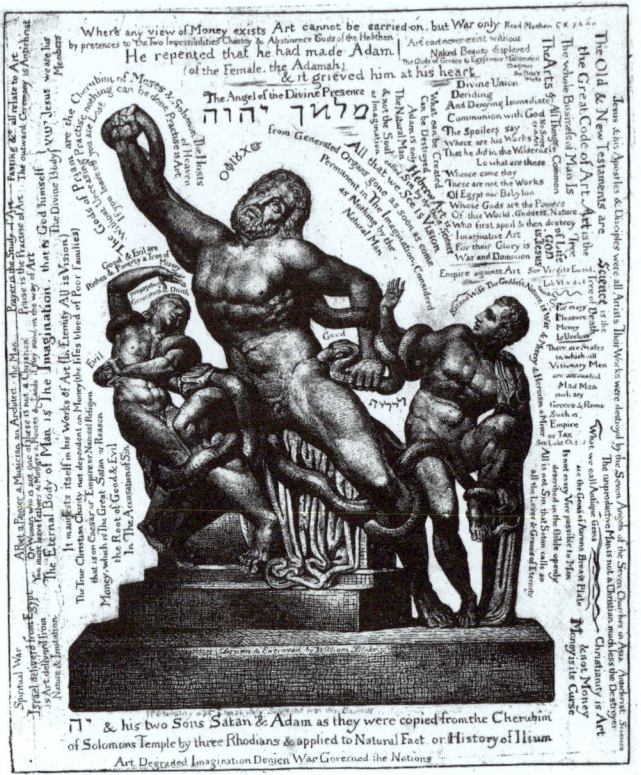

In *Paradise Lost*, Milton describes Raphael's loins and thighs as girt and skirted with a starry zone and downy gold of feathered mail. Such lusty legs lead us on; Blake has a thing about thighs, and is exceptionally good at them, offering us contorted torsos on muscular pillars in ecstatic poses of bondage and abandonment. He owes these living, lengthy marble muscles to Michelangelo, but they wouldn't look out of place in a drawing by Simeon Solomon or on a professional rugby player. They're enough to make you go all wiggly.

Blake is pure desire, an erogenous team zone of his own. In 1896, when W.H. Smith banned the *Savoy* magazine, it was not on account of Beardsley's perverse pictures inside, or the fact that it was named after the new luxury hotel where Wilde and Bosie shared a bed and any number of boys. Rather, the proprietors of the chain of bookstalls were outraged by the fact that an article by Yeats on Blake was illustrated by his naked giant Anthaeus arcing down to set Dante on a cliff edge like a scene from a Powell and Pressburger film.

Pl IX

There's nothing tentative about Blake's art. It doesn't flap or fuss. It is what it is. He reaches out, then stands back, and looks at us. Repulsion is attraction, switching between love and hate. He supplies what you need, not what you want. He gives you back moments of happiness you never knew you had, fills your head with terror fit to burst. There's no other artist so shocking in their welding of images and words. He is his own cause and effect.

Newton, nude and neoclassical too, posed like Madame Récamier on his rock. An utterly modern image, still filled with the power to shock: the arrogant refinement of the human versus the dark anarchy of Nature.

Nebuchadnezzar, another despot, hair fused to his flesh like feathers or roots, his nails become claws as he crawls out of his den, his muscle-plated body like Dürer's rhinoceros. His shaggy insanity, as Rossetti saw it, is subject to the same benthic pressure as Newton on the seabed.

Pl IX

Both labour under weather, whether a storm or a thermocline, caught in their own state of emergency, beyond human time. Bodies that can de-evolve, tipping over into the obscene.

The Ghost of a Flea contorts his Caliban shape into something that used to be, now all horny spine and finned ears; a humanoid dinosaur in a reptilian leotard, inanely curling his talons. Worst of all is that flickering tongue, licking at a cup of your blood, fit to lick you into quiescence as he sticks it down your throat.

In his breathless hopeless crazy Prophecies for America and Europe, in which he installed these masque-like characters, Blake foresaw the future and rehearsed the past. He did so in the true spirit of revolution and apocalypse,

Arise, O Orc, from thy deep den!

he summoned, as

The horrent Demon rose surrounded with red stars of fire
Whirling about in furious circles round the immortal fiend.

Blake's art is his one-man Unit One; instead of announcing it
in The Times, he publishes it in his Illuminated Books, broad-
sheets issued from the end of time.
Painters! on you I call! he cried,
Sculptors! Architects! Suffer not the fashionable Fools to
depress your powers.
He is surrounded by an aura. He's the magician a ten-year-
old girl meets when out walking with her father on the Strand.
He wears a brown coat and has uncommonly bright eyes, she
recalls, eyes she will remember all her life.
He is a strange man, her father tells her afterwards.
He thinks he sees spirits, he says.

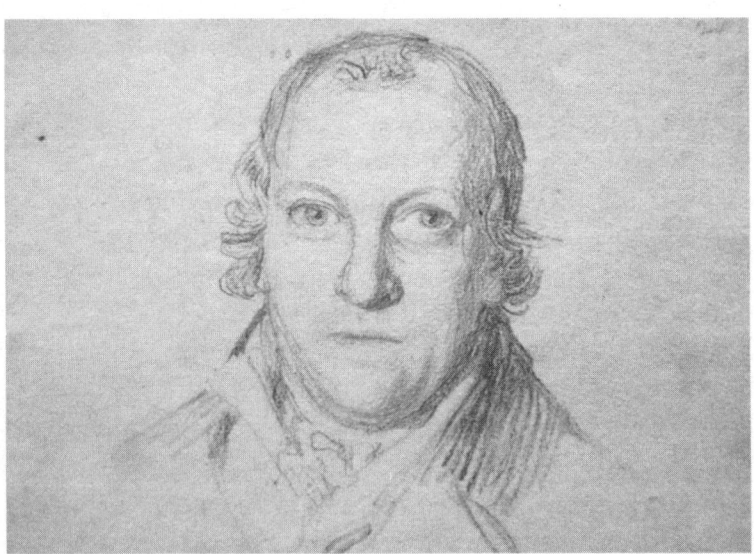

The child in his eyes. He'd take you by the hand, off in his time machine. Everyone knows that the mysterious, ageless Mr Blake, in his old-fashioned clothes, his pale broad face, is as familiar with angels as he is with human beings; they follow him round, like his beloved brother and the rest of his dead family. All those tygers and lions and birds? They're his eternal menagerie, his dream companions, his joy and despair. They fail and fall in mid-air or are tied down to the ground, caged and enslaved, awaiting release. Hell, like hate, is not the enemy but an energy itself. Everything exists because of its own paradox.

For every thing that lives is holy, he says.

Working backwards from that premise, everything is allowed. On one hand Blake's images are fantasies to exceed anything that Dürer or Fuseli imagined; on the other they're ferocious versions of the artist's real life and our own ordinary selves. They are multiples, repeated human-non-human beings, in a state of human being, becoming, attaining, still under construction, as we all are. Their stripped muscles and sinews work as machines; as mortals, not gods, in the bounding line of a medieval mural or an Aztec codex, ready to assume the shape of other beings: to be reborn as an eagle, an elephant, a dog, a horse, or a whale, just as we are all the same shape in the womb; evolving out of Blake's mirror-world as he writes behind his hand in class, in reverse, like Alice falling through the looking-glass. In one intensely strange and beautiful sequence in *Vala*, a Shadow rises like something out of a Pasolini film:

Of living gold, pure, perfect, holy; in white linen pure he hover'd,
A sweet, entrancing self delusion, a watry vision of Man,
Soft exulting in existence, all the Man absorbing.

        ★   ★   ★   ★

Then he beheld the forms of tygers & of Lions, dishumaniz'd men,
Many in serpents & in worms, stretch'd out enormous length

        ★   ★   ★   ★

And scaled monsters or arm'd in iron shell or shell of brass
Or gold, a glittering torment shining & hissing in eternal pain

★   ★   ★   ★

He knew they were his Children, ruin'd in his ruin'd world.

We're all cursed and blessed in Blake's ruin'd world, the moment a star falls out of the sky, a brief instant of unspecified pleasure, indefinable, the way a dream evaporates as you wake and you realise you're still here. Blake never left England all his life. He barely left London, caught in its canyons and squares, its alleys and hellholes and states of ecstasy and remorse. London was Blake and Blake was London: immortal, inspired, dark, disastrous; continually building & continually decaying, he said. He travelled through it in time and space, in his head. He saw the future, near and far; he was, quite clearly, a telepath, capable of second sight. When with his acolytes in Shoreham in Kent, he saw their leader, the handsome young Samuel Palmer, who had just left for London, walking back from the broken-down coach long before he came in through the door. Blake's apostles—Edward Calvert, George Richmond and Frederick Tatham among them—gathered round Palmer in his cottage, nicknamed Rat Abbey. Forerunners of the Pre-Raphaelites, they called themselves the Ancients in an ironic acknowledgement of their youth and, like New England utopians dressed in chintz shirts or Dürer's Nazarene fan boys in Germany copying their hero's medieval blouses, they enacted their cult of Blake by wearing amazing capes and declining to cut their hair. They swam in the translucent current of the river and roamed the Kentish countryside by night, like ghosts, as Blake said

look upon me
Not as another but as thy real Self. I am thy Spectre
. . . I view futurity in thee . . .

Worshipping Dürer and Michelangelo, with queer undertones (years after Palmer's death, his son claimed some of Samuel's sketchbooks displayed a mental condition full of danger, neither sufficiently masculine nor sufficiently reticent, and he burned them in a bonfire lasting five days), the Ancients took up the half-moons and mystic and dreamy glitter of Blake's woodcuts for Virgil, creating images of billowing, star-proofed trees and eerie figures that might or might not be what they seemed. Palmer even drew himself like Blake, like Dürer, in an unerring self-portrait made in 1824, when he was nineteen, the same year that he first visited Fountain Court, where he would seal his brotherhood's devotion by kissing Blake's doorbell each time he came to call.

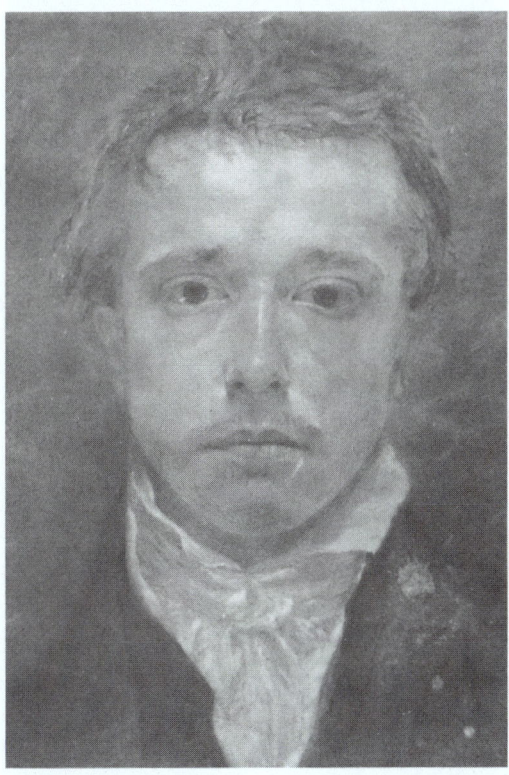

Their master, whose hair had been red and spiky once, appreciated such energy and enthusiasm. Who would not have been flattered by the attentions of such good-looking young men? He knew that through them, his art would carry on, almost genetically, in the contradictions and strange meetings of time, in people who came along, long after he'd gone.

A century later, Geoffrey Keynes, brother of the economist Maynard Keynes, become one of those disciples. He had been at Cambridge with Rupert Brooke and Ronald Firbank, then trained as a surgeon. Living in Bloomsbury in 1913, he had saved Virginia Woolf's life after she took an overdose of narcotics by pumping her stomach. As she had yet to write any of her novels, Keynes declared, we can now know what literature would never have existed had our efforts failed. During the war, when he helped develop new means of transfusing blood, Keynes saw men annihilated from the waist up, leaving only their lower halves in the mud. He mourned the early death of Brooke, whom he had loved, and, despite being married to a granddaughter of Charles Darwin, he counselled Siegfried Sassoon during his affair with the flighty Stephen Tennant by admitting his own Grand Passion for Serge Lifar, lithesome star of the Russian Ballet. Fascinated by entomology, bricklaying, mountaineering and good clothes, Keynes found the time to become an expert on Blake, acclaiming him as one of the greatest surrealists in the history of art.

They were Blake's new ancients, seeking transcendence through their trauma, as men fought for an illusory Albion and the Angels of Mons appeared in the clouds. Sassoon, who believed in angels, saw the infernal trenches as a vision of hell by Blake, and when David Jones, who said Blake was the greatest of all British artists, drew himself as a Blakean angel, a terrible Dance of Albion rising out of the trenches, naked save for his tin hat, his khaki uniform torn away by barbed wire and bombblast. Assailed by the tornado of violence, when Jones came home on leave he threw his lice-ridden uniform and underclothes out of the window. When his sister tried to pick them up, he shouted,

FOR CHRIST'S SAKE, LEAVE THE FUCKING THINGS ALONE

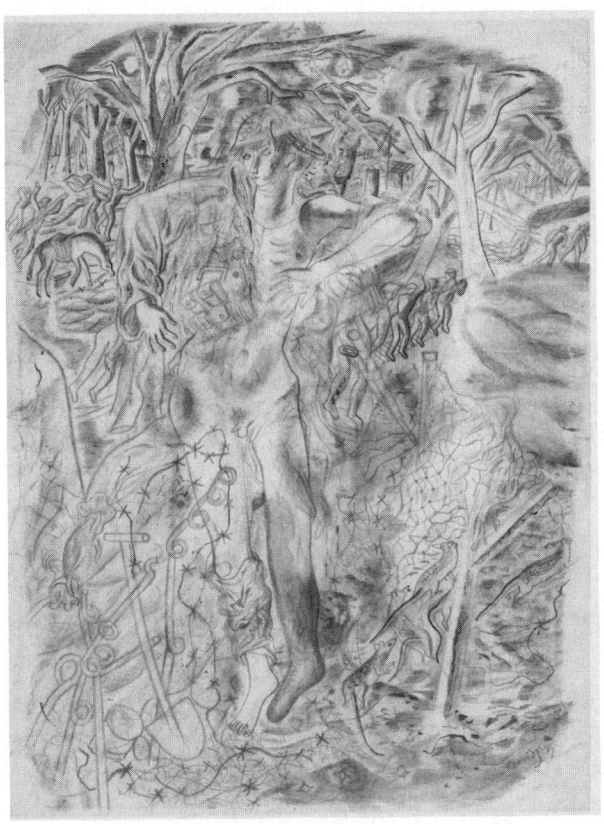

With nothing left to lose, they sought salvation and even oblivion in Blake, in the emblem of an England that had nothing to do with retribution or hate. They heard and felt him in their aftershock, in hospital wards and grand country houses and suburban sitting rooms, even though they could not stick their fingers in his side. Seldom, indeed, if ever, has there been another great artist who has subordinated reality to imagination so completely and so consistently, said Keynes. Other artists may be great, but their excitement was cool and impersonal, he said; only Blake retained this power to stimulate into our own time.

Over in Manhattan, perched on her sofa in her tiny Greenwich Village apartment around the time of Blake's centenary in 1927, the modernist poet Marianne Moore would agree. It was Blake's humanly personal approach to any subject that preserves him to us, she said. Demure to outsiders, Moore adopted Blake the way she engaged Dürer, as a courtier of her love, a physical ghost; the way that when Stephen Tennant was mourning his dead mother by dancing on his own in black in his empty manor house, he asked Sassoon, his lover, to decide which of her books he should keep. The first volume the poet chose was Gilchrist's biography of Blake. Tennant's mother, who conducted many seances in that house, had believed her son was spiritualistically inspired by Blake. Caught up in his fantasy world, he would go on to create elaborate ink-and-watercolour images of tattooed matelots and sick roses threaded through with poetic phrases, queer versions of Blake. They would still be lying there, strewn on the floor in that darkened room in that haunted house where I saw them, fifty years later.

The wreck of the twentieth century and its self-inflicted wounds could not undermine Blake's effect. His orderliness, set against his extraordinariness, resounded in our disorderliness. It was how he dealt with his chaotic mind. At the start of the twenty-first century, Robert A. Johnson, a Jungian analyst and Benedictine monk, told an interviewer in Chicago that Jung, whom he had known, liked to point out that Blake went further into the collective unconscious and lived to tell the tale than anybody else that he ever knew, and that he kept a very ordinary and human life.

Who can take it? Johnson asked. Blake married and he earned his living as an engraver and thereby saved his sanity in that manner, Johnson answered himself.

Blake transcends our travails. His visions survive because they came out of the Abyss of the Sea of Time and Space, not our venal and disputatious world. His art confronts and amazes us. Who could take it? Who could resist? He persisted and resisted for seventy years; it was a long apprenticeship and the pay was bad. Poverty was the price of his wild imagining, but the alternative was unthinkable. To labour under another's sway was to take the wages of sin. He'd already been reduced to drawing pottery for Josiah Wedgwood's catalogue. Apparently no one was concerned that the otherwise plain teapots and plates might start appearing emblazoned with fiery demons or serpentine leviathans or even the ominous Ancient of Days, ready to confront genteel hosts with their mortality as they sat down to their tea parties.

Respectable? Poor Blake, still poor, still Dirty, his friends said, though his linen was clean. He needed patrons, not patronising. He was irascible, resentful of advice or rebuffs, especially from other artists; quite rightly, since he knew he was right and they were wrong.

Their Pretence of Art was To Destroy Art, he said.

Blake remained right, right to the end, which came just in time.

His last view was squeezed between gloomy warehouses. The city had closed in around him. But he could still see the river from No. 3 Fountain Court, the Strand, his last earthly address. The Blakes moved there in 1820, by which time the Strand, London's beach, had been reclaimed from the Thames, leaving the Strand stranded. The street was once strung with lavish palaces, two of them owned by the earls of Essex and Southampton, a pair of dandy lords often found clad in corals and pearls: Robert, lover of the Queen; Harry, beloved of Shakespeare. But in 1601, in an act of brazen insurrection, they planned to seize Whitehall and the Tower in their Essex Rebellion. Instead, after a boat chase up the river when it seemed they might escape out to sea, Southampton ended up in the Tower and Essex lost his head, and the ruins of their former palaces now faced the newly built Waterloo Bridge.

Fountain Court was a dark terrace, itself a left-over place.

There was a pub on the corner, the Coal Hole, from where William would fetch his ale. London carried on being the same, its alleyways and rat-runs funnelling you down to the river, where narrow stairs ended in potential oblivion. One more step and you'd be swept away, into eternity or damnation. I slept there with a friend when we couldn't be bothered to go home after a night in Heaven. We only lived three miles up the road.

The Blakes' house was tucked away off the street like Scrooge's house that plays hide-and-seek with the other houses but has forgotten the way out again. Their lodgings lay on the first floor, over their landlord, who was also Kate's brother-in-law.

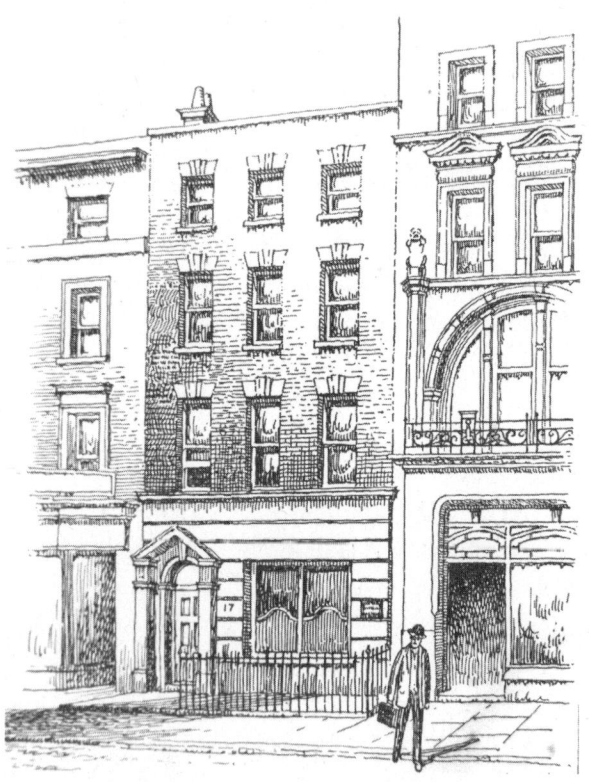

Mr & Mrs Blake, 3 Fountain Court

In their poverty, the Blakes were reduced to just two rooms. The one at the front was a kitchen; it doubled up as a showroom. Its walls were hung with William's art; in the corner, among the pots and pans, stood his press. He and Kate slept in the back room. It was bright in the morning sun, with light forced up from the river.

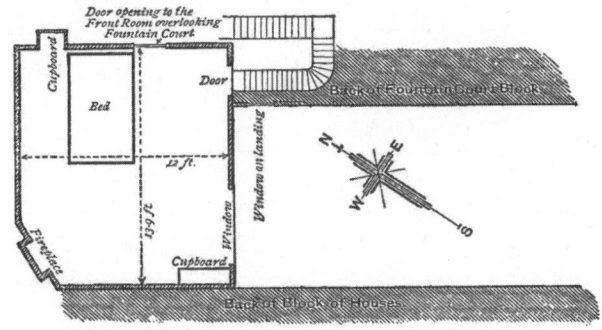

The place was tiny, but clean and orderly, as the young Ancients would attest. It was their island in the midst of the sea, they said, full of primitive grandeur. They called it the House of the Interpreter and he was their Michael Angelo Blake, sitting up in bed to draw. The nearest to God they could get. There was only one chair and one cupboard; his portfolios lay by his side on his desk, his books in a pile on the floor.

Fountain Court was the last refuge for the Blakes' art, never more cooperative than in this compressed space. Over his desk Blake hung Dürer's Melencolia, the only one of his antique prints he had kept, having been forced to sell the rest. Its eerie moonlight shone down as he painted the last version of his Ancient of Days.

There, that will do! he said.

He had come full circle. After all, as he wrote in someone's autograph book, he was born barely a mile away on 28 Novr 1757, and had died several times since. He was ready to fly. Leave all your belongings behind.

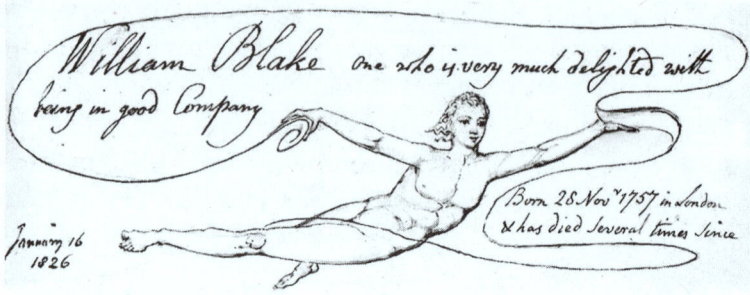

I wish to do nothing for profit. I wish to live for art. I want nothing whatever. I am quite happy, he said.

He'd drink his ale and listen to the children playing below his window. And there at his table, under the gaze of Dürer's ungendered angel surrounded by the clutter of the tools of their trade, he took up his burin like a lance and engraved a final series of pictures and words, inspired by the Book of Job.

At the end of his life he had created an entirely new way of representing his visions. He called them Inventions. The Book of Job is one of the Bible's most gruelling episodes, all plagues of boils and psychological trauma. To illustrate Job's terrible trials brought upon him by God, tribulations with which Blake readily identified, he produced gruesome depictions of what God had in store for Job, sitting there dolorously as he is confronted by a messenger informing him,

The fire of God is fallen from heaven & hath burned up the flocks & the Young Men & consumed them & I only am escaped alone to tell thee. Can'st thou bind the sweet influences of Pleiades or loose the bands of Orion?

Erasmus had said that Dürer could do in black and white what other artists could only do in colour; and as the German artist had made his sensational series of woodcuts illustrating the biblical Book of Revelations, so Blake engraved a collection of copperplates that surpassed anything else being done in his time. He dreamed in colour in his monochrome set. He may have been in his seventh decade, but he remained as excited as ever; Blake was capable of doing work as good as, and sometimes better than, any that he could do thirty years earlier, said Keynes. Always ahead of the rest. Ruskin said Blake's Book of Job was better than Rembrandt in expressing conditions of glaring and flickering light. The poet Kathleen Raine agreed. Looking at those same images, she too, like Marianne Moore, declared her love for Blake. She can't wait to write this all down.

It's 1968: another revolutionary year. Long-haired students are ripping up pavements to find the beach below. Guerre à la guerre impérialiste. Raine has spent all her life thinking about Blake. She has her own radical form, keeping company with the poet David Gascoyne, the artist and film-maker Humphrey Jennings and the critic Herbert Read. Her first husband, Hugh Sykes Davies, organised the International Surrealist Exhibition in 1936; her second, Charles Madge, helped set up Mass-Observation the following year. Raine claimed Blake for modernism, just as Read, who considered himself an anarchist, said Blake descended on him like an apocalypse. It was another Dürer reference. Blake is absolute, he said. Shakespeare is richer, Milton is more sonorous, Hopkins more sensuous; but Blake has no need of qualifying epithets.

Blake, first and last. They're all sold on him; it was a great advertising campaign. His name became so current in the twentieth century that Blake was seen as a contemporary by its artists and writers. When his fellow students came to wreck his college rooms, Stephen Spender read Blake aloud at his assailants, aiming the words at them like a phial of perfume. It was his equivalent of Stephen Dedalus throwing Blake's lines at British soldiers. As a teenager in an isolation ward in the London Fever Hospital, Spender felt he had been healed by a vision of Blake's angels, beautiful figures, innocuous in their incandescent nudity, he recalled, neither male nor female. And when he fell in love with a boy, he deployed a Blake couplet,

Come and lick/My white neck. (I spent an afternoon with Spender once, in the sitting room of his overgrown house in St John's Wood and its shelves of modernist texts. He didn't lick my neck.)

Blake allowed the unallowable. He gives us permission. The modernist romantic radical Blake, the word made flesh, appearing to Auden quite pragmatically as

Self-educated WILLIAM BLAKE

an egalitarian who took walks with tigers and

Spoke to Isaiah in the Strand,
And heard inside each mortal thing
Its holy emanation sing.

You can hear the voice-over, the train running over the border. Although Auden, always contrary under his shaggy blond hair, takes issue with Blake's statement that Science is the tree of death: Was he asking us to believe, Auden asks in 1957, that all the comforts of life from refrigerators to cheap books are fruits of death?

But Blake was beyond the rational and when Raine said that his illustrations to Job were masterworks to set alongside Bach's Mass and Shakespeare's Lear, she was only echoing what Gilchrist said back in 1863: that they exceeded all Christian art to that date. Raine saw the Tibetan mandala and elements of the Jewish Cabbala echoed in Blake's Job. Blake, setting the pace. By this time, no one knew what to believe any more; Blake's certainty and doubt suited a sceptical century.

The man who never alters his opinion is like standing water, and breeds reptiles of the mind, he said.

His figures grow out of sandy soil, burgeoning like bulbs, fields of life, uncurling and rising as abstract patterns of themselves. They could become anything in their graphic, animist power, even on the other side of the world, where Haida people carved ravens melded with orcas and otters on totem poles, while the Salish people wove intricate triangular designs that evoked the same spiritual states as Blake. When he laid out scenes from Job's life, it was a manifesto for a new tribal religion: a stripped-back Bible, a storyboard for God, an update of Dürer's Revelations. On the cover of his sketchbook for Job, Blake played with his initials next to his hero's monogram like a schoolboy practising their signature.

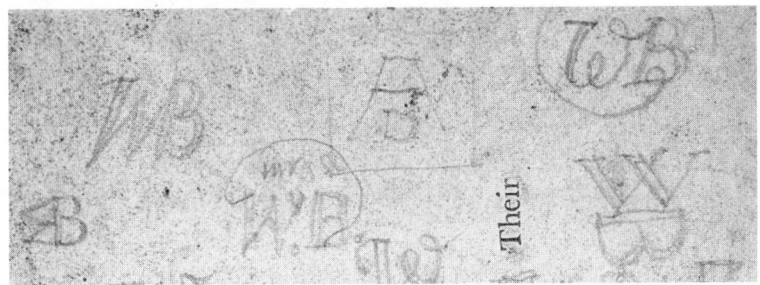

He was trademarking himself, becoming his own folklore, still playing with his identity, even now. He might have had the two emblems tattooed, one on each hand. His fan club—Moore, Auden, Spender, Raine—queue up to get theirs done. In paint, in water, in ink, in visions, on the stairway to heaven, Blake's genius endures. It just goes on and on. He is always young again. As Job confronts his elders under a starry sky, he says, in fear and trembling

I am Young and ye are very Old, wherefore I was afraid

Then Leviathan and Behemoth appear, and pausing for breath, Job asks,

Can any understand the spreadings of the Clouds?

echoing Hamlet's cloud like a whale. Blake's engravings are medieval medallions, Gilchrist says in awed tones, relishing the trees that stood and bowed like ghosts and citing intensely fully muscled figures of large-eyed and large-armed women whom a man may love with all his life. You can hear the joint voices of the Rossettis, Dante Gabriel and William Michael, Gilchrist's posthumous editors, in these lusty Pre-Raphaelite tones. Theirs is the hushed leer for a stunner; although they also note the odd detail, which we have already observed, that all of Blake's bodies have lines at the throats, wrists and ankles, as though they were bound with ligatures.

You can tell by the joins where Blake found his beasts. They had been put together from Dürer's rhino and Magnus's scaly sea monsters. One is naked, skinned, pseudo-elephantine, a sort of hippo with human ears; the other is a dragon stolen from the Brighton Pavilion. It's a Punch and Judy fight. The greatest of all Blake's depictions of evil, or energy, Raine said.

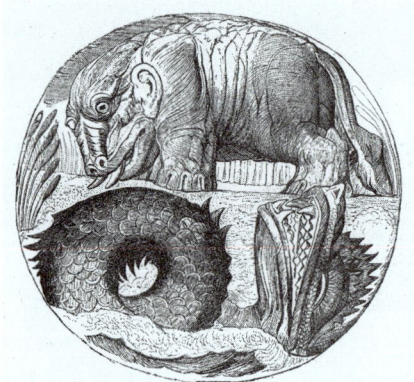

Of Behemoth, he said, He is the chief of the ways of God.

Of Leviathan, he said, He is King over all the Children of Pride.

Fantastical animals couldn't leave him alone. Soon after, in a stunning sequence of watercolours pouring out of him—an acid colour-burst after Job's black and white—Blake drew Dante being chased by a lion, a tiger and a panther. Less like big cats, more like humans under hairy skins in the Land of Oz. Blake might have been his admirer Aldous Huxley tripping in California, had he need of any psychedelic assistance.

You'd be forgiven for thinking that all this ambiguity was

because Blake was so far removed from the reality of such creatures. Yet directly across from Fountain Court a huge menagerie languished in hutch-like compartments, their roars and cries heard in the street, frightening passing horses and their riders. When Blake told a visitor to his rooms that his energies were being devoured by jackals and hyenas, he was not speaking figuratively for once.

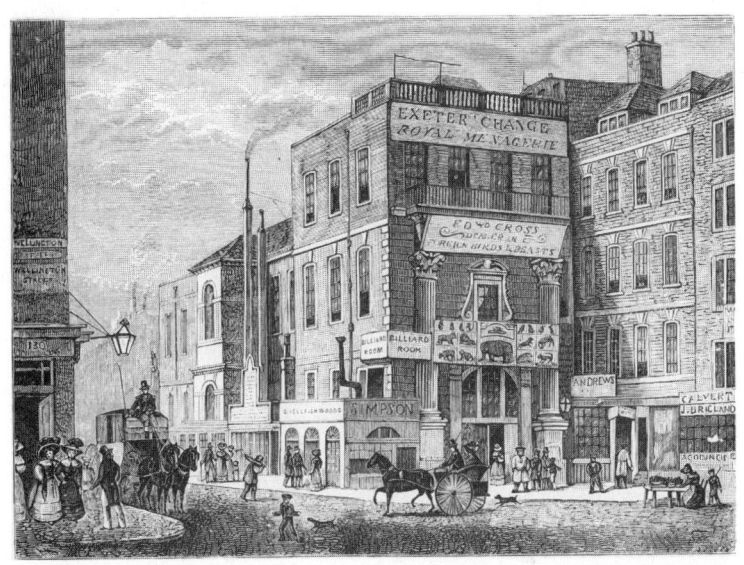

The Exeter Exchange, known as the 'Change, was a tall, rickety building that had replaced an earl's palace. At street level it housed an arcade of fancy-goods shops; upstairs, Foreign Birds, Beasts, &c, were Bought, Sold or Exchang'd. It was a livestock exchange, a zoological department store. Ground floor: umbrellas, canes and bibelots; first floor: hippopotamus, boa constrictor, porcupines and polar bears. In 1820, the year that the Blakes moved in over the road, a poster appeared, advertising a roll call of the attractions to be seen, by appointment to the King.

Arranged over three Apartments, it was promoted as the grandest National Depot of Animated Nature in the World. An ark stranded on the Strand. Jane Austen sent Mr Dashwood there to show his son the wild beasts; Lord Byron came to see the tygers eat their supper. Such a conversazione, he said. (and he would know, having his own menagerie of a bear, a wolf, a goat, innumerable birds and several enormous dogs, preferring their company to that of his own species). Yet the largest of its exhibits came at the end of the list as a postscript, squeezed in under the elephant

The Enormous Skeleton of a Spermaceti Whale, 60 *Feet long*.

the Leviathan, if not in the flesh then in their bones. Unignorable, the whale in the room. Blake had only to cross the street to see a real tyger and a sea monster. Perhaps that's where he got his idea of the whale as a serpentine creature, since a sperm whale's bones betray very little about their true shape: only a fearsomely toothed head and and a sinuous spine, like the one Urizen stood upon. Perhaps the 'Change's hippo also proved the model for Blake's Behemoth. But he may have declined on principle to pay half a crown to view this demeaning spectacle. Still more so since he must have known that until recently its displays had not been confined to non-human beings. In the 1790s the 'Change had exhibited a pair of Aethiopian Savages, as reported by the press. This curious Creature, when full grown, they said, is near six feet high, and in many respects a striking resemblance of the human species. The female they described as a kind of satyr.

If a chained boy in Astley's garden had aroused Blake's ire, this circus of cruelty on the Strand would have outraged his sense of humanity. Every Sunday afternoon, accompanied by zebra attendants, Chunee the Indian elephant was paraded down the street, then returned to his quarters where, like a captive orca, he could barely turn around. In February 1826, physically and mentally disordered by his imprisonment, Chunee accidentally killed one of his keepers, for which sin a platoon was summoned across the road from the garrison at Somerset House just across the road.

It was another good reason to dislike redcoats. Chunee's keeper ordered his charge to kneel; Chunee did as he was told. The soldiers got their orders; they did as they were told, shooting one hundred and fifty-two musket balls at his thick hide. When that didn't work, a harpoon was plunged into his side; being grey and ivory-toothed and imperial, elephants and whales were equally worthy of destruction on a grand scale.

The execution took place a year before Blake died. The commotion must have been intense: the sound of the shots, the shouts of the men. He would have been only too aware of the furore; the noise, not of innocent children playing outside, but of the death throes of Behemoth in his cage; stricken, bleeding, roaring, all Heaven in a rage. Eden in the Strand had become Hell on Earth.

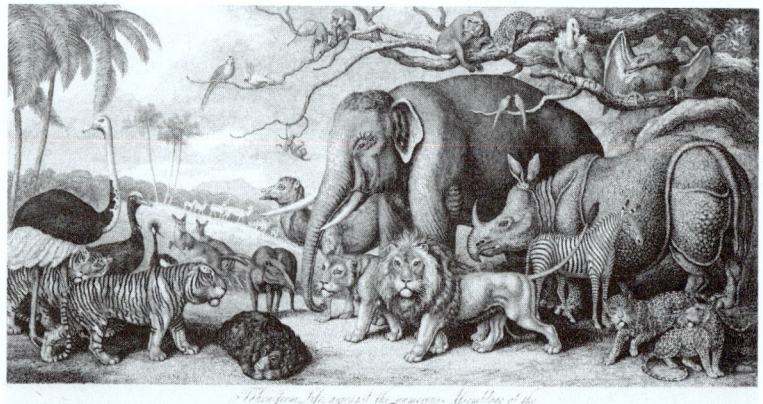

ROYAL MENAGERIE Exeter Change STRAND, LONDON.

After a public dissection, for which admission was charged, of course, Chunee's skin was sold off and his bones put on display.

Very like a whale.

I can't give you an account of Blake's daily life because he didn't leave one behind. No diary of what he ate or what he paid for his socks. His life was messy, like yours and mine.

Make no bones about it, he was no saint. He wasn't divine. He left nothing behind, not a single debt, no relics to be venerated. Only his art. We know almost nothing about what he did as a man and everything about what he did as an artist.

He had nothing to hide. He spoke for us all. He was not ashamed of being human.

Not always, anyhow.

As a boy, Paul Nash was haunted by deep water and disaster. He once nearly drowned in a moat in Devon, and then again off a Yorkshire beach, where he came close to being dragged in.

I can still hear the alarming rattle of the pebbles sucked back by the ebb, he wrote, and the frantic cries of paddling children and nursemaids confused with the yelling of the gulls. As the wave enveloped him, his nurse groped for him and grabbed him, just in time.

The sea came to him in his dreams. In 1912, he drew a pair of flooded pyramids, the waves rushing in like a tsunami, lit from within, swirling round their feet. You can almost hear it whoosh. A half-moon hangs over the scene, its dark side visible in second-hand sunlight. The whole picture is silent and full of noise, a sweeping symphony swelling up in a starry oasis; a surreal scene from prehistory, a prophecy of the sea rising at the end of time. It evokes Blake's visions, but it also came from another of Blackwood's tales in Pan's Garden.

Entitled Sand, the story starts with Felix Henriot in his lonely London flat on a foggy January night, dreaming of travelling. The roar of the traffic outside becomes the syren's call of the sea and soon Henriot finds himself in Egypt where, in a living dream, he sees flocks of pyramids sailing the Desert like weird grey solemn ships that make no earthly port. The scene, pale in the moon, was too huge for comfort or understanding, he says, and leagues of sand began to stir and rearrange themselves in a world of dim, huge, half-remembered wonders: the pyramid field, lost in this sea of an incalculable Past!

Nash explained his drawing to a friend. His brain seemed to become a hollow tunnel, he wrote, thro' which stupid meaningless trains of thought rushed, or just aimless winds of nothing at all. At last I nearly wept, indeed I <u>did</u> cry inside . . . but returned soon to my board and suddenly did a queer drawing of pyramids crashing about in the sea in uncanny eclipsed moon light.

Nash owed that moon to Blake. His picture was a psychic state, like automatic writing; uncertain and eerie, like his figure on the downs, an augury of the wavering in-betweenness of all his work to come. And just as that mysterious shape, with its bobbed head, echoes Margaret Odeh and her clairvoyant Eastern powers, so does this magical Egyptian scene, showing him the way. This promises, thank God, Nash said, as if he was only waiting for Blake and his own visionary energy to prove him right. Around this time, he sent his pictures to W.B. Yeats as possible illustrations, and was invited to a strange house in Bloomsbury.

There, in a shadowy upper room, with engravings by Blake and Rossetti on the walls, he found the poet sitting over a dying fire. Seated in the gloom which was growing darker by the minute, Yeats asked a few languid questions as he looked at Nash's drawings.

Did you really see these things? he asked.

He was hoping the boy would say yes.

Nash was all too attuned to the darkness, and it was only when he had seen Swanage that he saw the sea as blue and beguiling rather than a fearful rising roar. He had left Dymchurch because its ghosts had come to overwhelm him; he had painted

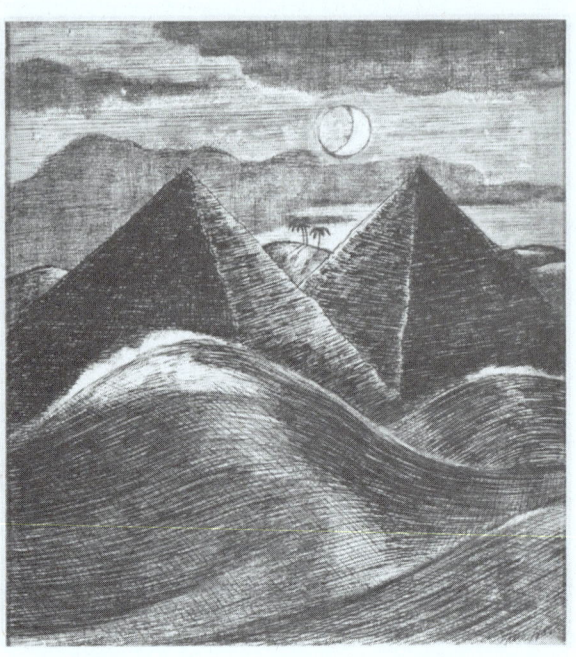

its sea as terrifying icy slabs, in a winter scene. Now, returning to the coast he had known from family holidays, everything changed; Dorset seemed a brighter place where he could be both melancholy and content, and, more importantly, be inspired by the clarity of its light.

It was a new world opening up, Nash said, a blessed escape; and he was finding new forms. They came out of the sea and the land, filling his head with new, strange shapes on the downs. He wanted to build a modernist house on Ballard Head overlooking Swanage Bay and settle down there with Margaret, who, like Catherine Blake, now acted as a psychic conduit for his art, speaking of the Past and the Future as only a confusion of thought. Time is a continual stream that curves and crosses and recrosses itself, she said; the waves are extraordinarily strong.

Reality was unreal. Fluidity suffused his work. The sea was a queer place.

But then, in the summer of 1935, in an episode quite unforeseen, Paul Nash met Eileen Agar, and everything changed again.

Eileen Agar was born in Buenos Aires of wealthy Scottish and American parents and therefore not ordinary from the start. Houses in London and Nairn; their friends were the Tennants, the Asquiths. She was educated in Dorset and at the Slade, a generation after Nash. Hers was the world of bright young things: her fellow students included Oliver Messel, Rex Whistler and Stephen Tennant; good dancers, she said, but not interested in girls; not like that, anyway. She was a wild creature too and declined to get in the Rolls-Royce her parents sent to fetch her home at the end of each day.

She was exotic and strange. Cecil Beaton stood her up against the silver wall where he'd photographed Tennant and the Sitwells. His lights caught the wrinkly surface, turning Agar all shiny and erotic in her velvet gown and Egyptian necklace that looked like sharks' teeth. She was a fish or an octopus, intense as the shimmery sea. A slippery customer.

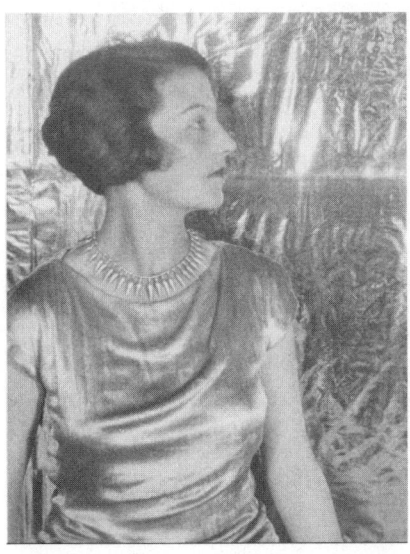

Agar's art was part of herself. Soon she became surreal; or rather, surrealism found her. She put things together. The first was a human skull acquired from the Slade's anatomy room; Agar painted it gold and covered it with a caul of cockle shells. It was a tribute to Ariel's song in *The Tempest*, but it could have been an echo of Charles Ryder in *Brideshead Revisited*, who buys a skull from the School of Medicine in Oxford and places it in a bowl of roses in his rooms with the motto *Et in Arcadia ego* inscribed on its forehead.

A skull worthy of worship. Agar was quicksilver and gold. She added a filigree whelk to a sea urchin and turned them into one baroque jewel. Like a prize presented to herself. She roamed from room to room. Her latest lover was a handsome Hungarian Jewish writer, Joseph Bard, a friend of Ezra Pound. He had thick wavy hair and was a beautiful man, she said.

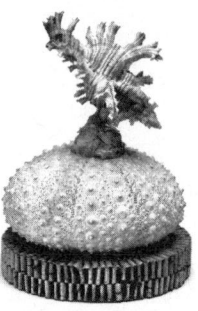

Summer, 1935. Agar and Bard and their bulldog Dandy were staying in Swanage in a rented cottage up on the hill. Nash was with Margaret at No. 2, The Parade, a Victorian terrace down on the seafront. Paul and Eileen met in a cocktail bar overlooking the bay. It was electric, a dream that had already happened, something they both recognised but couldn't say.

The distance between them diminished. Nash sent her a postcard. Then a letter. Then another letter. They began to meet. Agar decided that her suitor had a certain allure. Nash was transfixed.

You are obviously very delightful, he told her, as if to re-assure himself of the fact. It was refreshing, he went on, to find someone who will not rest upon being, but overflows with attractive actions—like a flower who could sing, or an exquisite stone which can fly.

She is art in action, not static. They are both small, trim, raven-haired, with a distinctive allure, a triangular look. She knows him by reputation, and the idea of meeting is exciting, somehow mixed up with her feelings for Dorset, she says.

In his eyes she is a miracle. One of those enchantments of his childhood, bound up in a place, in a time; an angel with the power to transform. One of Agar's closest friends was P.L. Travers, creator of Mary Poppins. Nash was overcome when Agar suddenly sent him a huge box of painted shells. She might have produced it from her carpet bag.

They sit in my tie drawer bewildering the inquisitive maid, Nash told her. He looked forward, very considerably, to receiving her promised present of a tern's skull, he said. He drew a little sketch of her face in half-light, his hand reaching to take the seabird's dead head. A surrogate exchange. The dumb mouth open, ready to peck a thumb. The space between them, a Michelangelo performance.

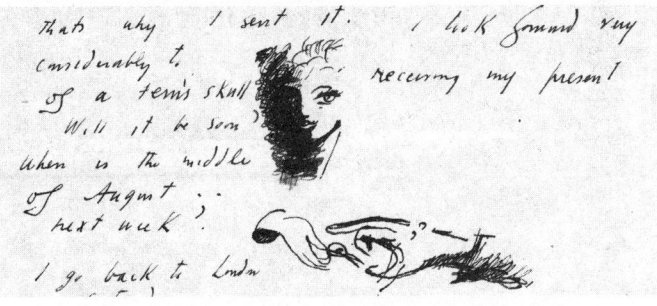

The letters and shells went to and fro. The sea was in on the act. Complicit, wide and open, but somewhere to hide too. For that one summer, everything fell into place as they fell into each other's arms, opening up like flowers. To mark his growing devotion, Nash brought Agar strange stones and marked pebbles from the shore. He told her that he felt like a penguin, laying them there at her feet.

They began to collaborate, breeding art between them. They made designs for veneers and debated other matters of aesthetic and interior indecision in which a young and energetic woman, as Agar knew herself to be, could help an ailing older man who had clearly fallen in love with her. She wrote all this down years later, after it had all passed away.

Nash had his art to offer. That and his swept-back mane of hair, his Spanish looks, his alien blue eyes, all a match for her own. His fantasies. In 1932 he had designed a bathroom for Tilly Losch, the dancer who had married the millionaire surrealist Edward James. Nash made a mirrored box for Losch's naked body out of chromium and purple-slate coloured glass, and tube lights in the shape of crescent moons. The towel rack was a ladder going nowhere. It was Dürer's Melencolia updated to the sadness of love in the twentieth century; a changing room conjured up by Prospero for Miranda. Later James had a carpet woven with Losch's wet footprint as she stepped out of the bath. Within a year she had stepped out of his life, and he replaced the pattern with the pawprints of his dog.

Agar is Nash's co-conspirator, free of any restraint. Her ambition matched his adulation, this ferocious angel of anarchy who wrapped a head in a mask of scarves like trophies from discarded lovers. The pair combed the beach together, finding new and exotic things, turning the shore into an emporium of the rich and strange. A stage set for their trysts, preordained by seaweed hanging on the wall. Nash told her they were like birds, making love in the sky.

In Swanage the radical photographer, Helen Muspratt—who was amazingly versed in Man Ray and Julia Margaret Cameron—turned Agar into a swooning astrological sign. When it came to his turn, Nash struck a more rational pose, looking concerned, with his beetled brow, as he wrestled with set squares. There was something of the obsessive examiner about him, like Ruskin in his working man's college. But you couldn't see what was going on in his head.

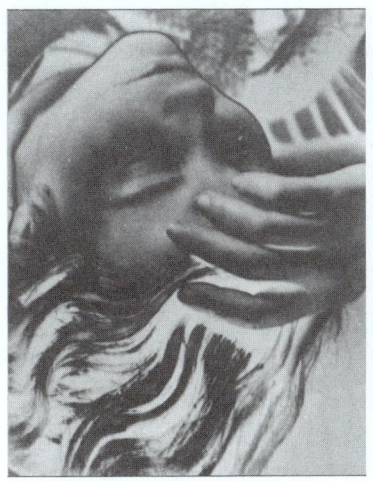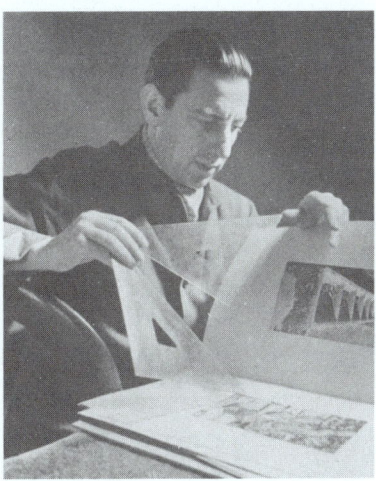

Agar and Nash went about their business; their affair proceeded inevitably on its course, *Brief Encounter* via Max Ernst.

They meet secretly in London at 12.30 pm at the bookstall at St James's Park tube station; Nash tells her to telephone him, but not to leave any messages if he wasn't in. He sends her risqué drawings of herself, the way he liked to see her, the way I like to picture you. All of this is happening randomly and privately. Their partners are aware of it, but the story would have to wait till they were all dead and had turned into archives.

In his essay, Swanage or Seaside Surrealism, published in the *Architectural Review* in 1936, Nash sought to recreate the resort in the spirit of the times. He insisted, as another of his gentle preliminary addresses (he set these things up nicely, like the narrator of a ghost story), that the pleasing but much-worried word surrealism was now so useful it ought not be capitalised or translated as super-realism and should be left in peace. He felt the same way about himself. He was really trying to quantify the effect of his affair.

Since arriving there, Nash says, he had begun gradually to discover that Swanage was definitely, as the saying is, surrealist. He quotes André Breton, who had declared, with the presumptuous precision of an archaeologist, that when a statue that should be standing in a street or some place wherever it would normally be found is found instead in a ditch or in the middle of a ploughed field, then that object is in a state of surrealism. Nash agrees, for the sake of convenience, since he now knew there was no state so super-real as the sea.

It was the cover for the dreams he and Agar shared. Their spiky studded affair played out on a shore stalked by stegosaurs and patrolled by ichthyosaurs with saucer eyes. The bizarre things that the lovers found on the beach were tokens of their unearthly vision, and all the things that would tear it apart.

Nash's essay coincided with the great International Surrealist Exhibition which opened at the New Burlington Galleries in London in the summer of 1936, on whose committee Nash presided and in which he and Agar exhibited a total of twenty works. The show was sensational; it even smelled like the street outside. It turned round the way people thought, like evolutionary theory. It was an invasion of dreams, or nightmares. Certainly for the police: tens of thousands of people attended the Mayfair gallery and the road had to be closed off. The cynical press, playing their part, underestimated the appeal of the shock of the new. In the catalogue, Herbert Read said no one should have been surprised: A nation which has produced two such superrealists as William Blake and Lewis Carroll is to the manner born, he declared.

At the exhibition, Nash erected some scaffolding in interstellar space, as the *Guardian* reported of his Mansions of the Dead, in which birdlike things flew through a strange structure like an aviary on the moon. In fact Nash was inspired by the building work going on at St Pancras, which he photographed from his flat at Queen Anne Mansions on Bidborough Street.

Agar showed her beachcombings still sandy from the shore, along with her painting of Leda and the swan. The sea flooded into Burlington Gardens as if London's terraces and monuments were pyramids or promenades, leaving the poets Ruthven Todd and David Gascoyne (I have a postcard from him to me from the Isle of Wight) to fetch a spanner to release Señor Dalí from his diving helmet. He had begun to gasp for air.

Nash remained ambivalent about this passing show; he was struggling for air himself. When he experienced a serious asthma attack, Margaret had to go to the chemist for an oxygen tent. She was buying time and air. She returned to find her husband gasping like a fish. He drew himself that way in a letter to Agar, to show he was feeble where she was strong.

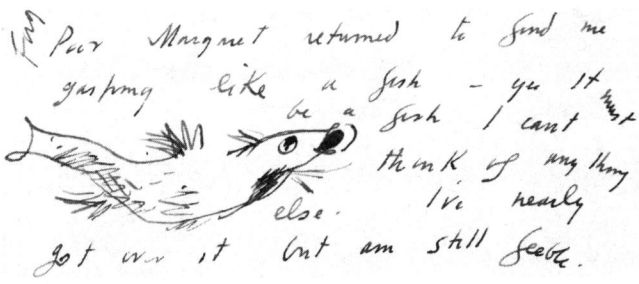

I like you best unencumbered, he told her, just as I like your pictures so. Darling be a drawing for me next, not a collage— remember I <u>may</u> be a surrealist or an invited visitor to an exhibition by the English Surrealist Group but so far as you are concerned I am practically a naturalist, a verisimilitudinist one might say.

They might have sat naked in a bower.

But of course I love you <u>all</u> ways and always. Ring me up at Kensington 6371 tomorrow, let me hear your sweet twitter somehow.

He called her his chaffinch and sent her a sketch on Braille paper. The sheet showed her naked through the feeling bumps as if he could blindly, like Milton, run his fingers over her remote body, sensually wrapped in a snake, a garter tied to her thigh. Eve to his Adam, caught in Satan's Blakean coils. A new order of temptation. A midnight cabaret, a serpent who courted her to his love. Agar declined to be an object; Nash was already lost. She always had the upper hand.

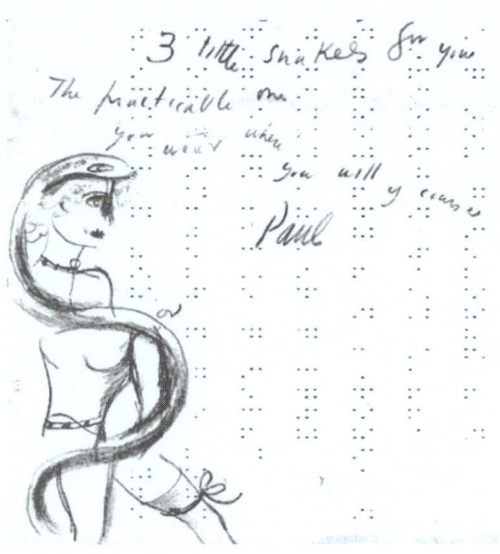

Nash saw Swanage remotely too, as once the haunt of turtles and crocodiles, as if he were peering at its prehistoric past through a penny telescope on the promenade. In the nineteenth century it had changed unbelievably into a *nice* watering-place, he said, quoting an historian from the eighteen-nineties who said that the resort's most debilitating ambitions of smugness came from the sense that it was safe from extravagant vulgarities or aristocratic roués and loafers who delight in corrupting all brought within their coils. Swanage was a snake.

The result of all this, Nash said, was a place of such extreme ugliness that the inhabitants instinctively looked out to sea or across the bay to avoid the hideous façade of the new Parade. To see Swanage in its true horror of Purbeck-Wesleyan-Gothic, you must approach it from the sea.

He posed as a shipwrecked stranger cast ashore, unwittingly hurled inland by angry waves on a dark night and flung onto the promenade. Clutching at a lamp-post to prevent himself from being dragged back out again, the incredulous, reluctant visitor discovers, as Nash writes, in the fitful light of lamps gleaming on the wet asphalt, a stone column with piles of cannonballs commemorating the arrival of Alfred the Great; a Wren façade of bad but genuine design; and a huge clockless Clock Tower, a repulsive Victorian-Gothic structure, grey and papery against the solid sea, he says. He was setting its sea-suburban clutter and chatter against the eerie austerity of Avebury.

It's all a bit de Chirico, a bit Magritte; a little bit Hitchcock too. A quota quickie, snatched in black and white. Trapped in such a scene, Nash's actor is convinced his reason has left him. Either that or he is merely part of a dream.

But he wakes from his stupor to realise he is not; and that he actually delights in the strangeness of it all. In the twilight the place has an atmosphere of doubtful enchantment, he says, made grotesque by indefinition. He expects Saxon invaders to stampede onto the shore.

Instead, a white swan rides into the bay.

It was a memorable fancy, beautiful and strange; the bird was probably a refugee from the nearby swannery at Abbotsbury. A swan appeared in the bay last Monday, Nash told a friend, and got badly hustled by some rude waves. A lonely love swan, buffeted by the waves, Agar said.

Nash, besotted, kept finding swan-shaped things in the town—bits of wood, postcards of the swan riding into the bay—as if Swanage was itself a quantity or a quality or a currency: an allowance of swans, the condition of being a swan, the age of the swan. He was remembering Blake's *Jerusalem*, in which the Daughters of Albion turn into fishes and serpent-necked swans. They look like Dalí's molten bodies; Agar's metamorphosis, love lying limp.

Nash, drunk on swans as mute and sinuous sea monsters. Swanage was surreal, but it was real, too, and the only modern things Nash could find that did not appal him were the concrete benches, and they looked like swans, too. He was not entirely serious about all of this. That was the point. His surrealism was playful, queer, almost amateur, in a way that Parisian surrealism was not. It would never occur to him to say, as Breton did, that homosexuals were mentally and morally deficient.

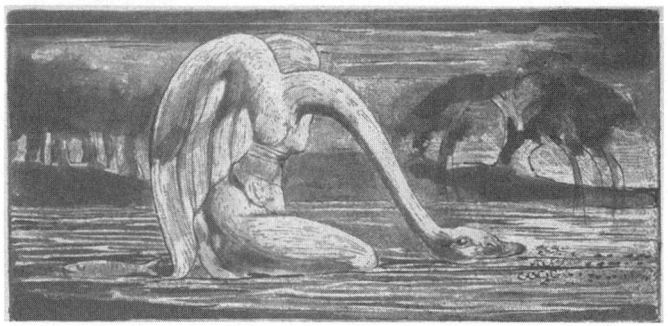

One day, in one of the curiosity shops, Agar found something extraordinary. It was a very splendid specimen of a crucifix fish, she said. She bought it and brought it home. In fact it was the skull of a catfish, whose splayed-out bones, by tradition, represented Christ's crucifixion. Agar proudly showed her trophy to Nash, who told her he already had one. They compared notes, and came to their own conclusions as to what it all meant.

Then a new creature came along. At Lulworth Cove, where the steep cliffs encircle a sea-within-a-sea, Agar unpebbled, as she put it, as if the beach were a bowl of cereal concealing a free toy, a long snakey monster with a bird's beak.

In fact, it was an old anchor chain, but it had been meta-morphosed by the sea into a bird snake, she said. She showed this totem to her lover, who was delighted and scared. Your stone & iron monster does not fly, Nash said, affecting to sound brave, and he duly photographed the thing to contain its spirit like a god in a bottle. Teasing out its inscape, he pasted it over the renegade swan bobbing about in the bay.

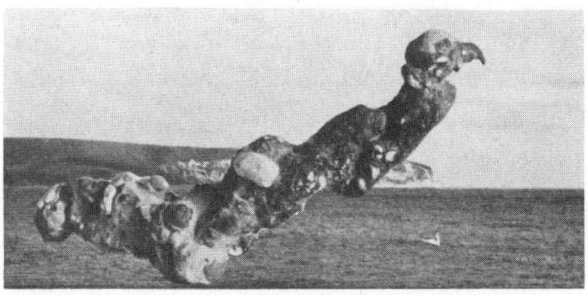

It was a moment of looming alchemy, of love and rust. Delighted, Nash added the collage to his essay: this surreality of the swan, he called it. Like an illustration to an unknown, surreal fable, the frail-necked swan is assailed by the bird-beaked monster, lurching over it like a dragon or a leviathan. Such tension was reminiscent of reports coming in from the far north, where Virginia Woolf recorded in her diary the remarks of a charming couple she had met on Loch Ness. They were in touch with the Monster, she said. They had seen him, they said. He is like several broken telegraph posts and swims at immense speed, Woolf said. He has no head. He is constantly seen.

The same beast also prompted Freud to write, in his 1936 essay on the disturbance of a memory, in which he imagined someone walking along Loch Ness suddenly seeing the body of the famous monster washed ashore and finding themselves forced to admit that the sea serpent that we didn't believe in really does exist. He might have been addressing Blake's whale slumped on the sand, or diagnosing Nash and Agar's collage as an emblem of their secret affair, as sea monsters in love.

Modern as it pretended to be, England was still haunted by monsters stirred up out of the silt and roused by storms. As Nash and Agar beachcombed in Dorset, new objects began to accumulate and, in a cluster of even stranger things, Nash reconfigured Swanage's edifices as votive monoliths, cartilaginous creatures discarded outside a takeaway on a Saturday night. A cabinet of monstrosities mutated into pre- or post-historic shapes, crusty, calcareous, mineralised; part animal, part geology, entirely worshipful, like dolmens spilling onto the downs in a parlour game. The unusual suspects lined up beside Agar's sea beast, an eerie array marching into the bay.

It was an uncanny cast. The crucifix fish hung there, a medieval relic in a gloomy nave. It was joined by bits of ore and stray bones and something that looked like a sail or a prayer on wing. Nash called it a personage and it stood proud like an ancient fetish; he'd found it on Romney Marsh, a watery site for gifts to the gods.

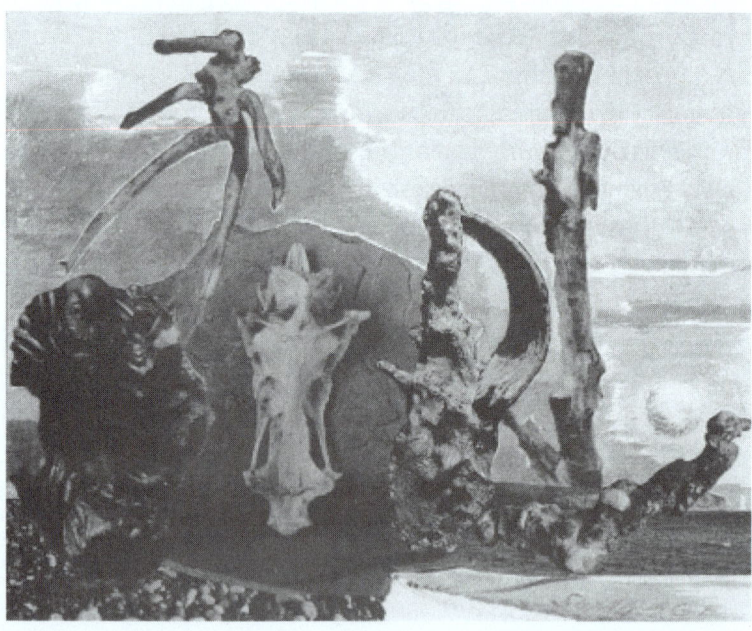

The moment I saw it I knew it had begun a new view for me, he said. And it was in turn accompanied by a wishbone-shaped stick he'd picked up. In his mind it became a leaping homunculus and he set it hovering in the sky, associating its power with tales he had heard from Francis Yeats-Brown, his yogic neighbour in Rye, of a Tibetan lama's ability to leap and glide in the sky.

Then, in order to cast a livid glow over the scene, Nash added a watery moon wandering out from the islands of long white clouds. It hung over Ballard Head like a dying star or exhausted light bulb, just as it lurks over Blake's blasted oak and slips into twilit paintings by Palmer, whose appetite for monstrous moons and an exuberance of stars Nash shared.

The same satellite would soon oversee an ominous dead sea of felled machines. But it also presided over another image, created by the visionary artist John Martin, as a frontispiece for Thomas Hawkins's *Book of the Great Sea-Dragons*, published in 1840 as a follow-up to his equally enticingly entitled *Memoirs of Ichthyosaurii and Plesiosaurii* of 1835, which somehow suggested that either Hawkins had a time machine or he was in spiritual contact with the tribal ghosts of the saurii.

Hawkins, born to a wealthy family in Glastonbury in 1810, had been a delicate and sensitive child who asked his aged grandmother to put on her satin dresses for him and collected wrens' pearl-like eggs, while other Wrenboys of the village killed the same birds on St Stephen's Day. The countryside he knew was a haunted place where people believed there was a dragon in the sun, and stories of the world about to end in fire seemed to come true as the peat was set aflame, driving young Thomas to the river, where he swooned and fell in, to be found by a dairymaid, his body half in the water and he half drowned.

Around the age of nineteen, suffering from a certain deafness, Hawkins was advised to try sea-bathing in Charmouth, Dorset, as a cure. While he was there a great storm rose up from the Channel, tearing up ledges of rock and exposing fossil dragons on the beach. As a result of this tempestuous revelation, Hawkins became an avid collector of sea dragons, one of the few to acknowledge one of his suppliers, Mary Anning of Lyme Regis, by name. He also liked to eat peacock eggs for breakfast. In his books he adopted a biblical rhetoric to retell prehistory as a palaeontological *Paradise Lost*, presenting images of the extinct reptiles he had uncovered as splayed angels in the strata, dread demons caught in stone as if still alive and writhing like snakes.

In fact, Hawkins rearranged many of the bones to make a better picture. Who can blame him? His commissioning of John Martin to imagine the unimaginable was equally adventurous. Martin was celebrated for paintings that portrayed the beginning and the ending of time in apocalyptic floods and earthquakes; in 1825 his engravings of Milton's *Paradise Lost* began to appear, darkly luminous, star war panoramas of the flame-lit palace of Pandemonium and the cracking-apart of Eden with which Blake was so familiar.

For Hawkins's book, Martin set to work creating similarly sensational scenes, fossil-born images of Dorset's origins as an anti-Eden, of Lyme crocodiles and swan-necked sea dragons, where ammonites were seen as snake-stones invested with magical powers. They came easily to Martin's feverish imagination, as he saw the tribes of the Ichthyosauri and Plesiosauri, truly ancient Britons, as needle-teethed, savaging beasts being savaged in turn by pterodactylian devils with bat-like wings. Claw-deep in gore, under Martin's fetid moon, these nightmarish monsters were not only like as not to snap up your terrier; they'd take you along with them too.

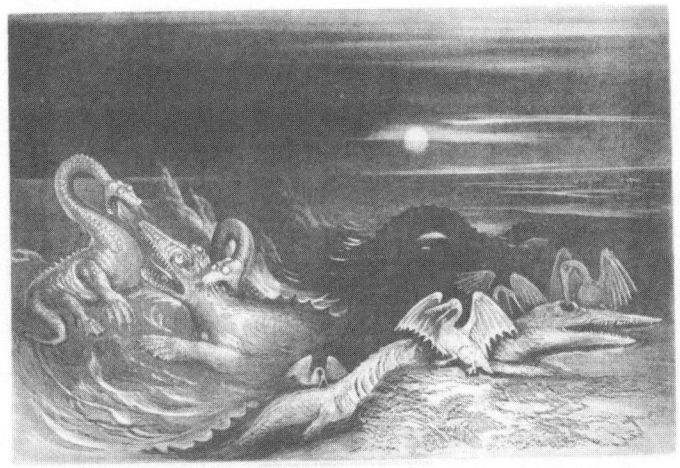

Every era has its own monsters and these ones were out-takes of Blake's Dragons of the Deep crawling out onto Felpham's shore. Hawkins supplied his rustic mechanicals with dialogue out of Thomas Hardy or a film by Ray Harryhausen.

O a viery dragern a-maa-be, says one quarryman, as they uncover a Triatarsostinus.

One that stinged Moses a-maa-be, says the other. How he do sound: I wonder if the stwoone be holler, as they manage to smash the specimen into eleven pieces.

Hawkins' demons were pre-industrial too, fossil frames to be smashed by Luddite workmen disguised in women's clothes. Like surrealist found objects, they embodied subconscious evolutionary fears. (How did we get there? What did we eat?) In vicious scenes of nameless seas, Hawkins created out of such remains his *Book of the Great Sea-Dragons*, as if he'd found them on another planet, patrolled by Robbie the Robot.

Satan was a pterosaur with his leathery wings, and he seems to have been thrice seized, as Hawkins wrote, generating Horrors and realising a teeming Spawn. His dark angels ruled the ridgy Deep, he said, and sank Empire and Life in the Profundity of pre-Adamic Times. As we upheave these remains from the Abyss of Ages, we hear them Roar. Serpents all—we behold.

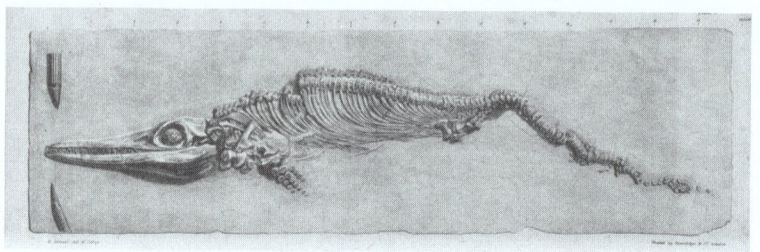

Hawkins's language grew ever more lavish and Blakean, the more bones he discovered to suit his story of his pre-creation creations. He might have been making Feegee mermaids to hawk to unwary sailors, filled with modern invention and atavistic despair at his beasts. He wrote of the cranial Caverns in which their brutal appetites lurked, employing teeth nursed from the cradle in blood; he talked of the Ghost of Chaos guiding us through the ancient Ossuary of the world, strown thick with the skeletons of these huge Dragons of the Ocean of the Past; and of the Powers of that Universe of which we were born co-gods.

Later, Hawkins's behaviour became even more bizarre, adopting, seemingly at random, Charles F. Bonney, a young man from Southampton, and declaring himself Earl of Kent. Hawkins's antediluvian sermons sounded more like florid extracts from *Moby-Dick*, delivered in the lee of the withdrawing sea of faith that left these beasts sealed in Dorset's rocks as though they'd burrowed there. Each of his extinct reptiles—faded Cartoons of Nature, as

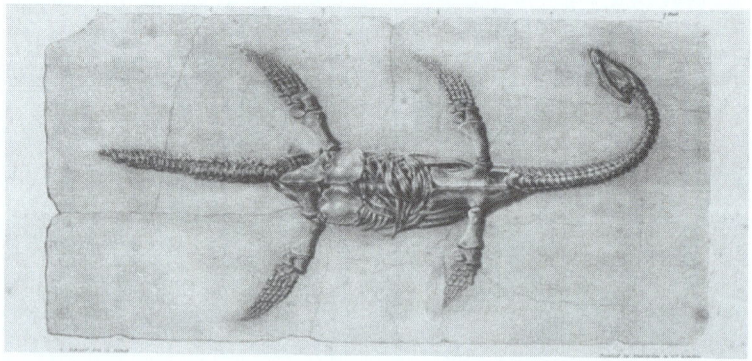

he called them—could have supplied Nash and Agar with acres of chimeric bones, slipping between scientific fact and artistic licence, through the x-ray of time, the ultrasound of outer space.

Such dim remembrances of the deep and pregnant past; such weirdness made real by fossilised fact; such eccentric examinations and arch transformations fertilised Nash's art. Having received a legacy of a small Victorian library, he was consulting other texts of that age, such as *Organic Remains of a Former World: An Examination of the Mineralised Remains of the Vegetables and Animals of the Antediluvian World, generally termed Extraneous Fossils*; and *The Gallery of Nature: A Pictorial and Descriptive Tour Through Creation*, in which he could read of the incessant pursuit of whales by man and how they had retreated to the poles, seeking the protection afforded by the ice, and how they could dive with prodigious rapidity to the bottom of the soundless sea.

Like Noah, Nash had to cram everything in there, stacking it all up like a warehouse with no room to spare: ivory tusks and imperial booty, seaside tat and palaeontology, talismans, surrealism, all bound up in his industry of design and the unerring grace of the eerie unknown. He was a witch doctor, fit to make a patient swoon, sensually archaic. After all, we'd soon discover that swans owed their own long necks to such ancestors.

Nash and Agar's fantasy image of Swanage was bursting out of itself. Its bony sentinels strode the shore like the living dead, voudou dummies that the pair of artists had summoned to life in their own outrageous scenario. The whole thing was a semi-buried construct of their subverse love affair. The fearful townsfolk had been forced to flee in the face of these horny riders of the apocalypse arriving in their quiet bay, leaving only that single swan to swim bravely along. You can see it there, in one corner, with its white dino-neck, not sure if it could survive very long itself when that uncanny crew finally tipped into the sea.

Nash's vision, like Hawkins's, half naive and half intended, created with Agar playing his South American Mary Anning, a Daughter of Buenos Aires as a fish or a swan, was hard to take. Quite exhausting, in fact, for the nervous, disconcerted viewer in the worrying times of 1936. It wasn't exactly consoling art; no one's desire is identifiably like this. Nash's pasted-down, pseudo-Victorian scraps were lurid and suspicious: a coshed, subconscious edition of Blake's dreams or Fuseli's nightmares spread out on Freud's couch. The dragons of our better nature subsumed to a surreal will; an unholy Jungian union of futurity as cluttered and crazy as Dürer's angel in their moon-lit attic. Or perhaps their twisted shapes were kin to Paul Klee's angel fluttering in history, caught in Walter Benjamin's storm, thrown out of paradise into an age of mechanical reproduction.

What on earth did anyone expect of artists and their subversive units and statements to the press? Rationality or consistency? Only the unearthly affects, had they consulted Nash's texts. It wasn't his business to be reassuring, despite his letter to The Times. He liked to disconcert, to address random objects, quite formally, as if addressing them in a town hall or asking them to dance. In another essay, The Life of the Inanimate Object, eccentrically placed in Country Life magazine in 1937, Nash confessed that it was certainly possible to be afraid of them. Like M.R. James (whose story, The Malice of Inanimate Objects, was published in 1933), Nash was creating supernatural landscapes stalked by the foul fiend. Monsters didn't have to move to have their effect. Mountains and seas could rise up from the horizon, and trees start to speak. He was the man whom they loved, after all.

I can look at a knot of wood till I am frightened at it, Blake said. Father Hopkins, putting his face in an icy puddle at a Lancashire seminary, would agree.

Here was a new kind of instress. The power of a pre-imagined site, newly plugged in; everything unsettled in its psycho-place. It was threatening, of course; but also oddly glorious and abandoned and even camp, in the way Nash wrote its title, Swanage, in his swashy Blakean-Omega Workshops hand.

What do you want? What have you got? Despite being reduced to a sliver in the background, it is the sea that is the essential component in this consensual arrangement on an operating table. He'd come a long way from the drowning sea of his childhood, from the sea of mud on the Western Front, from the slab-like haunted sea of Dymchurch. Agar had crawled up yelping like a siren on the promenade. And like the mute swan, the random things the two artists found reflected the random power of their love, in a theatre of complicity and hate.

Nash's collage was an oversized postcard sent to his beloved. Swanage had become their new Jerusalem, their solidarity. The spirit of surrealism had been born in Blake's Albion, where nothing stayed the same for a moment and where, as in all of his prophecies, bodies are caught in a God-given narrative, an endless loop; always driven on, like the artist himself. Blake had rehearsed all those chance encounters and associations long before Jung came along.

A man ploughs a field with human horses shaped like Assyrian bulls. People tumble in flames. A grown youth appears out of another's chest, popping out of the flesh in a bizarre Caesarean section. Pl XI

Most stupendous of all, a captive figure throws back his head in the throes of restraint or ecstasy. He's an illustrated man, a cosmic Ishmael recording the leviathan's dimensions on his skin, thighs tattooed with the sun and the moon and the stars, the same emblems inked into transportees' limbs as they were sent to the New World. He could be Queequeg. The sea is full of stars that have fallen there. Suns die and are immediately reborn, popping out of the firmament like roe from a fish. His umbilical cord is unwound by the Three Fates like the tail of a spermatazoa. He is unborn in their torture.

Born out of the darkness, Nash's repurposed objects slip into our world, mailed direct from Blake's imagination. Strange things shared, not static, but tumbling about like a lottery.

Something filthy and toxic too. Some kind of slag heap. A fine issued for littering, adding to the new ordure of the earth.

Tortured by his love for her, Nash loved Agar's gold and bundled hair, he told her, lustfully, breathlessly. He might fight for air, but she gave him reason to thrive. Her name was on his lips. He described her art and the arrangements she made as entire; almost Agar Agar, he quipped, as if she were a mermaid with a double tail preserved in something gelatinous, isinglass or mercury, like those solarised photographs. As if his collage were an in-joke, a fish tank fitted in a Victorian sash window and filled with slimy things to scare the parlourmaid.

He was her Blake, in a lounge suit; she was his Kate, in a snakeskin dress. Los and Enitharmon in Simpsons of Piccadilly and Schiaparelli of Paris. The sea is the epicentre of their affair, an heroic stage for a masque made to impress. Agar transforms again, shedding another skin, becoming a new sea creature, a bioluminescent constellation of surreal starfish and floating phytoplankton.

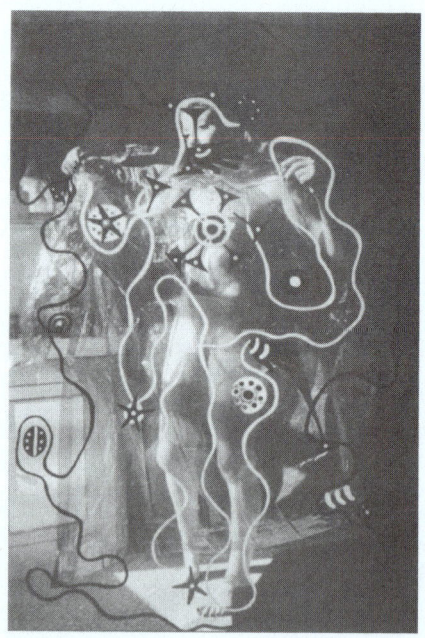

But she is sliding away from her lover, no longer connected, feeling the great pain they were causing to their respective partners like a hand put through a window, withdrawn in shock, cut by the glass; Catherine Earnshaw, or a scared parlourmaid. The following July, 1936, having agreed to call it all off, Nash admitted to Agar that he had wept with the intolerable ache of loss and gnawing desire of her.

But all that is no good, he wrote. Let us face what we have to do now. Shake off regrets, my dear, and enjoy yourself. I wish you everything you want. Think only happily of me. Paul.

Things weren't quite that simple, no matter how brave either affected to be. They were grown-ups, after all. They continued to meet, secretly. A year later, he was asking to see his imperious girl who was more like a star or a starfish than a girl, he said. It was as though they were now separated by different languages. Nash didn't care: he would give all the breath he'd fought for to taste the brine of her cool wet mouth just once again. As if she were an oyster.

Agar, knowing her power and his obsession with her myth, drifted further away. She stopped singing. It was all she could do. And even though they still wrote to each other and occasionally met, she evaded him, and when he asked to photograph her sea monster again she stood him up, leaving him on the doorstep, his Kodak camera, rather than a bouquet, growing heavy in his hands.

He could not forget or forgive. Nor could she.

There was an almost unconscious to- and fro-ness between us which continued until he died, Agar would confess at the end of her life. She was looking back, through the lens of her own memoir, as if the two of them were still conjoined, yet undone, by the strange things they found by the sea.

Beyond Swanage, Dorset gets bleaker and more brutal the further west you go. Rocks rise up like frozen waves against the sea's assault; their fissures and canyons turn the water darker and deeper, like the lump of petrified wood we had in our garden rockery. Geologists call these cliffs a discordant coastline as their strata run perpendicularly to the sea. They're permanently out of tune, out of joint, out of line. They buckle and curl, a discord in time.

In his Shell Guide to the county, written in 1935, the year he and Agar began their affair, Nash noted that both fin and killer whales had been seen in Dorset's waters, along with the blue shark, the thresher shark, and the electric ray and other outlandish creatures such as sea devils and sun fishes and a merman thirteen feet long.

His guide, ring-bound so that the motorist might lay it on the passenger seat ready to identify any passing stegosaur, had all the details and the information one might require to navigate and interrogate this place; but the artist's commentary and his photographs spin off wildly into another realm entirely. Like his essay on Swanage, they conspire to create a sense of the uncanny in a cheery holiday destination. Slender, nine inches tall, printed on different shades and weights of paper, the book feels handy in the hand; quite inviting at first glance. There's a gazetteer of sites to visit and tips about Dorset apple cake; but there are also intimidating photographs of funereal fossils and the dark interior of Winspit's worryingly top-heavy and quarried caves. The result is a sly Baedeker, wry Victoriana this side of camp, designed to confound. A secret code book produced by Unit One with messages for the initiated agents of modernism.

Nash was editing his guide for a century heading headlong into uncertainty and deceit. The publication of the book itself was underwritten by a petrochemical company that used as its logo the ancient shell from which it derived its wealth; it was now employing artists to lend respectability and allure to its output, which was slowly destroying the very scenes they portrayed. The car was the dinosaur, future fossil of a fossil economy. In 1936, the year that the guide was published, the first oil well was opened up on the Isle of Purbeck. It sucked on the same natural resource which had for millennia spontaneously ignited on the oil-saturated shale shore; a hellish, primeval sight, as if the sea itself had caught alight. Like Portland's quarries, these ancient products of ancient seas were sourced and processed: piers and refineries, stones and oil.

It was no coincidence that Nash's narrative was hardly the comforting Dorset on your doorstep, the familiar place you thought you knew as you drove through, past villages where you might buy ginger biscuits and currant buns. It didn't stack up, this vision, not even for the cover price of 2/6. William Blake and Algernon Blackwood, with a little help from Thomas Hardy and Marcel Duchamp, had taken over the tourist board and were issuing misinformation from their ministry of illusory dreams.

The chalk cliffs, which fall sheer from Ballard Down, Nash writes, continue in a ghostly perspective of concave walls and lonely monoliths where the owl and raven nest. It is a rather frightening landscape dwindling to those last outposts, he admitted, referring to Old Harry Rocks.

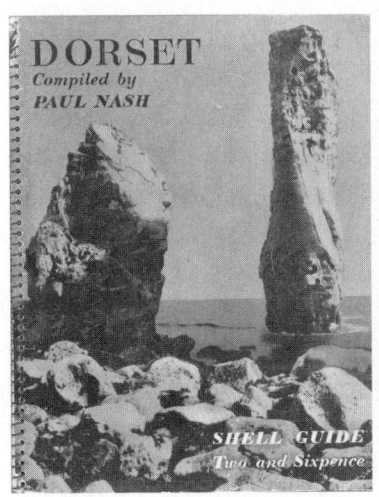

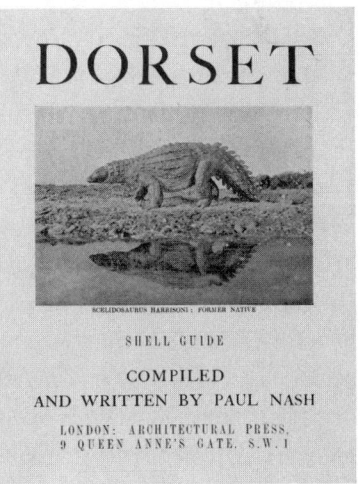

This was no place for your bucket and spade, but somewhere where sentinel stacks stirred from the shore and followed you home; where rock pools could suck you in, filled as they were with polypuses and spiky sea urchins. Nash's guide forces you to stop and stare, to address the fury of your spiritual existence as you wonder where you might stop for lunch. He had no need to collage this reality. It was already quite odd enough. All he had to do was to record it.

There are plenty of facts and figures and contributions from officers (Sport, by Brigadier F.R. Patch) and entomologists (Flora & Fauna, by Archibald G.B. Russell). But Nash subtly unsettles his readers motoring down from London by describing the county as a countenance, and draws their attention to Chalbury's prehistoric monuments as he travels through the valley at twilight; shut in by the ridged hills, seeing the long tombs cut against the afterglow, he says, is to experience an almost unnerving feeling of the latent force of the past. His photographs are even more disturbing, evoking the terror of Chesil Beach with a double-page spread of a wrecked hulk, a ghost ship slowly coming apart like an abandoned Ark overflown by cronking ravens. It's more Dantean hell than cosy Dorset; a boned and filleted land. One might abandon all hope, stepping out of one's Ford Popular, to be greeted by such sights.

All is wrack and ruin and melancholy. It lures you in. The alien landscape of Kimmeridge Bay appears near-demonic, when one learns that it could set itself on fire; those rocks possessed, in the irrational sense, as Nash says, a suggestion of super-reality. The world on fire, 1936. Picasso is painting Guernica. A year later a ship laden with four thousand children fleeing its bombing will arrive at nearby Southampton. It isn't exactly heaven to be alive. Hardly more encouraging is Nash's remark that Corfe Castle is a terrific personality that dominates the county like a calvary; or that at Badbury Rings, King Arthur's soul inhabited a raven's body which nested there. Nash recalls his teenage dreams, still kicking round in his head.

He wasn't alone. Even as he wrote his account, Mary Butts, the direct descendant of Thomas Butts whose family lived in the lea of the Isle of Purbeck, wrote in her diary about the same influences on herself. She had grown up with Blake; his works filled her childhood home. She slept with him next door: his butt-naked Newton sitting on the ocean floor, a mad king crawling on all fours; the careering white horses of Pity that would crash into Nash's monster field seemed to be riding over her own body. She felt that her life was governed by Badbury Rings, by the short turf & chalk hills that sprawl across counties, & our history & the history of man is written on them in flint & bronze & leaf & grey stone. Written on very short grass full of small black & white snail-shells. Also its secret history in letters too large to read. Secrets whose simplicity appals, chalk stripped of its grass, the bodies they have to take about.

Dorset embodied her desires, the way her hero Thomas Hardy wrote of the ache of modernism set against the ancient voices of inanimate things; the way he lay Tess on the altar of Stonehenge. Butts pulsated with the memory of Blake and would do so all of her short life. For Nash, too, it was as if Blake's Albion, with all its pagan foreboding, was carved into the land itself. When he came to the Cerne Abbas Giant, a naked god on the downs, rising like Nelson Guiding Leviathan, Nash hailed it as a spirited design of great character, very properly honoured and cherished by the local people—and was

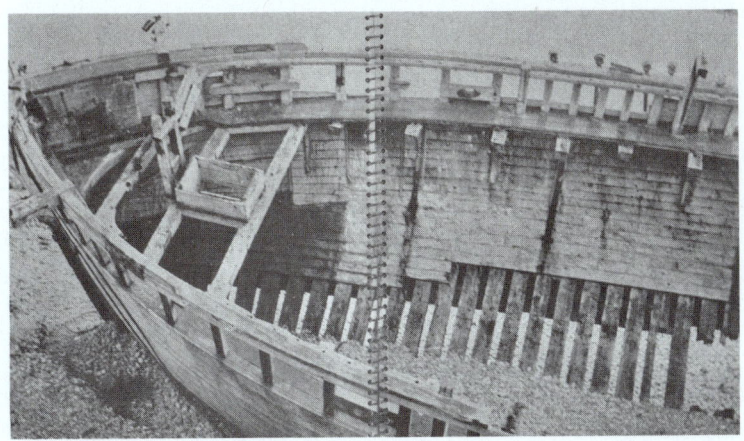

promptly forced by his editors to conceal the fact that the figure in question boasted an erection thirty-six feet high. Frustrated, Nash resorted to a footnote, informing readers that his sketch of the sight had been*

* Unfortunately suppressed.

Swanage's bay may have been pacified by a white swan, but Nash feared the open sea, with all its wandering rocks and sirens and leviathans living and dead. That much is evident from his images of Dorset beaches littered with coffin-like boulders and burning rocks. Like Blake, Nash was receiving intimations that he must leave this place; that it was becoming overwhelming, and that his visions were intuitions of the shape of things to come. In his notes for his unfinished memoir—a never-to-be-completed to-do list of things he'd already done—is a single cryptic line on his departure from Swanage

We are frightened from the sea.

It might have been a telegram from the front. There was no one reason for this fear. Nash had been told by a doctor in London that the air of the Isle of Purbeck was disastrous for his asthma. But his discontent also lay in the clamour of the crowds that descended when the sun came out; the way that the bay was a melancholic place over which the moon rose like a dirty pearl, the way its stones were embedded with dragons all too easily roused.

With the arrival of a new war, Nash became a war artist for the second time. The whole process of the defence of the country seemed to suck him in, not least because of his own vulnerable state. Summoned to a dump in Cowley, outside Oxford, Nash found a new monster field: one hundred acres of crashed enemy planes reduced to twisted skeletons in a burial pit. Like Avebury, but unholy. A vast fleet wrecked on an inland beach.

Seventy years before, Hopkins had lamented the felling of poplars on the nearby riverside where he had swum. In his words—the strokes of havoc—the trembling trees seemed to shake with the sense of their destruction. Now Nash turned a new nightmare into an image of his own. As he was driven round the site by possibly bemused and even suspicious RAF officers, who regarded him as a lefty artist, he tried to see it all as a sort of triumph; the tangle of metal was ready to be recycled in the car works to make more machines of war. But he could not ignore the wreckage as a shadow of his grounded, breath-shortened life.

As he stood there, drawing and photographing the scene, the thing looked to him suddenly like a great inundating sea, he told Kenneth Clark; under the moonlit night, a vast tide moving across the fields, the breakers rearing up and crashing on the plain. Blake's sightless horses had made an emergency landing.

The moon cast its palely light over the riderless, flightless machines, Nash wrote. Totes Meer, a Dead Sea, was an echo of his drowned pyramids. The wrecked planes rising like desert monuments; the moon mirrored in a junked undercarriage wheel. A trace memory of the dead sea of the Western Front. As if they had all come together—pyramids, poplars, planes— in one long unrolling sequence of disaster and ruin. Dishevelled and ploughed by barbaric machines: a vision of heaven and hell, of a world consuming itself.

The colours of the painting stretch across a gallery wall with the open-arm reach of the artist who made it. It's a yard and a half wide. I can feel him making it. I have to stand back to take it all in. This is not a domestic work. It's more manoeuvre than painting, daubed in military colours: grey, khaki, sand, mixed out of uniforms and surplus stores, drab and unglamorous. And although you might imagine that the planes could twist and turn as they did in the air, nothing moves, as Nash said; it is not water or even ice, it is something static and dead.

Tough and rigid structures had become bent and floppy and broken under their own weight, like a school of stranded whales. All the sensuality is left to that ominous moon, more watery star than familiar satellite, hovering there impassively. The same alien sentinel in the same half-lit skies that Blake and his Ancients saw; the same romantic omen of otherness at a moment of darkness, looking down on a scene made raw by war, overturned by a terrible tide.

Only on closer inspection, as I lean into the scene, risking the wrath of the gallery attendant and the electronic buzzer on the guard wire, do I see the sliver of the barn owl in flight who has given up hunting in that desolate place and flown on. Under the wire as it were. And, almost invisible, below the moon, at the dark upper centre of the image, a tiny crooked cross on one of the planes' flukes. A symbol already consigned to the dustbin, or so the artist hoped.

It was 1940. Everything had been tipped in there; it was the refuse tip of history and the earth-movers had moved in. The seashore is only just holding out; there might be a sphinx buried under the wreckage, ready to slouch over the sands. Far from triumph, there's a disturbing, unnatural air. Nash said he no longer wanted to control nature in his art. Dürer said the same thing at the end.

As Nash's asthma worsened and he fought for air, hopeless and helpless and considering suicide, he fantasised more and more about escaping by flying to the mansions of the dead, even though his disease forbade him from riding in an aircraft. Death, about which we are all thinking, he said, death, I believe, is the only solution to this problem of how to be able to fly. Personally, I feel that if death can give us that, death will be good.

He was now sleeping with seven pillows, propping him up like clouds.

The dead enemy planes Nash painted in Cowley were now echoed by the living bombers he saw revved up and ready for service on an air force station under the downs. Ready to deal death. He viewed these scenes by twilight too. It was his favourite time of day, when things were not quite what they seemed.

He peered at the planes in their hangars and saw them as mechanical creatures winged and finned indoors. They looked like a nest of wild planes to him. Rolled out onto the airfield, they stretched their great bellies and pointed their wings stiffly, outspread, with huge tail fins proudly erected, he said. And as he began to draw them there, their steady gaze as threatening as their huge jutting maws, they might have been asleep or dead or playing dead, he said.

Suddenly he had a vivid memory flooding in from his childhood, of the first time he had visited the alarming departments at the Natural History Museum in South Kensington, as he wrote, and the point where fish gradually cease and mammals begin and great sharks give place to small whales until all about one are the mighty whales. Nash saw these aerowhales in dreams, as flashbacks from an impossible deep. Having been supplied with photographs and spotter charts by the ministry, he began to create a new surreal guide: to the war in the air. The Wellington bomber so nearly resembled a whale that he saw no reason why it should not start spouting in the sky at any moment, he told the readers of Vogue.

It was 1942. To watch the dark silhouette of a Wellington riding the evening clouds, Nash said, was to see almost the exact image of the great killer whale hunting in unknown seas. It is clear where Nash saw that image. Like his penguin laying a stone at Agar's feet, it was a scene from a silent film first shown in London in its complete form in May and June 1924, and which seems to have made a great impact on him. It was created from sequences filmed by Herbert Ponting, the photographer on the Terra Nova expedition to Antarctica led by Robert Falcon Scott a decade before. The film's title, The Great White Silence, with its echoes of the newly reappraised Moby-Dick, sounded more like an accusation, as its inter-titles, praised for their letter-press elegance, announced a sterile and desolate place where no land animal could live, and where only ten human beings had stood since God made the World.

In this imperial anti-Eden, where the sea itself was hardened against the world, shards of ice rucked up around the expedition's ships, promising the same disaster and desolation Nash saw on the battlefields. It had haunted him, that notion of a solid yet not solid sea. A year later, in 1925, he had begun painting his Winter Sea at Dymchurch. It started out as a water-colour but was so deep in his imagination that it became another great arm's-span of an oil painting by 1937. It was thick with his dreams: the deep green-khaki-black sea, fatal, almost the colour of mud, seen by night or the low light of winter, where the waves are painted in slabs, their terror caught in frozen motion, as though pressed down by the dark. Anything could lie down there. Aeroplane wings and fuselages as floes, icebergs as the visible signs of the gods of the underworld.

> "Whilst at the glacier, we saw many Killer Whales — the most ferocious creatures in the ocean. They prey on Seals. Sailors call these monsters the 'Wolves of the Sea.' Here is one rising and blowing."

Ponting's camera, held in his gloved hand, follows the whales' dorsal fins scything through the Southern Ocean, the unknown sea of Nash's remembering, sea wolves circling ominously round the ship. In his diary, Scott recorded one close encounter. Ponting was out on the ice along with two of the expedition's dogs when six or seven whales appeared. Scott watched, horrified, as the ice heaved and split, as he wrote, as the animals rose beneath it. Only by leaping off did Ponting and the dogs escape being eaten, Scott thought. The whales' heads bobbed up afterwards, he noted, half in fear, half admir- ingly; they looked hideous to him as they showed off their small glistening eyes and their terrible array of teeth. But it was also clear they were as surprised by the encounter too, and Scott had to admit that they were endowed with singular intel- ligence, as he wrote, and in future we shall treat that intelligence with every respect.

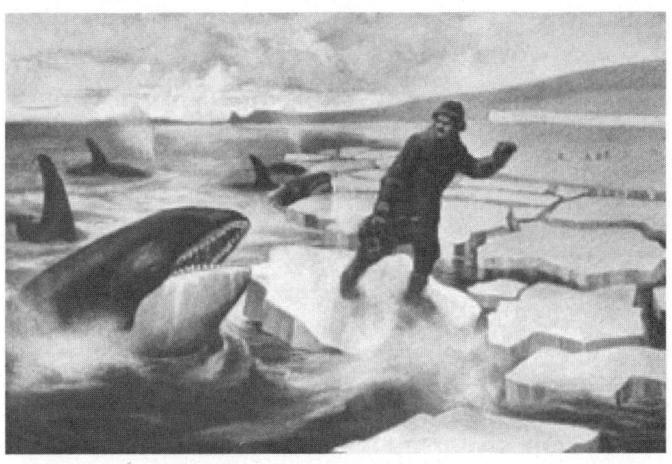

Nash never saw a whale, so far as I know, but they haunted him. Like the killer orca—their glossy black-and-whiteness; their sleekness as much machine as animal, the very concen- tration and essence of the beauty and terror of the sea—the planes Nash saw in a field by moonlight became exquisite and alarming monsters. Aerial creatures, as he identified them from charts and photographs as though flicking through an *Observer's Book of Birds* or consulting Ishmael's cetological library in which every kind of whale turns into any kind of shape endowed with the elements of other animals, as if their own defied definition.

Orca gladiator become gladiators of the skies. Nash lined up his air-whales like a boy with his Airfix toys, and attended to their characters. He did so with the same semi-seriousness he had applied to Swanage and the stones and shores of Dorset. The Wellington had a look of purpose, of unswerving concentration upon its goal, he thought. The long-nosed Blenheim appeared to be growing a face; with its livid coloured underparts and fish-like eyeball, it looked like the snarling face of a shark that he had photographed in Nice in 1934, the dead fish splayed out on a fisherman's trolley, mouth open wide.

The Hampden was more reptilian, Nash continued, in his modern animalium of aviation. It was some sort of pterodactyl, he decided; I love it because it is a devil. Perhaps he was thinking of Hawkins's chronicle of antediluvian dragons,

> Each from one Vortice to another,
> O weary Wings, and Space dreary ever.
> Sea-Dragons! Chase them in the Expanse of Heavens.
> Wild Lucifer Spirits our Companions through all Immensity.

And as he watched it take off, the plane soaring over the darkling fields as the moon rose, it became a flying lizard, Nash said, gliding across the cloud edge, its pale eyes flickering in the lunar ray.

Standing there in the hangar, he felt he had intruded into a whales' lair. And as he stood there, a pilot suddenly appeared at his side.

The artist said how wrong it was that people compared these sleeping animal-machines to birds.

Birds, the airman replied, with indignant emphasis, I always think my old girl looks like a ruddy whale.

Nash would never take off now. What the body is denied, he said, the mind must achieve. And so, like Blake, he began his last paintings. He created them out of memory, out of bright sunlight and melancholy eclipse, haunted by a gigantic sunflower floating in the air or rolling down a hill like a fire-wheel. A lifetime ago, as a teenager, he had begun with Blake's lines. Now, in his fifties, he ended with them.

Ah, Sun-flower! weary of time,
Who countest the steps of the Sun,
Seeking after that sweet golden clime
Where the traveller's journey is done:

Where the Youth pined away with desire,
And the pale Virgin shrouded in snow,
Arise from their graves and aspire
Where my Sun-flower wishes to go.   Pl XII

And as the black star pulsated with a halo of radiant petals,
Nash lent this last dreamscape a final burst of Blakean colour.
He had been reading Frazer's *The Golden Bough*, in which
Balder, the beautiful young god, becomes a sacrificial victim
like Melville's Billy Budd; a death required for the sun to
return. I cannot explain this picture, he said. It means only
what it says.

Summer, 1946. War is over. Nash goes on a tour of the Isle of
Purbeck. My kingdom, he calls it. His Avalon. He checks into
the Florida Hotel in Boscombe, a white deco building overlooking the sea. The Isle of Wight lay in the distance like a
white bar. He paints the view, goes to bed, and never checks
out again.

On his grave Margaret Nash placed a stone hawk: it was the
symbol of the Egyptian god Horus, to accompany Nash into
the afterlife; but also the same familiar spirit that had appeared
in his Landscape from a Dream before the war, perched over
Purbeck's shores. To the onlooker, it seemed that what was
missing in Nash's pictures were any representations of human
beings, let alone portraits of himself. But he's there, among
those enigmatic shapes: a melancholy angel, ready to spread
their wings.   Pl XII

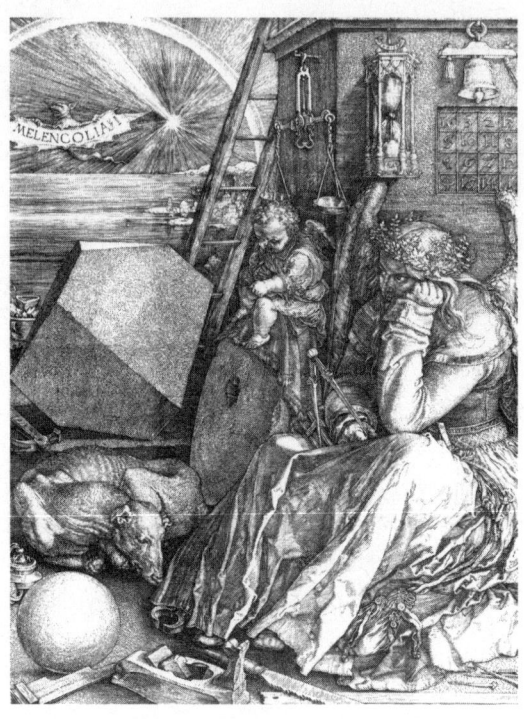

Towards the end, Blake was reduced to only bones & sinews, he told a friend. All string & bobbins like a Weaver's Loom. In his poverty, he had sold all his antique prints except one: Dürer's moon-age angel, still looking over him. To his intimate friends, the young Ancients, Blake's last view of the river, forced through the narrow channel of the tall dark buildings either side, was divine.

He seemed to see everything through it, as he saw everything through art, Palmer said; all framed by his symmetrical eye.

I should have liked to call on him there. The angel peering down on us, nowhere to sit but his bed. I would have given him five guineas for his Songs and waited two centuries for them to arrive, my mother calling upstairs, There's a Mr Blake with something for you, he looks a little pale, shall I ask him to sit down?

I admit it, here and now: I have never felt such solace from an artist. Once, at a party, in his old age, Blake said to a young girl, May God make this world to you, my child, as beautiful as it has been to me.

He would not move or change at the end; he was advised against it by his visions.

I only fear, he said, that I may be unlucky to my friends.

He had often seen his own end, having long since designed it like the rest of his life. That's the great benefit of visions. He budgeted for it, spending his last shilling by sending out for a new pencil. To him, each moment shorter than a pulse-beat was equivalent in its duration to six thousand years, as Joyce wrote, drawing extravagantly on Blake's words. All space larger than a red globule of blood was visionary.

Flying from the infinitely small to the infinitely large, Joyce went on, his soul is consumed by the rapidity of flight, and finds itself renewed and winged and immortal on the edge of the dark ocean of God.

Blake was ready to burst out like his luminous Dance of Albion, his Glad Day, his Albion Rose, shrugging off the angel's woes; a rainbow butterfly out of a monochrome chrysalis; someone he might yet become. He had first drawn it in 1780, as a lusty young man of twenty-two. An empty, naked outline he had been waiting to fill in. Unsheathed. Later he would colour it in, as his life filled up with his art. Up close, the picture explodes out of its sheet of paper, filled with itself, as if torn out of a book. An iridescent radiation, perfect and delicate like flesh. In the corner Blake has scratched through the melancholy blackness to indicate the rain the same way Nash would draw the wind. Blake is his own exultant unabashed self at last, triumphant, toes teetering on the multicoloured mountain, arms thrown wide to greet the dawn, the very ending and beginning of his life.

He was, said Palmer, energy itself.   Pl I

It was on Sunday, 12 August 1827, around six o'clock in the evening in Fountain Court, that William passed from one room to the next, on his long journey, singing to Kate from the angelic songs that ran continually through his head.

My beloved, they are not mine—no—they are not mine, he said.

His last act was to draw her, just as she was. Only Blake could make death sound like a perfect day. Only two biblical witnesses, Kate and a female friend. The friend said it was not the death of a man, but of a blessed angel. At the end, Blake's Countenance became fair—George Richmond, then eighteen years old, said—and he burst out in Singing of the things he Saw in Heaven. The lines had fallen away from his face, the way they do at the end. Richmond had arrived, just too late, at his deathbed, like the two children in *Whistle Down the Wind* who appear on the scene, having missed the arrest of the escaped prisoner they had all believed to be Christ.

Richmond kissed his master, then closed those eyes to keep the vision in. It was quite unnecessary. Blake had already gone, up to the stars. Forever ungoverned, he hadn't retired. He was living on heavenly time from now on.

There's nothing to show there now. The traffic runs past the alleyway where he left us behind. No one looks down from the top of the bus. There are no plaques on the wall. People are drinking cocktails in the Savoy. The steps lead down to Cleopatra's Needle. I climb down to the shore. The debris of centuries, timbers, cans, bottles, plastic cups, wash up in the corner. The river runs on.

They buried him to the east, in Bunhill Fields, a hill of bones outside the city walls, a dead centre for dissenters. It was a Friday, midday. He was huddled into a common grave, said Samuel Palmer. It cost 25 shillings. It was a convenient spot, William had said, pragmatic as ever: his mother and father and beloved Robert were buried in the same yard.

John Milton had lived next door. He wrote *Paradise Lost* there.

In his old age, totally blind, Milton would sit at his door on warm days, like Adam in his bow'r, receiving visitors who came to pay their respects. He could remember when Bunhill was a plague pit, when the afflicted were so desperate that they ran, clad in blankets and rags, and threw themselves, still living, into the pits.

A tumble of bones received Blake's remains. But he had lived and died at a good time. How different had he waited to be a Victorian! There would have been no space for him there. As a romantic he came from a looser age. He presided over the hopes of a new century and the despair of an old one, standing tiptoe on the top of the world, immortal for all. Born as a meteor landing in Soho, he died at the peak of the Perseids, on the summer night when all the stars fell out of the sky.

On the day of his interment there were just five mourners. Catherine Blake, John Linnell, Edward Calvert, George Richmond, and Frederick Tatham; Samuel Palmer was too distraught to attend. They said their prayers as he was lowered into the earth. Then they walked away to get on with their Blakeless lives. Kate lived on for four more years. William often returned to sit and talk with her. She only sold his work to people he approved of; he told her to keep back some of the best pieces and not show them all at once.

On 18 October 1831, she joined him, an irradiated saint, according to a friend. Her mortal body was laid beside Blake in the same field, with a bushel of slaked lime in her coffin to frustrate the resurrection men. It was quite unnecessary. She was already with William, beyond time and space.

When I lived in London, I walked over his grave every day. I felt close to him in my woe. It was the only green space I had and it was full of dead people. He lay down there, a few feet below my feet, in a cemetery named after a hill of bones, now overshadowed by the tower blocks that keep on rising all around. buried in a common grave. No one knew where his bones really lay. In 1878 Palmer uncovered a plot to plough up the field of the dead and douse the bones with carbolic acid; then, having tumbled them into a great pit in the corner, build houses instead. Blake wouldn't even have a grave to spin in.

It didn't happen, but it took a century to get him a memorial. The Blake Society gathered expectantly in their solemn beards and hats to mark the occasion, looking up into the air as if he might attend his own party. That would have made a great news story. But he wasn't there either. The stone only said that he was nearby, along with his wife, Catherine Sophia, as though they were sitting naked under the plane trees, feeding the pigeons.

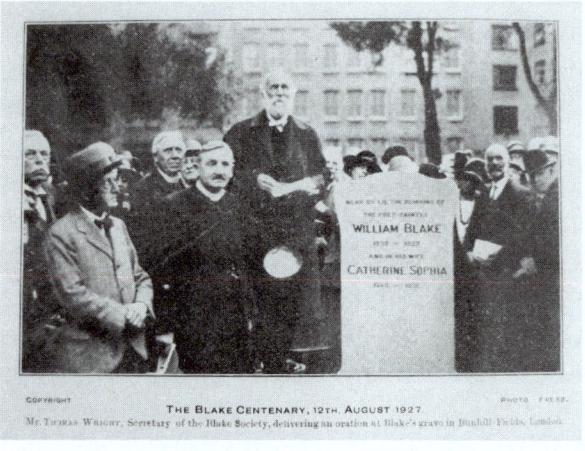

THE BLAKE CENTENARY, 12TH AUGUST 1927.
Mr. Thomas Wright, Secretary of the Blake Society, delivering an oration at Blake's grave in Bunhill Fields, London.

Recently they laid a gravestone on the right spot. It says

> I give you the end of a golden string
> Only wind it into a ball
> It will lead you in at Heavens gate
> Built in Jerusalems wall

I went to see it yesterday, and for want of anything to say, I sang the first verse of The Tyger. I pretended he'd given me the tune, out of the green air, over the grey stones.

And I realised, as I did when I first heard it as a boy, that it is the wildest poem ever written or read. The Y only makes it wilder; you can sing it that way if you like, like the Marseillaise or the Red Flag. Archaic, coloured-in: your child within, staring out through those glittering eyes, prowling in the grass.

An old man wandered into the graveyard and pissed against the wall. The leaves were falling on the path made of old gravestones, and I walked on.

Dorset, July 1972. It's pouring with rain, again. Crawling out of their cave, feeling guilty at having brought his friends all this way for nothing, Derek Jarman suggests they seek sanctuary with a friend of his: Michael Pinney, who lives in a seventeenth-century manor at Bettiscombe, not far away to the west. Jarman takes his crew there, to make amends for the temporary failure of his magic.

They drive down the narrow lanes, through the rain. Bettiscombe Manor is set deep in a valley. It has been in Michael Pinney's family for three hundred years. It is a haunted place. The Pinneys were related by marriage to Thomas Hawkins, the collector of sea dragons; Anna Maria Pinney had been a close friend to Mary Anning, helping her to search for Lyme crocodiles, clambering over the rocks; at one point Mary had to save her from the waves, catching her around the waist and carrying her away. The house is Jacobean, red brick with stone-flagged floors. Pinney, whom Jarman met through his friend, the artist Robert Medley, has recently published Jarman's first poems, A Finger in the Fishes Mouth. Its silver mirror cover is a photograph by Wilhelm von Gloeden, showing a smiling Sicilian youth wearing only a straw hat, holding a fish to his lips as if one or the other might speak.

Houses like this possess their own jealousies, some deca-dent disease, a fruiting body at their heart running under the floorboards, its tentacles reaching out around the timbers. Damp rooms, smelling of rot and sherry spilt before nine in the morning and game for lunch, full of shot. As a house guest I would pronounce the names of places and people erroneously and use the wrong cutlery and go red when corrected; which was the correct effect. I looked too young and was clearly not of their class. It was exciting for them. I felt like an interloper in a ghost story made for TV.

It's still raining when Jarman and friends arrive. They were soaked to the gills, Balet says. In the panelled library they find a dramatic cast arranged by Pinney to entertain them. There's the engraver, Reynolds Stone, an artist used to cutting into stone and printing banknotes and stamps with pretty pictures of the queen. Janet Stone, his wife, is a photographer; years later she will reply to my letter in her stylish italics, as if they were engraved too. And with these two people is their friend, Iris Murdoch, who has written fourteen novels and is famous.

I think I would have been afraid of her. She has big blue haunted eyes like the house. Soon she will write *The Sea, The Sea*. Its central character is Charles Arrowby, a theatre director-actor whose last role was Prospero in *The Tempest*. He has moved to a house beside the ocean; Murdoch says it's eastern England but it is clearly Dorset; she's covering her tracks the way that Virginia Woolf pretended her lighthouse was Scottish rather than set off St Ives; the way that everything both women wrote has the air of a fairy tale. The coast is full of rocks. Arrowby has wanted to live there all his life. But sitting on the shore, he sees a sea serpent writhing in the waters far out. He is appalled, and tries to reconcile this horror to reality. He could see through its coils, he says. The monster is Blakean and saurian, a fossil come to life, and the entire shore haunted, by Arrowby himself, even though he has never been there before.

I've always got *The Tempest* in my head; it was the idea of giving up magic, Murdoch said. As if one day she might lose her own to the sea. In *The Tempest*, Iris is a Greek goddess who appears, magically, in Prospero's masque; in *Paradise Lost*, Iris is the goddess of the rainbow. Our Iris is a drama queen; it's the way she runs her life.

You can see why she might be drawn to Jarman and his crew. She is only ever one step away from gothic camp or outrageous prophecy. Her novels, said George Steiner, had an immensity to which only Blake could provide a parallel in English literature. (But then again, Steiner told me his idea of easy reading was *Moby-Dick*.) Her works, he added, are luminous shades of Blake's holiness of the minute particular. As Daniel Read notes, one quarter of Murdoch's novels reference Blake, even though she disagrees with his philosophy, which she finds amoral. She agrees with her lover Brigid Brophy (a great defender of the gay and the non-human in her tigerskin print dress; I have a postcard from her to me, too, in her small neat hand) that much of Blake's prophecy was false & dangerous stuff. Murdoch is a philosophy of her own, working it out as she goes along, Shakespearean-modernist-Anglo-Irish-queer.

A potent mix. The mind can make a heaven of hell, as Milton wrote, and can make a hell of heaven; just as Blake turned angels into devils and devils into heroes. Murdoch's own head, she hoped, contained the jumbled cloud of thoughts whose self-protective and self-adjusting chemistry is known as mental health. But as an artist she was also prone to an overwhelming ennui, and Jarman and his troupe might have entered a scenario from one of her novels like a welcome, disruptive energy.

It's complicated, as all Murdoch stories are. Michael Pinney is bisexual; he and his wife Betty conduct an open marriage; she is an artist who had trained under John Nash, Paul's brother, who fell in love with her. She is also nursing a lasting dislike for Murdoch because, twenty years before, she had stolen her best friend. Meanwhile Janet Stone is in love with Kenneth Clark, an affair in which their mutual friend David Jones plays confidant.

I told you it was complicated.

Like Paul Nash, Iris Murdoch responds deeply to the spirit of place. Time stands still or goes into reverse in her world. Her friends, the aristocratic Cecils, Rachel and David, live nearby in another grand old house. They took her to dinner at Cecil Beaton's fantastically Edwardianised eighteenth-century house; the air of unreality was increased by the presence of Truman Capote, she said. He and Beaton had just been to visit Stephen Tennant at Wilsford, where Capote complained that he was served soup with candied violets in it. They're all incestuously vain. Beaton was having his portrait painted by Francis Bacon, who would destroy it before it could be delivered.

Murdoch stands outside it all, a little bit lost, for all her fame. Everything in Dorset, she wrote in her eleventh novel, *The Nice and the Good*, published in 1968 and dedicated to the Cecils, is *just the right size*, and rounded by time; even the old red bricks of the houses looked like playthings of the sea, she said.

In the book, she plays it all out like a game. Her erotic neurotic characters live communally in an old house called Trescombe. It's set back from the cliffs where the sea abides, a living, threatening presence on the edge of things. Mingo the family dog's sharp excited barks are seabarks, Murdoch writes, and despite being a confident and enthusiastic swimmer, he never seemed to get over his sheer surprise at the great restless watery phenomenon, she says.

Undermining the cliffs were the sea caves, accessible only at low tide before the water came rushing back in. Murdoch sees their blackness as a kind of consummation, in which treasure troves and death by drowning blended together into a buzzing vortex of divine unconsciousness.

It gives me the creeps, says one of the women in the Trescombe ménage, talking about the cave. I have a fantasy that it's full of drowned men who went in after treasure and got caught by the sea, she says.

Murdoch is always worrying about the sea. She asks, philosophically, does nature suffer here, in her extremities, on the stony beach, where the intention of God could reach only a little way through the opacity of matter? To Murdoch the beach and sea were quandaries. Her sea is sensual and hard. Uncle Theo carefully places round flat stones on the back of Pierce, his teenaged nephew, as the boy lies there in the sun after having swum naked in the sea. The stones accumulate as a pattern, a mosaic on the boy's brown body, like a ritual.

This sea is deadly too, offering extinguishment of precisely that sensual, selfish life, Murdoch says. A sea beyond caring, that will always exact its revenge. At the terrifying end of *The Nice and the Good*, as the waves swell in the darkness, up to the roof of the cave, they carry with them the main character, Ducane, who is faintly in love with his own Scottish manservant, a man with a big shaggy head and wide-apart eyes and red hair who claims to be the son of a mermaid born in a circus. With Ducane in the cave are young Pierce and Mingo the dog.

It's another Shakespearean scene (everyone steals from Shakespeare, even Shakespeare himself), and it is difficult to know what level of reality it may or may not suggest. As the rising water threatens to drown the three, man, boy and dog become a kind of offering to the gods of Murdoch's art, a sacrifice to love. There's something demonic, too, to this episode, so claustrophobic and compressed that I can't read it line by line but have to keep putting down the book to catch my breath.

Everywhere here, in her real and fantasy life, Murdoch's sea is a salvation, a witness, an invitation; a threat. Immortal, outrageous, always beyond. A drama of the author's invention, swirling about in her head. Like anyone transfixed by the sea, Murdoch is perpetually returning to it, like an offender to the scene of the crime, unable to leave it alone. To be caught in it, to drown in it, again and again and again. To pick at it like a scab on your knee.

You can see why she and Jarman might regard one another

curiously. With each new tide a new life, a new death. Destined to be. Curled up, like stones that once were snakes.

It happened when she was swimming off Chesil Beach. Chesil, eighteen miles of shingle connecting the mainland and Portland Bill, is unique in Europe, as Nash notes in his Dorset guide; a sea-wall constructed by the sea against itself, its human history both romantic and terrible, its geological formation still under debate; the result, as Nash wrote, of a mystical judgment known as the law of compensation. This beach beyond a beach seems to accelerate the high seas roaring round the Bill, where they meet the suddenly deep water off its steep rocks, creating dizzying vortices that might suck a kraken down.

The result of this maelstrom is the Portland Race, a current so strong that its presence is felt all the way to Winspit and St Aldhelm's Head. It races itself along the coast, running hard and fast, fit to wreck ships and whales, casting up surrealist refugees on the shore, leaving them bruised and battered and bewildered.

The Race picks up speed as it hits the steep beach, and the sea rolls and folds under itself. Nothing can stop it, this watery monster. It is difficult to stand on the beach, let alone swim. As Marianne Moore said, the sea has nothing to give but a well excavated grave.

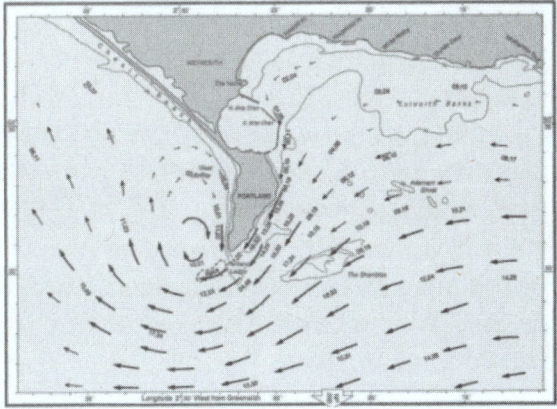

You cannot stand in the middle of this, she said.

That day, Murdoch's husband, John Bayley, and Reynolds Stone had got out of the water and were discussing classical music as they dressed on the beach, not realising that the sea had taken up Iris and was about to claim her for its own.

She knew she was about to be swept away. The stones were rolling beneath her like a street fight, defeating her attempts to retreat. It was a moment of incredulous surprise and terror, she told Bayley as they lay in bed that night, as she admitted to her fear of being drawn back under the smooth sea, of it closing over her like a cave.

It was deep over her head, she said, but she had kept her mouth tightly shut by instinct, and in another moment the next wave brought her ashore. Had she panicked and swallowed water, Bayley said, the next swell of the insidious undertow might well have carried her farther out and down; and then, easy swimmer as she was, she could have drowned in a few seconds.

Just along from that same shore, on a winter's afternoon, I was taken up by the same sea. The waves turned me over three hundred and sixty degrees (it happened in slow motion so I counted every one) till I too thought I was seeing my last of England. I felt the inexorable momentum, ripped raw by the water, the rattling stones, the waves dragging me down. I struggled uselessly and gave up. All I could see were the tall cliffs as though they were falling on top of me.

For a moment I felt I was on my way out. It got dark. Then the sea spat me out. I came ashore on my face, my features squashed in the shingle like a body found in a bog. That night, in the town, someone told me a young man had drowned there recently, in the same circumstances. I laughed, not heartlessly, but nervously, and turned my face away in embarrassment.

When she visited Dancing Ledge, looking down into its deep immediate water, as she called it, Murdoch said she was too afraid to go in. There was water in all her books, she told an interviewer in 1983, as if they were written autonomously,

248

by someone or something else. As if it might have escaped anyone's notice, as if she had something to hide, something inside herself that she felt compelled to betray.

I do love swimming, she confessed. I used to be absolutely fearless in the sea, but I nearly drowned once, and I'm now much more cautious.

I used to think the sea and I were great friends, she added, but one must fear the sea. As if she'd lost her greatest friend. I've only recently realised that I'm a kind of exile, she said, a displaced person.

She was regretting her removal from Ireland as a child at only a few weeks old, as if it were an outrage and a power she held to herself. The estrangement was easy to hide. Nonetheless, I identify with exiles, she said, as if that were the end of the matter, when in fact it was the beginning.

She was lost to it from the start. The first thing she could remember as a child was swimming in the salt-water baths at Dún Laoghaire. She often played on that heavenly coast on holiday, she said, climbing around the Martello tower and its rocks. (All this came to mind when she was trying to read *Ulysses* in 1983. She felt sick at the first page, purely an Irish reaction in fact, she said.) (I tried to read *Ulysses*; I got to the last chapter and had to give up.) Only her father could swim in the Forty Foot, since it was reserved for gentlemen; he described the experience reverentially. Iris and her mother had to make do with the sandy cove round the corner, where the ladies could besport themselves, albeit not quite as demurely as the gentlemen might imagine.

All of Murdoch's earliest memories were of swimming, singing, and of animals, as her friend Peter Conradi recalled. Swimming was the family's secret religion; it was mentioned on postcard after postcard, like another love affair. And although she was snatched away to England as a baby, before Irishness could really take hold, Murdoch would return with her family to Dublin for summer holidays in the twenties and thirties, staying with their relations at 15 Mellifont Avenue, Dún

Laoghaire. From their windows they could see the sea at the end of the street, the bay spread out before them, the great half-mile-long pair of granite piers of the harbour reaching out like a crab's claws.

She remembered, in her book *The Red and the Green*, set in Dublin, how the house seemed always full of a grey luminous light from the sea, and how the road ended casually in the water and the pavement turned into yellow rocks, and partook indeed of the hardness and cleanness of the rocks and the coldness and clearness of the water; and all the while the bulky headland with the Martello tower upon it rose like the Acropolis of the village.

And she remembered when, in the summer of 1934, everyone came out of their houses during a terrible storm as the maroon went up and the lifeboat went out and they ran to the end of the pier; and how they cheered when the yacht that seemed to be about to be smashed against the rocks was rescued, even though it was found to be empty, and two other yachts had sunk.

Ireland was the island of spells, a provincial pigsty, she said in 1945. Little brittle magic nation dim of mind, she called it. She was quoting Joyce, of course, she said, from *Finnegans Wake*. Despite living all her adult life in England, Iris insisted that she was profoundly Irish. Her family had lived there for three hundred years. She saw herself as an Irish writer, and claimed her accent remained Irish, that you could cut it with a knife. She may have had misleading Oxford overtones, but her vowels were Irish, she said.

It was what she felt inside. Her construction, her physical self, her political body. It was no more outrageous than Joyce retaining a British passport to the end of his life. She attributed her interest in the hauntings of history, of the gothic and magic and the occult, all these, to her Irishness. A collective past. And it was why, that summer evening at Bettiscombe, despite the fact that the visitors were soaking wet, she led them all up the hill to hold hands and dance around the wishing stone, with Iris like a seer, her blue eyes in the twilight.

Queer people often appear in Murdoch's books. She looks at Jarman and Pinney and their friends as material, as witnesses, as like-minded spirits of oddness. It's why flying saucers and sea monsters and the sons of mermaids also show up in her books; real and super-real at the same time, as they emerge in the culture of the sixties and seventies; strange things released at the edges and endings the way they would occupy my own mind as a boy growing up around that time, when I saw them rising and falling into my dreams from the sky to land in our suburban night garden, or rearing up sinuously from a dark loch head as I bent down to fill a bottle with alien water, hoping to catch monster genes.

In Murdoch's work these things appear as one long appari-tion, a performance of her inner self, her own philosophy, eruditely, the way she remembered Gerard Manley Hopkins, whose lines she could recite by heart,

There lives the dearest freshness deep down things

or the way she believed in the mysterious agencies of the human mind which, as she wrote, endow us with the ghostly power of appearing in other people's dreams; as she does.

It was all part of her antecedence: the swimming and the singing and the superstition and the life-saving dogs (she would weep uncontrollably at their loss, even as an adult). Above all, it was the water that embodied her otherness and her Irishness.

I'm *nothing* if not Irish, she says as she leans towards us; the way she keeps on insisting on the fact to the end of her life, as if that were the one overriding, justifying fact, the way that Virginia Woolf said no one from the future would believe all her work was inspired by the vision of a fin passing far out, or the way that Yeats believed all visionary poets had to be Irish. That deepness was always there, like the sea, even at the end, when everything else had fallen away, even as her husband had to lead her to the water and dress her in her swimming costume.

Her pale round face, like a moon with secret-violet eyes, seeing herself, peering back from her own past, alive or dead in the books she wrote, the words she chose to forget.

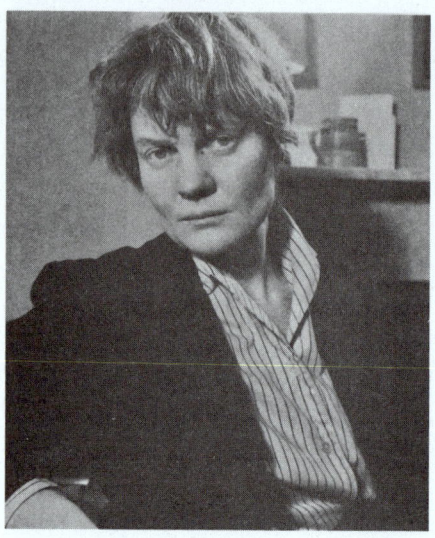

What is the alternative to a broken heart? Pierce the teenaged boy asks in *The Nice and the Good*. Art, he is told. Or more love.

Her disconcerting gaze remains. The space she left between being asked questions and answering them, looking hard. (It made you sound more clever, and gave you time for your witty reply. I met a famous writer who did the same, only his eyes were yellow like a leopard on the veldt.) Her crazy characters are undone by the sea. So is she. Her wildness, her feral, faerie presence under her rational skin. There is no admission that is not too great for her. She's collegiate-bohemian. Wearing a tangerine-coloured plastic mac with a purple outfit for a television interview.

Or, arriving for dinner at Frances Partridge's house, in a splendid antique military coat made of the finest black cloth with gilt buttons like Admiral Nelson. She was displaying her magnificent realism, said Partridge, who had the same broad face.

Murdoch's Joan-of-Arc-like quality held, attending to what

everyone said with her very Oxford Yes, yes, yes. Like Molly, like myself. She looked like a boy becoming a girl becoming a boy. A rebel, twice over. Her tousled blonde Tudor haircut, a cap for a principal boy. By the time she met Jarman, she was working on her fifteenth novel, *The Black Prince*, about a writer who declares, I am always defeated, always.

Every book is the wreck of a perfect idea, he says.

Murdoch's books appeared quite ordinary, on library shelves in the nineteen-seventies and now in charity shops, full of real or make-believe love affairs and excruciating or frankly crazy situations. But whatever she earned from them she was paying for mistakes she made in her past, the people she had betrayed; and her remorseful novels are deeply strange and obsessive. They hide what they really mean with new myths of their own.

The edition of *The Nice and the Good* I am reading is another former library book, still sealed against grubby public hands in its slightly sticky laminated cover from 1968, when readers had to notify librarians of any communicable disease. It is tightly bound but widely read. There are stains of biscuit crumbs, and every few pages there are kerb-like marks in blue biro at the end of a paragraph to indicate exactly where the reader had stopped reading for the night.

So I stop reading there too.

I start again, reading the wrong book. Same world.

Does it signify what really happened to Lawrence at Déraa? Arrowby's cousin James asks in his Kensington flat filled with exotic, votive objects. James Arrowby, an ambiguous figure in *The Sea, The Sea*, has left the army under a cloud. He is partly based on the elusive T.E. Lawrence, with whom Murdoch was obsessed. People often leave under clouds in Murdoch's world: clouds seem to follow them about, mysteriously.

If even a dog's tooth is truly worshipped it glows with light, James goes on. The venerated object is endowed with power, that is the simple sense of the ontological proof. And if there is art enough a lie can enlighten us as well as the truth.

As we know ourselves, we are fake objects, he says, fakes, bundles of illusions.

Can you determine exactly what you felt or thought or did?

In the seventeenth-century library at Bettiscombe, panelled and out-of-time, Iris Murdoch looks upon the ragged glamorous fetched-up visitors with her big blue-grey-violet eyes.

Over her glass of dry sherry, moderately amused, she seems to be struck by these fey young people with their amorphous optimism. She herself is entirely androgynous and Celtic in her heart, like a lithe god. Entirely Iris in her eyes. Detached yet curious, says Jarman. Those eyes, contracting and dilating in the candlelight. Querulous rather than bemused.

Over the amontillado she asks, What do you do?, like the Queen. They say they are making a film, leaving her none the wiser, and themselves too, Jarman says. For a long time he has been obsessed with Blake, and The Tempest. The house has a legendary screaming skull, he remembers; not studded with cockle shells, nor with pearls for eyes, but said to have belonged to an enslaved person brought back from the West Indies by Azariah Pinney in the early eighteenth century, where, using slaves, Pinney had founded the family fortune on a sugar plantation on the island of Nevis.

Since my arrival, John Pinney wrote in 1765, I've purchased 9 Negro slaves in St Kitts and can assure you I was shocked by the first appearance of human flesh for sale. But surely God ordained 'em for the use and benefit of us, he decided, otherwise his Divine Will would have been made manifest to us by some particular sign or token. (People said the same about whales.) Anna Maria Pinney, Mary Anning's close friend, claimed in 1847 that while the skull was kept, no ghost would ever invade Bettiscombe. If it should be removed, the family and the house would fall. It seemed like revenge. The visitors pass the skull around. A Black prince. Murdoch enters into the spirit of it all.

She's a magician, directing strange creatures. Actors are cave dwellers in a rich darkness which they love and hate, she will write in *The Sea, The Sea*. She stole the title. It's an incantation if you say it twice. One soon learns the limitations of the human soul, she says.

The profound truth, Charles Arrowby, the director, says in her book—as he swims precariously from the rocks, watching fearfully lest the sea monster reappear with the rising tide, like a gigantic eel, even though they laugh at him in the local pub—the profound truth, he realises, is that we are extended beings who yet can only exist in the present. He speaks in her voice. But who would take her advice as she lurches, like her characters, from the real to the improbable?

At the end of *The Nice and the Good*, the two youngest characters watch a UFO hovering overhead, over the sea cliffs.

The nine-year-old twins, who might be ninety years old, sigh and do not speak as it tilts in the sky, then disappears.

Isn't it odd how we know that it doesn't want to be photographed, says one.

Telepathy, I expect, says the other.

We'll come back tomorrow. You haven't lost that ammonite, have you?

Years later, I'd see her at parties for books. Across the room, kept in a corner, as if she were dangerous. An animal. Her face, her hair, her stature; her watery eyes, swimming in tears. Her mannishness. Looking back, angrily, unseeing, making my stare ruder with hers. I would have liked to talk to her, but I had no idea what to say. I was afraid of her, as if she might bite.

Even then she was still swimming. Iris in the Isis, the muddy banks where the cattle came down to drink, where Hopkins and Lawrence swam too. Our usual secret place, she said, in a last journal entry. Ducks, geese, swans, a delightful man came swimming in—we talked, no sign of the road on other side, cows wander.

Poor cows!, she said.

———

Jarman and his friends return to Dorset the following weekend. It was the only truly hot day of that summer, as Jarman remembers it. Radiant, as such stony places can be.

Out on the rocky shelf below the quarry, they finally stage their performance of The Siren and the Sailor.

As they go through the motions in mime, Jarman directs his crew aloud as Balet films, all the while watched by a single, random day-tripper who sits on a rock like a seal, only wearing sunglasses and reading a paperback book.

The camera picks out a trawler passing by. Its black shape and its rigging and its nets are ominous with dredged and dying fish and followed by a cloud of mourning gulls. The lens ranges up the cliff to find the sea god standing there.

Andrew Logan is wearing his mask of genius, made by Christopher Hobbs from scored and folded silver card. It looks like he sliced it out of sheet metal or found it at the foot of the Acropolis. Logan's arms are full of a diaphanous cloak-robe-dress, a deconstructed crinoline he'd worn for his Alternative Miss World that year, held in his Hackney studio on the Downham Road. The garment, much hacked and rent about, hangs around him like green and pink seaweed. He holds it up like a pair of wings. He looks divine. He's bare-chested and skinny, his white pantaloons flapping eighteenth-century sails held up by braces.

The camera follows his outstretched open hand, gesticulating like a dancer or a traffic policeman down to the sea. It is lapping into a rockpool in which the anonymous young man lies, the unknown sailor, all washed up, another lost soul fallen from the sun or a dive bar in the West End.

The siren sits on the rock looking out to sea, her long legs folded to one side. She is assuming, automatically, the pose of the Little Mermaid of her native land. She fixes the trawler in her stare, luring the oilskinned crew to their doom. They sail on regardless, chucking their cigarette butts over the side. She's naked except for her long blonde hair and a green fishing net as her weedy gown. Her pale blue eyes. She floats boats of silver paper on the surface of the pool.

The whole thing was very symbolic, says Balet. Ship wrecks. Mythical. It was totally Derek's idea, he tells me, although he isn't sure where it came from. The siren might be Miranda, gazing on a wrecked sailor from a brave new world, with Logan as another Prospero, casting his spells. In 1936, Paul Nash painted the porcelain head of a doll looking out to sea from this shore—a stand-in for his wife Margaret, who saw herself, as he saw her too, as a siren as well as a muse, fearful and miraculous to a man who cannot understand.

But most of all, the film is full of Blake and his lovely bodies and his noise, played out as they lay splayed out on the rocks. The intense inky colours, the camp romanticism, the theatrical licence of the sea, all tip towards Albion's shores where everything begins and ends . . . the way the sea forces you to perform, always rolling out endlessly; the way you are only ever lonely beside it. The way that the sea is the sound of a thousand broken hearts.

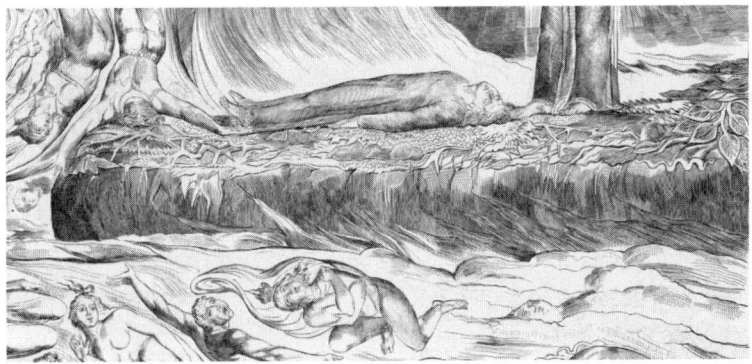

The handsome sailor lies in the pool, stripped to the waist. He is beautiful flotsam swaying in the sun with the ebb and flow, entangled in oozy weeds like Billy Budd. Everything is still and moving and opaque and wrecked. Adam on the rocks. His white bell-bottom trousers have a flap-front worthy of Billy;

the buttons are not pearly but bright orange with seventies allure. The way I wanted to look in the turquoise blue of Southampton lido, an eye of crumbling art deco trapped by the docks; my long blond hair, my white cotton Oxford bags.

Logan picks his way over the rocks with armfuls of his multi-coloured bridal train held out. An iridescent, sexy cormorant. The silver curves of his mask make him a cyber Orc, a space invader coming for you. The colours and textures, the sharp rocks and the ripped-up proto-punk clothes, stand opposed but also reflecting the bleakness of the time. Stranded bodies, exultant or resigned. The last of England. The demi-god, the siren, the drowned man. The sea spray, the sensuality, the sky, the nostalgia for something that never was. A continuum of queerness, threaded through countercultural time; time, passed on from hand to hand.

The god becomes the dance of Albion on England's shores, just as Logan had played Land of Hope and Glory on his gramophone. He embraces the siren as she mourns the sailor. Silencing her song, which we cannot hear. The colours close round her until we see no more of her. She's gone, and so is he. His mask and gown are left on the rocks like the skin of a selkie.

It's a wrap. The crew spend the rest of the day sunbathing, lolling around on the rocks. It's fifty years ago. It's all about how they feel. I see those scenes stilled now. They sum up all my longing of that time, as if I might appear in them, freeze-framed on the page by James Mackay, Jarman's producer, fragments of what I wanted to be.

Astonish me. The result was no home movie to be watched over cheese straws and sherry, but projected on the bare wall of a warehouse with a joint being passed round as the director played a record of Ravel's Lever du Jour from Daphnis et Chloé, composed for the Russian Ballet and set on the rocks of Lesbos. The lush wavelike chords rise to a crescendo. The dark Thames runs by as the film runs out.

———

Five years later, at college by the upper reaches of the same river, a friend shows me the script of a new film. It is set in a punk-infested apocalyptic England. It was another homage to Blake, to whom the director will dedicate his film. I thought it was ridiculous. Peter-Paul tells me they need extras for a crowd scene, would I like to come down? I was too haughty and too scared to say yes.

Jarman's *Jubilee* turns Blake's *Jerusalem* into his own prophecy, adopting the poet's hyperbole and exhortation; perhaps even the sense of his satire, An Island in the Moon. They make the film in the bombed-out wasteland of nineteen-seventies London, its wrecked streets and wharves patrolled by Elizabeth I and John Dee and gangs of punks. Dorset has become a separate country which has banned homosexuals, Blacks and Jews, a place so sleepy that a fascist dictator can retire there unnoticed, in a stately home.

It's the only safe place to live, he says.

The plot is wayward, to say the least. Jarman was just being astonishing. At the end of his extended allegory, his dark conceit, he returns to Winspit to film the queen and her magician strolling along the quarry's edge. Ariel, teleported from *The Tempest*, his next film, appears in a black leotard, with black curly hair, black contact lenses and black nail varnish.

We drift in a sea of stars, the spirit declares.

Then he lies back, splayed out on the same rocks. Three years later, in his own video, the most expensive ever made to that date, his version of heaven and hell, the starman will walk along a rocky shoreline in a pierrot costume stiff with sequins and pearls and his own legend, before affecting to drown in an irradiated sea. His honoured guest at the viewing is Derek Jarman, who is perfectly polite about it all.

This morning, as I was unpacking a box, I found another typescript I had entirely forgotten about. The first-year course guide to Dorset, where we were taken on a field trip in May 1977, just as Jarman was making *Jubilee*.

I didn't go to university. I got an E for my English A level. I wanted to go to art college but my parents, fearing the worst, persuaded me to attend a Catholic college in the suburbs of London, occupying a gothic house built by Horace Walpole. I was neither in the city nor out of it. But every week I took the train into the city to the Roxy Club, hidden under the streets of a darkened Covent Garden. My diary tells me that the night before we left for Dorset I'd been to see The Damned, and I was late delivering my essay on Joyce. I'd overslept and ran to my lecture with my clothes over my pyjamas. The guide instructed us to bring sensible footwear. I had none. I tramped round Dorset in Dr. Martens borrowed from a friend. They were two sizes too big.

Remember the Vicar, the village policeman and schoolmaster as sources of local information, the guide told us. We learn by looking, listening and asking questions, it said. It was printed on a Gestetner machine, the same rolling inked drum on which I would produce my fanzine announcing the imminent appearance of Jarman's film.

It was odd being in Dorset and not arriving in the family car. I felt sort of wild, irresponsible. My hair was dyed red. We were led up Maiden Castle's ramparts and down to Portland's quarries. I lay down in the abbot's stone coffin where Angel Clare laid Tess Durbeyfield. At the end of the guide was a section entitled The Founding of a Fortune which explained that the Pinney family of Bettiscombe had amassed one of the great plantation fortunes of the eighteenth century. It didn't say how.

Our invitation is to the house, and the person showing it to the party and telling its story is Mr. Michael Pinney, said the guide. It was the second of three invitations I declined that summer. Instead I got drunk on cider in the pubs and I walked for miles to St Aldhelm's Head in the summer heat with an art student with her long red hair who later propositioned me in the refectory before lunch.

Seven years later Jarman made a new film with a crew of shaven-headed young men in soldiers' uniforms. There was no script, but the intertitles quoted Blake in blood-red letters as Peter Pears sang Benjamin Britten's setting of The Sick Rose in a strained and haunting voice.

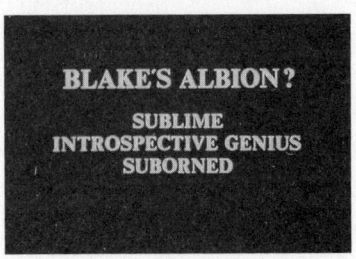

The Sick Rose

O Rose thou art sick.
The invisible worm,
That flies in the night
In the howling storm:

Has found out thy bed
Of crimson joy:
And his dark secret love
Does thy life destroy.

Imagining October was, Jarman thought, one of his most powerful films. It detailed the decay of the age, evoking oppression in the strangely optimistic art of the time. The way we held up placards in the street, demanding that everything must change.

BLAKE'S ALBION?

SUBLIME
INTROSPECTIVE GENIUS
SUBORNED

They seemed, all these episodes, like fantastical flash-lit scenes, like the radical music; fierce visions and ferocious statements, like our marches, our posters and badges, almost innocent, almost naive, like Blake. Despite all the darkness all around, they retained their hope: that they might change something, anything. Yet at the time I felt apprehensive of Jarman and what he signified. His life in the margins and in the newspapers; his indiscretion, his poshness, his queerness. I knew the people around him, I danced with them in nightclubs. But I didn't feel part of their gang. I didn't even feel very English or part of anything. The great thing about being young is taking nothing seriously except yourself. Things were speeding up. We didn't know where we were going, but we thought it must be a better place.

In 1986, Jarman found his cottage by the sea. His discovery was accompanied by the virus which seemed like the price for his ambition. The house was set on Dungeness, on the edge of Romney Marsh. Paul Nash had lived nearby. Blake's cottage lay some distance along the shore to the west.

It was the surreal seascape of Dorset of Jarman's childhood stripped down and transformed to this vast shingle peninsula. A queer place; some people called it the fifth quarter of England. Jarman's tarry fisherman's hut was a hundred years old, and stood in the shadow of a glowing nuclear plant. He called it Prospect Cottage and its blackness absorbed everything, all the energy and light around. It was his laboratory, a generator of power, calling things down like a lightning conductor. A deliberate experiment he undertook at the end of his life.

Outside the house he made circles of stones gathered from the beach in the canvas bag slung round his neck. He boiled up tar outside to make hellish paintings. Inside he wrote his journals, his account of modern nature which was already very old. He was a figure in the landscape, against nature, like Nash as a dandy in Avebury or Blake in his seaside garden. He strung holey stones onto leather thongs to be awarded to friends as prizes for making it all the way there.

The garden grew wild, almost of its own accord, with no boundaries, seeded with beach roses and acid-yellow poppies, with glaucous green sea kale and purple sea holly and found objects from the shore. The whole thing seemed left behind by the tide, as if it were the bottom of the sea only briefly reclaimed. The modern world passed by. He let it go. When his good friend Howard Sooley encouraged him to go out and buy a computer, Derek came back with a nice new pen.

The cottage is empty on an autumn afternoon. A note asks people not to knock on the door. Derek is in the churchyard, under the grass.

So small and almost suburban from the outside, the house expands like a film set inside. The rooms unfold, one by one. The kitchen is a ship's galley hung with pots and pans; they might start to sway. His rough-hewn bed, brought down from his London flat where I last saw it crammed into a tiny dark space, floats like a raft. There's a crucifix on the wall and rosaries of stones, and at the back is the sun room where he lay in state, clad in a sequinned gown. He wanted the house razed to the ground; its tarry walls would burn well.

A cine camera lies next to the clapperboard for The Tempest, next to a tiara worn by Miranda. My books on his shelves. I walk into his study, its view of the distant sea a disrupted line on the horizon. I half expect him to turn round from his desk. His ink and pens stand ready in a mug. A net curtain filters the blue twilight. I apologise for interrupting and shut the door.

I last saw him in Heaven, in his boiler suit. I watched his eyes as my friend sang about parties in the nineteen-twenties. Afterwards I wondered if I ought to tell him I'd already written his obituary. He was talking quicker than ever.

Soon he would lose his sight but not his vision. His last film was the last colour he saw. That was all he had left. He owned virtually nothing. The blue flooded the screen. All the sea and all his experience concentrated into that one frame.

If the doors of Perception were cleansed, he said, quoting Blake, then everything would be seen as it is.

The pleasure of film is the pleasure of seeing language put through the magic lantern, you don't know what you have to say until you've said it.

You can dream of lands far distant, he said.

On Sunday evenings our father would project slides in our front room, feeding the little cardboard-framed images like eyes into the machine, throwing them on a shaky screen. Holidays and days out, the seaside, my sisters in identical new dresses; our second-hand car in its chrome and navy blue livery. No one shows them now. But out of the box leaps a giant animal, all shiny and slick.

I remember that day very well. The dolphins had left the pool. A banner advertised Embassy cigarettes. Ramu, frozen in Kodak celluloid, performed in the Royal Windsor Dolphinarium, as if all whales belonged to the Queen. The god of the under-world reduced to a theme-park ride. An Apollo mission gone wrong, headbutting a basketball. Impossible.

I never played ball. I dressed up all the time. It was my only means of escape. A superhero in my sister's green woollen tights, a pair of emerald-green swimming trunks and my broth-er's motorbike goggles. A Red Indian in feather headdress and loincloth. A tea towel and dressing-gown cord round my head as Lawrence of Arabia. A Tudor prince in a black velvet doublet made from a woman's jacket, the sleeves slit to the elbow, a floppy black velvet hat with pearls on it. I was left to my own devices. All I lacked was a stage.

I had the clothes, stolen from dead people. I was a grave-robber at jumble sales. A matador's gilt-embroidered jacket; a grey fedora hat. My mother made me pink satin Oxford bags. I wore them with platforms with four-inch heels, clattering down from the upper deck of the bus on my way into town. A green woman's jacket from the forties with aircraft-carrier shoulders, a diamante clip on the lapel. The green of my eyes, photo-boothed in black and white for the boy that I loved.

Fancy dress: a wonderful phrase, like parade or charade or gown. It wasn't a phase; it was a protest against the suburbia outside. I dressed up my room too. With eau-de-nil whiplash art nouveau wallpaper and a pewter dish from Liberty's that I found in the garage among my grandfather's rusty old tools. A poster of Beardsley's orange Isolde on the wall. A pale green art deco nude statue and a palm tree that would grow with me as I moved from room to room. A cardboard display from a record shop showing a blue siren crawling on the rocks clad in claws and pearls. How did she get there? What did she eat?

I pull out a pair of boots from the back of the wardrobe, from the nineteen-twenties via a junk shop. I'd dyed them black to look all shiny up to my shins. I'd tuck my jeans into them and walk the streets of Twickenham through the autumn leaves, thinking I looked like someone I'd seen in a magazine. They made me feel invincible. Now they're cracked, the heels worn out. I put them back in the wardrobe and wonder at what I've lost and what I've found. I had no expectations of the time I was living in. I wanted to live before I was born.

I had no idea of who I was or what I wanted to be.

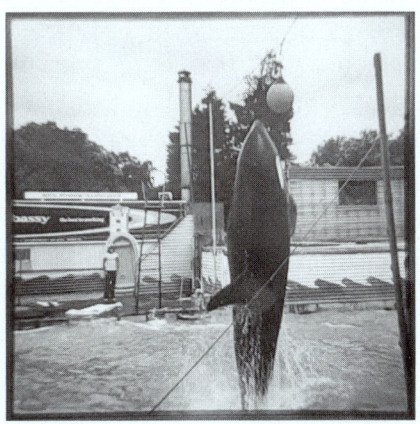

The park is dark and strange, decayed, like the city, like a black pool. Trees hide the statues and paths. People move between the railings and rhododendrons dangerously, like birds. The buildings are tall, on a plane, sliced by northern light.

I arrived late and I've had virtually no sleep. I wake at two am with a headache so intense I think my eyes are about to fall out. I stumble out of the hotel and into empty streets full of people stumbling about. They're looking for another drink. I'm in search of drugs. Something to dampen it all down. I remember how to act in a city, marching straight ahead, ignoring the shouts of abandoned people and boys on their feral bikes. The sky is black. The shop is bright white. I return with my prize and lie down in the darkened room, making out the cracks in the ceiling over my head, waiting for the plaster to fall and the pills to work.

This room is three hundred years old.

I get up and go out again.

The man in the tea shop is demanding a table. It is against the current rules. He shows his papers like a collaborator; he's masked, in disguise like the rest of us. He's tall and blond and old-young, willowy, preserved. He has an English voice and a folded-up paper under his arm. We must show our passports to eat.

He looks familiar, like someone I've seen in a book or a film or on the street. I see him again a few days later on the train, reading the paper. I begin to wonder if all the people in this town are the same, reduced by history to recycling themselves, walking round the block, surprised to see each other again and again.

The tanned women on the tram in their summer frocks. The boys in their football shorts and pink shirts. Everyone striding or lolloping along. Giant poets in the windows of empty banks. Travellers sitting on steps. A Georgian Manhattan or a whaling port or a data start-up, everyone stepping in and out of their lives. The past is always present and never correct.

On the other side of the park the street is wide and empty of cars, then suddenly full of them, then suddenly empty again. I cross over, stop and look up.

The building tips up before me, grey and flat. Monumental like everything else on the square, except for the bright wound in one corner where the shopping precinct is filled with people with placards protesting against the cure. My head feels airy and the building a façade. There might not be anything behind it at all.

I hurry up the steps, worried I'm late. I always run when I can walk, people say. Dead centre over the door, abandoning all hope of anyone ever taking the thorn from his paw, is a dolorous lion, looking down as he sits slumped on a ledge.

He gave up roaring long ago. All those geniuses passing by, they make him want to yawn.

Father Gerard walks in through the big door. He's fresh off the boat. They ferried him over from England. They didn't know what else to do. How do you solve a problem like him? At school his nickname was Skins. Forever jumping in the sea or the river or whatever. Relying on the kindness of strangers on a train. Watching porpoises from the ferry. Those big boyish eyes taking everything in. This city will be his last posting, by the sea.

Anyone else would be pleased. He's in despair.

It was good training, for a poet, to expect the unexpected. One Jesuit was sent to China for the rest of his life with twenty-four hours' notice. Fr Hopkins SJ arrives via Oxford's quads, Roehampton lawns, Welsh mountains and Glasgow slums, coming to rest here in this black city, compressed under his duties and sins, looking like a teenager in a Jesuit gown. He is a skinny slip of a thing; from a distance people think he's a teenage boy. He cuts his hair short with a fringe. He tells his superior he did it to look like Chaucer.

The university is a joke. Decaying salons and cracked plasterwork depicting indecent women. The Jesuits covered them up, putting plaster straps over their busts. The whole place is rotten with the past. It was not built to last. There's no library: the students have to use the one round the corner.

The clock ticks away the emptiness of mid-afternoon. The leaves fall in the park, curling up like your hand.

He gave it all up for this. He used to lunch with Walter Pater, meet Swinburne at the Royal Academy, go back to Simeon Solomon's studio. He wanted to be an artist but was afraid of what he'd see in the life class. He wrote out his sins, crossing them out as he confessed them.

~~Looking at and thinking of stallions. Looking at a man who tempted me.~~
~~Lateness to bed. Looking at Fyffe.~~
~~Fyffe. Wicked feeling.~~
~~Looking at Fyffe.~~
~~Looking at Fyffe.~~
~~Looking at Fyffe.~~
~~Wicked curiosity abt Buchanan and Fyffe.~~

Looking at Fyffe. Looking at a chorister at Magdalen and evil thoughts.
Tempt fr. Fyffe and fr pictures in Blake.

I did much the same, only I didn't cross them out.

Turned on by Blake's bodies and by his fellow students, Hopkins was even wary of getting excited when the family spaniel sat on his lap. He was right to be afraid. Years later, Fyffe—a big handsome cowlike boy who'd played cricket and took female roles in college productions, all dumbly decked out in flowers like a prize breed—would be charged with interfering with a young man on a commuter train going into London. Fyffe tried to cut his throat before his court appearance; he had to be wheeled in with a bandaged neck. Sent to an asylum in Edinburgh, a year later he succeeded in taking his life on the railway track.

Hopkins met Digby Dolben at Oxford, just for one day. Thereafter, he was the only boy he ever loved, though they never met again. Dolben—petulant, intelligent, beautiful; I imagine him played by Rupert Everett—became a priest too, but a rather vainglorious one, displaying his piety by walking miles in his bare feet. Hopkins didn't cry when he heard the news. Dolben had drowned in the river, teaching a boy to swim, the two of them tethered together. Dolben, suffering some kind of attack, began to sink. The boy felt Dolben push him up to the surface. Dolben disappeared. It took hours before his beautiful body was found, dragged up onto the bank, like Ophelia or Narcissus.

A year later Hopkins became a Jesuit. From then on, he could own no books or anything else. It was his lifelong penance.

He is dreaming of leaving even before he gets upstairs. The ebony banisters wind to the top like bones. His last room; at least it has a view. The mountains in the distance, barren and calm.

He puts his black bag down on the table. There hardly seems

any point unpacking. There's nothing in it anyway. He sits on his bed, trying to think of reasons to stay. He had counted on his faith but relied on his art. The things he had to say. At the age of thirty-nine he is little more than a child. In a hundred years' time Elizabeth Taylor will have his work read out at her funeral and his words will appear in A Clockwork Orange. In the meantime the critics declare him a dangerous literary model, as if he were a suspect device.

After he left college, Wilde came back for a stay. He was already famous, even when he was away in America, being famous for being himself. He'd only published one poem. That was enough. Anything more might display too much effort. The residents of Manhattan and Milwaukee didn't want poems anyway. They wanted instructions on how to live from a sleek sophisticate in a seal-and-otter-fur coat (which his brother would later pawn for drink). Back in this strange and dark city, Oscar returned as a star. How that must have hurt everyone, especially his mother, who had been more famous than him.

They owned the tallest house on the square; they made sure of that. It rose up from the dusty street like an aquarium. Its unnecessarily numerous windows were studded with imported glass; ruby red and gold and blue to filter out the grey light and throw a rosy glow over the inside like a womb. Just enough to allow passers-by to wonder what was going on inside.

His father's surgery was on the first floor. It had opposing windows on two sides like lenses, to throw greater light on the eyes he examined there. Eyes came from all over Europe to be looked at. Almost independently of their owners. They might have sent them in cardboard boxes by post. Sir William Wilde's glass cabinet was a bow window with all his instruments on display, a selection showing exactly what he would do to return the light to your eyes, slicing in to let it out. It was said that he took out one patient's eyeball and left it to dangle on his cheek when someone came to the door. Both he and his wife were obsessed with faeries, that sort of thing.

The rooms shrink as you rise up the building. By the time you reach the third floor the doors are two-thirds size. Martin shows me the beam where Oscar must have hit his head as he grew to his full height like a sunflower. Lanky, prone to weight, always turning towards the light.

The attic window is low and squeezes in the grey light. Wilde looks down at a bad statue of himself, sprawled on a rock in the park, peering back up at himself.

At college he wrote Blake's name in his commonplace book and hung Blake's drawings on his wall. Twenty years later, in the darkness of his cell, he quoted Blake in his piteous letter to Bosie, calling forlornly for a new dawn.

When I arrived at the airport I presented my papers, expecting, as I always do, to be sent back on the next plane. I was once backroomed at Newark for having the same name as a wanted man from this place. But this morning the garda just looked at me and the name in my passport and said, Let's have a look at your face now, Patrick.

I took off my mask and he smiled. No one had stretched out the A in my name like that before. Open wide. AAAAA. It had been silent and flat up until now.

Let's have a look at your face now.

An hour before dawn, the train moves through the stations, darting along. I'm the only one awake. The train is keen to get on, but also sleepy at the same time, like its passengers. Keen to get off, I get out and walk along the esplanade.

It's clear where I have to go. There are people with bags slung over their shoulders, going the same way, walking quietly in the dark. It is impossible to get lost. The path gets narrower and narrower and ends in huge boulders tumbling into the sea. Too late to turn back now. We undress by a wall painted white as a ship. There are little puddles of clothes on the bench and lumpy pegs on which to hang our kecks.

My heart skips a beat. Still that tic. Wave-polished rocks thrown out to the bay, dice to decide our fate. More bones than boulders. More brutal than I thought. Land turned round to look at the sea. A port for people, built to tip them in.

The excitement rises inside of me. There's no choice. Down with, out with, in. Rusty banisters lead down a slippery stairway. Heavenly. We might step out onto the seabed below.

There's no flirting here; at least, not with the sea. No humming or haaing or hanging about or dipping your toes or splashing your face. Either you're in or you aren't. Here one moment, gone the next. From Sandycove station to another green world. The water rises up, sucks me in.

There are no instructions. No one tells you what to do. It is perfectly obvious to wrinkly old people and pale young people, all our bones all the same underneath, all dashing to get our kit off, to be borne up and carried off, held up by the swell as it surges in and out. The tide has only one demand: yield up all earthly control. Why do something once when you can do it again? After nine months when the only animate thing that touched me was a jellyfish who wrapped their tentacles around my belly in the sea, leaving me with a red welt like a love bite, I'd forgotten how exciting it is to be human.

Summer 1876. I ride sometimes after six, Oscar tells Bouncer, his friend. I don't do much but bathe, he says; and although always feeling slightly immortal when in the sea, he feels sometimes slightly heretical when good Roman Catholic boys enter the water with little amulets and crosses round their necks and arms that the good S. Christopher may hold them up. He goes to bed reading S. Thomas à Kempis. Gets up and does it all over again.

I hope Gerard pulled off his jumper on these stones, kicked off his sandals and socks and, drawn in by the shouts, lowered his puny body into the water.

Today at the Forty Foot it's somebody's birthday. A circle of women sing in the dark at six am. Sloshing and swishing about. Stephen Dedalus saw a priest in a loincloth down there, his tonsured head marking him out from above. This is the centre of my world, the place I was destined to come. I waited to be invited, and so I came. This deep dark green hole in the world, waiting for me to fall in. I might come out the other side, somewhere completely different, someone completely different, the me I was waiting to find.

By night the gulls come wheeling into the city to wreak their revenge. They cry through the night, bringing the sea with them, to fill in the gaps in the street. The city could turn avian at any point: cormorants perching on the library dome, streaking the dull lead with their white shit; oystercatchers pecking outside the oyster bars; terns plucking tufts of hair from passing students' heads.

I draw my curtains like the Queen of Scots' bed. The ceiling is definitely cracked. The gulls argue through the night. I buy a bike.

The university lies at the end of a line of semi-detached houses, after a long ride during which I stop regularly to ask for directions, mostly for the pleasure of doing so in a place that has not forgotten its manners and where greetings sound less like a threat and more like a promise. The library rises in concrete over a turbid ornamental lake, an inland sea slowly going green.

Up here on the top floor, Hopkins's letters have been sealed in plastic as if to waterproof them. I turn them over like tarot cards. They tell his fortune.

By the bye, he tells Robert Bridges, as he writes from this watery city; by the bye, some geologists say, he goes on, the last end of all continents and dry land altogether is to be washed into the sea and that when all are gone 'water will be the world', as in the Flood, will still be deep and have to spare.

I work steadily through the pathetic pile of pleas and asser-
tions and one-sided arguments. His writing grows steadily
smaller as life bears down on him. His words shrink till they
are confined to cards smaller than a packet of ten cigarettes,
inscribed in script so microscopic that it has almost vanished,
like him. I can barely read them at all.

. . . you will no doubt understand what I mean by saying
that the <u>sordidness</u> of things,
wh. one is compelled perpetually
to feel, is per-
haps

Then he crosses it all out.

~~By all means come to-~~
~~morrow. I too am per-~~
~~ishing of a cold, let us~~
~~call it a catarrh/ I~~
~~left Sunday letters at~~
~~both clubs sending this~~
~~I suppose they are not~~
~~delivered~~

Crossing out is the most modern thing he can do.

I put him back in his folder and fold him away. I wanted to
write a book about him, how as a young man in England he
had visited the shore where I swim and the abbey nearby; how
as a schoolboy I read his poems and saw the world through his
eyes; how he loved to swim in the river and the sea. But there
were just too many sins that escaped him, and I was afraid of
what I might find. I was afraid of his last, darkest poems, afraid
of myself.

No worst, there is none. Pitched past pitch of grief,

he wrote,

all

Life death does end and each day dies with sleep.

He tells Bridges about James Gannon, a former pupil from their Jesuit school, Clongowes Wood, outside the city, now a medical student in Dublin, who went into a field between the canal and the railway and tore out his eyes with his fingers and a piece of wire then threw them in the nettles. He was found staggering about, covered with blood in an awful state of agony, the news-paper said. He was conveyed to the Mater Misericordiae hospital, but the reason for the act the unfortunate young fellow had not disclosed. The police found his eyes in the ditch, two feet apart.

> Pull out his eyes,
> Apologise,

Dedalus was told as a boy.

Back at the hotel I eat food from my drawer. Is the crack in my ceiling getting bigger? I fall asleep in it.

This city makes me want to cry. Like I've been here before. I ride out before dawn, past the grubby stucco terrace where Oscar was born with its inconsequential plaque. No sign of an alien visitation on the doorstep. They all came down this street. Wilde, Hopkins, Yeats, Beckett; Bacon was born up the road. So many geniuses to the square mile. Can't have them getting above themselves. The city confers these privileges. It can take them away again.

The first square green train of the morning runs slowly onto the platform as if it were still waking up. A woman says her prayers to a video on her phone, crossing herself and mouthing the words. The windows are black. From trains you can see the guts of a place, houses from behind, all the rubbish dumped round the back. How dozy youths put their feet on the seats, how pink is the colour for boys this year, how the empires of the new reality are doing, not from headlines, because people no longer have them to hide behind, but from the buildings going up and down to house new memories once the old ones have been destroyed. But in the darkness I can see none of that.

Sandymount

Every station is announced like a surprise. The poet wrote me a postcard from here about *Moby-Dick*; the big fella, he called him. There's a whale bone arch at the end of his street, giant jaws tied tight at the top with blue nylon rope to keep them quiet. The power station chimneys like rugby goalposts. This place is pulling me in.

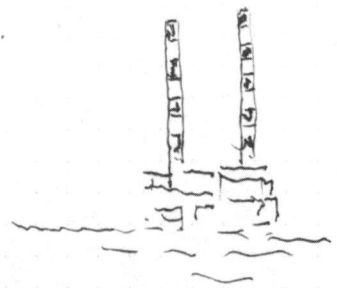

Uh-oh. There it is again. Waiting for me.

The sea, thrown round the bay. The cormorants on the rocks, guarding it with their sea-dragon wings.

The distant headland tips its mist into the sea. The measure of how the day will be. I ask myself idle questions as we roll along in the dark. What comes out of those chimney stacks? Where exactly did Hopkins die? Who held his hand?

Blackrock

Getting closer. The water's the colour of a roof.

The pterodactyls slide slyly under the waves.

Sandycove & Glasthule

6:31:30

Seachain an bhearna, le do thoil

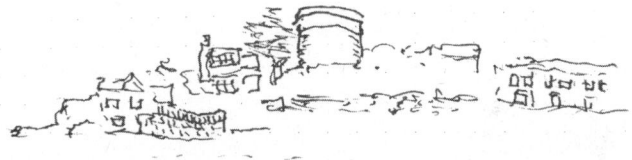

Afterwards my hand shakes from the cold as I try to write on the train. The words look lovely, like a seismograph, jagged with breath. I try to explain to myself something about the place. The unprettiness of it, the pragmatic people, their bones, the history like the sea so old. None of your, is it cold?

Eyes, pale as the sea the wind had freshened, says Dedalus, paler, firm and prudent. He watches a young man move his legs like a frog in the water. They're green, like the deep jelly, he says.

The time flickers on the digital display in the stations as we pass. The crack in my ceiling is getting bigger. I'm getting older by the minute. I forget who I was.

I cycle out of the city to arrive halfway through morning Mass. I sit at the back. There are no disapproving looks over shoulders. It's Friday and no one has to be here. The church is full of saints. A pair of confessionals at the back. Cupboards stacked with sins and omissions. At the end of Mass the monstrance is brought out. The rays of God. We all fall to our knees. The faithful sing a prayer they know by heart. It appears old and strange to me. Afterwards I ask the man clearing the altar if I could have a word with Father. The man takes me to a side door and shows me backstage.

Father is taking off his vestments. As he turns into an ordinary person again, he directs a parishioner to unlock a cabinet, and out come the big red books. I trace my finger across the page, as another priest wrote it in sepia ink, a century before I was born.

14 May 1856. There I am, dead and alive in a book.

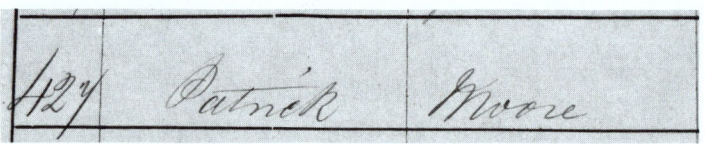

Newly baptised. The names I was born with. My great-grandfather, my namesake, born in the Lower Road. I ask where that is. They tell me it's called the Strawberry Beds. It sounds strange, romantic. It is a dark wooded valley, I discover, just out of town; steep, river-run, low cottages hidden among its trees. It doesn't feel like the twentieth, let alone the twenty-first century.

I find the house on the hill where Patrick Moore was born. Two rooms, three windows, one door. Eleven members of my family ate and slept and procreated there. It was made from mud dredged up from the river, down there, where I just swam. Inside, I can almost touch both walls without moving. Where did they sleep? What did they eat? They put the boys in the loft, I'm told. I say another prayer.

In the pub overlooking the weir, there is a beam dated 1588. I arrive with my sisters and we meet people related to us. Separated by a century or more. One of them, who looks so much like my younger sister that people gasp when they meet, produces a photograph. It seems impossible. It shows our family, outside their cottage at the end of the nineteenth century. They had lived there since Blake lived in London. The pub, owned by our cousins, appears in *Finnegans Wake*. When they went into town they could have passed Wilde and Yeats and Joyce in the street. They would have said a prayer for Fr Hopkins at mass when he passed away.

In the photograph, our uncles and aunts—they look like us and we look like them, the same bones—are arrayed around our great-great-grandmother, Rose, a widow these past twenty years; her husband Denis, who worked as a blacksmith and had a brown dog, had died of bronchitis and asthma in this damp valley. Rose sits as a matriarch, limbs outstretched, as if they all came out of her womb. She was born in 1821, six years before Blake died. Portland Row. Standing behind is my great-uncle Willie, with an ivy leaf in his lapel. It shows his loyalty to Parnell, who had died in 1891. In front of him is his sister, my great-aunt Lizzie. She will die, unmarried, in 1947 at St Joseph's Asylum for Aged and Virtuous Females, Portland Row. The formality they present—a wedding group, perhaps from the young couple's buttonholes and their Sunday best—is almost a parody of the rich people who live in the big houses on the hill and own all the land around. All they own, it seems, is the bowl of cherries in the young woman's lap, and the potted plant in the little boy's hands.

Patrick, Rose's younger son, left before this photograph was taken. An unprodigal son, sailing away to work as a coachman and a fisherman in Whitby, where my grandfather was born; then to the mills of Saltaire, where my father was born; then to Bradford, where the mills were darker and more satanic, before ending his working life as a gardener to another wealthy family. He died on New Year's Day 1936 in St Joseph's Home. His heart and his lungs had given up.

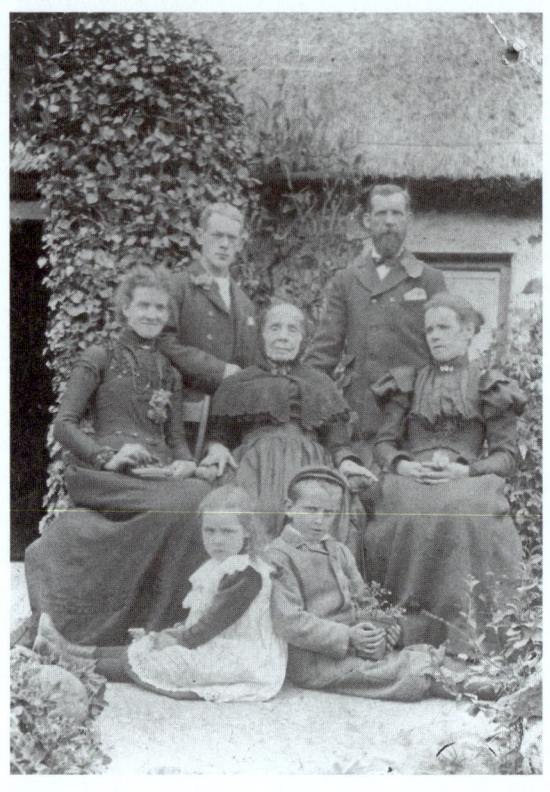

In the little chapel of ease up the mass path, past the holy well let into the hillside, my sister finds a brass plaque fixed to a pew, engraved with Rose and Denis's names. With my name, Patrick Kevin Moore, the most Irish thing I could possess, you'd think I would have worked out all this belonging long ago. Patrick, Pádraig, sending the snakes away. Kevin, Caomhín, standing in his lough to pray. Swimming in the brown rivers of Wicklow and the grey waters of Bray. Just look at you, someone says. My Irish eyes and bones. But our father never spoke of his family back in Ireland. It was not respectable to be Irish in England; he came south to leave all that behind. I realise now that when our three-bedroom house was filled with eleven people too, it was an echo of how his family had lived, even though it meant he had to shave over the kitchen sink where we were bathed as children.

I preferred it to the bath because the water was less scarily deep, and because my mother was near. It was strange to be as shy as I was, in such a big family. Perhaps that's why I kept so many secrets. The only private space I had was my bed.

I prayed to the statue of glorious St Patrick in our church as the serpent squirmed beneath his feet. Alien clumps of shamrock appeared in a box at the back of the church on his feast day like divine seaweed, magical talismans to keep the devil at bay. We sang about being true to thee till death and I wore green, not blue. I still do. Let's have a look at your face. The little boy in the photograph, holding his potted plant. Aunt Lizzie living on, alone in that little cottage overlooking the river, while Bryan and Diana Guinness listen to *Finnegans Wake* on the gramophone in their stately home up on the hill.

Leaving Hopkins's room, where they burned his papers in the black grate as soon as they could in a rite of purification, I ride over the river and up the hill, past betting shops and barbers and the pillared church where they left his body outside and took an empty coffin in for fear he would infect the mourners with his disease. Poor Fr Gerard. So shy he didn't even attend his own funeral.

In the bright white gallery down the hill, founded by Hugh Lane, they reassembled the deeply ordered chaos, as Francis Bacon called it, of his studio.

When I'm dead, he said, put me in a plastic bag and throw me in the gutter. Stand in this diorama and you place yourself in his place. All that ash and trash, all those ripped-up photographs of handsome men and women and beasts. From Muybridge's studies of motion to the *Sunday Times Magazine*. A bombsite of art, an explosion of sins; some weird seabed.

Among the great waves of paint and blackness, the slabs of light and bodies squeezed out of tubes like soft cheese, his sitter victims sit freeze-framed in fluorescent cages. Businessmen in suits, lovers in Y-fronts. There might be any kind of animal in there with them, scrabbling and foraging in their own waste.

Bacon trips down the stairs, closes the door behind him and gets on the bus, giving me a stare as it pulls off.

I alone saw him. His florid face, his fish-shot eyes.

Born in Dublin, round the corner from Wilde, he grew up next door to Clongowes Wood College, south of the city. Joyce and Hopkins walked down those dark avenues of beeches, past the lush green aprons of playing fields, into the gothic buildings. I went to a school like that as a scholarship boy. The corridors patrolled by grown men in dusty black cassocks and crucifixes round their necks, leather straps hanging on their office walls ready to punish any misdemeanour; the big white house next door where Jane Austen was a visitor. Our secular English master, a harried man in Harris tweed jacket with leather patches on its elbows, setting us to read Joyce's book where first I read that strange name, Clongowes Wood, and the weird sing-song beginning with a nicens little boy named baby tuckoo and Stephen Dedalus wetting the bed.

It never struck me as odd that we should be taught such a subversive book in such a place. It was where we read Hopkins's poetry too, only dimly aware that his hovering kestrel had anything to do with Jesus Christ. And it was where I read The Tyger, in that classroom with its windows to the corridors that kept us under permanent surveillance. Blake's dreams seemed even stranger to me, creating a dark animal with glittering eyes that had a power beyond anything human. It was the first verse I ever learned by heart. I had no idea it was about revolution; but I sort of felt it, anyway. Long-dead people and their words registered because I always felt out of place in the places I was supposed to be. I had no idea that two of those people, the priest-poet and the sinful boy, existed in the same time and space; that Hopkins had often visited the school at the same time that the young Joyce was there. That they would have passed each other in the same places but in different worlds.

Clongowes Wood rises on the road ahead of me at the end of a long ride. It smells exactly the same as my school. The boys are the same boys in their uniforms. As I wait in the hall, two or three come out to see if there are any packages from home. They leave empty handed. I'm led to the library where my reward is brought out of a drawer: a battered photograph on a cracked, torn piece of cardboard of people who look just like the people who taught me. It is the last image of Fr Hopkins. He sits in the front row, to the right of the rector, hanging his head as if it had become too heavy. He holds his own hands. It looks as though one of his eyes has been blacked out.

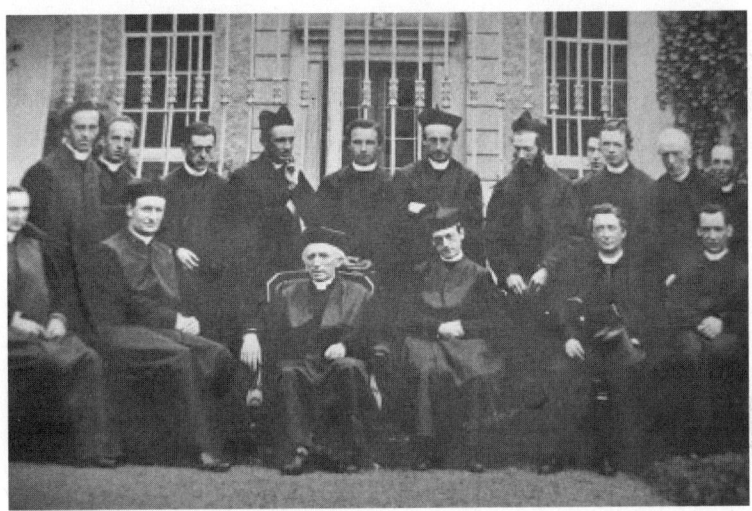

We never really went to school, Bacon recalled. I don't know whether that's a good thing or a bad thing. I'm not Irish, unfortunately, he said, but I'm very attached to Ireland. Yeats and Joyce are my greatest literary influences, he said. They created stronger images than any thing that I saw, he said.

He grew up there, in that green outland out of Dublin, but stayed oddly the same with his big round face in the big square house. His father trained racehorses and his mother threw parties. Francis spent his time in the stables, full of boys and

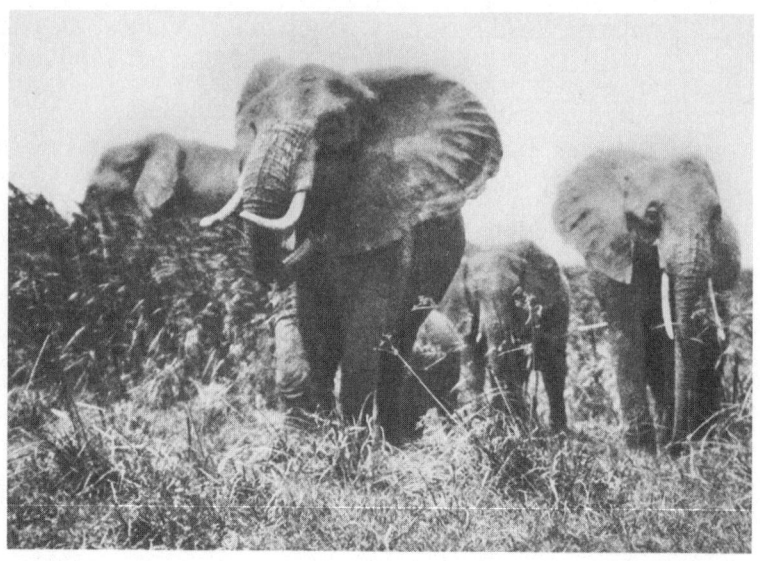

men with whips. Next door Stephen Dedalus was pandied with leather-covered whalebone; Francis was whipped for dressing up in his mother's underwear. As an adult he sold his body through personal ads in The Times. He lived by petty theft and living off other people, he said. His Irish nanny still lived with him. She'd go out shoplifting when they got poor.

As a boy he had pored over Marius Maxwell's book, Stalking Big Game with a Camera in Equatorial Africa, published in 1924. It was a manual of extinction: animals advertising their beauty in order to die in shame. Maxwell's silver camera snaps scenes of beasts from the dominions. Having shot them with his camera, he takes up his gun and shoots them again. They rise, fall, die, rise, fall and die again. As advertised. Men get excited by such things.

Picking up my 0.600 bore, Maxwell reports, I emptied both barrels in rapid succession on the biggest bull.

He falls as if injected, the way an epidural makes you buckle under yourself as you fall out of bed; the way Chunee fell to his knees as the soldiers spent their lead on him.

Bewildered at first, the other elephants crowded aimlessly round the carcase of their fallen leader, Maxwell says, until they finally moved away in sedate and stately fashion. Honour in death. When he visits Africa as a young man, Bacon will acquire a dozen whips made of rhino hide, for his hide to be beaten.

Maxwell's book becomes a pattern of Bacon's art; Francis, patron saint of dead animals. The black-and-white plates betray the source of his beasts as he copied them in his paintings. Photographs were more real than real things. A poet ought not to pick nature's pocket, Samuel Taylor Coleridge advised; let him borrow, and so borrow as to repay by the very act of borrowing. Examine nature accurately, but write from recollection, and trust more to your imagination than to your memory.

The preface to Maxwell's book is written by Sidney Harmer of the Natural History Museum. The curator grandly extols the explorer's enterprise as an expression of Sport in its highest form. In the future, Harmer maintains, when perhaps the animals of which Maxwell gives faithful portraits will have become extinct, the value of his services will be even more

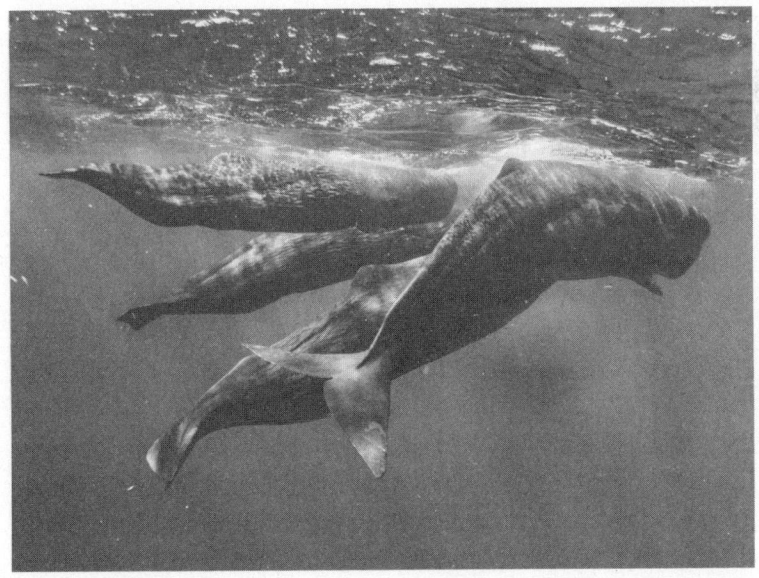

appreciated. During the Great War Harmer had invited the press to the museum to eat a dolphin that had stranded in the Thames. It was a way of addressing wartime shortages. Harmer's preface was an epitaph for the shadows on the veldt. Jeroen sends me his picture of grand hooded phantoms from the Caribbean. Their sea has just been declared a sanctuary, but it's a bit late for apologies. Someone suggests talking to them using AI, but we don't have a good record when it comes to first contact, and anyway, what would we say?

Summer 1966. I'm at primary school, innocent with a pudding-bowl haircut on my big head, excited to write the date that our teacher tells us will never happen again in our lives: 6/6/66. In London, Bacon is a priest dressed in existential black; Left Bank in South Kensington, polo-neck from Marks & Spencer. His carefully coiffured quiff is an extravagant affront to the chaos that lies around him. His studio bed is a raft washed up on a tide of images torn out of books and his head. Dirt and paint and rags and ideas and rejected canvases to be slashed with the Stanley knife he kept ready in his pocket like his dodgy friends from the East End. It comes up to his knees, this tsunami of trash. A compost heap of newsprint and paint. The underlying violence is his art. He's hiding behind it.

London sprawls in dirty stucco. Dirt finely laid everywhere, in your lungs and up your nose. Up the walls. Its buildings still blackened with centuries of soot, rubbed in like grit in a wound. Cities are unfair wherever you go. South Ken is a slum, a sepulchre, and Bacon is Sally Bowles: his tarty face. Pushes up his sleeves to show off his meaty arms. He's surprisingly thin yet somehow chubby; tall, faintly hunched like his portraits. The beaten, defensive slope of his shoulders, the weight of his big head. His dealer says he was not the same shape as any other human being, there was the sense of an aura about him—something radiant, he said. Keith Vaughan attested to his ardour and natural grace, his extraordinary physical beauty—supple—gentle—sensuous.

He gave up the lipstick before the war; apocalypse rendered red lips obsolete. But the memory remains like a smear, like a cure and he still pats his hamster cheeks with pancake make-up like George and Marilyn in the Wolseley, handing round the powder puff to thrill the diners. He coaxes his quiff into tumescence with boot polish. He says he wants to paint a mouth like a Monet. They put artists in warehouses and mews because they make too much mess.

In the corner of Bacon's stable-room, he sits on his bed, a divan covered by a dark green silk tapestry from Morocco, as if he were in a brothel window in Amsterdam, the painter for sale, his own model. He leans back on one elbow, a Freudian odalisque, mid-dialogue, smokes a series of Gitanes, recreating the swirls on the packet. The thin white smoke spirals up to his quiff. Byron in slacks and silk socks, a hyena on a dirt road.

I want a very ordered image, he declares, in his plummy voice, but I want it to come about by chance.

That's why he loves casinos. They're still illegal, and they leave everything left to chance, like his art. He doesn't believe he will live too long. Harrowed, toxic South Ken is still going on outside, post-war grey. It's still the same when I get there ten years later. Summoned to my lofty agent's lofty office, he tells me, through a cloud of Senior Service, that no, it's not Earl's Court. He was Waugh's last editor and his great advice to me is that you spell it c-a-r-c-a-s-e. Over lunch he nods conspiratorially about the stories and says he was like that once.

I watch the bus pull away, Bacon's vivid face in the dark well of its door. He fixes his eye on me across the street as he stands there with his hand wrapped round the white pole, as if he might dance for me in the morning.

One wants a thing to be as factual as possible, he stresses, sprawling his aristo-drawl over the adjective, drawing it out with the smoke, and at the same time, he goes on, telling his audience, a single black-clad critic in a crumpled suit perched on the other end of the bed like a corpulent crow, as deeply suggestive, he stresses, or deeply <u>unlocking</u> of areas of sensation <u>other</u> than simple illustration of the object that you set out to do.

Do you see?

The reflexive phrase of his class, expressing condescension, politely. I murmur.

He takes another drag of his cigarette, curls one leg behind the other twice as an actor with big blue Irish eyes would do for me, sitting on a banquette twisting round on himself.

Bacon's body is a coquettish come-on for the camera; he has all the charisma there is in the room. He sucks it all up the way stars do. He's a black hole and they all said they always knew he was going to be famous, as if he was just doing it to please them. It's all the same to him. Balancing his big wobbly head and those big watery eyes, he says the words you are longing to hear, delivered from that dishevelled bed:

Isn't that what all art is about?

You'd expect the camera would stop at that point, out of respect. But it just keeps on rolling as if he were advertising margarine. The critic at the other end of the bed balances out Bacon on the seesaw divan. So little stability in this world. That's why he throws frames round his subjects like cages for hawks.

The two men cling to the mattress for dear life. Sylvester, the critic, like as big cat, lights his next fag from the last, shifting his weight so as not to fall off. An importunate suitor at the artist's feet in an unpressed suit. Bacon knows he's being weighed up. It's historic. He's made up. Complicit, artist and critic.

And isn't that in a way, Bacon goes on—

Sylvester sat for his portrait once, until he realised Bacon's attention was fixed on the photograph of a rhino's grey skin

—Isn't that why, Bacon goes on, that abstract art has to always remain on one level, because it is entirely the aesthetic sense of the artist that is involved?

The whole scenario: a bedsit blur of Victorian poses and Renaissance popes and leather jackets, instant coffee and powdered milk in the galley kitchen (Rothko's was the same, albeit all tidy and tucked away as if he were on a boat); the absence of any real possessions at all other than paint, squeezed out and used up and tossed aside like contraceptives. The ravishing decadent restraint of an ascetic who spent his casino gains on a week in a villa stocked with good food and wine and lots of friends who lasted for about the same time.

We know where all this would end up, as it always does. His beady stare from the bus, his raptor eye fixed on me from the platform, that eye flickering up and down. Editing his life as it went along, cutting out the bad bits with that Stanley knife whipped out for a little artistic violence. The Brando of art.

Isn't that what art is all about?

He's deluding himself, he does it very well. His mews is cobbled for horses. He feels at home there, back in Kildare. Stable boys, unstable boys, mad dogs. Trips down the stairs, hauling himself up the rope banister, pissed again. He's a priest, everything's allowed.

You see, the very fact of being born is a very ferocious thing, he says. Unless you put a veil between yourself and life, it is just filled, really, with suffering and despair.

The bus pulls away. While he was out at the Colony Room, entertaining his sham friends, his real friends crept into his studio and moved it all back to Ireland.

On the shelf, next to a cracked mirror, is a plaster cast of Blake's life mask. Bacon painted the original floating against inky black, all drawn mouth and clamped eyes, an alien in real life, a silenced pope of art. He claims to hate Blake's paintings but loves his poetry. Blake hangs in the velvet fluidity, heart beats up love. Jarman passes Bacon on Old Compton Street. They both have posh voices. Jarman hopes he will still be wearing a leather jacket at that age. Something else to hide behind. Soho, the same psycho-arena for Blake's performance, and mine. All those gutter. All those stars.   Pl XIV

I think that if I'd been born later, rather than trying to paint, Bacon says, I'd have attempted to make films.

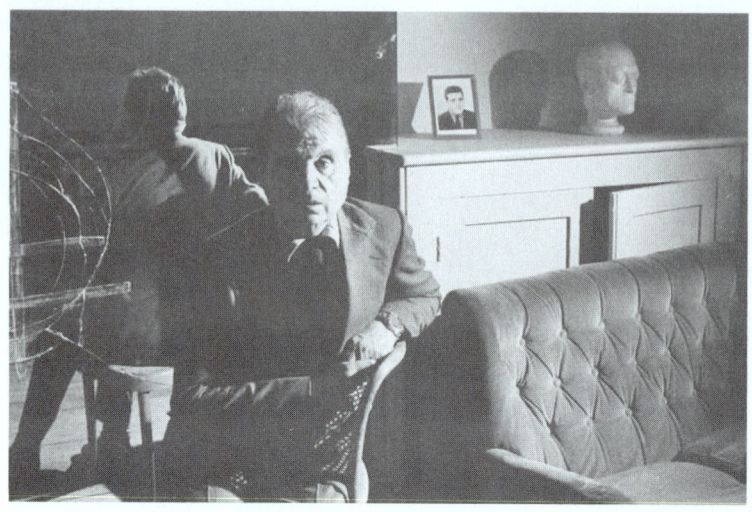

In the back room of the gallery, Blake's precious head is lifted out of the box, everyone's darling. His life mask was made in 1823 to enable a phrenologist to examine the artist's skull and discern the source of his imaginative flare.

He grimaces with the slapped-on plaster, breathing through straws, the way the starman snorted as he called for tissues to wipe his eyes. Bacon succumbed to the same procedure, lying absolutely still for an hour for the sake of immortality. Like going to the barber's for a shave. As the cast came away from Blake's face, so did a few hairs.

Now it stands on a pedestal of its own, this weird paperweight; an unhanged man, an unshrunken head. There's a dab of outrageous lilac on his plaster cheek; Bacon-pink, like glam-rock make-up. He'd smear Max Factor on his face in the mirror to get the right blurred effect for his portraits.

Blake's eyes bulge under their lids, looking through the blood vessels, bursting to open again. You can see how big they really were, like flowers. You can see why his disciple George Richmond closed them. They were just too powerful. The pressure of the plaster tugs at Blake's features like a plastic bag. Cling-filmed, pushing out of the womb, fully formed; his own 3D-printed memorial, the way I used to make papi-er-mâché masks, ripping up the evening paper, all those classified ads and football results telling me the way I was supposed to live, all torn to pieces and pasted onto a polysty-rene dummy for wigs. The soggy mush dried into a thin imitation of a face which I painted with streaks of enamel paint, sticking on slashes of gold foil from a chocolate bar. I carefully cut two holes for eyes and held it up to my face, then hung it on the wall. Getting old, you are forced to parody yourself, your age as your disguise.

Yeats claimed no one could look at Blake's mask without seeing that he was an Irishman. I draw it quickly in my little black book before they take him away, for fear his face should grow faint and fade.

For a moment he hovers there like a saint. I'm his disciple and his smile serene. I feel I ought to kneel in adoration or, as the staff turn their backs, bend down and kiss his cheek, to see his eyelids flicker open, those big blue eyes staring back.

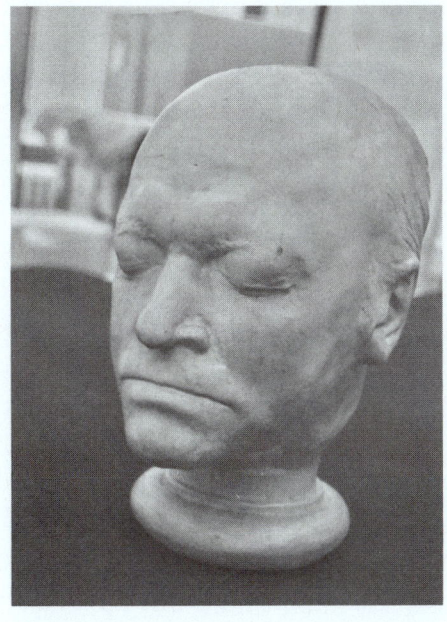

In the museum across the road from my room, five bodies slumber in separate chambers, curled up in climate-controlled glass cells. Discreetly surrounded by circular wooden enclosures to protect their dignity, they lie there, hushed out of the world as silently as they came into it.

Or at least, bits of them do, these blackened bags of bones and sinews pulled out of the bog; Irish, the surprise of death still on their faces. Their sleep exceeds Enitharmon's or Orlando's. They've been dozing for two thousand years.

Oldcroghan Man was old at twenty-five. He stood naked and six foot six inches tall, towering like a god. He threw up his arm in self-defence as the knife entered his chest. Then they chopped him in half and cut off his head. His twisted armlet of leather and bronze is still wrapped round his bicep, defiantly; but his nipples were removed so no one could suck on them and demonstrate their loyalty to a king. It was a tradition: St Patrick was asked to do it by the captain of a boat he was boarding to prove he was in good faith. It's a novel way to catch a ferry.

No one could suck on Oldcroghan now. He was composted deep in the peat of the past like a crow, down there in the dark, his suntanned skin turning into tannined hide. Like other offerings to the gods, these remains were never intended to be retrieved or see the light again. The label says so as it displays them for all to see. I walk into each enclosure in turn and stand over the contorted human assemblies gathered up in their cosy moorland nests. The lights are dimmed to allow them to doze, like a premature ward rather than the end, the intensive care where they twisted my mother's hair up into a knot. I look at each one only once, then I turn round and walk away.

In a nearby vitrine, on full view to the school groups as they career past, is a wooden post. It's roughly carved with elongated arms, legs clenched and knees bent. A head with deep gashes for eyes, a block for a nose. The mouth is full and pursed, almost sewn shut. A dumb expression, full of defiance.

I can't stop looking at it. The wood is hacked about, pitted and scarred; charred by time, dark as basalt or jet. A totem, a mask on a stick, cracked like an actor's face. The whole thing is barely a metre high but it looms as a giant statue or a machine from far away. The label says it acted as a boundary marker, but it could be a fetish made to order or a water god pushing up from the marsh. I draw it again and again but the face just seems to blur and change. I end up with a scratchy mess.

As I leave the museum, passing rooms of ancient gold, I lean over the desk of the attendant at the door and tell her how amazing it all is.

Yes, she says, smiling, adding, and it's all ours.

Everything, I realise, is already fossilised, all these scenes I'm showing you, dug up for our pleasure at their expense. Our plastic bottle tops in future strata as ammonites. I think of the teeth in my skull as exposed bones, the beast beneath my skin. You couldn't tell my shape, unskinned, unleathern, flayed.

I cycle back up the hill to the cemetery and pace down the plots, following the coordinates I've been given, the latitude and longitude of the long and the recently dead. It takes me a while to find what I'm looking for, weaving my way through all the angels standing upright in stone like lighthouses. I park my bike and watch from a distance as a burial party, all tugged-together suits and skirts, gather round an open grave, murmuring along with the priest's prayers. They're all trying to ignore the big hole in the ground. You might chuck anything in there. I find the spot nearby. It's marked with a cross and the words St Joseph's, Portland Row and four columns of names. Fr Conmee passes by, saying a prayer for them. Dozens of them, all aged and virtuous, laid in the same grave. And there is Aunt Lizzie, part of the consignment for 1947. Dying on charity, no one left to wear an ivy leaf for her. But she's lying next door to Fr Hopkins in his Jesuit pit. I imagine him popping across to borrow a cup of sugar. Aunt Lizzie was always ready to help her neighbours.

Then I go down to swim at the cove as the sun comes out and there's a lady drying herself next to me. She's elderly, as they say, which is to say she's older than me. She has long hair. As we both shiver from the sea, we see the cracks of each other's bodies, carelessly as her towel flicks away. She tells me she used to teach English in a Limerick school; her favourite was Yeats.

I'm a spinster, she says, twisting up her hair. That's a nice word, I reply. I'm a bachelor, I say. Today it is her birthday, she says. I wish her many happy returns. Various scenarios run through our heads. The train runs by. A cloud passes and the sun comes out again to make us good and dry.

1967. Peter Beard arrives from New York with his photographs of dead elephants in his book. It's called *The End of the Game*. Handsome, wealthy, well read and well connected (Warhol, the Jaggers, Jackie O), at seventeen he was taken on safari by Quentin Keynes, eccentric explorer son of Geoffrey Keynes. He likes to quote from Blake's *Marriage of Heaven and Hell*: You never know what is enough unless you know what is more than enough. He lives on Montauk Point at the end of Long Island, where he has a diving board installed at the edge of the hundred-foot cliff. He walks out to the end, it's a daredevil act. He is the most handsome man Bacon has ever seen. He paints him, again and again.

> Versions of Bodies into other Bodies.
> Making of new Species.
> Transplanting of one Species into another.
> Force of the Imagination, either upon another Body, or upon the Body itself.
> Making rich Composts for the Earth.
>
> Sir Francis Bacon, *New Atlantis*, 1627

Art is the ordering and disordering of all things. The way we make it out of our skin and bones and flesh and stones and thoughts in proportion to our presence on earth. Francis relishes his queer ancestor in black bombazine, whose rationality so enraged Blake. The tide of trash on his studio floor steadily rises. Continually building and continually decaying like this city, as Blake says, as my friend George reminds me. Briefly exiled to a cottage in the country, Bacon can't bear all those birds singing in the morning. To hell with them, he says, crawling back to town. He thinks man is nothing more or less than an animal. And there's no one more unnatural than me, he says.

David Sylvester says his friend is the religious priest of an atheistic age.

Man realises that he's an accident and his futility, that he's a completely futile being, that he has to play out the game without reason, Bacon replies.

March 1972. Bacon and Beard sit on a rooftop in Limehouse, the East End, overlooking the Thames. They're talking about dead elephants. They could be talking about dead whales. The river is lined with empty barges and dead-eyed warehouses.

Beard says London and New York are the real wildernesses. Wasn't A Clockwork Orange set in this city?

Bacon says the places he lives in are his autobiography, memory tracks of himself. He likes perfection, but also damage. Like bones left in the sea or the sand.

The river runs on.

Back in his studio, he tries to explain his fascination for old photographs. All those people thought they were eternal, but soon they would be swept away, like the elephants.

Sepia people walking in the streets.

Now they're all dead, he said.

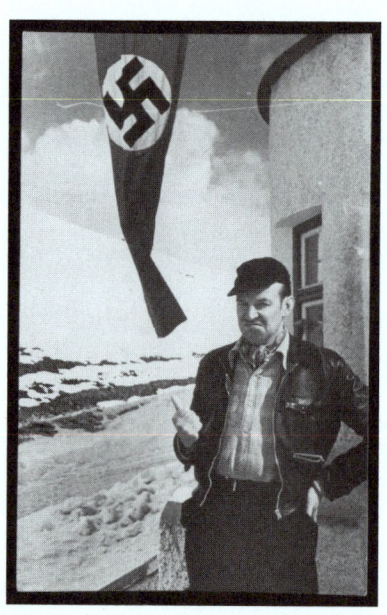

March 1938. John Banting stands in the Tyrolean snow on the eve of the Anschluss. He's wearing a leather jacket and a po'boy cap, expressing distaste for the flag behind him with a dismissive thumb and a mocking grimace. He and his friends Nancy Cunard and Brian Howard oppose everything. They're irresistibly foreign: European, even American in their ambition to be different. All better alternatives to the Home Counties and going home on your own.

Banting, Irish by descent and surreal by choice, dyes his hair green and paints toes on his shoes. Howard, American parents, part Jewish, wears rather good Oxford bags. His alter ego, Anthony Blanche in *Brideshead Revisited*, paints his toenails the same colour as the Duchesse du Vincennes. Divine decadence. He recites *The Waste Land* from a balcony through a megaphone and addresses the rather juicy leader of a gang of hearties who try to duck him in the college fountain.

My dear, I may be inverted, but I am not insatiable. Come back when you are *alone*.

He carries a bottle of cheap perfume in his pocket and if anyone abuses him in the street, he dabs it behind their ears, saying, Now that you smell like a tart, your arguments carry *very* little weight, don't you think? He is an inveterate instigator of illicit performances; in 1949, he will introduce Francis Bacon to the Colony Room, a couple of streets away from the Chevalier d'Éon's salon. He wears Visconti fancy dress; sultry eyes look great framed by a ruff. He's a modern poet. He wants to abandon the purple mists. A little less Mallarmé, a little more Blake?— don't you think? He adores *The Marriage of Heaven and Hell*. They all hate fascism. They're not taking any of that shit.

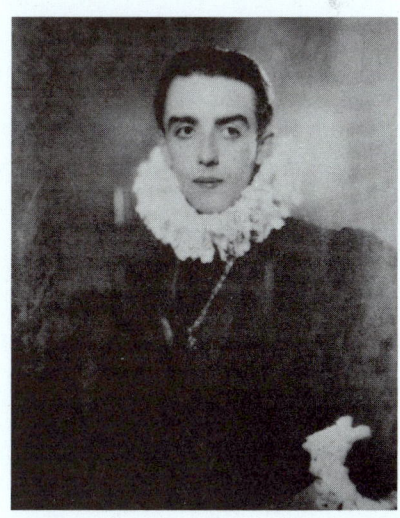

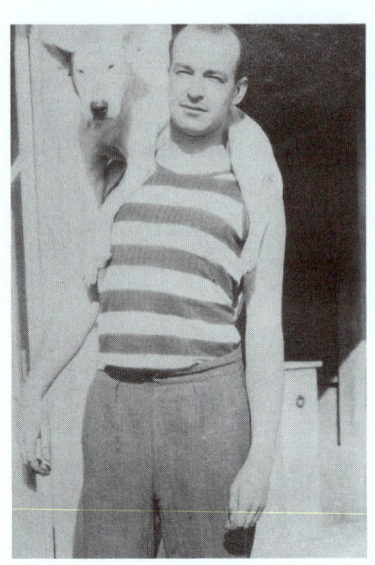

Banting is a wild creature, according to Eileen Agar. She says he dances all night in nightclubs then gets the tube home to his mother's house in the suburbs. He shaves his head and wears a bull terrier round his neck. It's a good look. Ruff-ruff. He's also inclined to Stalinism. Nancy Cunard says he's her Irish brother. Queer and tough. He rages against war memorials, says Humphrey Spender, becomes hysterically abusive in their presence. Arrested for stealing their geraniums, he's jailed for three days, which he finds very interesting.

He's a great dancer. Smokes hashish and tells Spender that Cab Calloway's Kickin' the Gong Around is actually about opium and cocaine. His calling card—he does a little interior decor on the side—is a poem by Hopkins or an album note for a dream home. I have wasted my life, he would say, years later—I mean that I have not contributed to your silly civilisation (Jesus would spit on it).

He's still protesting. He admits to being swept up in those wild parties of the Bright Young People. Admittance was by your good looks, true bi-sexual behaviour, fearless drinking (and later on occasional drugs), he says.

Livid cosomoramas sooty purple henna – snagged
dizzy in hairy skies : icy courtyards : roast
gourds : turkeycock spools : piebald leaves
pungent veins coiling : clumsy slabs
of rancid saffron rife in blown faded wastes :
P a s s p o r t r a i t p o s t e r s :
varied
downy
milky
purely glazed
brushed smoothed
scrumbled etched modelled
clear advancing speaking warm
velvet mouths phosphorescent cheekbones :
Interiors flooded with lambent consoling colours
glossy plastered gnarled climatically rounded habitual

We danced all night and it was bitterly miserable to go to one's room alone. We danced mouth to mouth, and rucked a lot (all kinds of sexes). And not even the hearties were bothered by the queens, or vice versa.

We hated go-getters and teasers and money-whores. Class was disregarded. Charm, looks and personality were all that mattered. Fucking and buggering were sometimes enjoyed in lavatories or out of sight. There were casualties, of course: some to fame and fortune, others to drink and drugs.

Nothing was taboo. Banting had no time to remember it all at the time. He shows a dozen works at the International Surrealist Exhibition of 1936 alongside Agar and Nash; Francis Bacon is turned down for not being surreal enough. Banting persuades Harry Quashi to pose naked for his lens.

Harry's a young actor, via Ghana, doubly exposed and discovered, his ghost-self on the wall. Everyone loved him, says Spender, himself seduced by Essie Robeson. Their friend Anthony Butts, great-grandson of Blake's patron, is wild about Harry, too. Queequeg-Quashi finds himself arranged by them, again and again. His blackness is a bargaining chip. His body tilts like a megalith.

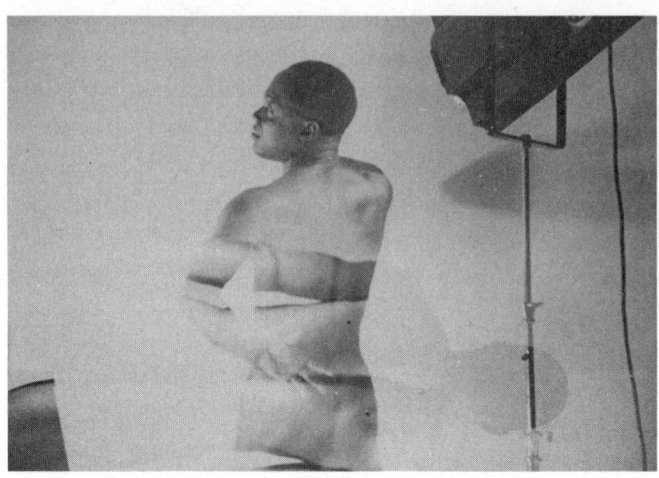

They are a new type of person.

Transmetropolitan, transhuman, transformed by their art. It's no game for Nancy Cunard: her sailorish name is a siren call for a mannish woman of modernism. All fingers and eyes, a mannequin, she stalks like a queen, acting in her own masque, so tall and long-limbed she could be an insect too. She is busy inventing herself out of aristocracy and onto the street.

She is her own currency. She switches denominations and time zones. So thin that people stare right through her steel-blue eyes. She shares a finishing school with Agar (as if women like paintings have to be finished off) who sees her as slim and undulating like a slinky grass snake. When they meet her people aren't quite sure; she uses their discomfort and her allure.

Just what is it? She's certainly animal: a tyger on vaseline, a wild horse, a bird of paradise; a poet, a provocateur, a unit of her own. A one-woman revolution. But what does she actually mean? She defies her decorative qualities and her genes. She is her own calling card:

defy mother
outrage society
burn with radical fire

She's half American, with Irish eyes, a a stacked-up portmanteau of desire. Her bones, her face, her irascibility. Her causes are many, like her amours. She publishes two volumes of poems, *Outlaws* and *Sublunary*, and demands of God in two lines,

> Make me symbolically iconoclast,
> The ideal Antichrist, the Paradox.

She's England's dreaming, under arrest for swimming in the Serpentine at dawn. Our figurehead, precisely what she means. How can she expect to be taken seriously? It's not rocket science. She is what she seems. Her sex is a weapon and a defence. Her lovers are of any gender or none. She's a ghost in the twentieth-century machine; she leaves it behind while everyone else gets old. Her teenage agenda is to stand alone in fabulous rooms, looking over the abyss. A telegram of uncanny glamour from the front line of art. She stands in their works of art, making them new. She takes Pound for her lover. He makes Eliot take her out of his *Waste Land*—an unflattering section about a society woman who dabbles in poetry and sex. Coward would call her a poor little rich girl. Her name precedes her, advertising her wealth.

Her pedigree is immaculately conflicted. Her ancestors were whalers and sailors and anti-slave Quakers. Boycotting herself, Nancy declined to travel by Cunard. Beaton throws her shadow on the wall. She's more surreal than any thing. That's why he took her photograph: to prove she was no illusion (she was) and to capture her (he couldn't). She belongs to the lens, ivory-armoured from the barrel of Maxwell's gun. How many elephants died to encircle her white arms? Mon amour. She's so thin she could walk through a crack in the door. So thin she wears two dressing gowns at the same time; she recommends it to Ronald Firbank, who paints his nails carmine and says she's a charming woman with a hard and cruel face. One of her lovers discovers that when warmed by the human body, her

301

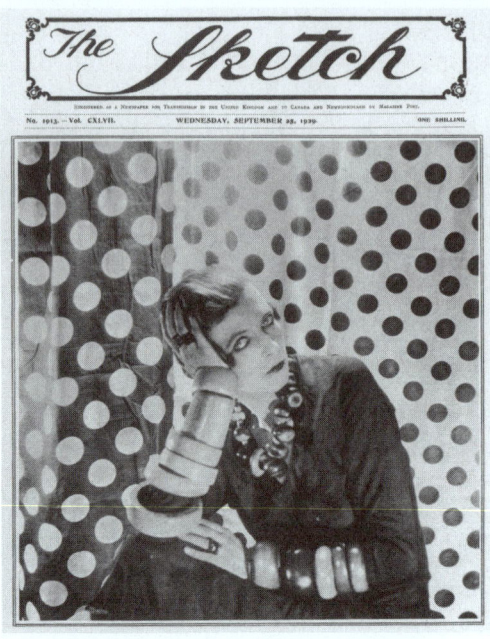

ivory bracelets smell like semen. Like the musk of a spermaceti whale. She's Ishmael in silver lamé, an existential orphan clinging to a coffin.

She achieves her paradox in the way that she looks back at us. Her life is a theatre set, with a little casual violence. She's antiqued, tusked, masked. The after-effects of her hysterectomy—she felt as if the steel things had been left inside her—makes sex complicated. Pierced. So she takes Michael Arlen and Aldous Huxley as her lovers; they put her in their books as a reward, or a punishment. *The Green Hat, Crome Yellow*, colour-coded, stripped down. Caricatures, venereal disease, drugs, fast cars. She's far more than the sum of these parts. Brancusi sculpts her, reducing her to a slender bronze cloud. Curtis Moffat snaps her in a Sonia Delaunay deco coat. She's a walking dazzleship, camouflaged for the city: it's impossible to get any more modern. She lives on chocolate and cigarettes and concepts and the occasional slice of smoked salmon.

Fucking food, darling, she says, if only one didn't have to eat. Being boring is the greatest crime. She never is. Nor consistent or obvious. She will be consistently arrested, and obviously gaoled eleven times, earning almost enough points to earn a swallow on her hand. She slips out between the bars, between the wars, like Harry Southampton getting out of the Tower free after the Essex Rebellion. Her life is a throw of the dice. She's in bars, free, drinking, rebelling all the time. In search of ecstasy and social justice, never knowing, consciously, what she is for; never knowingly satisfied, no matter how hard she tries. She is enough to drive anyone insane.

Dragging a bouquet of dead roses, waiting for her man, calling for a cab, a stray straw tangled at the back of her hair. Everything else is so tentative; no one else understands. Her eyes are arctic, exotic. She drops belladonna in them to dilate them all the more, to take in the whole of the world. Snapped against a tyger skin, burning bright. On the front page, snarling, like a cover of the NME. Everyone stares, she stares back. Fearsomely veiled, fierce as you like.

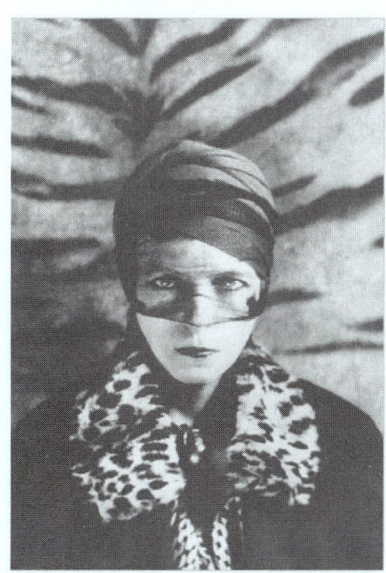

No one realises she's the enemy before it's too late. She wears her black veil in mourning for the society she seeks to destroy. An anarchist bride, masked against capitalism. Out for revenge: auto-erotic, auto-artefact; part human, part angel, obscure object of desire. Furred and feathered, an egret ready to strike. She might run off to the circus in her black-and-white maquillage. She deserves all these metaphors. She is greedy for context after all this time. She looks divine.

Straight as any stick, emaciated, holding herself erect, as William Carlos Williams describes her; her blue eyes completely untroubled, inviolable in her virginity of pure act, he says. How would he know? He's never seen her drunk, but suspects she's never sober either. She feels so ill in the mornings, she complains, so exhausted most of the time.

Seldom seen in daylight, like a vampire, invisible in the mirror, she has no regrets. Of what possible use would they be? Tristan Tzara kneels before her to kiss her hand; Man Ray takes her photograph again. They think they're being ironic, but they're slaves to her love. She is armed against the arrows like a female Sebastian: my armful of ivories, she calls them.

The silver hat, a blue angel; the silver backdrop, the tired silver on Wilde's edition of Salome, Orlando's silver room in her many-roomed palace, furnished when she had a passion for that metal, like a shell that has lain empty at the bottom of the sea. It's her turn to have her shadow thrown on the wall. Back-projected, contingent, a banshee; the enemy within, wrapping her head tightly to keep her thoughts in, staring through her veil like a mourner for her own past. Trapped in leopardskin. It's easier than a ruff or terrier round your neck, but just as feral.

What is she fighting for? Whatever you've got. She is her own lost cause. She owns her own press, The Hours, taking lessons from Virginia and Leonard Woolf. Like Blake, she does it to defy the censors and create total works of art, broken

English in Paris, France. At the controls, her hands on the printing press wheel, churning out radical texts, the captain of her fate, straddling on skinny legs that barely support even her wasted frame. She's a model looking good for the end of time. A mannequin with a personality crisis and a tight skirt, driving fast in a fast car, the wind in her hair, throwing off her selves as she goes.

Imagine her dancing: like a praying mantis in slow motion. Mina Loy loves her from near and afar. She puts Nancy in a hard-edged frame of words. Loy, who sports a thermometer dangling from her ear, is radically modern, too. Her *Lunar Baedeker* poems of 1923 are full of chimera like the crab-angel

An atomic sprite / perched on a polished monster-stallion... / a minnikin of masquerade sex

They call her an electric-age Blake. She sees Cunard

Your eyes diffused with holly lights
of ancient Christmas
helmeted with masks

beyond your moonstone whiteness,
Your chiffon voice
tears with soft mystery . . .

Your lone fragility
of mythological queens
conjures long-vanished dragons—

Hotel Cristal, Paris, 1930. Joyce knocks on Nancy's door. Today she's a decaying queen, brittle as ice. She can't talk easily, has an abscess in her throat. Joyce's thin fingers falter to find the furniture; he's already nearly blind. He seem'd to find his way without his eyes. She can see right through him. Tall, glowing in his white jacket that helps him to read by reflecting light on the page; it pours out of him and his electric blue eyes. A cathedral-spire of a man, she says. He has come to tell her to intercede with her mother to get his friend, an Irish opera singer, hired in London. It's barely a request.

Nancy's mother is Irish-American, an heiress in her own right. Her name is Maud, but she's reinvented herself as Emerald Cunard, as if she were an ornament in a turban or the glittering superstructure of a liner; Nancy refers to her bitterly as Her Ladyship. Irony makes for a great distance. Lady Cunard is spending her sea fortune on art and parties and affairs. She's what's left over when all the guests have gone. Her lover is the Irish writer George Moore, said to be Nancy's father; Nancy wishes it were true. She was twelve years old when her dog Bouncer, a terrier with a withered leg, bit Moore on his unwithered leg. When Moore kicked Bouncer back, Nancy, in a rage, slapped him in the face.

Cavendish Square, W1, 1916. Prompted by Pound and Yeats, Emerald Cunard sends copies of Joyce's books to her friend Edward Marsh, who is considering Joyce for a grant from the British government.

Eddie, as he's known to his friends, of whom there are many, on account of his patronage and love — they include Siegfried Sassoon and Ivor Novello, Paul Nash and T.E. Lawrence — is a great collector of art; Catherine's portrait of William as a rebellious young man hangs on his wall.

Eddie had a way of rearing his handsome head like a horse, Nash remembered; only with the addition of a monocle; he sang poetry, loudly, in the bath. He's also private secretary to Winston Churchill, who had his moments, too, with Novello: he said it was musical. Marsh, in his official capacity, reports on the pros and cons. Joyce was the author of a good book yet-to-be, *Portrait of an Artist*, he says. He used to drink too much when he was young, but seems to have made a very creditable recovery, and to be now without reproach.

I ought to mention also that his writings are occasionally what is called outspoken, Eddie adds, but I think not excessively so.

It is the end of an age of grand delusions. Remarkably, given that there is a world war going on, not to mention the little matter of an uprising in Ireland, the grant is agreed. A Royal Bounty of one hundred pounds is to be sent to Joyce overseas. He is living wild in Europe, now in Zurich, lately Trieste, where he lectured on Blake. He is subverting the state by making it pay for its own instrument of destruction, like the forty pounds a week Margaret Thatcher gave me in her enterprise allowance scheme when I was unemployed and which I used to undermine her tyrannical estate.

Joyce considers the bounty a down payment on reparations. Emerald Cunard professes herself simply thrilled at the news; she had been sending money via Pound to Joyce, and would continue to collect sums from her friends to enable him to write *Ulysses*. The cheque goes off to Zurich. None of them have any idea their money is going to pay for filth and drunken nights in foreign bars and the greatest work of modernist literature in the twentieth century.

It is six months after the Easter Rising of 1916. Joyce is still a British citizen. It would be a tabloid story these days. But everyone is behaving terribly well. Joyce writes to the prime minister, hoping, as he says, that you will allow me to thank you most sincerely for this generous gift made to me in His Majesty's name and to assure you that I am deeply sensible of the honour which your recommendation confers upon me. Either he was expecting to be knighted, going down on bended knee, or he was taking the piss.

Meanwhile Eddie Marsh remembers being a soft fifteen-year-old boy back in 1888, visiting Robert Bridges at Boars Hill. The poet took him for a walk, talking about poetry—he was wearing a bright tie and spoke with a lisp—telling Marsh about his friend's poems. When they got back he brought the manuscripts out into the light; Gerard Manley Hopkins was still alive in Dublin at that point, and would be for just one more year. Marsh recalled one line as if the Jesuit had read it out loud to him, as he sang in the bath,

O look at all the fire-folk sitting in the air!

Approaching Nancy Cunard in her hotel room, Joyce has no idea of the enmity between her and her mother. If he had he might not have bothered. He suggests that if she is successful in getting his friend to Covent Garden, a piece of his writing might come the way of her Hours Press. Everyone wants a piece of him. As he leaves, she is horrified to see how he gropes his way out of the room, the miraculous way he walks down the stairs.

Nothing comes her way from Joyce. She has bigger things on her mind. Her mother is trying to get Nancy's lover Henry Crowder, an African-American musician, deported. Nancy reacts by deporting herself, sailing across the Atlantic, not by Cunard line, and checks into the Grampion Hotel in Harlem. She's arrived in time for the renaissance. They wear leopardskin to assert their African legacy; she's so white she might fade in the sun.

2 May 1932. Miss Cunard's association with coloured friends is a bombshell to titled London, says the *New York Daily Mirror*

CUNARD HEIRESS FOUND IN HARLEM!

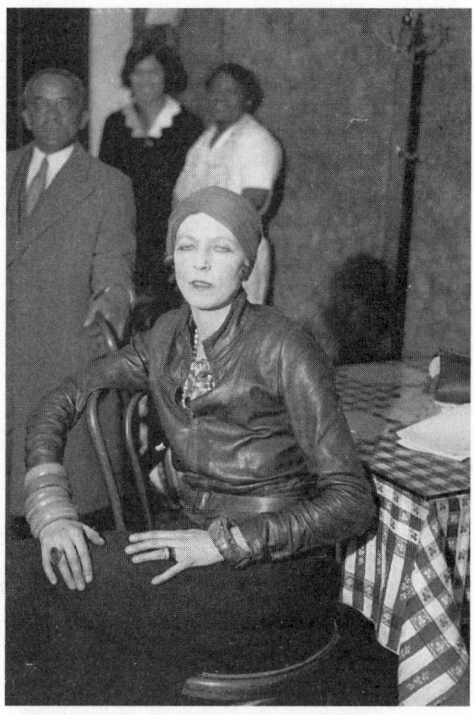

UN AUTRE «GRAND SCANDALE » !

adds the press back in France, claiming the high society of New York was actuellement scandalisée by the sensational conduct of the daughter of Lady Cunard de la Cunard-Line who had descendu à l'hôtel Grampien in the heart of Harlem, cité nègre, the first white person of honour to have done so. The outrage is compounded by the fact that she has announced she is there to campaign against the execution of seven young Blacks who had been accused of attacking and manhandling two young whites in Scottsboro, Alabama.

It's no pose. Their lives matter to her. She deploys her fame against infamy, setting her celebrity against the fate of nine men and boys accused of raping two white women on a train. Eight of the defendants had been sentenced to death; only the youngest, a boy of thirteen, was not convicted by the all-white jury; in court, one of the alleged victims admitted to having made the whole story up.

She calls a press conference in the hotel. The camera-flashes light up her face. She hands out a defiant statement. It denies any relationship between her and Paul Robeson. It is outrageous to suggest that a performer of his calibre should require her patronage, it says. She has travelled to New York third class on a German liner and she insists,

Press Gentlemen, my name is NOT the Hon. Nancy, it is Nancy Cunard.

And now, after your interest in my private affairs, I want something in return. I want money for the defence of the nine Negro framed-up boys held under death sentence in prison.

Why are you Americans so uneasy of the Negro race?

Why should one have to waste time with the vultures gassing about the rottenness of America etc when they're going to fabricate their own crap? she tells Claude McKay. He's the queer Black Bolshevik poet from Jamaica who is, inevitably, being monitored by the FBI. He will turn Blake's Tyger, which he read as a boy, into bitter paradox

> The white man is a tiger at my throat,
> Drinking my blood as my life ebbs away,
> And muttering that his terrible striped coat
> Is Freedom's and portends the Light of Day.

All of Nancy's friends are Black or queer, preferably both. They step out into the Harlem sun for the photographers. Her turban is wrapped round her head and her leather jacket is another skin wrapped round her thinness. She might be about to escape on her motorbike.

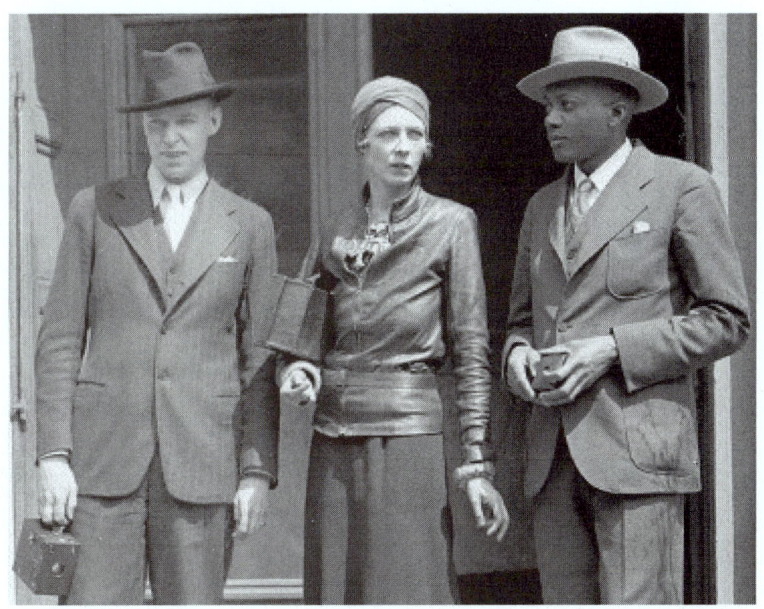

They're a post-punk trio. There's something of the shark about Nancy Cunard, well hard. A film camera rolls. I'd love to see that newsreel. On her right is Banting. He's dressed formally, gangsta style, his camera a violin case. To her left is Taylor Gordon, singer and actor, dandy darling of the Harlem Renaissance. His autobiography, *Born to Be*, has attracted the attention of Gertrude Stein in Paris; in England, he sang for Radclyffe Hall and Una Troubridge and Somerset Maugham. His Manhattan profile is enhanced by the white promoter of Black art Carl Van Vechten. You get the picture. Yes, we see.

Taylor Gordon knows his audience. He's about to appear on Broadway in *Gay Divorce* with Fred Astaire, and after that, Noël Coward's *Conversation Piece*. Then he'll leave for Soviet Russia with Langston Hughes to make a film about US treatment of African-Americans. The trio pose in the Harlem sun. The shadow of a lone tree falls on Gordon's jacket. Cunard might as well have a hammer and sickle painted on the back of hers.

She's known Hughes since he worked the clubs in Paris in '24. He's about to publish his polemic *Scottsboro Limited*, illustrated by his white friend Prentiss Taylor, who is in love with Aaron Copland. Hughes riffs on *The Tempest*, bitterly

That Justice is a blind goddess
Is a thing to which we black are wise
Her bandage hides two festering sores
That once perhaps were eyes.

PARTIES

They go out dancing, of course. Speakeasies and dance halls and nightclubs, cabarets and rent parties. In his memoir *The Big Sea*, Hughes quotes a Harlem gossip column on all Taylor Gordon's fabulous parties.

What a crowd! ultra aristocrats, Bourgeois, Communists, Park Avenuers galores, bookers, publishers, Broadway celebs, and Harlemites giving each other the once over. The social revolution was on. And yes, Lady Nancy Cunard was there all in black (she would) with 12 of her grand bracelets.

Into swell dance music was injected African drums that played havoc with blood pressure, the celebrated reporter Geraldyn Dismond went on. Jimmy Daniels sang his gigolo hits. Gus Simons, the Harlem crooner, made the River Stay Away From His Door, and Taylor himself brought out everything from Hot Dog to Bravo when he made high C.

The past is so much more exciting when we edit it in our heads, leaving out the boring bits. A year later Edward Burra, Paul Nash's friend and neighbour in Rye (where he found the great artist at work in the garden, at one with the nature he so tenderly portrays. he was robed in a seamans jersey and kerchief bought at the village shoppie; I like Paul he is quite a petty; they'd all run off to the South of France together, where they admired the men on the beach in their futurist-patterned shirts), tells his mother he is going out into the garden and doesn't return for six months.

It transpired that all this time he had been living in New York, making drawings of Negro dives in Harlem, John Rothenstein reports, when he goes to interview Burra in Rye. When questioned about the truth of this story, Rothenstein adds, the artist admitted that it was not entirely apocryphal, but, apocryphal or not, it was psychologically true.

Isn't that enough?

Burra writes back to Billy Chappell, his best friend. Says he is staying on Seventh Avenue with Edna Lloyd Thomas, a renowned Black actress. Theres so much talent at the partys here that its more like non stop Variety, Burra says, in his breathless stylee. They go to an outrageous place called the theatrical grill, a cellar done up to look like Napoleons tomb and lit in such a way that all the white people look like corpses.

Zombies.

Ive never seen such faces the best gangster pictures are far outdone, says Burra. The chief attracles of the cabaret was 'Gloria Swanson', he says; a mountainous Black man in a crepe de chine dress trimmed with sequins who rushed about screaming Clappy weather, just cant keep my old arse together keeps runnin all the time etc and rush up to the table dragging his sequins up and disclosing a filthy dirty pair of pink silk panties how he managed I dont know no balls or anything else so far as I could see.

If you want a nice record dearie buy 'Harlem on my mind' by Ethel Waters, he advises Billy, other side is Heat Wave.

It's getting hot in here. Burra meets Taylor Gordon at a party, and finds him delightful. He goes to the Savoy dance hall, you would go mad Ive never in my life seen such a display an enormous floor half dark surrounded by chairs & tables and promenade on one side and the band on the other with a trailing cloud effect behind Ive never seen such wonderful dancing. The city is full of gossip. Tilly Losch has been in a taxi accident. Tallulah is so ill her life is despaired of its too awful. Bankhead leaves the hospital weighing seventy pounds, telling the doctor, Don't think this has taught me a lesson.

Burra goes to Boston. The port is full of sailors and gangsters and whores and queens, he says, just what he likes; they're wrangling over the sailors like gulls over something thats been thrown off a boat. Camping up Melville he invents Betty Tosspot Boorsqueeg of Beacon Hill and later stays on Cape Cod getting drunk in a thunderstorm which he describes as a gorgeous multiscreen 3 dimensional masterpiece by C B de Mille before ending up in Provincetown at the very end of America. He is always returning to Rye, a place he professes to hate. He is never well. He makes his watercolour paintings the same way as Blake, on a table, spread out like a quilt. He's described by John Rothenstein as pale and silent in person, a machine who had run down. He could not stand up for long, so easels were out of the question. If he could have painted lying down, he would have, he said.

Like someone aping insanity for fun, said Christopher Neve.

Standing there on the doorstep of the hotel, Cunard reminds the reporters that it was in the house of her ancestor Thones Kunders—a Mennonite Quaker from Germany living in Germantown, Pennsylvania—that the first protest against slavery in a New World colony was proclaimed in 1688, after some of the Quaker settlers proposed taking up slaves. The dissenters issued their own press release. Nancy in Harlem might as well be reading out the same statement.

These are the reasons why we are against this traffik of men-body . . . for we hear that ye most part of such negers are brought heither against their will & consent and that many of them are stollen . . . How fearful and faint-hearted are many on sea when they see a strange vassel . . . if this is done well, what shall we say is done evil?

The document, later suppressed by the Quakers, was witnessed by Kunders, who went on to change his name to Cunard and whose descendants' wealth was founded on strange vessels serving not slavery but luxury. In 1840, Samuel Cunard, Nancy's great-grandfather, owner of timber and whaling ships in Nova Scotia, was processing dead trees and dead whales in his trade. In 1847 he is obliged to issue an apology, via a damage-limiting letter to The Times, when he learns that Frederick Douglass, on his campaign against slavery, had been forced to travel steerage on a Cunard liner because his presence would give offence to American passengers in first class.

On Douglass's outward passage, the ship's captain had invited him to address the passengers. As he spoke to the assembly, this fiercely handsome man, Douglass was heckled by five or six republican slaveholders who threatened to administer to him the code of Judge Lynch, as Douglass reported drily in his own letter to The Times. The captain, taking Douglass's part, had threatened in turn to put the abusers in irons; an irony which was not lost on Douglass.

But when he boarded the same liner on his return journey, after his wildly successful lecture tour, Douglass was denied the first-class cabin he had paid for. It was on account of the colour of my skin, he told The Times. For the whole of his journey home he was segregated. I must eat alone—sleep alone—be alone, he said; even to the point of being denied Sunday worship. He was the hero of the Underground Railroad, a shining hope to the enslaved. He had spoken to crowds all over Ireland and Britain.

Now all he could do was to stand on deck and look up at the stars.

Nancy Cunard wields whatever weapons are to hand. Especially her privilege. Her championing of the Scottsboro boys is set against the obscenity of their wrecked lives. They escaped execution but served long prison sentences. As if they should be grateful. Cunard in turn is told that she was making a lousy hoor of herself, can't you get a white man to satisfy you, you dirty betraying lowdown piece of mucus, your number is up, you're going for a ride very shortly.

We shall call for you just as soon as the necessary plans have been completed for your reception.

For the sake of her own safety, Cunard has to leave the Grampion. She too is under surveillance by the FBI as a suspected subversive. She sails to Cuba and Jamaica, but not in steerage. The press report that she is accompanied by her unmistakable blackamoor without bothering to find out the man's name. As if A.A. Colebrooke, an erudite Bostonian, were her servant in a Georgian drawing room.

Nancy has a new literary project in mind. It is designed to offend. She tells Banting that she intends to include a selection of the less obscene letters she has received in Negro, her anthology of Black issues. She fires off invitations for contributions and persuades Wishart & Co. to publish it, funded by money she has won in libel cases. This all seems perfectly elegant, but she neglects to pay her contributors. Claude McKay withdraws his essay in disgust; as if they should all be grateful for all of this. Taylor Gordon delivers his but talks about Malicious Lies Magnifying the Truth. The caucasians are queer people, he writes. They think that any other people that can't see things as they do are to be pitied and cared for. That if there's ever an eternal peace among men, it will be because of their generosity.

There are scholarly essays on the eighteenth-century slave trade from white people, and Anthony Butts contributes a piece on his experience of the colour bar in England, despite being white. He has china blue eyes and Stephen Spender is a little

316

in love with him. At Oxford Butts bought a large motorbike but didn't learn how to stop it and just rode on till he reached Blenheim Palace, which he used as a roundabout. He writes plays and learns to paint with Sickert and starts a business designing surrealist hats. He has hated colonisation in all its forms since he was a child, he tells his sister Mary, but thinks *Negro* would have been better if it was less subjective and more scientific. Beckett translates the French essays for Cunard's book. He will recite her name six times in one speech in *Waiting for Godot* as a mantra or product placement

alas the stones Cunard [*mêlée, final vociferations*] tennis . . . the stones . . . so calm . . . Cunard . . . unfinished . . .

Negro is Cunard's *Jerusalem* or *America*; her Blakean prophecy. She has to fit everything in there. It is over-excited, patronising, often distressing, veering from a guide to Negro slang to images of lynchings which, like Blake's Surinam horrors, do not bear reprinting here. Like Joyce and his *Ulysses*, she oversees every detail, down to the cloth specially woven for the cover dyed black to her demands, with red lettering and a red map of the Black Belt of America on the back as if it were another promised land. People don't take it seriously. It has no precedent, and that pisses everyone off.

She attends demos for the Scottsboro boys; Banting paints the banners. They're their own anti-Nazi league. She gets in another fight with the police. Sir Thomas Beecham, her mother's lover, says Nancy Cunard should be tarred and feathered. She's a witch, full of grief. The papers satirise her belief in Sur-realism as if she made it up herself. Her art is performance. She joins the hunger march from Jarrow in disguise, wearing a man's overcoat, an aviator's helmet and several scarves, as her admirable biographer Anne Chisholm describes her. Like Banting, she also carries a cine camera in her hand. She's acting up, under surveillance, returning the compliment. The revolution will be filmed. Her obsessive compulsion is slowly destroying her friendships, one by one. Her sublunary lovers fall away but they keep coming back.

I have loved this woman since I was a teenager. My sister and I, my partner-in-punk-crime, recreated her pose in our suburban bedroom, my sister in a gold-tinsel, fur-collared coat from a jumble sale. In London I hung Cunard's picture on my wall, nine floors up in the East End: Man Ray's photograph, twice life-size like an advertisement on the Woolworth Building. She was my ivory-armed guardian angel, protecting me from the police helicopters peering in through the windows.

London, summer 1934. Cyril Connolly and Evelyn Waugh are at a cocktail party. They fulminate about Brian Howard and Mr Banting—worthless, no talent, homosexual sewer rats, they say. Nancy's socialist nancies. Connolly leaves for Dartmoor, where Waugh is writing in a country hotel; he complains that it rains all the time. The hotel is very odd, he says, run by a deserter from the Foreign Legion and a woman who mixes menthol with her cigarettes. Waugh suspects the place is a distributing centre for white slaves or cocaine or something like that. Back in London, Emerald Cunard says sex plays no part in modern life. At a pretentious lunch the day before, Madame de Margerie, the wife of the first secretary at the French embassy, like a nightmare, a hotted-up Lady Colefax, says, I am mystic myself and can tell when a room has been used by Böchine or Gerard Manley Hopkins. Ireland must be the least homosexual country in the world, Connolly says, just back from Cork. Evan Morgan, unaccountably loved by Firbank, says the East End is utterly promiscuous and bisexual. It is amazing to see how extinct the upper class appears to be becoming. The Jews have got in there, it won't ever be clean again. The café in Old Compton Street is entirely full of n—s, he says. V. Woolf

asks Elizabeth Bowen what unnatural vice is—I mean what do they *do?*
They might as well be on an island in the moon.

Barcelona, summer 1936. Nancy leaves her bracelets in Paris for the civil war. It's not a social engagement or the surrealist exhibition in Belgravia or an erotic encounter with the men and women she continually picks up and discards. She's perfectly willing to pay for pleasure, hiring boys and whores. It's the most offensive way she can think of spending Her Ladyship's money.

She's imperial in her disconnection from every norm. Off to Spain, carrying her possessions wrapped up in a coloured handkerchief, her typewriter slung over her shoulder. Always ready to go one step further, she declares herself an anarchist. To piss people off some more. She meets Neruda in Madrid. He says she's quixotic, unalterable, fearless and pathetic. She publishes his poetry and Lorca's. Soon the streets of Barcelona will see machine guns on top of churches, Durruti Columnists on La Rambla, anarchist cells in Poblenou. It wasn't a summer for sketching. No wonder she has to shout. Fired with opposition, she too summons Blake to her cause.

I'm of a mood tonight, boy, marked DO NOT TOUCH,

she writes in her poem, speaking of artists

Who brooked no nonsense, who wrote and painted and said
Their NO against foolery, NO against lying . . .
. . . their NO to the living-dead,

Blake too—you'll do well to remember that naked man's
                                        announcement:
'It is impossible, yes, for truth to be told *so's understood*

And not be believed'. Great Blake is the Day of Judgement,
Vengeful, oppressive, peculiar—Blake's all to the good.

Banting takes her photograph on the carrer. It's his favourite
picture of her. So fragile, so strong. He can find alcohol
wherever they go. Drinking makes them hard and invulnerable,
heroic. They write about it all, all of the time. Spain is her
apotheosis, her perfect state of beauty and conflict. Her body
hangs off her shoulder pads like snipers on chimney stacks.

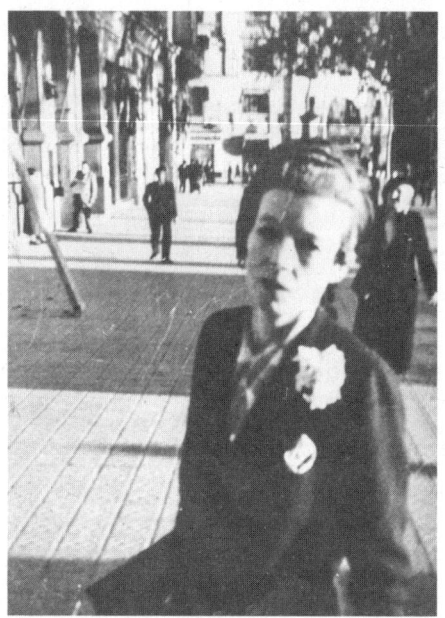

William Plomer, the poet, describes her eyes as like those
of some cats, lucent among their dark lashes, a pale and
precious enamel in which had been fused a suggestion of gold-
dust. And on her thin, fine-boned arms, those bangles, he says.
When she walked, Plomer writes, they made a clacking sound,
as of billiard balls or the casual cakewalk of skeletons.

Her own bony soundtrack. Plomer is a white South African
who protests against the regime. Anthony Butts writes to him

on 22 May 1928, praising him for speaking of Africa and the folly of the euro-american machine. They become lovers. Woolf introduces Plomer to her friends at Charleston and embarrasses everyone by declaring that he claims descent from Shakespeare and William Blake.

The cakewalk is a mocking Black parody of white society dancing. Nancy is slave to the capitalist inheritance on which her insurrection relies. The Cunard Line pays for Cunard's lines of cocaine. She holds her hands before her face like a martyr, her bracelets a pair of handcuffs snapped on her wrists by the police. A manacled visionary, staggering from room to room, scratching in the sand, taking you by the hand in White Trash at the Embassy Club with Divine's boyfriend, kicking you out in the morning as you wear her Westwood dress down to McDonald's on Kensington High Street.

Cunard & Beckett become sublunary lovers. She publishes his first poem, says he looks like an Aztec eagle. A lovely Irish young man. She takes him out on her long drunken rambles into the night. He looks up gloomily and bursts out saying, What, in God's name, am I *doing* here?, as if they were Estragon and Vladimir.

Nowhere is safe now. Beckett gets stabbed in the street in Paris while walking home from the cinema; the blade only just missed his heart. Cunard visits him in hospital. She bounced in from Spain to his bed, he says. She and Banting are just back from the war. They escaped on the back of a truck; her bones shook like sticks.

Langston Hughes is in town. Banting found him magnificent and magnetising when they met in Valencia. Friends reunited. The trouble they've seen. Backstage after an event: Langston in slashback lapels and tight tie-knot; Nancy in cap borrowed from Banting and a Schiaparelli sweater with rhinestones raining down her sleeves like falling stars; très sportif or kabuki. It's difficult to tell who's performing and who is not.

They might be plotting the downfall of western civilisation, demanding reparation, or just falling about laughing at her joke.

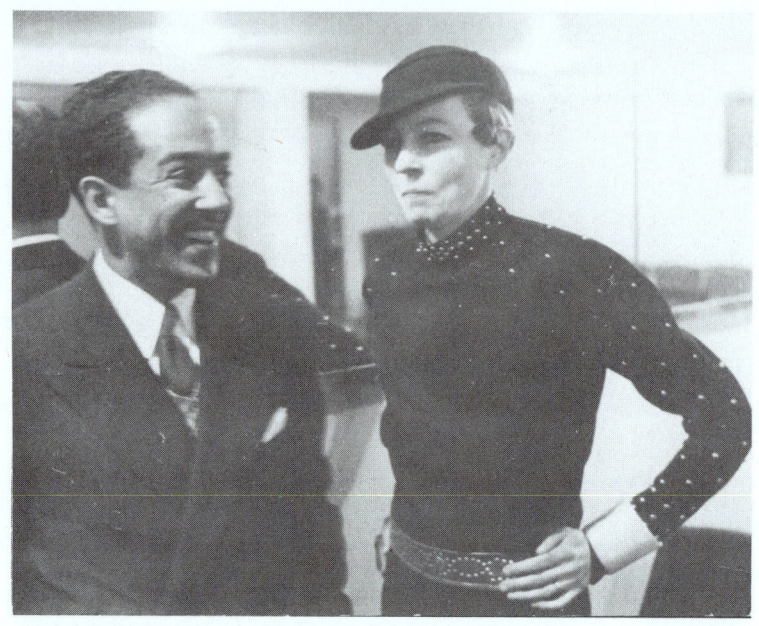

She's thinner than ever. Give her a decade and another mission and she'll disappear entirely. She is perpetually open to protest, professionally defiant on behalf of Black people and queers and communists. A lost cause of her own, an allegory of bones. Her fingers have turned into sea claws like Sam's. She doesn't hang around for applause. She holds on to herself. She doesn't travel, a friend says: she is driven, by the force of her own personality.

She goes back to the war to report on it for the *Guardian*. No-one in England realises what's going on, she tells the editor. She writes dozens of reports, notes, postcards, and letters signed in emerald green ink. She demands that they start a fund for the Spanish refugees, half a million of them. Cities collapse, one by one. Bodies are left in ditches or laid out alive under barbed wire in the sun.

Spurning the clouds written with curses, stamps the stony
   law to dust,

Blake writes in *The Marriage of Heaven and Hell*,

loosing the eternal horses from the dens of night, crying,
Empire is no more!

The painter Michael Wishart, whose father published *Negro*, knew Nancy Cunard late in her life. She was lonely and already rather mad by then, he said. I don't so much mind not knowing *where* to live, or *how* to live, but I'm so tired of not knowing *why* to live, she told him. She wore more mascara than anyone I have ever known, he said, with the exception of the Marchesa Casati and Prince Felix Youssoupoff.

I met Wishart at a funeral for his friend. He apologised for arriving in tweeds, having spent the weekend somewhere grand. Later he would send me a postcard telling me he had fallen in love with Michael Jackson and had no idea how he was to live without him. One afternoon, after lunch, he took me up to his bedroom in the Chelsea Arts Club and told me I looked like Lawrence of Arabia, while Eduardo Paolozzi played pool upstairs (the balls clicked like Nancy's bracelets). With his solemn, ruined-angel face and bricklayer's build, Michael had the air of William Blake in a leather jacket. When asked to lecture in public, he prepared for it with a cocktail and two lines of speed.

South Kensington, 17 July 1950. Francis Bacon gives the wedding party for Michael's marriage to Anne Dunn, artist and daughter of a millionaire; she kept a flying fox in her apartment, Michael recalled, as well as an ageing night-club hostess of whom she was fond. The party went on for three days and three nights. It was held in the vast black billiard room of Bacon's first studio at Cromwell Place in South Kensington. He turned his paintings face to the wall, for fear they would be shocked by what was going on. There were one hundred golden chairs and he had painted the cut-glass chandeliers bright pink.

The guests just keep on coming in: drug dealers and aristocrats and thieves; critics and artists and rent boys; actors and directors and Bacon's Irish nanny, who never left him, always there, looking on, providing one, two, three bottles of champagne for each of Francis's real friends while his fake friends circled around. The bride and the groom spent their wedding night separately with lovers of their own sex: Michael with Lucian Freud, Anne with Michael's mother, Lorna, who was also a former lover of Freud; as was Anne. There was only so much love to go around, so why not share it out?

You got your money's worth with Michael. It was only after he died that I realised he had been Bacon's lover as well; he'd sit watching Francis make up his face before launching out into the night. Freud painted Michael as a young man in a blue coat, holding a dove like a sacrifice. I met the eyes of all three of these artists: Freud's were narrow and evasive; Bacon's, sad and full of lust. But Wishart's gaze, looking into an unknown distance, even to the end of his life, was that of a wide-eyed deer, innocent and irrevocably lost.

Clearing out my flat, I find a little chrome-plated compact with a glass slab cover on which there is a reproduction of a Joshua Reynolds painting of an innocent boy. He has golden curly hair and a ruff-like collar above his red coat and white breeches, and he holds a fluffy white lapdog in his arms. Blake would have snorted at the winsomeness. I open the little case, which feels familiar and weighty in my hand, for all that it is hardly larger than a credit card. It once held face powder when it lived in an evening bag; inside is a mirror, just the right size for checking your face. As I hold it, I remember what I used it for, how precious it felt in my pocket. The silver gilt of the mirror has begun to flake under the glass, as though corroded by the ghost of the cocaine it once contained. I look into it and see my young face and the powder on my nose. My green eyes, getting paler by the day.

Leaving London after forty years, the home and the family I tried to make there of the friends and all the people I loved. I made all my own choices and my own mistakes. You shouldn't go disturbing the dust that obscured all your desires. The Soho Brasserie, standing on a chair to see the princess going into the theatre across the street. Dancing in the Hippodrome as the drug kicked in. Never wanting to go home alone. Never knowing where or what it was. I close up the case and put it in my pocket. You never know your luck.

Tilbury Docks, 1948. Nancy Cunard returns from the Caribbean, sailing back to London on a battered ex-troopship. It's the *Empire Windrush* and the beginning of a new Britain. Full of neat young men in neat young suits and young women in smart cotton dresses. They are not the first. Two ships bringing similar groups of Caribbean people had arrived in Southampton the previous year. They are all interviewed, politely, when they arrive, replying politely in turn. They do not complain about their cabins, down in the hold.

During the voyage of *Empire Windrush*, Evelyn Wauchope, a Jamaican dressmaker, is discovered as a stowaway. In a reverse of Douglass's experience—Cunard was making amends a century after the family firm's mistake—it is reported that Wauchope is given a first-class cabin and offered a job as a maid. In fact a general collection is made for her fare to prevent her from being arrested on arrival. Nancy returns to Valencia where she's jailed for organising protests and is expelled by the fascist regime. In London she's suspected of carrying explosives for Spanish revolutionairies and using a flame-thrower in the street She digs out her ivory necklaces and bracelets from her ruined house in France. She's ready for the fight. A thief in the night. Fire, the next time. She knew she was right.

She's thinner than ever before. Anorexic, drunk in Chelsea, assaulting a police officer, arrested again, this time for soliciting sex in public, flicking up her dress. Throws her shoes at the magistrate. Her cousin has her certified as insane. She is sent to a sanatorium in Virginia Water, from where she writes to Nikita Khrushchev, telling him her confinement is politically motivated. The Soviet leader does not reply, but her allegations are not entirely unfounded. On leave from the asylum, Banting takes her off for the weekend. They consider running away. He is loyal to the end. Inspired by the civil rights movement, she says she's going back to the States. James Baldwin is quoting Blake about the dog starved at the gate.

On her last visit to England, her friend Charles Burkhart drives her south-west so that she can admire the stones at Avebury and the Cerne Abbas Giant. Her taste in art remained pre-historical to the end, Burkhart said. She declined to use the word primitive. She believed she was African. Tribal. Her clanking bracelets, her bones sticking up out of her skin. Burkhart remembered her cool laughter, her great amusement at things, the dear pure presence of her.

What a nuisance fucking food was.

On 16 March 1965, at the age of sixty-nine, Nancy dies in an oxygen tent, alone in the public ward of a hospital in Paris. The warm wind was no longer in her hair.

They'd found her face down in the gutter, weighing fifty pounds. Martin Luther King is marching from Selma to Montgomery. People are still getting shot on the streets. Louis Aragon, the only man who ever really loved her, she said, says it's impossible to discuss the intellectual history of the twentieth century without mentioning her name.

One of the last people to see Nancy, Raymond Michelet, another lover, said he could not shield his eyes from that last great glare. There was no one to close hers as she lay there, waiting for someone to come and pick her up.

The stars above her weighed nothing at all.

––––

Seven years before, in 1958, Brian Howard, who had long ago succumbed to alcoholism, died in France from an overdose of morphine. John Banting was with him at the end. He lived on, mourning his two best friends in a hard-scrabble life, drinking, retreating to his native Ireland, where he was reduced to extreme poverty. People told him they liked his paintings from the nineteen-thirties best. So, like the modern artist he was, he just dated the new ones that way too. When he and Burra and George Melly went to a show at the ICA in 1969, they saw lots of assemblages of old bits & DADA, as Burra reported. Banting went round writing Marcel Du Champ & M. Du Champ on all the exhibits, but nothing happend, it was a happening, Burra said.

In the winter of 1972, Banting undergoes drastic surgery, for the rehabilitation of his arse, as Burra says, which will be combined with his cock and he says its distinctly Picasso cum Heath Robinson. Banting lies there, Burra writes, with a pipe up his nose stuck on with sticky paper, one arm done up in gauze and a peice of plastic with a pipe in it connected to a plastic sack under the bed. He is talking between gasps but talking.

This weather is getting a little trying just in time for power cut tayme, Burra tells Chappell. Blackouts tomorrow honey I hear by courtesy of the Daily mirror on Radio Luxembourg.

He doesn't know that Banting had died that day, alone in his hospital bed.

Nancy Cunard's picture still hangs in my hall, over the telephone. She's waiting for me to give her a call.

London, 1923. 15 Cheyne Gardens, Chelsea, 17 June, 11.30 pm. Being dead is boring, announces Oscar Wilde.

He's only been gone twenty-two years. Now he's broadcasting from beyond, responding in automatic writing recorded by the mysterious Mr V, a scholar sent to spy on the spirit world. With her hand resting on Mr V's is Hester Dowden, an Irish medium, who records his words for a book: Oscar Wilde from Purgatory, in lurid blood-red blocking on matt black binding. A wicked book about a wicked man.

She is also the daughter of Edward Dowden, an eminent Shakespearean from Dublin who had refused to recommend young James Joyce for a job at the National Library in 1903. Dowden was also a Blake enthusiast. In 1884 Anne Gilchrist told Walt Whitman that Edward Dowden had just visited her to see Blake's drawings.

Hester had left her husband in Dublin and was now living in London with her own literary circle, most of whom were dead. Her first book, Voices from the Void, was the result of a conversation with the gallerist Hugh Lane, after he had drowned on the Lusitania. Her living friends included Yeats and Bram Stoker.

At her home in Cheyne Gardens, by the river, she and Mr

V awaited their guest. Oscar knew the way; he lived just down the road. They'd thrown him out after his bother with those boys and the law, and put all his belongings on the street. Peacock feathers, blue-and-white china, all chucked out the door. Like Blake he died in poverty. But he'd moved on from all that, of course, in the neon glow of his dead fame.

Oscar Wilde is speaking. I have come, he announced, as if to a servant who had answered the door.

Being dead is the most boring experience in life, he says.

He's been rehearsing the line in eternity, retying his cravat, adjusting the brim of his floppy hat, ready to attend this remote private view.

To think of what is going on in the world is terrible for me, he said. Now the mere memory of the beauty of the world is an exquisite pain, he confessed.

I worshipped at the shrine of things seen. There was not a blood stripe on a tulip or a curve on a shell or a tone on the sea that but had for me its meaning and its mystery.

What do you think of the Sitwells? his hosts ask. His comment is too rude to publish, says Hester. Mr V can hardly keep up. Oscar may be dead, but he still does the voices.

What is your opinion of *Ulysses*, by James Joyce?

I have smeared my fingers with that vast work, he replies. In it he finds a monster who cannot contain the monstrosities of his own brain. It has given me one exquisite moment of amusement, he says.

But he does not say what it is. Nor does Dowden tell us that she is secretly avenging Joyce's comments in his book about her father, who had died in 1913. Instead she issues a fabulously ambiguous disclaimer: The opinions expressed by 'Oscar Wilde' are not mine. I leave it to my readers to pronounce on the case. I speak with assurance of Oscar Wilde's continued existence, merely for convenience; my own feeling is that of a diver who has pulled up a strange creature from the deep and wonders of what nature he may be!

Inside the copy of the book that he gave me, my friend Neil wrote a note about a seance he and his friends conducted in the nineteen-seventies, when Wilde told them, My dear children, you are so young, do not make my mistakes.

A shop-soiled Wilde. I once shook the hand of a man who shook the hand of a man who shook the hand of Wilde in a Dublin street.

Dowden will go on to transcribe a new three-act play by Wilde and give forty thousand sittings to clients, including Queen Eugenia of Spain. Her career in the spirit world is one long dream, a charade doused in savage perfume, the glittering gutter gloom of drawing-room curtains drawn on long afternoons. Her daughter, Dolly, a stage designer, will also become a practising medium, talents that came in useful in her role in the nineteen-sixties as curator of the Martello tower at Sandycove, where Joyce's disgraced ghost hung around the Forty Foot like a tramp, and where Mulligan, who in his real-life persona as Oliver St John Gogarty saved many men from drowning, proceeds to shave his chin on the top of the tower, summoning up the rage of Caliban at not seeing his face in a mirror, telling Stephen Dedalus, If Wilde were only alive to see you.

By that time Mr V had been revealed as Samuel G. Soal, a mathematician who turned psychic researcher after losing his brother in the First World War, and who would himself admit that his transcriptions of Wilde's words were probably the product of cryptoamnesia, the emergence of a forgotten memory.

Paris, 1929. Connolly interviews Joyce, who is wearing a white cricketing blazer and blue trousers as ironic commentary on his British passport. They talk about Clontarf, where Joyce liked to swim, and about Brian Boru's legendary sword with which Boru sliced off one hundred Viking heads before breakfast.

I am afraid I am more interested in little things like that than the problems of the solar system, Joyce tells Connolly.

He is writing *Finnegans Wake*, his narrative of the living and the dead. It is another seance, drawing directly on Hester Dowden's book; a revenge on her revenge as they both draw on the indiscretions of Wilde. It expands into a vastness that takes everything in. It is not about something, says Beckett, it is that something itself. It is absolutely modern, with scenes that Joyce describes as televised on a screen. Revolutionised. Cathode rays as ectoplasm. When an advance section appears that year, Connolly sees it as a kind of air photograph of Irish history.

We are looking at the earth from a long way away, he writes, perhaps as one might look at it by overtaking the light rays by turning a telescope on the Dark Ages, from some planet so far that it still could watch them going on.

My cousins swim in the Liffey. Joyce wraps his white blazer around himself, tries not to rub his eyes, crosses his long blue-trousered legs, twining them round and round, as if he were sitting on a banquette in a vegetarian restaurant in Brighton. He's keen to get rid of Connolly and his pompous Anglo-Irish tales. Joyce is only being polite. Just for the sake of a few more column inches. A little more adulation, a little less to say himself.

1 Martello Terrace, Bray, September 1888. From their house that ends in the beach, where the shingle rattles in the purple light of dawn and the sea is cold and grey and deep and floods the street at spring tide as it chills your bones; from here, at the age of half-past six, wearing his sailor suit, Joyce is packed off to Clongowes Wood. Alone. When a boy breaks his glasses, Joyce is unjustly punished for someone else's sins. At eleven, he is a blond, frail boy, the thinnest thing you ever saw. He has a scar on his chin inflicted when he was five years old by a

mongrel dog. He used to play at being Satan and the serpent. His eyes are already failing him. Pull out his eyes, Apologize.

By the time he makes it to university, walking up the steps and under the lion, Father Hopkins is a decade dead. But his poems are still in the building, locked in his little room, unread, pulsating, suppurating, waiting to be read. Joyce is across the hall, in a classroom on the same floor, the same floorboards. He is a difficult, brilliant student. He seldom washes if he can help it. They call him Disgustin' Joyce.

Gerard Manley Joyce. Gerard/Joyce. Skins/Disgustin'.

They cancel each other out. One fallen Jesuit, the other falling. Joyce disdains analysis, Jungian or otherwise. If you're going to do that, you might as well go to confession, he says. He asks for forgiveness, as if Fr Hopkins was hearing his litany of sins, then crossing them out.

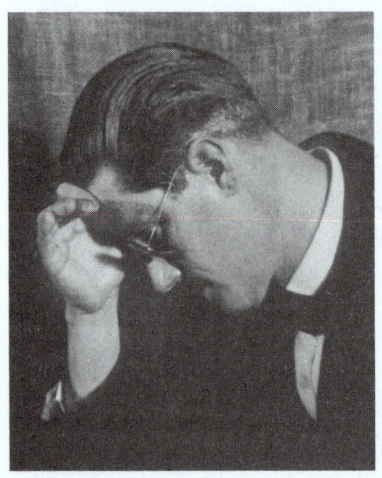 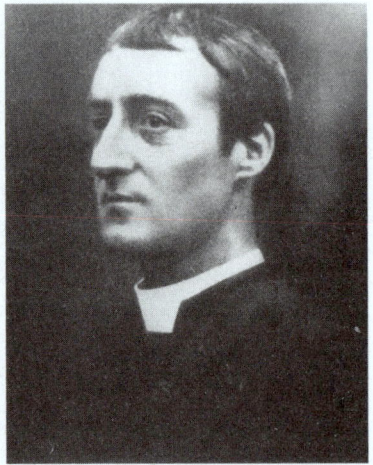

Disgustin'   Skins

His English teacher is Father Darlington, the same priest who remarked on Gerard's girlish shoes with a strap. He disapproves of Joyce, too, too smart for the good of his soul. Joyce sees himself as a womanly man and dedicates his first work, a play called A *Brilliant Career*, to himself and his own soul. He's so clever he hurts himself. He's so thin he asks someone what he looks like, then answers himself: Hunger, he says. He laughs out loud at his own jokes, with his whooping laugh, drawing attention to himself.

The Adriatic coast, 1912. Joyce is lecturing on Blake. England is not truly represented by John Bull, he tells his audience, as Richard Ellmann reports: Joyce sees himself in Blake, in his outsider status; both regarded as mad, estranged, yet deeply, fantastically drawn to the islands from which they came. Like Blake, Joyce is fearful of the sea but he's still by it, in Trieste, reading *The common objects of the sea-shore; including hints for an aquarium* by Reverend John George Wood, M.A., F.L.S., first published 1857. Joyce flicks through the text and the colour plates, seeing weird fringed things, changing shape like Blake's polypuses, someone's guts, the organs in *Ulysses*.

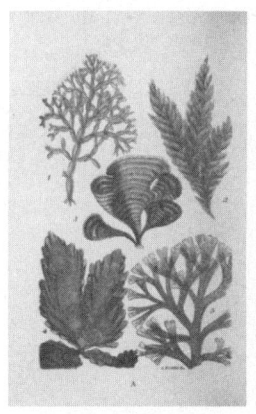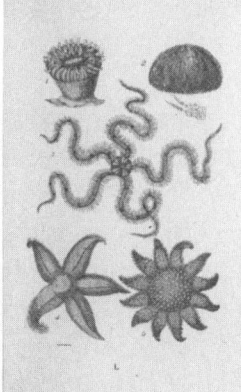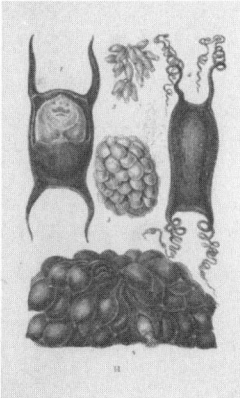

On some days, the Reverend Wood writes, the electric clouds that skirt the cliffs map out, as it were, the sea-coast; and when such signs fail, the marine birds give evident tokens that the sea, their great store-house, is close at hand.

Some little distance from the shore a number of black objects may be seen partly emerging from the water, executing a summersault, and disappearing below the surface, the reverend continues. These are Porpesses, he says. Some people say, that as it looks like a fish, and lives like a fish, to all intents and purposes it is a fish. So it is, says the priest, if the diver at the Polytechnic Institution is a fish. Both diver and porpesse must breathe atmospheric air, or they would die.

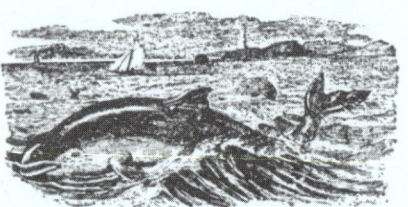

PORPOISE (OR PORPESSE).

I want to be famous while I am alive, Joyce says. He doesn't want to be a dead superstar, cigarettes and lipstick in Père-Lachaise. He must escape. Mr Wood goes on to describe the various seabirds that provide Joyce with his lists. Seaswans, seahawk, seagull, wild geese; all sighing and sobbing, and listening, Joyce says. The cormorant, the gannet and the common shag, all representatives of the Pelican family, as Mr Wood notes. They accompany Joyce's journey from *Ulysses* to *Finnegans Wake*. The pelican plucks her breast to feed its young with her own blood. Ireland is eating itself.

It was a very good idea of God, to make blood red.

Joyce's career as a cinema proprietor is over before it began. Instead, he plans to take to the south coast of England with a lute, singing old English songs from Falmouth to Margate.

My tour will not be a success, he admits, but it will prove the inadequacy of the English. Like Blake's lyrics, another way of subverting the state. Instead he goes outside Wilde's house, waiting for Nora Barnacle, a sea creature herself, to come along. (I just walked past; I think he's still standing there.) Wild, outspoken, she is his muse, his Kate. He sees himself as a deer from the family coat of arms—pale, silent, bayed about—or a bird, both in its song and in its flight. Doe-eyed, short-sighted, deer-man-bird. As thin and dandy as Nancy Cunard. A match for each other. He walks into Shakespeare and Company, a movie set where he's playing himself.

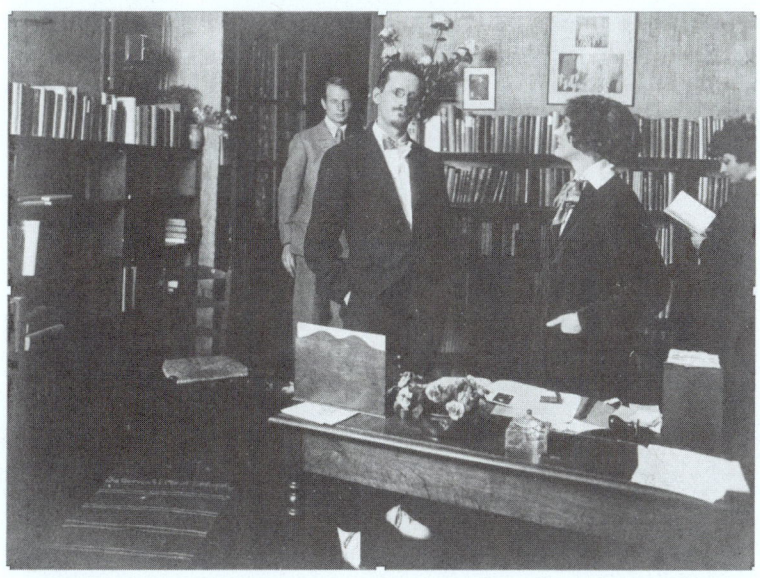

The lights go on. Who is he, where is he, who do I see about the rights? That tilt of his head, the cock of the north. I knew boys like that. Sixth-formers, lanky, all nervy self-confidence and jokes. Hands in pockets, white shoes. Sylvia Beach raises her chin to take him in. He takes her in.

Can you stand me a buck, 20 livres? he says.

Paris, 1922. *Ulysses* is published, thick as a brick. Its cover is the colour of the sea, specially dyed for the occasion, like Yves Klein blue or a tin of Farrow & Ball paint. It is composed of uncrossed-out sins. A book based on a myth turns him into a myth. They say he wears black gloves, surrounds himself with mirrors. That he swims in the river every day, a lad in the Seine.

I am not a literary Jesus Christ, he protests. Some say he's the Antichrist.

Imperial Hotel, Torquay, August 1929. In another stunt, arranged on his behalf by Sylvia Beach, Joyce leaves Torquay—where he'd spent two months on the beach fingering the great pebbles for texture and weight like Molloy—and goes to Cambridge to record an LP of himself reading from Anna Livia Plurabelle. He can barely read the script and someone has to whisper prompts to him. His voice is oddly elfin and childlike; the feminine way he says Flip! and rolls his RRRs at 78 rpm, as if he'd only just discovered the words. It's his master's Dada voice. Price, two guineas, in a plain paper sleeve so no one sees it when you leave the shop. It's mischievous and complicit. He's winding us up. David Jones, the artist, listens to it in his London bed-sitting room, playing it over and over again, till he learns it by heart. Joyce mentions the Strawberry Beds six times in his book. Anselm Kiefer chalks them on a gallery wall.

strubbely beds   fraiseberry beds
strawbirry reds   fraisey beds
strawberry bedspread   Strubry Bess

As he loses sight of the world, Joyce crams more words in, in references that escape almost everyone, including himself.

Well, old Humber was as glommen as grampus.

Grampus being another alias used by the killer whale. Whales disguised by whales. He makes a note of whales in his notebook in 1924, the year *Moby-Dick* and *Billy Budd* resurfaced. They are scattered through *Finnegans Wake*, one long watery wake, with its rivery references to Hopkins's alliteration

Can't hear with the waters of. The chittering waters of. Flittering bats.

and

rockbound (hoahoahoah!) in swimswamswum and all the livvy-long night, the delldale dalppling night, the night of bluerybells,

as your eyes run over *Finnegans Wake* like the river it embodies. The book fills up as it goes along, water flowing underground as Joyce calls on the waters to part to reveal the island of Manhattan as

a waalworth of a skyerscape of most eyeful hoyth entowerly

comparing the Woolworth Building, the tallest building in the world, to the world's biggest animal, using the Danish for whale.

He will never go to New York.

I should have been reading Moby Dick, Virginia Woolf tells her diary in the summer of 1928; she sees her nephew's new gramophone, painted white like Moby Dick, she says (later she will see herself as a spirit flying over the ocean to New York, where she too will never go). The white whale, the shores of Albion, the angels of God.

With pale blake I write tintingface, Joyce writes, as if he were dancing with a whale in lieu of a hovering kestrel

Lave a whale a while in a whillbarrow

while everything is collapsing all together as

Grampupus is fallen down

while

fins and flippers that shimmy and shake . . .

We're not sure what's human or non-human

Me seemeth a dragon man

Blending in their Blakean ambiguity, like a god of disorder

What a quhare soort of a mahan.

There are dozens more queer and whalish things in *Finnegans Wake*, in the wake of the whale, innuendos scattered like scars, strewn with dark entries and pale bodies dragged back from the dead, under the stars.

1922–1939

Give him a search engine and he'd never have finished it.

Joyce couldn't bear to end it, so the last words of his book are left hanging—

a last a loved a long the

—turning back to the first ones—

riverrun, past Eve and Adam's, from swerve of shore.

Starting all over again, the book eats itself like a shark. I collect up all the references the best that I can, telling a story of their own:

the hill of the
Himmalehan
whale of whom
Ishmael speaks

Whalebones and buskbutts may hurt you

(thwackaway thwuck!)

the woman's body
constricted by the
whalebone busk
used to pandy
Dedalus's hand or
perhaps his arse

I feel like that hill of a whaler

The great fin may cumule!

Finnegan's wake,
the fin whale,
employing
the whalers'
shorthand for
the long whale

Finner! How did he bank it up,

swank it up, the whaler in the punt

Jonah, left behind
in the ship's wake

Wherry like the whaled prophet

1132 A.D. Men like to ants or emmets wondern upon a
groot hwide Whallfisk which lay in a Runnel. Blubby
wares upat Ublanium

from a queer sub-
librarian

the pourquose of which

a sweet unclose to the

Narwhealian captol

but low, boys low, he rises

queerest man in the
benighted queendom

two Whales of the Sea of Deceit

his Thing went the wholyway

retup Suffrogate Strate

wham-bam

a part of the whole as a port for a whale

the hill of the
Himmalehan
whale of whom
Ishmael speaks

Whalebones and buskbutts may hurt you

(thwackaway thwuck!)

the woman's body
constricted by the
whalebone busk
used to pandy
Dedalus's hand or
perhaps his arse

I feel like that hill of a whaler

The great fin may cumule!

Someone accuses the humpback Norwegian captain, you wutan whaal, sayd he, saying he's a white whale.

And the tavern turns into a ferry boat, like a moon-ark careering down the Liffey from the Strawberry Beds where my great-grandparents, my Adam and Eve, sit in their cottage as my cousins are drinking in the Wren's Nest and the women are washing their clothes, down to Dublin Bay as the four dodos of the gospel apocalypse bob about; a ship of fools, this Ship-le-Zoyd, bouncing from *Finnegans Wake* to William Blake, endlessly added to like Blake's prophecies (as the critics Northrop Frye and Karl Kiralis would say in the nineteen-fifties), words making more sense than they say, rushing on till they reach the sea. Joyce throws everything in there, making it up as he goes along. It's a test of endurance: ours, and his own. He's Jonah thrown overboard, not wanted on voyage.

Drowning in his own words.

Autumn, 1932. Joyce's vision is in full retreat. He can barely see his own shoes. His condition, glaucoma, is the same one that dimmed Milton's sight and turned my mother's eyes misty sea-green. They test my eyes for it by blowing puffs of air at them. Like having someone whisper in your eyes instead of your ears.

Beckett leaves Paris, playing secretary to Joyce, for London. He reads *Moby-Dick*. He prefers it to Huxley. That's more like the real stuff, he says; white whales and natural piety.

In *Waiting for Godot*, Lucky puffs like a grampus.

Winter 1939. Joyce moves from Paris towards the sea. Exiled again and again, by himself. He lies on the beach. He keeps its pebbles in his pockets not in his head, not to be sucked but to be used as ammunition against dogs. Someone asks him why he dislikes dogs. Because they have no souls, he says. It's more an accusation than a critique. He doesn't realise that dogs hear everything you say. It's just that sometimes they quietly ignore it, for your own sake, and theirs. Generally we are more like dogs than dogs are like us. This demonstrates their superiority over us.

Joyce dies quickly, escaping Paris for Zurich. He's here, then he's gone. No one sees him leaving. He just slips away. The anonymity of Switzerland ensures the anonymity of his departure. He likes it that way. The doctor who sees him off will perform the same duties for Thomas Mann. Nora, who has never read any of her husband's books, is annoyed that everyone ignores *Finnegans Wake* in favour of *Ulysses*. It's not his passport.

Modernism: old-fashioned even before it began.

Summer 1981. A man walks into a bookshop on Madison Avenue. Actually, he runs into it from the street. It's about to close. It's no joke. Saturday afternoon in midtown Manhattan; it's been a long day. It's annoying when they do that. But at least this tricky customer knows what he wants. A copy of *Finnegans Wake*. He's read it before, he tells the assistant, describing it as a work of literature that is actually music. The way he cuts and pastes his own words. He's half Irish himself. Having delivered his lecture, he goes on his way. He's the starman, and he's a thief.

Karachi, summer 1927. Thomas Edward Lawrence is lying face down on his bunk. It's his preferred position. He's reading *Ulysses*, the book of the century, so heavy he has to pull up a table to prop it up. He's wearing khaki shorts and long socks. Playing himself. He decides Joyce is a genius, but an unlucky one. His writing has the architectural merit of Balham, he says. It goes on for ever, and needn't ever vary in spirit.

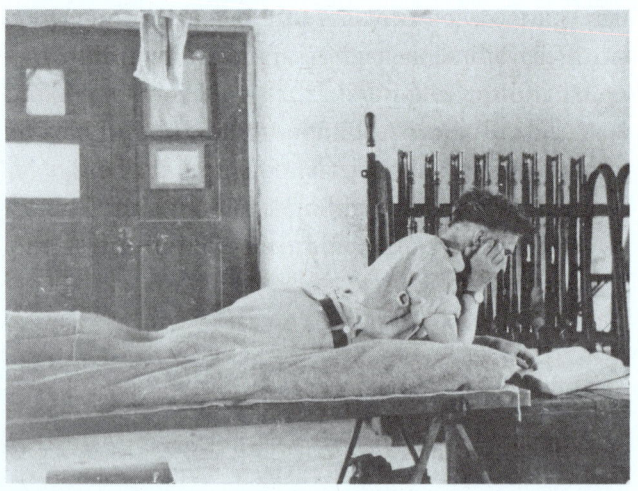

The Solent, 1929. Why did you join the RAF? someone asks him at Calshot, where Lawrence and his fellow airmen are qualifying for their swimming badges like boy scouts. He has had a fear of swimming ever since his experiences in Arabia, where he had to run into the sea to wash the stain away. Now he's back on the same shore where he learned to swim as a boy. He knows it well; he grew up in a house between the New Forest and Southampton Water. This waterway, my backyard.

He's staying on his friend's yacht. She hears the splash in the night. Icarus overboard.

I like the life, it suits me, Lawrence tells the other airmen. Then he proceeds to imitate a frolicking porpoise.

Plymouth Sound, 1932. Lawrence writes to a friend from Mount Batten, Plymouth, where he is stationed, on a rocky peninsula, along with a hundred airmen. The place looks like a fossil lizard swimming out into the Sound, he says. He is just back from racing secret speedboats on Southampton Water. He says he lost his character there. The water allowed him to become anonymous.

He is surrounded by as many myths as Joyce, most of them of his own making. He's well connected: George Bernard Shaw, Thomas Hardy, Winston Churchill; E.M. Forster, Noël Coward, Siegfried Sassoon. He is happy in queer company. He preys upon them like a lion. He loves to be loved but hates to be touched and will not sit on anyone else's bed. Eddie Marsh is a charming joke, so kind and nice. Nice is his word, Lawrence says. He retreats, deep into Dorset. Stephen Tennant comes tottering up his path. None of them really know him, or that he's the bastard son of an Anglo-Irish baronet.

You would laugh at my cottage, he tells Edward Elgar. It's just two rooms, really, one on top of the other, in the woods. One room upstairs (gramophone and records) and one room downstairs (books): but there is also a bath, and we sleep anywhere we feel inclined, he said. A one-man house, he says.

But there are two sleeping bags; and at Christmas, late one night an airman arrived to spend the holiday with me, he tells Nancy Astor. That was a nice present, all wrapped up. That Christmas two men and four women sent me fervent messages of love, he says. Love carnal, not love rarefied.

Dorset, 1933. He's got the builders in. So I couldn't find the Wilfred Owen, he reports. Of the Hopkins, I found two copies: one was the large paper, with portraits: the other this scruffy little edition. But Hopkins is a fine poet, he says, and I value him—The Deutschland and the Epithalamion are both sustained efforts. Every now and then he is astonishing. Very 'repressed-sexy',* I feel (he adds a footnote). Celibacy has its dangers!

* homo-?

Afghanistan, 1928. Standing like that: thin, cinched in, big head, holding on to himself. Arthurian-alien in the desert sands. As D.H. Lawrence said of Melville, there's something too keen and abstract about blue-eyed people. In his jumpsuit, short-back-and-sides, fallen to earth again. He has wasted away with all that nervous energy, consumed in flames that do not burn him. I estimate his waist at twenty-six inches. The photographer is Flight Lieutenant Stanley James Smetham, named after his ancestor, the artist James Smetham, a staunch defender of Blake. Smetham poses Lawrence like a doll, a desert saint in drab, a visionary in fatigues. Holding his wrist, hair disarrayed, unbuttoned to the waist, a thorn in his side. Looks at his watch, thanks God he's still alive.

His *Seven Pillars of Wisdom* was published in 1926; it was named after a mountain and he intended it to be a titanic book, to emulate *Moby-Dick*, he said. With him starring in it, like Rudolph Valentino or Ivor Novello or the kohl-eyed starlet Theda Bara, her name an anagram of arab death. You must see the movie. He spends all his money on his secret epic, the source of all this fatal glamour. It is illustrated by, among others, Eric Kennington and Paul Nash. The two artists were at school together; Nash recalled Kennington as a swarthy boy who lived

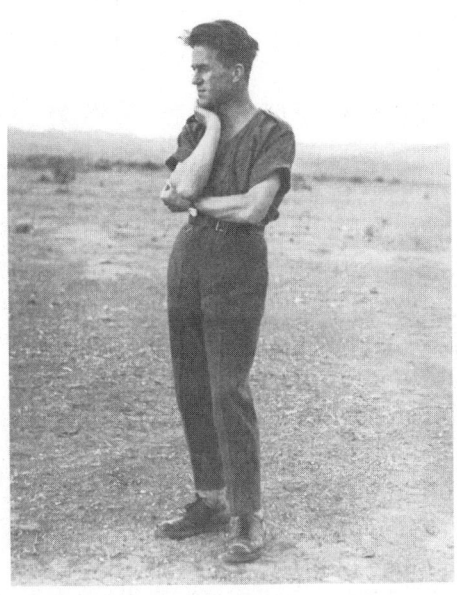

on a perch like a bird. Kennington was now a very handsome man. Lawrence curated his artists to give his text modernity and romance. It was his tribute to Blake, this attention to words and images on a page. He wrote paragraphs so they would fit neatly without breaking in half. He was making no widows or orphans in his book, although he had made plenty in the desert. He spent hundreds of pounds on commissions, asking artists to illustrate that which he could no longer bear to see in his dreams.

The result was a kind of prophecy. William Roberts, Edward Wadsworth, Nash and Kennington draw Lawrence's nightmares. They record what he felt rather than what he saw. They respond to his desires, filling the book with the naked bodies of men.

I don't know what they mean, Lawrence said; they're mad; the war was mad, he said. The amazing thing is that he stayed sane and so innocent. But his obsession meant that every page ended with a full stop.

I am a disciple of Blake, he declared, and called Kennington's contributions wonderful imaginative things in colour—drawings, Blake-like, of states of mind. Cyborg-erotic updates of the Book of Job. He empathises with Job's tribulations.

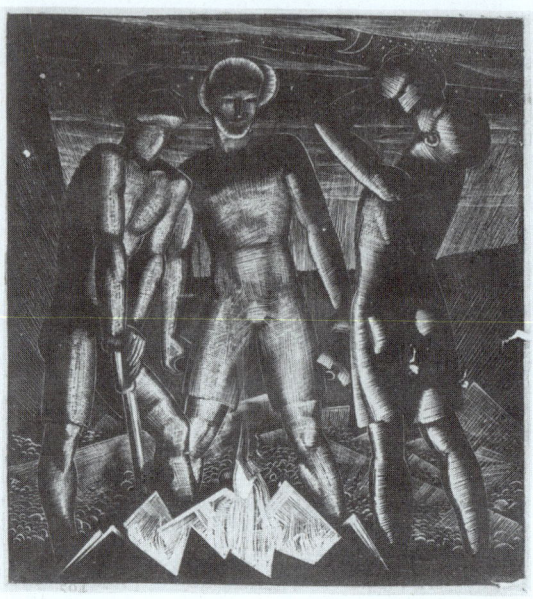

Paul Nash is introduced to Lawrence by Eddie Marsh, whose patronage and loyalty had no limits, like his undeclared lust. He put people together to see what they would do. Nash had given up painting for a while, and has just begun again, painting the sea and the shore.

T.E.L. buys my first sea painting to hang in the Colonial Office and annoy the officials, Nash says.

I want it: very much, Lawrence tells him, and pays for it in instalments. He has a lust for art, if not for life.

I'm very glad you agree to sell the Ocean in bits, he says.

Lawrence asks if he would work from photographs, and arrives at Nash's house, bringing two hundred with him.

He is the ultimate modernist: not in his words, but in his deeds. Editing his life and his passions. He needed to be beaten for sins he had not crossed out. He submitted his body to the cold sea for the same reason. It was a lifelong campaign. The sea versus the desert. Who would win? John E. Mack, a Harvard psychiatrist who won the Pulitzer for his book *A Prince of Our Disorder* in 1976, believed that Lawrence was trying to destroy his own sexuality.

Mack saw Lawrence for his strangeness, not despite it. It is hardly surprising (although it shocked his colleagues to the point of distraction) that Mack's other great subject of scrutiny was truly out of this world: after writing Lawrence's biography, he devoted his energies to examining accounts of alien abduction, having been alerted to them by the experiences of Budd Hopkins, an abstract expressionist artist on Cape Cod where, together with two other people, Hopkins had seen a UFO hovering over the dunes in the summer of 1964.

Hopkins and his friends had set off from Truro to attend a cocktail party in neighbouring Provincetown, driving on the narrow causeway that connects the end of the Cape to the rest of the world. Ahead lay the Pilgrim Monument, an improbable Italianate tower in the distance, like this was Venice. On one side of the causeway is the usually calm bay; on the other is a lagoon. Beyond that is the great ocean where the pilgrims had come from. The strand nearby is called First Encounter Beach. This slip of land, held out to sea in a vast curl, an early-warning system of what is happening out there. Or perhaps a landing strip. The end of America, so Thoreau thought. As they drove to their party, along the thin ribbon of road, Hopkins and his two passengers saw an elliptical, aluminum-coloured shape in the sky.

At first they thought it was a balloon tethered to the ground. But as the clouds passed over it, it seemed ghosted like a ship in a fog bank, Hopkins said; it was not moving with the same wind that made the clouds roll by. He stopped the car and he and his passengers got out to watch as the object began to move, heading east against the wind, towards the ocean. It was clearly not a balloon, although a military airbase stood nearby.

They watched until it disappeared behind the clouds, and was gone. It was only when he got to the party and talked to friends who lived out there on the Cape tip, who had also seen strange lights in the sky, that Hopkins realised there was more to what he had seen than met the eye. I knew two of those people. One was Mary Oliver; the other, her partner, Molly Cook. They did not disbelieve him. Hopkins felt the object was surveying the area, possibly for intelligence purposes.

Mack was convinced by Hopkins's story; or at least, that none of this was quite what it seemed. He thought that the reports of alien abductions which Hopkins had begun to explore could not all be dismissed as the products of fanciful imagination or delusion. Mack had already been investigated by the FBI for his plans as a young student to visit the USSR in the nineteen-fifties, and for his activities with anti-war and civil-rights movements in the nineteen-sixties. Later, his own employers at Harvard Medical School would also censure him for seeing two hundred patients who claimed to have been abducted by aliens.

Mack said these case histories, which formed the basis for two books on the subject that he published in the nineteen-nineties, were a logical development from his studies of Lawrence, of suicide, and of the threat of nuclear war. The connection resides in the matter of identity, he said, who we are in the deepest and broadest sense. Conspiracies or coincidences did not explain everything.

But in 2004 Mack was killed crossing the road in north London. He was on his way to address the T.E. Lawrence Society.

I've never been inside somewhere so dark and so bright, like a box full of mirrors, pulling in the light, some kind of trick. It all comes flooding in. Magnetic, electric, hypnotic. The cottage consists of four rooms, two up, two down, set at the foot of a hill, surrounded by rhododendrons, overlooked by pines. The road runs right by it, fast and empty. Except for the tanks.

I haul myself upstairs by the rope banister like an artist dragging himself up to his mews. A tough rope stay, thick as my arm, stained and polished in its twists by many hands. The place is animal-nautical-cryptic; a stable or an abattoir or a black cabin on a shingle beach. The doorway is hung with a rough piece of hide to keep out the draughts and the spies and the sea gods. Sealed like a submarine or a bordello. The first floor is a secret attic, with a state-of-the-art gramophone installed. You can hear it from under the floorboards.

The fireplace comes up to my ribs. Lawrence had no time-wasting dining table; the mantelpiece built wide enough for a plate. He stood there to eat, talking all the time. Stephen Tennant said it sounded like Morse code. Like Blake, Lawrence was delighted with his cottage: it was called Clouds Hill and he was happy up there, closer to heaven. On his mantel-altar, where he left his last supper plate and knife and fork and empty tin of baked beans (there was no one to clear up after him), stands a pair of stainless-steel art deco candlesticks, presented to him on Southampton Water by servicemen who loved him. All these devoted men, under his thrall; at least, that's how he saw them. The local blacksmith made a guard for the fire of sprouting arts-and-crafts lilies; the local carpenter lined the room with dark square wooden panels to keep out the demons that moved through the trees outside.

The light pours in from the skylight like a burglar landing on the big leather sofa. It falls on an airman bedding down on the floor. The gramophone has a horn the size of a stinking lily made of papier mâché so as not to reverberate with Mozart and Beethoven as the rain drummed at the window. It used a wooden needle; Lawrence claimed a record sounded better the more it was played.

The neighbouring room, cupboard-like, is covered in silver foil. A giant cool box. The bed is a boxed shelf on a set of drawers, exactly the length of his body. He was three inches shorter than me. He came up to my nose. He lied about his size to become an officer, at the regulation five-foot-five or above.

The drawers contain his clothes as well as the body that wore them. Like sleeping on top of a wardrobe. A bunk for Billy Budd; the entire British army stands guard outside. Inside, Lawrence sits in his customised armchair, also built to his shape. He is electric even when doing nothing, a state of melancholia, surrounded by nothing that does not work. Everything bends to his will.

A painting over the fireplace shows a scene from a beach in Falmouth, Cornwall. Lawrence had run away there as a teenager and joined a regiment in 1905. A boy swims in a rock pool at high tide. No one's filming it. A second young man sits on the sand, getting undressed. His head is unmistakable.

The painter was Henry Scott Tuke, who knew Wilde and exhibited his work in London at the same time as Graham Robertson. Tuke's student, Philip Streatfeild, had painted a similar nude portrait of Noël Coward as a boy on a Cornish beach in 1914. Both Streatfeild and Coward were close friends with Sydney Lomer, a poet and captain in the Sherwood Foresters who had been involved in a scandal in 1912 when a nineteen-year-old bandsman shot himself in Lomer's bedroom. There are currents here that remain unknown to us. In 1922, Lomer bought Stuke's picture (under an assumed name, Scott) of Lawrence; Lawrence in turn bought it (under an assumed name, Gray) from Lomer's estate after he died in 1926. Secrets and lies were necessary.

Stuke recorded the picture as a Portrait of Gray. It was a pun, a disguise; Gray was the name Lawrence used when he ran away. He denied nothing. It was his game. The artist worked what was left of his study of me into a beach picture after, he said, giving me a new head, several sizes smaller. The second painting showed him naked on the rocks while another boy bobs like a seal.

Apparently I am shaped rather like a tadpole, Lawrence said.

The cottage is a ship in the woods. Fixed and fitted and

sealed up tight. The amount of leather in the house is perverse. Animal skins covering chairs, covering mattresses. Dubbin for leather, wax for brass rubbings from gothic churches, frottage. Skins, skinned for the lover who never arrived. The sergeant who was hired to beat him, face down on the leather bed.

Stories swirled around him like a cloud. He lay in his cabin, all shiny and narcissistic. I see my silvery ghost reflected in his silvery room. This place was tailored to him, bespoke to his body. There was no one to tuck him in. But there's a brick-red sleeping bag of thin cloth, the kind of material you'd make curtains from, fastened round with a thick zip. He could zip himself up. It's one of a pair. On one he embroidered, in careful chain stitch, the word Meum; on the other, the word Tuum. An intimate invitation. For you and him. Often, he just slept on the floor where he fell, as if under desert stars rather than Dorset skies.

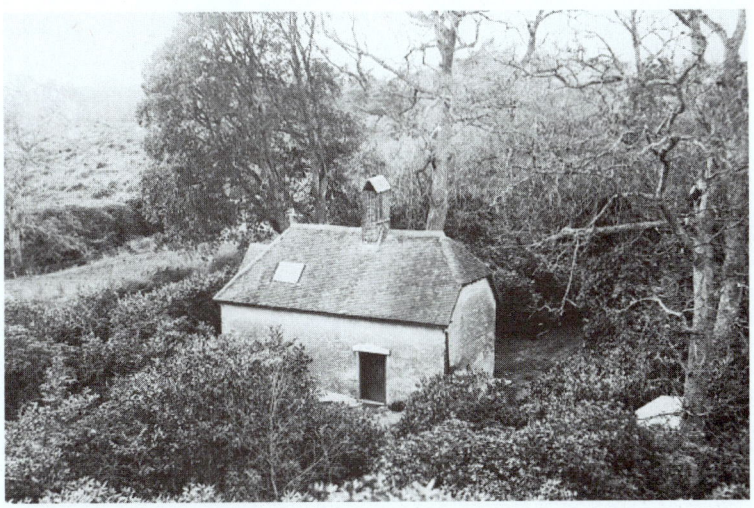

His dead-or-alive eyes follow you about. He is the sort of person I would leave anything to follow, said Iris Murdoch, rereading *Seven Pillars of Wisdom* in 1943. I feel a sort of reverence for that book—for that man—which is hard to describe, she says, breathlessly. To live such a swift life of action, and yet <u>not</u>

simplify everything to the point of inhumanity—to let the agonising complexities of situations twist your heart instead of tying your hands—that is real human greatness.

He knew what he was doing. Some suspected him of super powers. He had a latent psychic superiority, a sense of his own greatness, said his friend, the writer Francis Yeats-Brown.

One morning, failing to meet his friend as arranged on the Plymouth quayside, Yeats-Brown leaves the Drake Steps and drives round to the dock at Mount Batten, where Lawrence is getting off the boat, bare to the buff, wearing only a bathing slip on his small brown body, his hair wet (Yeats-Brown says it's red. The viking in him). He has a fiendish look on his face, and is attended by two airmen, fully dressed, much taller than him, yet under his spell, as was Yeats-Brown, a former major fascinated by Indian mysticism who had told Paul Nash about Tibetan lamas. He was also a supporter of fascism, attuned to the notion of a magnetic personality. He will later meet the German leader in Nuremberg.

I was paralysed, Yeats-Brown reports. Lawrence seemed full of the possibilities of destruction, he says. I wanted to avoid this cosmic force, yet was rooted to the spot. The moment passes; Lawrence says something had gone wrong.

He goes off to dress. Yeats-Brown lights a cigarette with a shaky hand.

Eric Kennington came to believe Lawrence could affect events remotely, even if he was thousands of miles away, or just in another room. That he exhibited the talents of a faith healer. They're all hypnotised.

He was a stranger to himself, Yeats-Brown said. He was not human enough to do anything else.

When I go outside for a pee behind his shed, I can feel him standing beside me. By the road, by the garage-stable he built for his bikes. He wrote his book in a borrowed attic room in Westminster, living on chocolate and tea, checking into the Savoy for a night when he needed someone to do his laundry.

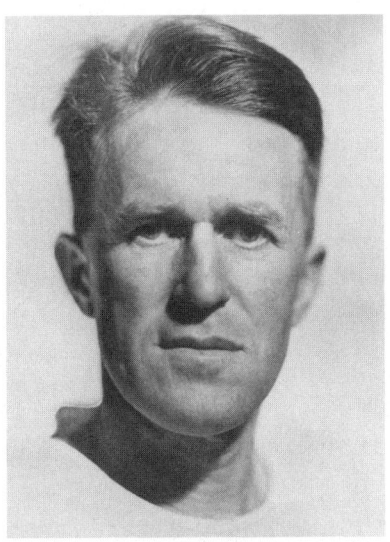

He crashed out there, neuro-sublime, on the lane where the cars career round the bend. Someone said they saw a mysterious black car. He took six days to die. Dying and dying again. Comatose, a nine-inch opening in his head for his spirit to get out. Hurled over the handlebars and across the road. Propped up by a tree, pointing up at the sky. He never regained consciousness. They put grass from Akaba, the site of his greatest triumph, in his coffin, the way Jackie put a whale tooth in JFK's casket. Everyone wondered: grass from the desert? Was that just another of his miracles, this martyr, this saint?

T.E. was attended, even in his own private rank, by aides-de-camp, said George Bernard Shaw. They were his guardian angels in buff uniforms, hench henchmen, hired to beat the devil out of him. He rode out like the devil on his custom-built motorbike. It was bigger than him, worth as much as a house, drawing even more attention to its reclusive rider as he revved up its bestial roar.

He rode through the tram tunnel under Kingsway in Holborn and down the Duke of York's Steps to the Mall. Or he cycled like a boy scout. To get away from himself and everyone else. He was poor, by choice; a vow, like his chastity. Bernard Shaw thought he never actually came to maturity in that very curious arrest of his physical development. Shaw's wife, Charlotte, the woman closest to Lawrence, called him an infernal liar. He made the army his monastery, said his friend Lewis Namier, and said he wanted to be like a brown paper parcel, with no decisions to make.

He said Melville was the man. He's all there. He's Moby Dick, the ghostly whale of revenge; Ahab, the wounded captain, his sex maimed; Ishmael, the suicidal onlooker, running away to lose himself himself, rejecting, rejecting any rank or responsibility; Bartleby looking at the wall, preferring not to do anything. Billy Budd, flawed, doomed by his own charisma. I always felt there was something tragic in Lawrence's youth, said Will Rothenstein, Wilde's friend.

Soho, 1935. Morgan Forster and T.E. dine at a French restaurant in Wardour Street, discussing the impending prosecution of James Hanley's novel Boy.

Lawrence is a fan of Hanley's works; he wrote out of the blue to tell him so. Your writing is hot, he said. When Hanley sent him the typescript draft of Boy for his advice, Lawrence told him his characters were drawn with blistering vividness.

Hanley, born in Liverpool of Irish parents in 1897, had spent his early life at sea. He too worshipped the work of Melville. His first novel, Drift, published in 1930, was influenced by Joyce's Portrait of the Artist. Boy was his second published book. It was dedicated to Nancy Cunard, who gave him the typewriter to write it.

The book is the story of a thirteen-year-old boy, Arthur Fearon, described as thin and undersized, who flees his abusive father and stows away on a ship, only to be assaulted by a steward, and interfered with by two other men.

It is another retelling of Billy Budd. Hanley insisted the story was not autobiographical; he claimed he had overheard it on the bridge of a ship. After visiting a brothel when the ship calls at Alexandria in Egypt, Arthur contracts syphilis, and in extreme pain and all the while calling for his mother, tries to throw himself over the side of the ship. The captain, with a mixture of gruffness and compassion, takes Arthur into his cabin, and tenderly smothers him with his greatcoat to put him out of his misery, all the while whispering, Boy. Come Boy. Billy in Starry Vere's dreams.

Then he throws the boy's poisoned body into the sea. The book is prosecuted for depicting intimacy between members of the male sex.

I will not throw *Boy* away, Lawrence told Hanley, because I like men, and ships and Alexandria! You leave nothing unsaid or undone, do you? I can't understand how you find brave men to publish you.

Devon, 1931. Lawrence visits Hanley in Exeter. He was simple, charming, unaffected, Hanley says, quite ordinary-looking with a cap on. He sat in an armchair drinking a cup of tea and eating a slice of bread and butter, like any ordinary person. A small terrier belonging to the house sat on his knee, but he would not have it removed, and it seemed to prefer his knee to anybody else's. During the course of conversation Lawrence tells Hanley he felt best when he was moving about amongst crowds, thinking of nothing in particular, excepting patterns, shapes and colours.

He does not want to advance, Hanley said, but is slowly retreating.

August 1922. Lawrence enlists in the air force under the name of Ross. He is trying to escape his public and private self. He will write it up as a fictionalised memoir, *The Mint*, the Joycean antidote to his *Seven Pillars of Wisdom*. In it he vomits his dinner silently into the barrack latrine, wrestles late in the night, dog-fighting with Dickson who has him arched back over a bed, shifting his hand to that fatal bollock-hold, as Lawrence writes—You bunch the things tightly and knead them, he says. I'm learning him, Dickson says; would he keep step when marching down town? Would he fuck? he says. When Ross falls, his friend Sailor is one of the gang who undressed me after gym, he says. They feel and flex their lithe bodies, even in spare hours, for delight in them, Lawrence writes admiringly, regretfully, of this person he sees but cannot be.

I wrote it tightly, he told Forster, because our clothes are so tight, and our lives so tight in the service. He's a tease. That winter, he meets a young airman who is described, by a fellow serviceman, as beautiful, like a Greek God. He's from Birmingham, about to be posted to a new aircraft carrier, HMS *Hermes*, in Portsmouth. Saturday quite convenient, says Lawrence in a telegram. His name is Robert Austen Marston Guy; R.A.M. Guy. A piston. Bob, for short.

Lawrence calls him Poppet or Rabbit and orders a new overcoat for him from a Savile Row tailor. The receipts are found stuffed in a sealed envelope, as Desmond Stewart writes, long after Lawrence has gone. His generosity was saint-like, Mack said. Not wanting to be seen, constantly seeing himself.

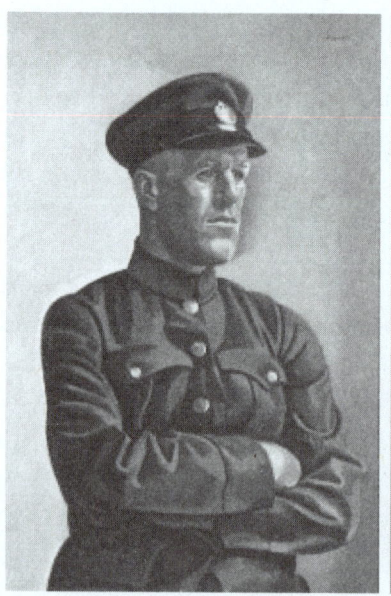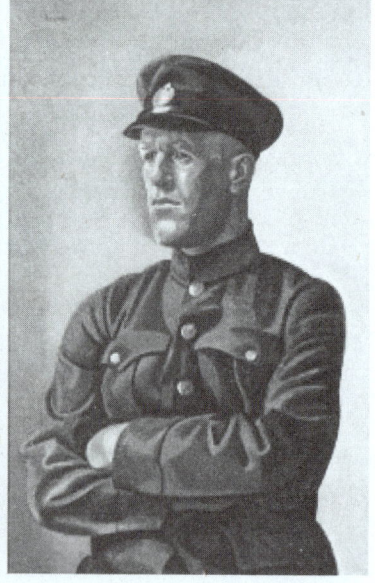

Poppet   Rabbit

I stand like a burglar in his library, between his leather-covered bed and his boxed armchair, surrounded by his books that have since disappeared. Caught in the act, they gave too much away. *The Mirror of the Sea* signed by Conrad, with the greatest regard. Noël Coward's *Post-Mortem* in eight acts. Gerard Manley Hopkins's poems, 1930, limited edition, number 86, the gift of Robert Bridges. Poems by Gogarty and Yeats. Blake's *Poetry and Prose*, inscribed, T.E.S. August, 1927, quoting the poet in the year of his hundredth anniversary

> He who bends to himself a joy
> Does the winged life destroy;
> But he who kisses the joy as it flies
> Lives in eternity's sunrise

along with other Blake works, including the *Book of Job*, signed to Lawrence by the editor, Geoffrey Keynes, in 1935. They'd met at Sassoon's wedding in Christchurch, Dorset. Keynes sat across from Lawrence, gazing his fill at the small but strongly built man, with a pink face and a shock of yellow hair. Blake's astonishing cry, Lawrence had noted in Bovington Camp, Every thing that is, is holy! The best words ever said, Lawrence said, even though he had rewritten them and he had no visible God.

The secret life of books, viz: *Anna Livia Plurabelle*, 1928, signed by Joyce; *Tales Told of Shem and Shaun*, 1929; *Haveth Childers Everywhere*, 1931; *Ulysses*, signed by Joyce, 1922, limited edition, number 36. Herman Melville's *Collected Works*, all of them, 1924. *Moby-Dick*, illustrated by Rockwell Kent, 1930. Books by Lord Alfred Douglas and Huysmans and Firbank; Whitman's *Leaves of Grass*, one of my big books, he said. And next to Mann's *The Magic Mountain*—joining *Moby-Dick* and *Ulysses* in a monumental queer trio—is its prelude, *Der Tod in Venedig*, in the original German, with T.E.L.'s initials and the date, '1913.'

Ulysses is a wicked book but he feels as spotless as the lamb, lying down on his army bed. He'd ordered two copies from Shakespeare and Company in 1922—the high-end limited edition, 350 francs each, signed by the author. They didn't arrive, so he wrote to the bookshop asking where they were. They were delivered to his address in Westminster eventually. Then one was shipped all the way to Afghanistan.

Years later, Richard Aldington, Joyce's friend and lover of Nancy Cunard (he was obsessed with her, entering her room grabbing his balls), writes a book exposing the stories Lawrence made up about himself, as Aldington said. In his *Biographical Enquiry*—as the author subtitled his book, as if it were an act of forensic assassination—Aldington conducts a modern analysis that sees Lawrence as an autofact and starts off with an epigraph quoting Wilde:

Untruthful! My nephew Algernon?
Impossible! He is an Oxonian.

Aldington makes much of such queer equations. He finds ambiguity everywhere. Call me Ishmael! he says, putting words in Lawrence's mouth. He defines Lawrence's psychology as an Ishmael complex. But he discovers, like everyone else, that scepticism only adds to the allure, another guise. In the desert, crossing borders, Lawrence dressed up as a woman to avoid being taken for a spy. The embroidered veil. The hitched robe. The masked eyes. A ghost haunting himself.

Carchemish, 1913. The site of the ancient capital, now on the border between Turkey and Syria. Divided by the Euphrates. A fault line. Lawrence is excavating artefacts from an ancient mound and shifting great stones about with the help of a derrick of his own design. He relies on the labour of dozens of Arabian men and boys who, he boasts, are pleased to do as they are told. It was here that he was at his happiest, living in the archaeologists' cottage.

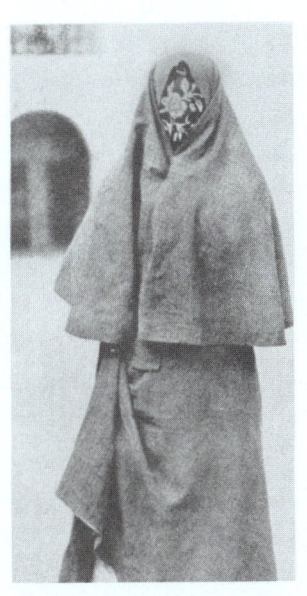

He furnishes it with a pair of chairs designed by the Austrian consul—he was a very good designer, Lawrence says—in black wood and buff leather and straight lines; they went very well with the jet-black floor. Very modern; it might be a radical room in Bloomsbury. There are rugs from the market and a Morris tapestry from Oxford; the curtains are red leather. He wants to melt Roman glass on the walls of the house to give it lustre like a jewel in the desert. He bathes frequently in the Euphrates, which turns his hair even more golden as it dries and is burnished by the sun. No one has ever seen such intensely blue eyes. He comes out of the sea like a god. Someone tries to shoot him as he is getting dressed. Lawrence picks up his revolver, takes aim and shoots back, wounding the man enough on the hand to send him off. He sails out to the island with the usual object, as he says, of returning with armfuls of wild flowers in his canoe, roses and daisies and forget-me-nots.

He is flamboyant, recessive and careless, in his love of dressing up. For the desert he wears a blazer of French grey trimmed with pink and a gaudy Arab belt with provocatively swinging tassels; he had them made bigger than anyone else's: traditionally, they indicated that he was seeking a wife. The ensemble was completed with white football shorts, long grey stockings, red Arab slippers and no hat. A lord of the desert flies. His hair was very long and in wild disorder, said Leonard Woolley, director of archaeology, and it used to get in his mouth at mealtimes.

In the evening, in their house, said Woolley, half-reproving, secretly approving, Lawrence changed into a white and gold embroidered Arab waistcoat and a magnificent cloak of gold and silver thread, a sixty-pound garment that he had picked up from a thief in the market at Aleppo. His hair now carefully brushed, his sleek head, with an air of luxury, he sat by the winter fire reading Blake.

He was a beautifully made man, a friend said, admiringly.

Dahûm is his constant companion. He's fifteen years old. His name means darkness or sea monster. They try on each other's clothes. There's a pistol in the boy's hand. It's a dangerous game. There are no trees to hide them, there's nowhere else to go. Lawrence is pleased to see him, like the handsome young Arabian men he admires whose clean limbs quiver on the yielding sand as they lie clasped together. Like Roman centurions. The Arabs were tolerantly scandalised by the friendship, Woolley says, especially when Lawrence brought Dahûm into the house to live with them. The scandal about Lawrence was widely spread and firmly believed, Woolley recalls, but he insists his friend was in no sense a pervert. In fact, he had a remarkably clean mind, he said. Greek homosexuality interested him, but in a detached way. Like everything else.

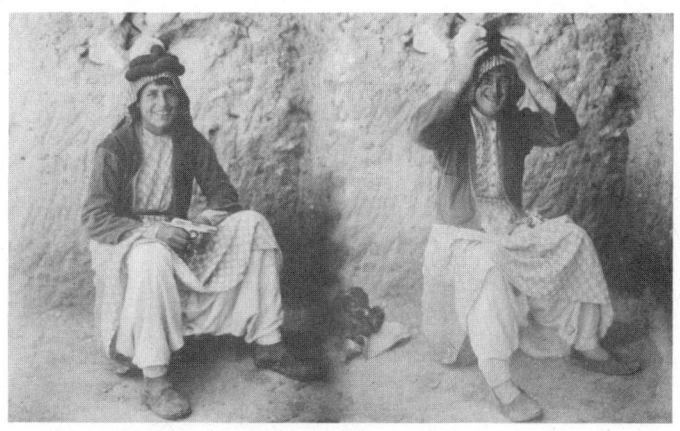

roses and daisies and forget-me-nots

Lawrence always felt himself beyond the law, and, as Woolley adds, he liked to shock. He brings Dahûm home to Oxford as a souvenir, like a shard of Hittite pot. Installs the boy in his bungalow at the bottom of the garden. He knew perfectly well what people thought. He didn't care. He said Dahûm saved his life three times. The boy's reward was death by typhoid. When he told a fellow soldier the news, Lawrence drew his kuffieh over his face and said,
I loved that boy.
When he turned back, it was clear he had been crying.
He dedicates *Seven Pillars of Wisdom* to Dahûm.

I loved you, so I drew these tides of men into my hands
and wrote my will across the sky in stars
To earn you Freedom, the seven pillared worthy house,
that your eyes might be shining for me
When we came.

Beirut, August 1911. Lawrence meets James Elroy Flecker, a handsome young man then serving as a diplomat. He's a protégé of John Addington Symonds, the first man to use the word homosexual in a book. Lawrence already knew Flecker's friend, the tall and languid John Beazley. At Oxford Beazley and Flecker were inseparable, notorious for provocative stunts and their secret club. Flecker introduced healthy sports. The town wasn't big enough for them in their overcoats and shorts. It was a memorable look.

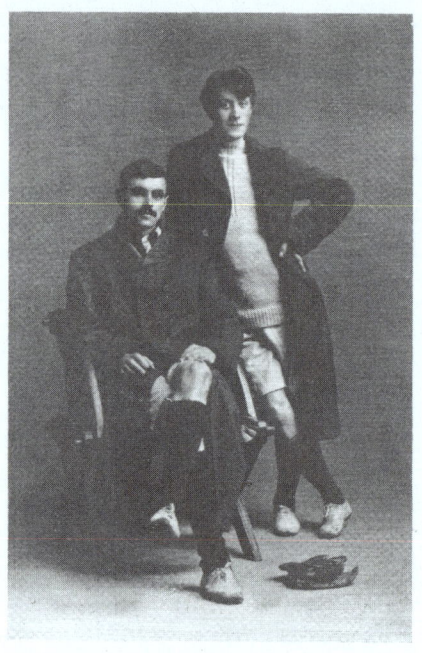

Flecker's parents banned Beazley from the house. Flecker wrote poems to other lovers, such as the anonymous dedicatee: G.T.B., Drowned among reeds at Wisbech. Flecker is too good-looking for his own good. An ad for men's grooming products; more Scott Fitzgerald than Yellow Book; exotic, of Polish Jewish descent. His black hair only makes his vivid blue eyes stand out even more. I had rather be told that I had beautiful eyes than that I pulled all the wires in the university, he said. Flecker, caught in the flicker; a lustrous young man,

362

those dark pupils the very pool of decadence. In his most famous poem, Flecker wrote perfervid verse about an imaginary golden journey to Samarkand as if fitting his eyes to his words of yearning

> Always a little further: it may be
> Beyond that last blue mountain barred with snow,
> Across that angry or that glimmering sea,

as if he knew he would always be leaving too. The packing must have been a chore. His Oxford rooms were filled with mountainous piles of rare books, strange fruits, bottles of liqueur, curious nicknacks and pictures in luxuriant disorder, as his

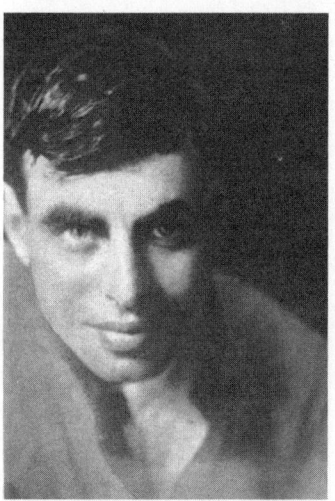

biographer, John Sherwood, wrote. There is something barbaric about you, a friend told Flecker, when I saw your taste for those lurid pictures: the monstrous shapes: the weird castle on a steep impossible cliff: a blue obscene moon leering from a purple sky. Flecker learns German, becomes a diplomat in Beirut. He's already afflicted with consumption. The light of the future was on his face. But it was fading fast.

He wasn't built to last. In Beirut Flecker assumes loose Arab dress. Lawrence arrives with his camera. Flecker stands on his balcony. Holds his robe round himself as though just out of the bath. His feet are bare in red leather slippers.

Lawrence is taking notes.

The secret life of Areya. Soon he'll be consigned to another balcony: Flecker's final address is a sanatorium in Davos. Thomas Mann is there at the same time. In December 1913, Flecker writes to Lawrence in the desert, recommending radical books for his friend's library. Among them is Mann's *Death in Venice*, published the year before in Berlin, a story of the love for a young boy in a time of cholera, the same disease even then sweeping through Carchemish.

Do write me a word, Flecker writes to Lawrence. I'm sick and very miserable.

It was his last postcard. Flecker died in Davos on 3 January 1915, aged thirty years old. With him there went out the sweetest singer of the war generation, said Lawrence. He recalled talking with Flecker, carelessly flung beneath a tree, of women's slippers and of being beaten.

In 1908 Flecker had written a speculative novel, *The Last Generation*, set in a future state, in which a man named Joshua Harris has become King of Britain and Emperor of the two Americas, making proclamations in a huge elliptical hall bigger than the Colosseum, lit by a thousand electric discs, attended by an International Police Force in tunics and boots. Birmingham has become a city that never sees the sun or the moon, and a Vertildungsverein has been established in Germany, a Club for Mutual Extermination in a pseudo-Chinese erection that looks like a cricket pavilion but which turns out to be a rifle range set up by Teutonic scientists disappointed by the evolution of the human race. There a passion-wrecked woman is being shot dead by a young man, while the club members draw lots to shoot each other.

Embroidered on the badge on the white, gold-edged blazer

that Flecker still wore from the club he and Beazley devised at Oxford was the crooked cross, then still the sign of mystical Eastern divinity, worn on a Jewish breast.

One can only live in the future or the past, Lawrence tells his mother. At Carchemish he keeps a snow leopard for the winter. The beast escapes and puts the fear of Allah into the Arabs, he says. That summer, 1914, digging in the sand, disturbing stuff from the ground, they find a demon with horns and bull's legs.

At school he would assess boys' physiques from behind, the way they walked off to the river or the football pitch, then tell them how they looked. He was obsessed with clothes and speed. He designed his own travelling shirt of thin delaine, fastened by tiny glove buttons to fold up into the size of a matchbox, and wore a suit of strong lightweight material, said his mother, with many pockets, in which he carried all his things. He designed it himself. He cycled down to the shore where I swim and inspected the ruins of the abbey behind it, making the same notes about it that Hopkins made forty years before. He fitted his motorboat with car headlights to make it go faster in the dark. When he came to dinner he talked of the many tastes of water. Or sat silently on the couch.

Vyvyan Richards, who sounds like a friend of Dorian Gray, recalls the image of Ned in the dark, when he became active, like a cat, creeping out into the freezing winter night to swim in the same river in which Hopkins, then Murdoch, swam. He relished the momentary thrill, Richards said, of finding whether the ice he dived into would be thin enough to let him in—and out again; and then the pleasure of seeing the astonishment of orthodox folk and policemen as Ned appeared grinning and dripping like a river god.

In photographs of him, after it all happened, after the fame and the violence, his rape in the desert, which may or may not have been what it seemed, his fists are often clenched, or clutching at each other; his arm wraps around his chest, holding himself tight, from within. He strikes strange poses, cradling his fingers, knuckled and tense. I shook the hand of a man who shook that hand. A little boy in fancy dress, standing in line-ups of grown-up men.

Other veterans declined to recall their trauma; he wrote about his at great length, again and again, not quite believing any of it was true (which some people said was true). Secrets never seen. He slept naked in the desert to avoid fleas. His sublimation, like a lion. His big blue eyes burnt open like Regulus's in the sun. He'll squint for ever from now on. It makes him look perpetually sceptical about everything and everyone.

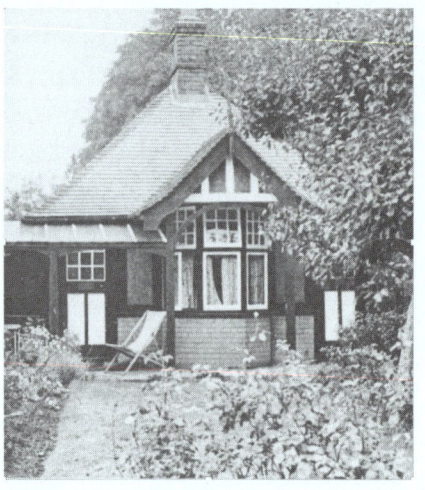

As a student, his parents built a bungalow for him at the bottom of the garden, hung with dyed Bolton sheeting, used in theatres for soundproofing. It turned the interior into a tent or a stage. There was only one ornament-prop, in the bay window, a bronze head of Hypnos brought back from Naples. He would lie on the floor to contemplate the ruined god of sleep. Nothing, not even the dawn, can disturb me in my curtains, he said. The silence of the desert in suburban Oxford, his secret life. It was the most silent place I have ever been in, said his friend.

It was there that Vyvyan Richards, who was in love with him, found him one afternoon, sitting in the nude on the rug by the fire, placidly sketching his own foot and leg. It was a private performance: Lawrence as a faun, falling to the floor, the coals glowing red, reflecting on Hypnos's head.

The god did the sleeping for him, keeping everything else at bay.

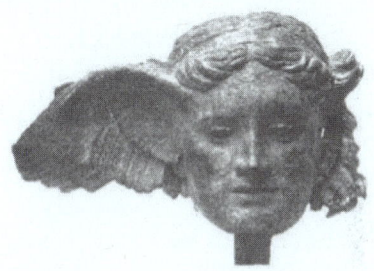

In 1933, two years before he died, Lawrence built a new retreat at Clouds Hill, on land he had leased just across the road from his cottage to prevent other people building there. The project grew out of necessity and invention and resentment.

Lawrence had channelled a water supply from the spring and stream in the valley, pumping it into a tank and then running it under the road and into his house so that he could have a hot bath. He had always managed to have a hot bath everywhere he went, even in the desert. It purged his flesh, sweated out the soul and the sin. Having regained his love of swimming, he turned the tank itself into a bathing pool—a tiny one, he said, but splashable into.

The reality was a dark dank trench, a dugout lined in cement, forty feet long by seven feet wide and five feet deep, holding seven thousand gallons, sunk among the chestnut trees. To protect his new pool from falling leaves and to warm the water, he built a glasshouse over his holy well. It was a machine for swimming in, financed by his translation of the *Odyssey*, for a hero who was going nowhere.

At one end stood a pair of ornate inlaid doors from Jeddah, opening onto Lawrence's little study, like the balcony in a play. The whole place was a memory of when his Arab guide, Nasir, led him through the moonlit and starry desert, telling him about his family's stone-paved home that had a great vine-trellised swimming tank, lined with shining cement, into which Nasir and his brother used to plunge in the heat of noon.

Aligned east to west like a chapel, painted blue and white inside like a cold Turkish bath, the pool in the woods allowed the ritual immersion of his body, another punishment leading to ecstasy. He was religious by temperament, said his brother, but without a creed. He would swim there, up and down, furiously, the way he did everything else, especially in winter when the water was bitterly cold. It was a medicinal facility, a spa for his traumatised self.

And in the ultimate contraction of his life, at the end of his watery conservatory, where his brown body swerved like a trout or a carp, he set up a printing press. The dampness would be good for printing, he said. Like a Manchester cotton mill or an infernal press in a cave. Heaven or hell. It was the only component still within his control: to make his own books in his own environment, excluding the whole of the world.

Like Blake he would exert absolute agency over the process: the words from his head via the pool to the press. He even fantasised, only half-jokingly, in order to avoid the press who hung round all the time, cameras slung around their necks and notebooks ready for him to put a foot wrong (one day he opened the door to a reporter and punched him in the face), that he would build a chute direct from his bedroom, over the road and down to the pool, thereby bypassing the doorstepping hounds and landing him in his tank so that he could swim into his office, followed on behind by his books and papers in a clockwork boat and kept dry in a waterproof bag. His drowned bunker, an escape room, in advance of what he knew was to come.

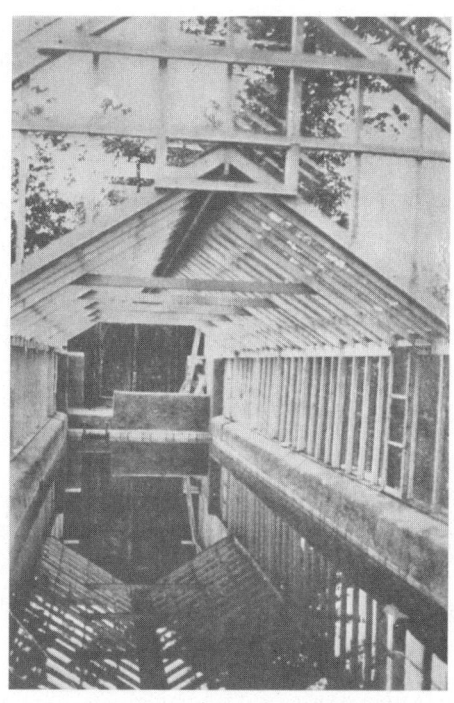

But the words did not come and the tanks kept rolling over the legend he had made. He knew he wouldn't make fifty: he had only a few years left, he said. Mr Lawrence never observes Christmas, they said. He buries his head in the sand. Probably it would be wholesome for me to lose my heart, he told Nancy Astor in December 1934, adding, if that monstrous piece of machinery is capable of losing itself. Returning on the last day of the year to his lonely lodgings in Southampton, where the grey water lapped the quayside, he felt he had come to the end.

Do you ever feel that there is a wall of glass between you and the street? he said to another friend. You see the people scurrying and waving their arms—but no noise, no eddy of air and no touch?

My mother, fourteen years old, would have passed him in the town's high street that ran down to the sea, a ghost in the crowd, going into the same bookshop where Robertson bought his biography of Blake. Her father had served in Arabia at the same time as Lawrence; in our family album was a little card he sent back from Jerusalem, containing a photograph of the golden dome and a pressed flower; I'd touch it as if I could feel the exoticness of what he had seen through pale petals. The house in which I was born was named Akaba. At the hour of his death, my grandfather, whom I never knew, appeared to my mother in the doorway of the front room to tell her everything would be all right. Soon after I was born, we were forced to leave that dark Victorian house at the crossroads which was demolished to make another road.

In 1934, a last portrait of Lawrence was commissioned by his distant cousin, Desmond Chapman-Huston, an Irishman of means; a writer, a soldier, a socialite, he'd known Lawrence's brother in the air force during the Great War, when there were parties for young airmen in a private pool in Chelsea owned by Captain Leo Charlton, a friend of Lomer, Streatfeild and Coward. Chapman-Huston was also a frequent visitor to Bavaria and wrote a biography of mad king Ludwig. His chosen artist was an Austrian, Herbert Gurschner, who had recently painted St Sebastian pierced by arrows and tied to a tree. Lawrence is said to have sat for the picture; which may be true, since Gurschner painted Corfe Castle that year. All these people connect covert networks; one of Chapman-Huston's close friends was Maud Allan, the Salome dancer. I might imagine Coward and Lawrence meeting in that pool, the light reflecting on the ceiling, on the young West Indian boys who were Charlton's gymnastic pupils.

In the belly of the National Gallery of Ireland, behind a metal door thick as a castle wall, Adrian Le Harivel, the elegant and erudite curator, has the portrait set up for me. It is disconcertingly larger than life-size. The desert hero peers at us through his sad blue eyes as the heroine dies. He might be playing himself on film (any prettier and they'd have called it *Florence of Arabia*, quipped Coward). The plaque screwed to the frame says

Presented by Major D. CHAPMAN-HUSTON Pl XIV
Author of *NED: A STUDY OF LAWRENCE of IRELAND and ARABIA*

Ned gestures like a saint beating his chest with a rock. A raven perches on a branch, ready to bring him bread or pick his bones. The pose, with a cape strung tensely across his chest, is a direct echo of Dürer's self-portrait as a young man; so are the hands, only here sand is running out through his fingers. You might think it an intimation of mortality. There are pyramids on the horizon, a sense of terrible beauty. Two years before, Yeats had nominated Lawrence for the Irish Academy of Letters. Lawrence wrote back to tell the poet he'd set eyes on him once in Oxford, many years ago. He'd wanted to call the street to attention, for lack of power to make the sun blare out, Lawrence said. But he did nothing, and let the moment pass.

I am Irish, he told Yeats. He saw the offer as a chance to admit it publicly. He was grateful for the honour, but added, I'm afraid the truth—if people could look inside—would destroy the flattering picture of myself that I have put about.

The fascists and their union had already invited him to dinner. Lawrence had the right look for them: square jaw, blond hair, blue eyes. He replied with a smirk: he'd join them, he said, if they'd take over public ownership of all the sea-beaches. But when Morgan Forster ran into him at a concert at the Queen's Hall, Lawrence was with some men whose faces Forster instinctively distrusted. All his friends will agree that he had some queer friends, Forster said. Ned was a wanted man. In 1929, a banner depicting Lawrence had been burned on Tower Hill by communists protesting at imperial rule in India where he had been serving, it was said, as a British spy. As the flames curled up from his chin, finally obliterating his face like a guy on a bonfire, the *New York Times* reported that cheers broke out from the crowd of British reds. The icon they carried was folkloric, a portrait by a spirit artist or Andy Warhol. The hero in his robes versus men in their caps. Impending disaster. The windows are barricaded. The reporters chased his taxi through the streets for an hour. They're waiting for the crash.

BURN LAWRENCE IN EFFIGY

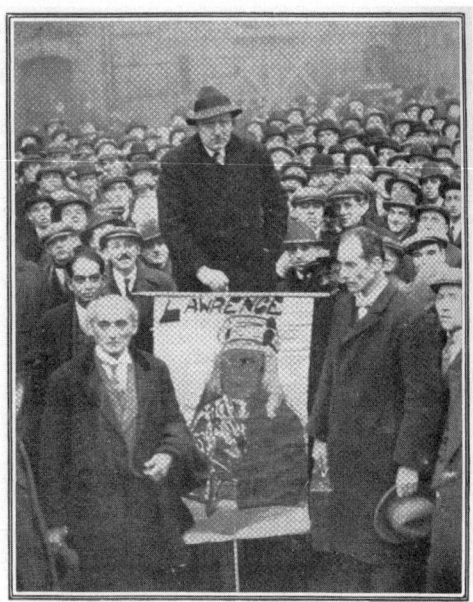

Is it true, the press who hounded him asked, that you plan to make yourself Dictator of England?

It's medieval, this martyrdom in the face of fame. Those hands were as familiar with guns as they were with the poems of Blake. You wouldn't suspect he'd fired a revolver at random out of an Oxford college room after working for forty-five hours at a stretch without food. Or that out in the desert, he had felt it his duty to execute a murderer in order to avoid a blood feud. He ordered the offender into a ravine. It took three fumbled shots: to the chest, to the wrist and finally to the head. The man squirmed in the dust.

The sand in his eyes, the sun in his brain. He couldn't forget, as he picked up his fish and chips from the shop outside Bovington Camp or got his short-back-and-sides at the barbers, the memory of blowing up trains full of hundreds of people and laying them out in rows in the sun; then photographing them. He was the most famous man in the western world and a failure to himself.

As he lay there on the road, his body splayed on the gravel like a wounded white hart, the blood pouring out of the crack in his head and onto the road, Lawrence appeared to regain consciousness for a moment.

The men who found him said he opened his eyes and, looking up, lifted his hand and held up a finger, as if to indicate the number one. Some sort of victory or blessing. A pietà in the sergeant's arms. Then he fell back again.

And again.

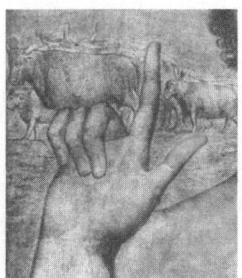

Trembling, into my arms.

A week or so before, Lawrence had invited Paul and Margaret Nash, down in Swanage, to come up and see him at Clouds Hill. Margaret was looking forward to seeing Ned again; her father had taught him at Oxford. Just before their visit, they received the news. Instead of going to tea, they attended his funeral. The little country church was filled with the most distinguished men and women, she said. She didn't hear Churchill, outside the church door, taking aside one of Lawrence's soldier friends to tell him it was his patriotic duty to keep his secrets.

In the village bakery soldiers in camouflage stand behind me in the queue as I buy a box-full of cakes. You've got an army to feed, I apologise, but so have I.

The cottage is up the road. You're just in time, we're told. It's his anniversary. I had no idea. Across the road is a little garden gate, made with a metal sunburst design as if we were in suburbia rather than on the wild heath. His pool is covered over and his office has rotted away. They took away the Arabian doors for their safety's sake. All that is left is a disembodied brick wall. But the stream still runs under the road and the tanks still run by, and the sound of a different engine pulls into the drive.

It stands there, cooling off, low-slung and sleek like a panther. Its leather saddle is sunk below the petrol tank and the back wheel lowered to accommodate the stature of its former owner and his short-back-and-sides. The rider unscrews the petrol cap to show us the half-crown kept inside for emergency fuel. The machine has the deep sheen of a Rolls-Royce. Glossy, revved up by its provenance, it stands patiently waiting for him to come out of the door and hop on. Astride, in control, purring between his legs.

A Brough Superior, number four in a series of eight. Other editions of Lawrence, stretched out, black lacquered versions of his body, chrome-plated and ready to go. Roaring, rearing up, they'd outrun him: one was buried in the earth out of respect, like a warrior king with his nipples cut off. They dug it up and sold it for a million pounds.

As he signed off from his last job, the officer's attention was distracted for a moment, and he realised T.E. had gone.

No one seems to have seen him actually leave, Sims said.

South London is a different place. Cross the river and you're in another country. It scares me. I turn off the main road and into the tarmac courtyard of a huge warehouse. A young man from Japan conducts me inside. His hair is long and his eyes are dark like a loaded cat. He leads me to a table the height of my waist. Two or three workers are busy behind me. It's an ordinary morning. They have to be there. Trailing trolleys with crates, stacking shelves that recede I don't know where, full of I don't know what.

My guide lifts a cover and it's like a lightbox has been switched on.

Three golden-framed pictures lie before me, glowing. Newton, Nebuchadnezzar and Pity: a trio of strangeness, not so much printed as impressed. All three look sub-aquatic. My guide agrees; he's an underwater diver, he says.

They are laid flat, the way Blake made them. Impenetrable trap doors. Resting here, from their last moment in the spotlight. They haven't travelled far in the past two hundred years. Hercules Road is only five minutes' ride from here, by horse or bike. These pictures, waiting for me on a Tuesday morning, changed the people who saw them, and now they're changing me.

It's like meeting a rock star in the flesh. Not knowing where to look or what to say, I recite The Tyger to my new friend, in honour of the ecstatic art at our side. He's somewhat mystified, and his colleagues working behind us have gone quiet. Then, because I've forgotten the other verses, I get out my battered book and read the rest, reeling in the tyger's eyes as I fix my gaze on his. Maybe he thinks it's a come-on. Which it is, but not to him, lovely as he is. Complicit, even as he is. Art is always on our side, he seems to suggest, unlike time, which, at any given moment, is not.

I ask for a magnifying glass. Instead a huge standing light appears, an incandescent rectangular lens fit to floodlight a small stadium. The effect is intense. For an hour I peer at the naked pictures, a peep show, nothing between them and me but Blake himself. He's standing over my shoulder, wondering what I think. I can't put it into words, and photography is forbidden for fear of spoiling the surprise, so I draw little details in my notebook.

It's the eyes, I realise. Pity's pitying gaze, Nebuchadnezzar's desperate stare; Newton's almond orb, almost Egyptian, staring down at his compasses.

Encompassing everything. The design he's drawing on the sea floor is a simple mathematical symbol, but it might summon up the devil in a swimming pool. I realise, from a scene in Civilisation, delivered through Kenneth Clark's folded arms but ignored by the critic, that Blake drew on the figure of Euclid teaching geometry in Raphael's fresco, The School of Athens; and that the same compasses appear in the hands of Dürer's melancholy angel in their damask dress.

But Blake's Newton is stripped of classical robes and his instruments are ultimately useless. His fingers flex, his muscles tense, his body perches on the rock. He's a beautiful man, despite or because of it all. Illusory, like his situation, down there, under the sea. Not seeing things he could never have seen: crinoids waving in the current, skeins of seaweed and clusters of corals, mottled with pigment, abstract and intensely beautiful.

In 1941 the artist and Tate curator, Robin Ironside, described this print, which had been sent into hiding like the rest of these works, as having rock formations granulated like some rare variety of quartz; he compared them to accidental effects in drawings by Henry Moore, who was busy sketching troglodyte Londoners sheltering in the Underground. In the corner of Newton's dark chaos is Blake's signature: five letters, neatly inscribed, taking responsibility for it all.

A hundred and fifty years ago Dante Gabriel Rossetti looked at this same object and was defeated by its technique. It seemed like alchemy to him. It cannot possibly be all handwork, he said, and yet I can conceive no mechanical process, short of photography, which is really capable of explaining it. It is no less than a complete mystery.

The rocks in particular perplexed Rossetti in their intricacy. I peer over them as if over his velvet shoulder, and again through the illuminated lens, scanning the abyss for clues. They are space and time, at low tide

—in the blue-lit basement of the oceanographic building are nurseries growing corals. I peer into the shallow tanks, seas in miniature, seminal and warm. Shelf-like luminous green and pink growths, ever so slightly obscene, cling to little rocks. The ocean in a tray. The sound of filtration systems like the sound of their collective breath. Tentacles wave. The young man showing us round occasionally climbs into the bigger tanks, he says. For work, that is, not for fun. His wetsuit is drying on the side as if it were on a Newquay beach; he has partly bleached blond hair, the pipefish twist and turn on themselves. They dance in the artificial current that makes the diver's body sway and his work difficult to do. It's an experiment in a brave new world—

Newton ignores the beauty around him. He sees only a certain ratio of things. To the poet Adrian Mitchell he looked like a monk who has landed on a whale, blithely unaware the leviathan is about to sink below the waves. But what has settled down there, along with the aeon-long fall of marine snow, is rich and strange and internal. Peter Ackroyd points out the similarity between the encrusted rocks and the urinary tract stones Blake engraved for a medical textbook in 1793. For Ackroyd they echo the fall of man within the human body. To me they're the bit of shingle rattling round inside of me which, as I watch on a screen, the surgeon zaps like an asteroid.

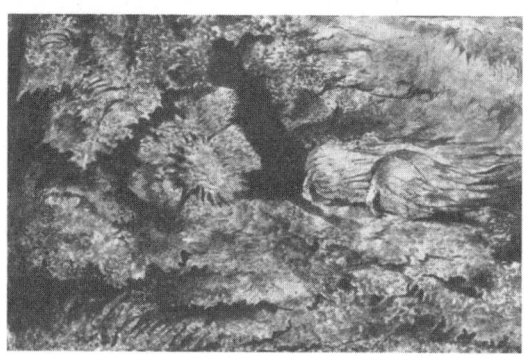
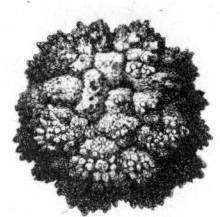

Newton is sunk by his discoveries. From whales to phytoplankton, the ocean's denizens share the same density as the salty sea. They defy gravity, floating free. No such luck for Newton anchored on the bedrock. Shackled by his own ingenuity, he's nothing so much as a stuffed trout in a taxidermy case. Down there in the abyss, his compasses are as fateful as those of the Ancient of Days, up there in the air. You cannot measure an unencompassable sea. It's impossible to stand there. He's waiting for the remote operated vehicle to come along and catch him in its beam.

I move on to Pity, for pity's sake. A pair of airborne horses career over a young woman, her body laid out on another mossy bed. Rain pours from thunderous clouds, rendered in violent scratches in the paint, gouged and clawed. All the power of this picture lies in those marks from Blake's hands

—in the shed-like building next to the reef-birthing room are jars and jars of strange things, lined up on rows of floor-to-ceiling shelves, their contents collected a hundred years ago, preserved like false teeth in a glass. Anglerfish deflated by their sudden summoning to the surface, mouths open wider than themselves. Goose barnacles squashed together like ingredients for a gothic bouillabaisse; the little vials of liquid act as miniature seas, as if they might still be alive a century after they were gathered, protesting, from the abyss.

One bottle contains dozens of squids' lenses, swilling about like marbles. There's a number on the label—1574—the number of the whale from whose stomach they came. The one thousand, five hundred and seventy-fourth victim of the cull that enabled this scientific expedition, like the energy companies still financing such exploration in order to exploit the resources of the seabed. Last week, Dr Horton tells me, she discovered a new family of worms. Not a single species, but an entire new family. She hands me a little jar. Inside is a caramel-coloured lump of mud. She invites me to dip my finger in it. It feels silky smooth but with a faintly gritty texture, like foundation make-up. I say it would make a good face mask. She tells me it is composed of crushed invertebrates from the Porcupine Abyssal Plain, four thousand, eight hundred and fifty metres down at the bottom of the Atlantic Ocean. It is like touching a rock from the moon—

the pity of it all. God has inflicted all this on us, again. Blake turns the Bible pagan, according to his means and ends. He does not believe in God but saw him anyway, at the top of his stairs. I consult my notes. Yes, it's all true. What Milton foresaw in *Paradise Lost*, what Blake recorded in *Jerusalem*, what Jennings diarised in *Pandæmonium* and what Thoreau set his body against: it's all set to be re-enacted down there in the depths, to be mined to power the machine.

If I had a phone the battery levels would be faltering. I've got forty minutes left on my supermarket sweep in this emporium of dead-or-alive art. I don't know which way to turn.

On another table Nebuchadnezzar is crawling out of his cave, a grizzly bear eating grass. A famine victim out of their scrape. He's transhuman too, out of his mind, going the wrong way round the gallery. Wild-eyed and aghast, on his knees, but not to pray. His hair flows out of his eyes, like tears, like locks; his forehead, like his muscles and the rest of him, is segmented like the carapace of a crustacean, formed out of so much clay. Made out of abyssal mud.

It's not enough. It never is. He's ripped by grief, debased by sin, the state we're in. He will never escape: he's a study in biblical PTSD, a victim of industry. His face and body a living autopsy; stripped back, animal muscles tensed and flensed. He fills the frame like a flayed rhino, grazing on paint, a mutant pachyderm. Beauty as nightmare, a sensational circus at the end of the street or the bottom of the sea, something that used to be, to meet you and your friend.

All these pictures scare me as much as they astonish you. They never end. That's the definition of dread, someone said. The fear that draws you to it, like a magnet. The centuries that have passed by between this being made and me standing over it in an art facility, a holding point between Blake and me and eternity. 1795 to 2022. (I've been writing this book for a long time.) Every kind of inhumanity and exploitation. Every dictator and torturer. Every spy and betrayer. Every slave and enslaver. Every kind of evil that is real and that exists. Turned into something so beautiful that I cannot turn my back on it.

You pity him, this bedraggled king, but not so much as you would a dog. Don't be taken in. He will be taken away and shot. He is deranged by the knowledge of his fate. The most terrible detail is the fact that he is dragging his beard on the floor as he crawls. That's how much he cares. Then I notice how his arms have thickened into shins as he fell to the floor, felled by sin, to crawl on all fours. His legs are Neanderthal. His uncut toenails have grown into claws. He needs a good chiropodist. He moves like a defeated tyger among these three works; a bestial partner to Newton and his melancholy; a predator to Pity, defied by his human animality. Pursued and pathetic. Ready to bay at the moon. Death cannot come too soon. It would be too merciful a release. Better install him in Bedlam (it's just down the road), chained to a wall or a bed.

For a century these three pictures, along with dozens of others by Blake, had slumbered at Salterns, the Dorset home of Thomas Butts's descendants, where they were given refuge in a specially built three-storey wing overlooking the sea.

It was an amazing survival—not least because Frederick Tatham, the Ancient who claimed that Catherine Blake had left him all her husband's other works, had joined a mille-narian sect and burned many of Blake's paintings and writings as unholy works inspired by the devil, not God (he'd already tried to rub out the rude bits in Blake's erotic manuscript *Vala*). That narrow escape explained the Rossettis' passion when they discovered this cache, then still in Butts's London house. It was a transactional act of fate: from Blake's commer-cial failure as an artist, via their appreciation, to the potency of his true worth.

I also enclose the account I mentioned between Blake & Butts, William Michael Rossetti had written, in amazement, in 1861. It is an authentic record of the scale of prices—& such prices!—received by Blake, Rossetti said.

DR.		Mr. BUTTS		
May 12, 1805		£.	s.	d.
12 Drawings . . .		12	12	0
7 Sept.				
4 Prints, viz—				
1. Nebuchadnezzar. 2. Newton. 3. God				
creating Adam. 4. Christ appearing		4	4	0
Dec. 12—				
Drawings sent from Felpham		14	14	0
Urizen, Heaven, &c. and Songs of				
Experience, for balance		0	10	6
Dec. 25, 1805.				
On account of teaching your son, at				
26 Guineas per annum, to commence				
on this day		26	5	0
CR.				
By Coals, to 5 Oct. 1805		12	19	0

Who would not confess their Pre-Raphaelite lust at this bargain Blakean receipt? Imagine gathering them up at the checkout, stuffing armfuls of eternity into a carrier bag.

As Captain Butts's collection was moved to Dorset, to the sea, it began a new reaction. His daughter Mary and his son Anthony grew up in Blake's shadow; in their own remarkable way, they would live out his bohemian regard for the way to live. It was their great-grandfather who had come upon William and Kate sitting naked in the afternoon. Their father, Frederick

Butts, hero of the Crimea, was as eccentric. He had bought the house in 1861, along with twenty-one acres of land, because it enabled him to walk down to the shore in his night-shirt and swim. He had his yacht, the *Vanity*, tethered to the old pier. The marshy land turned into the sea there, almost imperceptibly, looking out over Brownsea Island and Poole Harbour to the distant Isle of Purbeck.

Anthony Butts later wrote an account of his family, *Curious Relations*, under an assumed name, William D'Arfey, in which the house becomes a fictional Marsh Hall, a gothic site, a Dorset Manderley. The book, which I bought in a jumble sale years ago, largely for its strange orange cover with a hermit crab with a sea anemone growing on top of its shell, was published in 1945.

Until now, I had no idea who had written it. Butts describes the house as low, long and white, vaguely Regency with green-shuttered windows and a vaulted avenue of rhododendrons forty feet high that spattered white blossoms on the gravel drive like snow. The heath gave way to the salt marshes of the harbour where dozens of bird species lived, and in the winter gales the house itself seemed to rock and pitch with the same sea fit that blew through Blackwood's story set on the same beach. My mother's family had lived close by, in Corfe Mullen, and had done for hundreds of years, as carpenters and soldiers; as a teenage girl before the First World War, my grandmother, acted as children's nurse to the daughter of the Spanish ambassador, in one of those big houses.

Perhaps that's why I found Dorset so magnetic, with its embedded mysteries and eccentric families, its radioactive sense of somewhere remote and close at the same time. A powerful place for Blake's art to end up. Lying there ticking, patiently waiting to wake up, while thirteen clocks chimed and the garden succumbed to sleeping-beauty vines and briars, and the sea grew ever closer with each day.

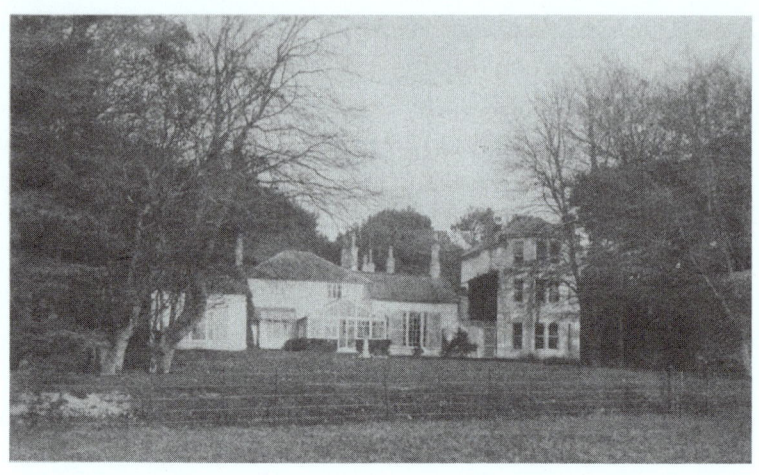

In his book, Butts made no direct reference to Blake's haunting of the house, on account of wishing to disguise his family tales of gluttony, adultery and other oddities, especially those of his father, who wore so many rings that his wife insisted he take some off before she married him, and who scored Wagner's Siegfried Idyll for concertina and accordion, a composition which could only be played by his Black coachman. As a doomed specimen himself, Anthony said, he vastly preferred his father to the average enemy of art and passion, and he recalled, to underline the point, that it was a member of his family who created opportunity for one of England's greatest men of genius. This house, long since demolished to make way for suburban villas, is Blake's ground zero. Without that Victorian extension, he might have been eaten by rats.

Anthony Butts would never wholly resolve his own life, either, despite his gay charm and his storytelling and those china-blue eyes and the fantastic hats he designed. His sister Mary, ten years older than him, remembered Blake's pictures all too well: the way that they filled the room as she looked out to the Purbeck Hills, which seemed to her to be a naked god laid down asleep while Corfe Castle sat like a black crown on a bright hill or spun like the hub of a wheel. She spent her childhood saturated in Blake, she said, but she was unconsoled by his presence. All those automaton figures, sleepwalking across the walls, made her feel uncomfortable. She wanted ghosts to haunt her house but not these. As a girl she used to stand in the Blake Room and scowl at the pictures. She couldn't understand why people kept coming to see them, or why Newton should be naked and sitting on a rock like a sub-aquatic Michelangelo; though she admitted Nebuchadnezzar might have looked like that, all hairy and hoary on all fours.

She would hurry past the dimly lit Blakes, the way I did when I saw the scary old pictures in my grandmother's bungalow in the forest. She knew many more images were tucked away in Blake's engraving cabinet which was also on display, like any ordinary brown furniture, for all that it might have been made of crystal. Only Blake's Pity drew her appreciation, its dreadful night sky all scratched out; she felt pity for herself as she brooded on it and it possessed her. There was a lot of Mary Shelley's self-drama to Mary Butts, as if she were laid out under those ghostly horses as they galloped in from the sea.

In 1905, when she was fourteen years old, Mary's father died. The following year her mother sold the best works by England's greatest unknown artist to pay death duties. Graham Robertson paid nine thousand pounds for them. Yeats told Mary they should have fetched fifty thousand.

Only later did she realise the power of that loss, that un-making, as she called it.

She came to see how Blake had affected her unconsciously and profoundly, how he became her visionary guide in her own art. He had set her on her own wild course: of female lovers and clairaudience and clairvoyance, dealing in dark magic with the wickedest man in the world; slashing crosses into her wrists and going on astral journeys with or without the aid of hashish and cocaine, injecting heroin in her thighs. She claimed to have sheltered IRA rebels on the run from the Easter Rising and wore her red hair tangled up with a single green jade hoop in her ear; she smoked opium with Jean Cocteau, Christopher Wood and Francis Rose. She was photographed by Man Ray and married John Rodker, another of Nancy Cunard's lovers, then she married Gabriel Atkin, serial lover to Siegfried Sassoon and Maynard Keynes.

She also, almost by the by (where did she find the time? what did she eat?) wrote intense occultish books influenced by *Ulysses*, by Jung, by Badbury Rings, by Dancing Ledge and by Land's End where she would end up, drawn there as on a golden string. She longed to know Lawrence of Arabia, and over dinner in Paris, Joyce told her to take care of her eyes.

Avoid worry of any kind, he said.

It was the touch of truth, between us & the world, she said.

Then she travelled back to England, arriving in Southampton Water which looked like a blue pearl. By the time she reached Sennen Cove in Cornwall—a good place to hide, where the land dwindles down to a point before it vanishes in the Atlantic, the same point where Blake imagined his great god Albion, straddling the British Isles like Leviathan, setting his right foot, the other being on the Rocks of Bognor; by that time Butts's life was falling apart. Atkin, her husband, went off with other men, and she had become estranged from her brother Anthony over their unequally shared inheritance. He would commit suicide in 1941, during the London Blitz.

Queer people always had to plan for disaster. Suffering from terminal cancer, Anthony Butts saw it as his duty to terminate himself rather than take up a hospital bed from casualties of the bombing. He threw himself from the fourth floor of his hotel, leaving his lover, William Plomer, to edit his memoir of his Curious Relations. War took its casualties sideways, surreptitiously. That year Virginia Woolf left her house in Sussex and, having filled her pockets full of stones, stepped into the river that ran down to the sea. The War killed Virginia, Plomer told Stephen Tennant. Two years later, in a sanatorium in Kent, Simone Weil stopped eating in order to honour those suffering in France. The deceased did kill and slay herself by refusing to eat, the inquest concluded. She stopped consuming the world to leave it. As the bombers flew overhead, even Orlando, in the persona of Vita Sackville-West, asked their doctor for the most effective pills to take should the enemy arrive at Sissinghurst's gates. Pity was on the ration book, blind horses careering in the night.

But for Mary there was always the sea, the mirror of the sky: dangerous, vulnerable, beautiful. I want the sea, the sea, she said. The southern English coast was a grey-pearl in Cornwall, she wrote in her journal; the whole world cut out of grey pearl & black; dead white. Remember, she said, addressing herself in the third person, double-underlining the instruction to make herself think twice: Last night, the moon again, on its back like a boat beside its star. Remember: What frightened me, she wrote in the storm, once again, looking down as I hurried into the bay, was the dreadful whiteness of the surf; the same white-ness she remembered in *Moby-Dick*. And like Sylvia Plath contemplating Cape Cod Bay in a storm on a yellow day when she was a young girl—the sea molten, steely-slick, as Plath wrote shortly before her own suicide—so in Sennen Cove the sea seemed unravelled to Mary Butts, white against ink-purple & ink-indigo & ink-slate. A dreadfulness.

Her vivid imagining may have been the result of the opium tea she made in Cornwall by boiling poppy heads. But she could not forget the loss of her childhood home and those strange pictures, that disputed inheritance. What time had done in its demanding order she wished to disrupt. It is this splitting up of events into an irregular, inconvenient, positively demented time sequence that bitches things up, she complained. Why can't relative things happen together, simultaneously or in close sequence?

And how angry it made Blake! she said. As she wrote about her life in a book which, like her brother's, would be published posthumously, a few months after her death in Penzance from a perforated gastric ulcer in 1937 at the age of forty-six, Mary spoke of the crystal cabinet like the one Blake wanted to live inside and outside of at once. Perhaps that was the way to live, she said. I look at their pictures, Mary and Anthony, the pair of them. They look like photographs from our family album. Curious relations, ordinary people like you and me.

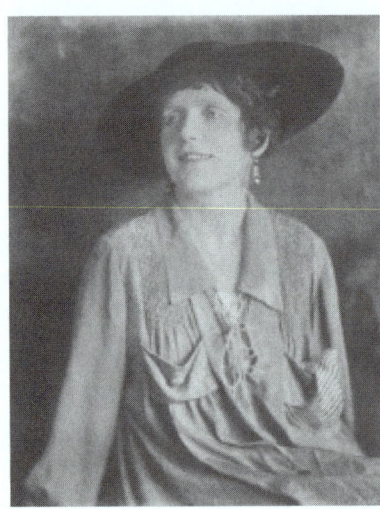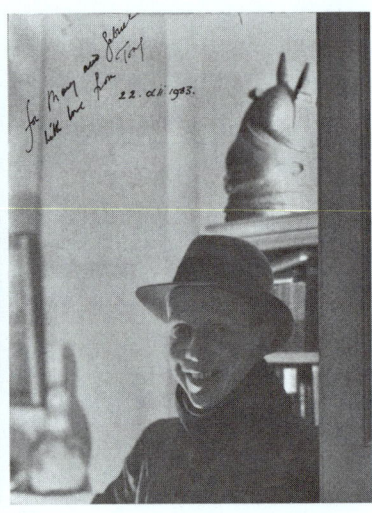

For the first half of the twentieth century Blake's pictures hung in Robertson's London residence on Argyll Road, off Kensington High Street, alongside Sargent's portrait of him as a young man. He was now an aged boy, a relic of the decadence, living mostly with his dogs in his gasless, electric-lightless, bathroomless, motorless house in the country, where he would reread his letters from Wilde and entertain Noël Coward or John Gielgud to tea, or receive a flying visit from Geoffrey Keynes, who arrived wearing a beautiful blue RAF overcoat with silver buttons.

Much too beautiful for a respectable surgeon, Robertson said, with his gentle sense of irony. He still loved a good overcoat: it was akin to wearing a dress, and it concealed so many sins. And although he lived in rural seclusion, he was still directing elaborate village performances worthy of Inigo Jones. For one Arabian fantasy he requisitioned a gigantic young man to play a slave.

He had the most perfect figure I have ever seen, he said.

When he appears for a moment between yellow curtains against deep blue, dressed more or less like Blake's Glad Day, he is really divinely beautiful, even though, in his clothes he was quite an ordinary, pudding-y boy.

Robertson thought the boy should be cast in bronze as an example of what poor humanity can attain.

Glad Day is evidently his natural and proper attire, for after I had dressed him (his costume is put on with a sponge) he disappeared and was rediscovered watching a football match in the next field, having merely added a blue worsted comforter to his toilette.

He attracted no attention whatever, Robertson reported, with satisfaction.

Blake remained Robertson's god; he was now Blake's representative on earth, always being asked for his opinion or advice as if he had the artist's supernatual ear, passing judgement on fakes or wrong 'uns on which he was an expert, not least because Robertson had once faked his own; colour prints which, he discovered, were now being sold as the real thing.

What was real or make-believe? Who could be sure?

2.30 pm, 2 December 1938. With the international situation worsening, Robertson takes a cab to Christie's, where he'd just bought a last, long-lost Blake to add to his collection: Christ appearing to the Apostles after the Resurrection. The final piece of the jigsaw.

And it's a beauty, he said, as it was knocked down for seventy-five guineas. It was a bit dirty but it would scrub up well. He took it home by taxi like a refugee, to join the other colour prints on his wall, just in time for John Rothenstein's visit that afternoon.

The Tate's director, whose father, William, had also been a close friend of Wilde's, arrives promptly at 4.30 pm. Rothenstein, brought up with artists, thought he knew what to expect. He is used to visiting their houses. Burra's childhood attic in Rye, where he practically lay down to paint; Barbara Hepworth and Ben Nicholson's Hampstead studios, which they occupied like ballet dancers, spaces as spare and meticulous as themselves. When he'd called on Paul Nash, his friend and neighbour, he was warned by Margaret Nash not to sit down as his chosen chair was already occupied by a stuffed hawk. It was not your usual north London interior: there were more stuffed birds scattered about, along with stones sculpted by the ocean, fossils and roots and other objects allusive to the childhood of the earth and Nash's dream world of occult correspondences, as Rothenstein wrote.

But when he knocks on the door of this grey terraced house in Kensington, off its noisy High Street, he is taken aback by what he sees on the other side. Something even more haunting than beady-eyed birds.

Newton and Nebuchadnezzar and Pity, glittering on the dim gold walls. An entirely different register of correspondences that barely seemed to belong to this world, let alone this age, Rothenstein said.

Over tea, Robertson tells him, somewhat teasingly, that the Tate had a magnificent Blake gallery without a single first-class Blake in it. Something of the dandy still lingered about the spare person of this courteously scholarly old man who had played many parts besides that of collector, Rothenstein said.

There was one part Robertson still seemed to be playing, even though Oscar had told him to stay away from that portrait in the attic. Some people develop a new and quite presentable face later in life, Robertson complained. I only possess the devastated ruin of my old one. He claimed not to believe in magic now, but he still tied a skein of red silk round his waist to protect against lumbago, the way Beardsley had worn a girdle in a forlorn gesture against consumption. Mary Butts had embraced magic and modernism as a way of working herself out; but Robertson distrusted all modern art, except, grudgingly, the works of Graham Sutherland.

I don't think I like pictures any more, really, he said, ever contrary. He'd learned well from Wilde. He had bought his last Blake. He couldn't buy any more, he said, any more than he would buy another dog for the same fear: of their being left a homeless stray.

Ten months later, on 3 September 1939, on the day war was declared, Robertson wrote to Rothenstein, offering to donate his nine Blake colour prints to the Tate—which you much admired at my house—to save them from the bombs. They were Blake's most important pictures, Robertson said, and the flower of his work. I am rising 74, and pretty shaky, and the return of peace is not likely to find me here—so if you can find a harbour of refuge for these pictures—I could present them to the Tate at once.

Rothenstein lost no time in accepting this gift to the nation; there could hardly be a more patriotic act. Saving Albion. Delivered directly from Argyll Road to the stores of the gallery, they stood there in a row, in a dim corridor, gleaming like a string of jewels, Rothenstein said. But there was no time to display them or show off these first-class attractions. To avoid the bombs which would soon fall on the gallery, they were taken out of their frames, like the rest of the collection, and packed up in anonymous crates—the King himself came down to say goodbye to them; then they were sealed in railway containers and sent off to secret locations around the country. Almost exactly a year later the gallery's east side would be reduced to a spectacle of devastation that reminded Rothenstein of pictures of the Western Front painted by Paul Nash.

Robertson died in his utility-free house (imagine how few

the bills were) in the country in September 1948. He was paralysed and no longer able to speak. Everything had been taken away from him. He spoke of death as joining the majority. As if it was just another act. Another golden room.

All those billions of people who have gone before; as my friend Michael points out, who represents them? Robertson left half a million pounds to ensure the safe upkeep of his Blakes, to keep them alive; and as they came out of hiding, to hang in the Tate's cavernous rooms alongside his portrait as a young man, he would step out of his frame at night when the doors had closed, a narrow shadowy figure in a tight coat with a velvet collar, evading the security cameras as he paced up and down, admiring, deliciously, his legacy.

Nebuchadnezzar crawled into the bunker. It's a wonder he ever crawled out.

But he did, and that is why, along with the fact that the seventeen-year-old Robertson found Gilchrist's biography in a Southampton bookshop, I'm standing over Blake, in a vast concrete and steel facility in south London, in the disorder of time and space.

The cumulative effect of the three pictures in front of me is dumbfounding, hypnotic. They exceed anything else. They are prints, but they are beyond any painting, and we have little idea, any more than Dante Gabriel Rossetti did, of how they resolved themselves as the perfect manifestation of Blake's art.

Un-two-dimensional, physical, emotional, they are active evocations of his hand, his sense of discretion and grace, of immaculate composition and spiritual wealth. A man who never lacked life. Even his movement, the way he held himself, is echoed in these kinetic records of his nervous system. Everything is caught in these acts of God. Art: the fear of a divine child, wilful and wild. Their surface is everything, so is their depth: I want to dive in.

I can't tear myself away. I might never escape them, never stop staring at them. These are the pictures passed on from Blake's devoted friend to Wilde's lover. These are the pictures Paul Nash saw, before the beginning of the First World War, that launched him into a new magical imagining. I see them now through his eyes, I'm seventeen again. Falling in love with someone I shouldn't have fallen in love with. Like Mary Butts growing up under their gaze, I'm both deeply uncomfortable and worried I'll never be happy again without them.

So I stop staring, using up their precious energy and mine, and I ask my guide if I can see the other works. Be reasonable, demand the impossible. Like an angel, he takes me by the hand deeper into the building, down into the London earth and out the other side. I follow one step behind him, apprehensive at what we might find. I have no idea where I am in the building, which level I am on, or how I would get out if I were left alone in here. It could be heaven or hell in a video game. What are they trying to hatch? I might die down among the serried racks and shelves, surrounded by beautiful things whose monetary value could buy me a city but which would be useless in my final hours as I sucked the last air out of here. Reduced to a skeleton by art, the shreds of my shorts and my Vexed Generation fleece still wrapped around my bones for warmth in this cavern, this corner of the ocean. When I ask, my guide says that yes, sometimes, when it's quiet, he does come down here and pull out the paintings. They come alive, as if he'd tripped an infra-red ray. They stare at him with their big eyes.

There's another table standing in the middle of the room. There's no one else about but me and my guide and the humanoid beast tiptoeing across the white melamine. I tell my guide that Blake saw this thing, in his house, on the stairs, only a mile or so away from here.

Do you believe in ghosts? the young man asks me, directly, matter-of-factly. He looks into my eyes. I know from his steady gaze what the correct answer is. He says he has a friend who sees spirits all the time. When he came to London, my guide took him to the Tower. As you would with any visitor to the capital. His friend saw many ghosts there, my guide says. A man in armour with an axe on the battlements. In Tokyo, another friend was playing the piano when she realised she'd been joined by a ghost at her side.

Ghosts are just memories we lost. I want to tell him that sometimes I feel them standing over me on the sea wall, on a beach where there is nothing at all, nothing but wreckage and lost souls, or that once, in a dilapidated Victorian house I was living in, I heard a long-dead woman sobbing downstairs for her long-dead man who died in the First World War; but then we'd be here all day and night and my time is running out. I have just one hour here and we're ignoring what lies between us, what we both came here for.

Something seen in the microscope, something science got wrong; something creeping out of the wings, ghoulishly poking out his tongue, holding a curved blade in his fingers in a lascivious, barbarous gesture, disgusting like the rest of him, the whole of his body and mind. His phallic lizard head, the crustacean bumps of his spine. That horrid sideways stare. Everything crude and lost. Everything alien, future and past, Assyrian, contained in that archaic shape.

A gargoyle calling at your front door; Nosferatu in the waiting room of hell, a psycho killer, a perverted act out of Astley's circus, a creature from the black lagoon. The Flea told Blake that if, in attempting to leap from one island to another, he should fall in the sea, he could swim. It's Fuseli's nightmare, a demon from Jung's *Red Book*; the frightful shape that follows the ancient mariner, a robot born out of lightning in *Metropolis*, a classical satyr with blood-red eyes.

It is the gothic fiend of our legends, Blake decided, the true devil; all else are apocryphal.

It's no surprise that the dandy performer in Robertson was drawn to this image or that Wilde warned him not to read *Dorian*

Gray. When he had the picture cleaned in 1906, Robertson discovered, perhaps to his disgust, a tiny flea on the floor, representing the earthly body of the monstrous Spirit of Evil. Thereafter, Robertson was haunted; he saw the flea everywhere.

There's something utterly abandoned and theatrical about it all: behind this unnumbered beast, on the wall, is a surprisingly glorious scattering of stars, bold enough to brighten up any ice cream parlour or pearly unicorn. The stars that fell around William are still starting to fall, in paint, in wood, in gilt, in the sky. A comet zooms down like the beginning or the ending of the world, casting a green glow; bursting like the fireball I saw this morning, tumbling into the sea in the dark, all forlorn. These heavenly bodies represent the only brightness in this dark icon of an unheavenly body, barely bigger than this book. Glossy and nocturnal, obscure and obscene, a heaving dream.

It's disconcerting enough on a postcard; in the varnished flesh it's so fearfully made, so opaquely inhuman, that it makes me want to look away; then look back again, hoping it will have gone, only to find it filling its thick frame like a rhino, pushing at the bounds of reality, swelling and unashamed of what it may or may not have done. Uncontained, stalking down the Old Kent Road, a dino-man swinging on the sign to Dover. A keratinous perversion, an unbordered version of some other self, all the worse for its ignorance and its mindless plight.

Do you, sir,

Blake addresses his student,

work in fear and trembling?

Beside the Flea, resplendent and naked and suspended under an even more gelatinous coat of varnish, like spilt vanilla syrup or a thin slivery veneer of tortoiseshell, is Nelson. He is dreaming in colour: a beauteous sight in every regard, in contrast to the beastly humanoid insect by his side. A naval archangel to that prancing Orc. Peering out through his yellowy film, the admiral is a butterfly Apollo and bold as you like, a funny bunched strip of linen shielding his private parts. Another glad day at the village fete. All around him the venomous, fierce-toothed sea beast curls round the hero, while dead-eyed souls writhe in torment, their bodies carelessly caught in the coils like so many virgins abducted in tritons' arms.

But it is at Nelson's saintly feet, dainty enough for a dancer, a murderer in the ballroom, that the most terrible sight awaits: an enslaved person cowering, bare head buried in their arms, face too agonised to show. It makes you selfishly grateful for that act of guilt and ignorance on the artist's behalf, and ours. Don't expect me to educate you. I never learned anything about slavery at school.

Standing there, on tiptoe myself, I can make neither head nor tail of these visions, these reliquaries of pain in paint. Their glazed gaze and double centuries stand between me and what they purport to portray. I see them all as if I had eyes inside myself, buried in my belly or my chest. But they also make me laugh, wicked as they are. Why should we take him so seriously? He's the great performer, performing his own art. A performance artist. The funniest visionary around. I'd forgotten how funny he could be. A stand-up on the Lambeth Road.

What are they even doing in here, in this industrial installation which might as well be supplying internet customers with the stuff of their dreams only to find that they've ordered a nightmare? We walk past crates of stuff being shipped out or being brought back. Clustered like chimneys and buildings. Skylines of the modern world. Stencilled with familiar names, as if they contained people I had met in a bar, or a club— **GALLAGHER – POLLOCK – HIRST**—leaning over a table to say hi, now reduced to flat-packs, with only an Allen key required to unlock their meaning. They might as well contain self-assembly beds as anarchic works of art.

Art as export and import. Art as tokens of love. Paintings propped up like pillows on a posh hotel bed. Piled on the floor, not wanted on voyage. A Turner leans wearily against the wall, an actor awaiting their call: a bursting furnace of a picture, glowing red-hot like a plasma screen. Not far from here, an artist is burning his paintings to make them more valuable. A few streets away from him is the site of the house where these pictures were made. My guide pulls out another rack. Look at this, he says, as if it were only found yesterday. Flying out of the stack is a panel Blake painted for a fireplace in a Norfolk rectory: a bearded Ancient in his gown, representing Winter.

I remain outwardly cool, like the Londoner I was; but under my breath I say,

BLAKE ffs

still the provincial boy at the back of the hall, overawed in the presence of a god.

The egos must be intense down here after dark. Shuffling round the room like zombies. So much wood and canvas, staples and spit and sweat, interchangeable assemblies of the minds that left them behind. Unlooked at, they are inert, as my friend Peter says. Pull one out and it suddenly changes, radically. Do these things only mean what we say? In the future they may mean nothing at all. They may even disappear, like the people and the animals and the world they portray. Blake's works, so frail and so fragile that I fear I'm wearing them out by looking at them. That in my allotted sixty-minute audience, I have used up an infinitesimal part of Blake's half-life.

We're still working him out. His imagination did not diminish; it merely got more intense the older he got, the more he had to work on. His teenage energy. Why shouldn't his pictures do the same after he's gone? They get more intense, the more we look at them, the more that we've lost. They're not going away; not yet, anyway. They still have a job to do. We're his future and today I am his only audience.

Time's up. I'm escorted off the premises. No one frisks me, there's nothing under my shirt. I resort to my default position: a nobody with no expertise, in shorts, on a bike, like a boy. I ride off down the street, round the roundabout, past his house which is no longer there, back to the station and its steel and glass. But I have the sense I'm being followed. Shadowed, benevolently. That someone is looking out for me.

And it's not the ghost of a flea.

Three thousand miles and an ocean away, the waves roar beneath the crumbling cliff. Same as it ever was. I stumble down it. There's nothing human there. Nothing permanent, either. Nothing between me and home.

This place is exposed, like flesh, held out. Excavated. It does not leave you alone. The storms run day and night, chasing each other across the bay. All the houses are wooden and they shake like ships. I ride to the shore, the backside of the cape. The snow needles my eyes and face. It gathers in the dunes in fluffy white clumps like plucked cotton. The sea is stripped back. I strip off and run in, forced there by the wind.

The gulls rise up. The ocean is another order of time entirely.

I pull my clothes back on and my thick black workers' mitts last of all, with their rubber grips, then clamp them to the handlebars. The two miles back to town might as well be the two hundred miles to the mainland. I wonder if it was a good idea.

At night I shake, but not from the cold. I move my head repeatedly from side to side when I am thinking of something I can't deal with or that has embarrassed me, or something which I have done wrong. Something I have been told. The way that when I am excited or pleased I bang my wrists together.

We are not organised for this world. There are no words for the way you and I are. The sea is my tic, happening all the time in my head. My reassurance, the way I have come to terms with the world. To only feel comfortable when I am suspended in it. There are no issues that it cannot dissolve or resolve.

The storm goes on night and day. The snow comes and goes like a locked-off shot. Everything is reduced to the sea and the wind and the light. The waves and the sand and the air. Another time lapse, too beautiful to know, too fearful to behold.

I ride back to the edge of town, sit at the bar of a diner and drink hot tea, clutching the mug in my hands to stop them shaking. The server, a man in an apron and a mask, leans over gently to ask if everything is OK.

I arrive the next day at the same beach, on my bike, leaving it in the sand, and look down from the dunes into the navy-blue waves and see them part

> to
>
> reveal
>
> a whale
>
> unfolding, before my eyes.

The golden callosities on their head like a coronet, something triumphant, rising. Their snout thrusting up as they ride the waves, as improbable as a medieval hippocampus, half-fish, half-god. Their tiny eye, their glossy black body, the curve of their tail. The first cetacean I've seen for five years: there, barely twenty yards from the shore.

Did they see me arrive? How did they get here? What do they eat? After all this time it strikes me as strange how a whale lives in the sea. Buoyed up by their own density, the same as the ocean's. How they occupy its oceanic size, this nowhere place without anywhere to hide. The way I've seen them held there, before my eyes, suspended in perpetuity, touching nothing except for each other, yet feeling everything through the water, their medium of being and connection.

That's where the longing lies.

I watch as the whale plays in the surf the way a dog runs around a field. There are less than three hundred and forty of their kind left, set against the teeming multitude of the whole human race. Too few whales now to fill this great ocean, or animate it enough to save themselves. Too few to fertilise it, with their living excretions or their dead bodies. Too few females to continue the line. An insufficiency of whales. Day by day, line by line by sonic boom, fewer and fewer till they reach vanishing point like an old TV closing down. The greatest miracle is that any survive. Precious, enamelled, gilded and crowned, bright and alive: the whale, framed there in the waves.

In the afternoon Dennis and Dory and I walk to Sal Del Deo's studio in the woods. He's been painting my portrait, fixing me with his bright, ninety-five year-old eyes. We talk of Blake and Michelangelo and Sal's Irish wife. Josephine, whose hand he reaches for in the night, even though it is no longer there. The light fails and we climb the hill to his house to sit in front of the roaring red fire. Dory looks at us with her big black eyes. The power of this audience lies in the fact that this place is so full of people I love. She's a little bit slow now, and her sand-coloured coat is flecked with white like snow. She is exactly one with the beach. Her hind legs bow out, as if with all the beauty she bears in her old age. Where she once leapt out of the car, Dennis now has to give her a helping hand, the way he and I groan when we get out too. But she's still the same. Dogs only look sad because they take our sadness away. When Dory leads me down to the sea, she sits there patiently, waiting for me to come out. Sometimes I think she is only technically a dog, or that I am only technically not.

I like being me. Which is not to say I wouldn't have been perfectly happy being something else. You forget that you're a human out here, even as you're never so aware of your own body and its frailty and strength. How you hold yourself. How you stand. There's nothing else to compare yourself to. On a beach I always feel someone is leading me by the hand. Standing beside me, or walking in my wake. But when I look around there's no one there. You can believe anything in this place. Everything slips away here, at the edge of the known world.

A single fin appears out at sea, once, twice, breathless, gone. Then everything is empty again.

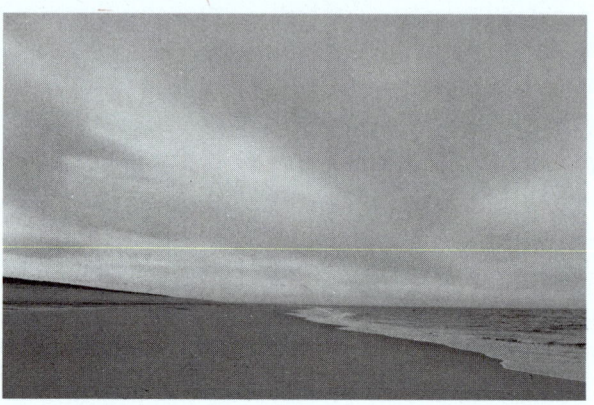

In the bustle of summer this place has all the services and compliances and the crowds, all falling in love and leaving again. In the winter it's a frontier town, denuded eroded and bare, bleached of colour, drained. A damaged place under constant repair, assailed on all sides by the sea, its houses, its people, its sands slowly curling back north-west, to return to the mother--land from which they came. Every winter that I can, I migrate here, to get myself good and cold, like a brent goose, the fierce cold sky beside not above me, as if it might eat me up.

Yesterday Mary and I went from beach to beach, up and down the backshore. The sea knocked us back. It didn't want us there. We looked at waves that could hardly be described as waves, more collapsing buildings or mountains slowly held in the chill air. We crouched on the cold sand as the cold sea rose over our heads, clearing everything in its wake, withdrawing, then coming on, back with all the energy of the turning world behind it, beating us back.

How can you live in a place like this? How can you not? It exhausts and restores, takes away all the pain. You can't think of anything else when you're so cold. Not to think is the greatest luxury. The sea doesn't think at all. It bites away at me, leaving bits of me feeling nothing but the cold itself. You reach a register beyond which sensation is arbitrary. The retrieval of life like blood. The cold is a great editor; it takes everything away. It allows you to become nothing again. The best thing about getting cold is what it proposes: the prospect of getting warm again. Of knowing you are alive. It is the best reminder: that the body you carry about with you is a miracle. Unrepeatable and unique, like an ultrasound. When I first came here, twenty-four years ago, invited by my friend John, my literary godfather, he knew it would be good for my ultrasoul.

At night, in the next storm, the trees shake and bend round this house in the woods. All the trees here are seeded in dunes, turning sand into earth, as if they were growing on the seabed. The houses stand among them like shanties or sheds, lifted up by the rich on stilts to accommodate the rising sea. In the dark, packs of coyotes howl at the full moon. Wild turkeys as iridescent as peacocks cross the highway, bronzed heads held high like velociraptors. Primeval. When Thoreau walked these shores, he reached the end and said, A man may stand there and put all America behind him. He was beyond any human jurisdiction.

Nothing is permanent here. Even the police station is made of wood. These province lands are still unclaimed. They belong to no province of Jesuits, this flick of isolated sand, hanging on to the mainland, stolen from people who called the entire continent Turtle Island, as if it might paddle away one day. They named the coyotes too. Duane Slick paints their shadows, the way he saw a shadow cross his bedroom as a boy. He is Meskwaki and he knows the coyote for a trickster. Dennis and I see them through the trees at night, much more wolflike than I thought, their coats shaggy with the winter cold. They move slowly, possessively, assured. One stops to look back at us, the way a fox does, with an imperious stare. Then they walk on, into the woods, into the edge of the night.

Nothing is what it is for. Nothing is what I came here for. At night Nauset Light sweeps its beam over the bay, searching the shiny black sea for escapees like me. There's an icy smudge in the sky, a comet passing through. It has its own registration mark, to tell us where it's come from and where it's going to, C/2022 E3 (ZTF) Like a whale, numbered and tracked. Next time it appears, all of this will have gone. Blake raises his stick to the stars and rearranges them for me. I can be me here, because I'm a long way away from myself. I think of the whales' nakedness and of what Stormy Mayo said to me last night in Mac's restaurant.

That there is no bridge between us and the right whales. That they may be the most enigmatic of their kind. That they have a sense of the oceanographic world that we cannot understand. It is a moment of revelation, talking to Stormy, seeing the whales through the decades of his grey-blue eyes.

Other whales seem to him to be quite comprehensible; humpbacks, sperm whales, fin whales: we know what they do, he says. But these creatures, which he has been studying all his life, are set apart. For all the data he and his colleagues have collected on them since the nineteen-seventies; for all that we know precisely how many of them there are left and where they might be at any given point in their migratory lives; for all of this, they seem almost completely unknown and alone. Out there in the bay or off the backside shore, moving slowly through the ocean, straining its surface for the tiny copepods that provide their only source of nourishment. Living in a world of taste and scent and sound. With no apparent interest in us at all.

Perhaps that's their fatal flaw, these three hundred and seventy-two cousins of ours, fewer each year, outrageously ignoring all our power and might. They could live to two hundred years old, like their Arctic cousins, some of whom were alive when Blake was. But these whales, hit by ships, entangled in fishing gear, subjected to warming seas and our cacophony, have been brought to the brink of extinction. Yet yards off these shores, I have seen them rolling round each other, sleek black, slate black blubber and skin and fins, engaging in mating rituals for hours on end. The memory of all the whales I ever saw.

The temperature drops to minus thirty in the wind. The sky swirls with the cold. A huge tree trunk appears in the water, like a felled mast. It bobs there in the dark as I get in. By the morning it has disappeared. It's the coldest it's been for seventy years. The sea also swirls with the cold. I go back to the beach. In thirty minutes exposed skin will become frostbitten, says the severe weather alert. Smoke rises from the surface like human forms. The sea is edged with sluggish ice, slowed down to a slush. My face freezes and burns. I take off my clothes under the bulkhead, stash them under the timbers and slide in.

I didn't expect the sand to be frozen under the water; it's varnished with ice. It's more like skating than swimming. A new winter sport. No one's making you do it. I swim through the strands of sea smoke. Turning back, I can't get out. My feet slip helplessly on the slope of the shore.

For a moment, I wonder, is this it? The fatal, stupid mistake? I try crawling like a Precambrian creature. Then I grab on to the wooden piling of the bulkhead. Hauling myself out, I stand on my clothes in an attempt to defrost my feet. Haven't you got a fridge at home? I look down and see that the water in my body hair has turned to ice, like little crystal beads. I laugh at myself as I shiver, not so much from the cold as from ecstasy.

With nothing to the contrary to convince me, I place all my faith in the power of the sea. It's as close to God as I can get.

Three hours down the coast, a snowy bus ride away, in a clinically bright white room on a cold afternoon with more snow coming on outside, a dozen pictures are propped up on a shelf, unframed and unglazed, as though they're for sale.

It's the kind of display you'd see in the department store of your dreams, a counter in Macy's, or a Shinto shrine. There's a watercolour by Dürer I've never seen before. It shows two buttercups, some plantains and clovers. They sit in a clod of dirt and look like they were dug up yesterday from the fields of Providence. Next to them the Virgin Mary dandles the Christ Child on her knee, a capuchin monkey perched at her feet, proud as a cat. The angel of Melencolia peers at us from the folds of their gown, wings folded against the storm outside.

At the centre of the room on a white table lies a portfolio propped up by wedges of grey foam. The label has a date, March 1826, and a price, five guineas. I finger the credit card in my pocket. As Christin opens it up, a light comes on inside. For twenty-one pages we follow the story. It's all here in black and white. Film noir.

The trials and torments of Job. In Blake's own words, as if he'd experienced the trauma himself, which he did. It's an outrageous act of faith: a poet reordering the Bible the way Milton wrote its backstory. A year before his death, Blake was retelling his own life as if it were rushing before his eyes. Each black image could have been his exquisite stone, drawn the nearer he got to his end. His autobiography, his visual memoir, his final perfection. His are the sufferings as Job receives the plague of boils and the betrayal of friends; the fate of poor Job, whose vexations felt heavier than the sand of the sea. But also his the triumph, his the ecstasy as he reaches the end, standing there with his wife in the benevolent glow of God.

Nothing prepared me for this. You'd have thought I'd be used to it by now. For disappointment or communion, in this white room full of absolute black-and-whiteness, a velvety light from under the ground. Black through white through light through dark. His use of white space was more outrageous than Dürer before him or Beardsley afterwards. W.G. Sebald called it echo space.

It took his whole life to be able to do this. To be this extravagant. Andrew tells us how Blake returned to his first love, the art of engraving in which he'd been trained. He'd tried everything else. Miniatures for private customers, giant images for the general public to behold. Now he's carving through the black to let out the light. He scratches urgently, carefully. He has found the final formula at the end. His greatest work, reproduced. Released. He's ready for heaven now.

As Christin slowly turns the pages, almost like an ordinary book, the scenes leap out. The words around them act as captions or commentaries; inter-titles for a silent film, frame by frame, woven with dreams, winged demons and scaly serpents; with complacent sheep and gentle lions and proud peacocks and dangling spiders crawling and creeping in from the Blakean menagerie. They're what he found trawling through other dimensions, on his travels beyond the material world. Whatever he imagined, as Bronowski says, Blake also saw.

In 1969, Bronowski made a film for BBC Two, a dramatised essay with a soundtrack from the radiophonic workshop. He called it *As a Man is—So He Sees*. Humans were about to set foot on the moon and more than ever

9.5 COLOUR

WILLIAM BLAKE
1757—1827

Dr. Jacob Bronowski
presents a dramatised essay on the man and his work

AS A MAN IS—SO HE SEES

William Blake as a boy.....Oscar Peck
William Blake...............Paul Kermack
Catherine Blake...........Pamela Craig
John Scofield................Richard Henry

For thirty-five years of his life Blake lived under the iron heel of war and three revolutions—in France, in America, and in the growing industry of Britain. He was a rebel against political and religious dogma, a mystic who dined with Isaiah, a poet of the stature of Milton. As an artist, he considered himself in the company of Michelangelo and Raphael —a presumption, maybe, but all his life he struggled to convey extraordinary visions: he saw the plight of twentieth-century man crushed by the Machine of State. Yet he lived with the hope that man's imagination would enable him to rise free. He believed Jerusalem *could* be built among the satanic mills.

Like most men ahead of their time he was deemed mad. Only today can we see him as a prophet whose work is as relevant to our time as that of any modern thinker.

Music by Dudley Simpson
Commentary by
Dr. Jacob Bronowski
Dramatised and produced by
Adrian Malone
A co-production with N.E.T., U.S.A.

Blake seemed like a prophet, up there in his capsule, looking back at the blue planet.

Three years later, in his *Ascent of Man*, the irony of his being a scientist and Blake's great champion did not escape Dr Bronowski. Reaching up to the fitted bookshelves of his mid-century modern home in California, he pulls down Newton's *Principia*, followed by Blake's *Songs of Innocence and Experience*.

It's 1972, again. Here in his room overlooking the ocean (exposed brick painted purple, Bertoia chairs, purple and scarlet striped sofa, ancient works of art; glass sliding doors with the Pacific light falling through them), Bronowski holds the two books together—Newton's and Blake's—and declares them part of the same impetus. Then he walks out into his garden with its palm trees and looks up at the sun, and by the miracle of the edit suite, steps into a European graveyard where he holds a handful of earth to the camera and recites, not a chemical formula, but the words of his favourite poet, the greatest statement ever made

> To see a World in a Grain of Sand
> And a Heaven in a Wild Flower
> Hold Infinity in the palm of your hand
> And Eternity in an hour.

Here, now, in this room overlooking the ocean, in the echo space of the School of Design, they delay our gratification, these angels and animals moving in the margins of Blake's book. There's even a leviathan threading their scaly way into the frame. They stop you making sense of the main event, making it all the more powerful when your line of vision drifts back to the centre of it all. In the middle of every page are images so black that their blackness blocks off all the white around them, like a pinhole camera or an eclipsed black sun. I burble out words at each new image, apologising as I do so. I should curb my enthusiasm, play it cool among all these professionals. But

Dürer's comet is streaking across the room and there are angels in front of me in black and white. It's four o'clock on a January afternoon, and Blake's alter ego unfolds.

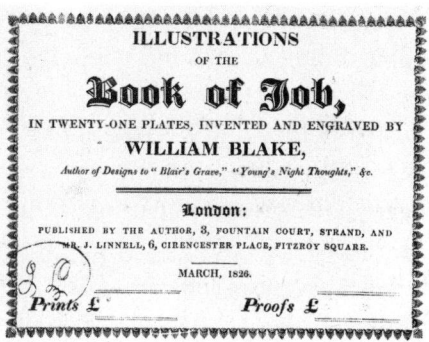

1. There was a Man in the Land of Uz whose Name was Job.
2. I beheld the Ancient of Days.
3. The Fire of God is fallen from Heaven.
4. And there came a Messenger unto Job & said The Oxen were plowing & the Sabeans came down & they have slain the Young Men with the Sword. And I only am escaped alone to tell thee.
5. Then went Satan forth from the presence of the Lord. And it grieved him at his heart.
6. And smote Job with sore Boils.
7. What! shall we recieve Good at the hand of God & shall we not also recieve Evil.
8. Lo let that night be solitary & let no joyful voice come therein.
9. Shall mortal Man be more Just than God?
10. The Just Upright Man is laughed to scorn.
11. With Dreams upon my bed thou scarest me & affrightest me with Visions.
12. For his eyes are upon the ways of Man & he observeth all his goings. I am Young & ye are very Old wherefore I was afraid.

13. Then the Lord answered Job out of the Whirlwind.
14. Canst thou bind the sweet influences of Pleiades or loose the bands of Orion. When the morning Stars sang together, & all the Sons of God shouted for joy.
15. Can any understand the spreadings of the Clouds, the noise of his Tabernacle. Behold now Behemoth which I made with thee.
16. Hell is naked before him & Destruction has no covering. Thou hast fulfilled the Judgment of the Wicked.
17. I have heard thee with the hearing of the Ear but now my Eye seeth thee.
18. Also the Lord accepted Job.
19. The Lord maketh Poor & maketh Rich, who provideth for the Raven his Food, When his young ones cry unto God.
20. How precious are thy thoughts unto me O God, how great is the sum of them. There were not found Women fair as the Daughters of Job in all the Land & their Father gave them Inheritance among their Brethren.
21. Great & Marvellous are thy Works, Lord God Almighty, Just & True are thy Ways, O thou King of Saints. And then Satan went from me.

I feel a bit giddy and want to lie down. As Christin turns each page and Andrew continues his narration, the scenes power up, flashing into life. I write all this down in my notebook later, my laptop, my illuminated book, having lost its ability to plug into the grid. The extravagance of Blake's images lies in the bright depth of their glorious blackness, the way that whiteness appalled Ishmael. It's benthic, this squid-inkiness. A swirl of long-bearded prophets proclaiming woe, Satan casting his plagues with a malevolent glee, before being cast into the eternal fires for his trickery, while angels rise as a chorus to provide the soundtrack for this expressionist film. There's so much ink so lavishly concentrated in these postcard-size images; you couldn't possibly fit any more ink into them.

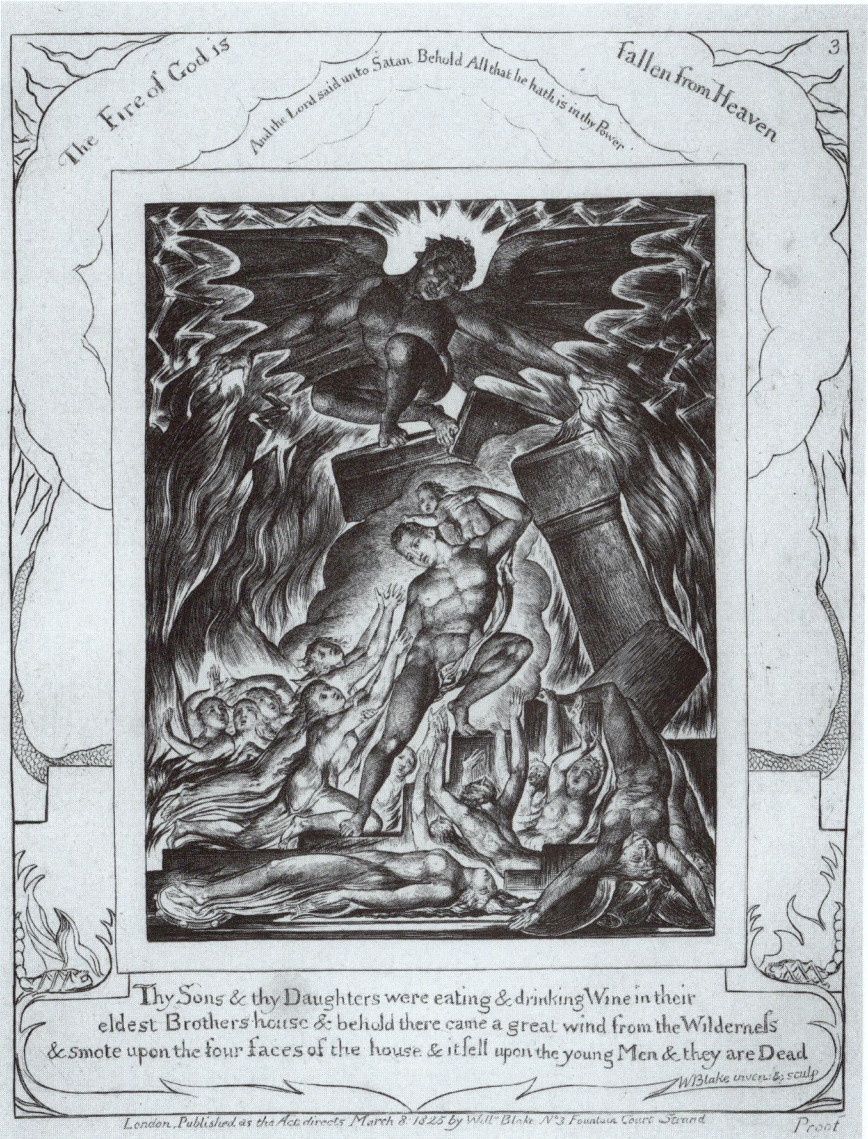

3

The Fire of God is

And the Lord said unto Satan Behold All that he hath is in thy Power

Fallen from Heaven

Thy Sons & thy Daughters were eating & drinking Wine in their
eldest Brothers house & behold there came a great wind from the Wilderness
& smote upon the four faces of the house & it fell upon the young Men & they are Dead

W Blake inven & sculp

London, Published as the Act directs March 8: 1825 by Willm Blake N° 3 Fountain Court Strand

Proof

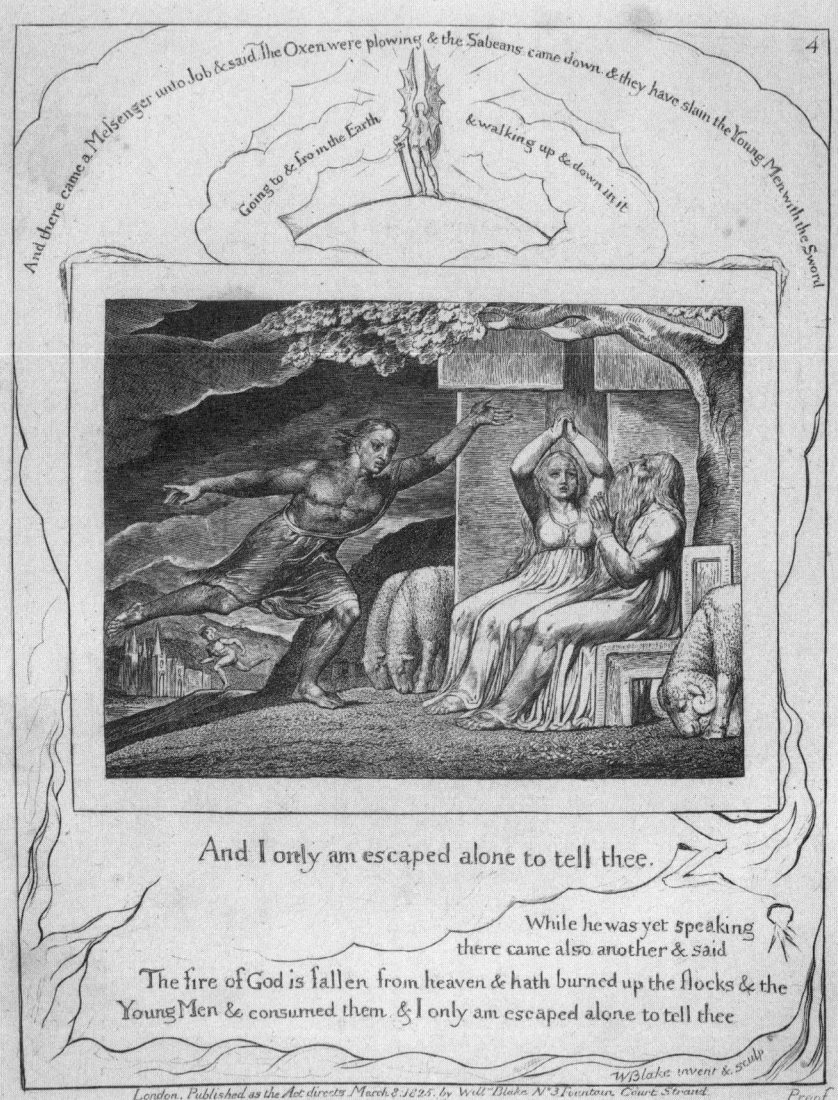

And there came a Messenger unto Job & said. The Oxen were plowing & the Sabeans came down. & they have slain the Young Men with the Sword

Going to & fro in the Earth & walking up & down in it

4

And I only am escaped alone to tell thee.

While he was yet speaking
there came also another & said

The fire of God is fallen from heaven & hath burned up the flocks & the
Young Men & consumed them. & I only am escaped alone to tell thee

W Blake invent & sculp

London. Published as the Act directs March 8. 1825. by Willm Blake N.º 3 Fountain Court Strand.

Proof

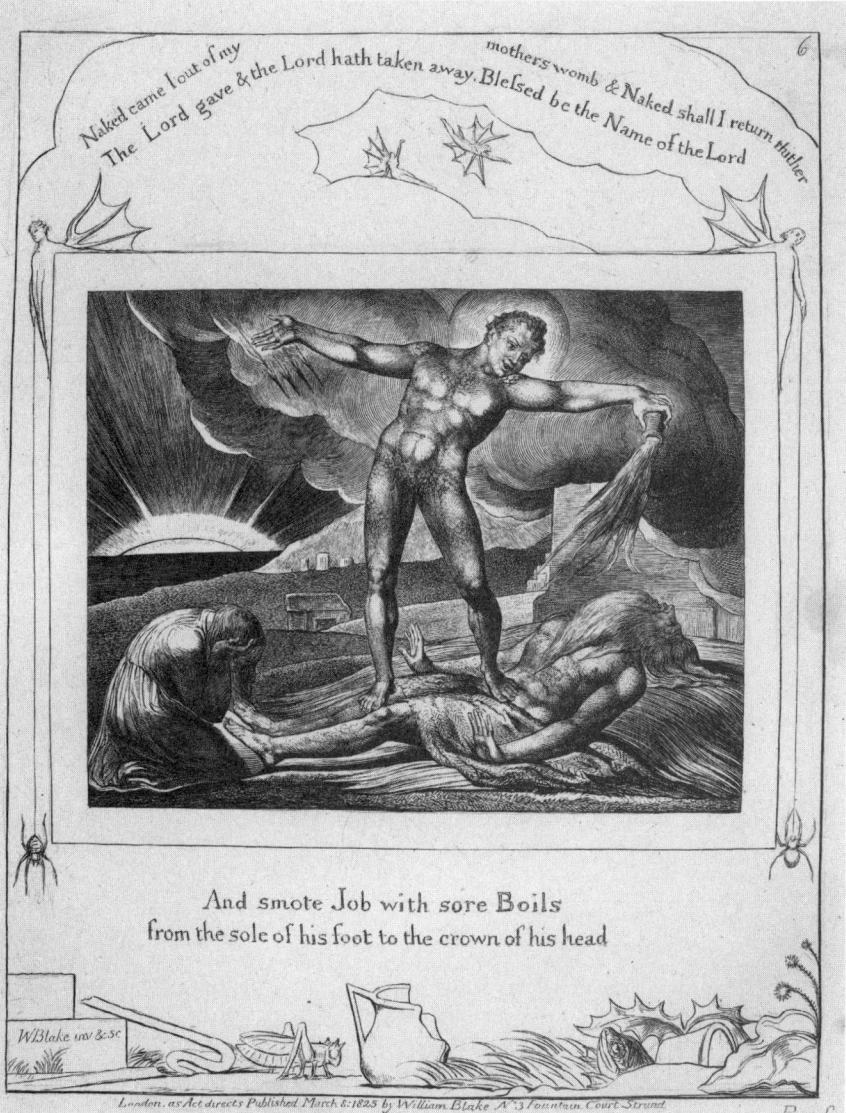

Naked came I out of my mothers womb & Naked shall I return thither
The Lord gave & the Lord hath taken away. Blessed be the Name of the Lord

And smote Job with sore Boils
from the sole of his foot to the crown of his head

WBlake inv & sc

London, as Act directs Published March 8:1825 by William Blake N.º 3 Fountain Court Strand.

Proof

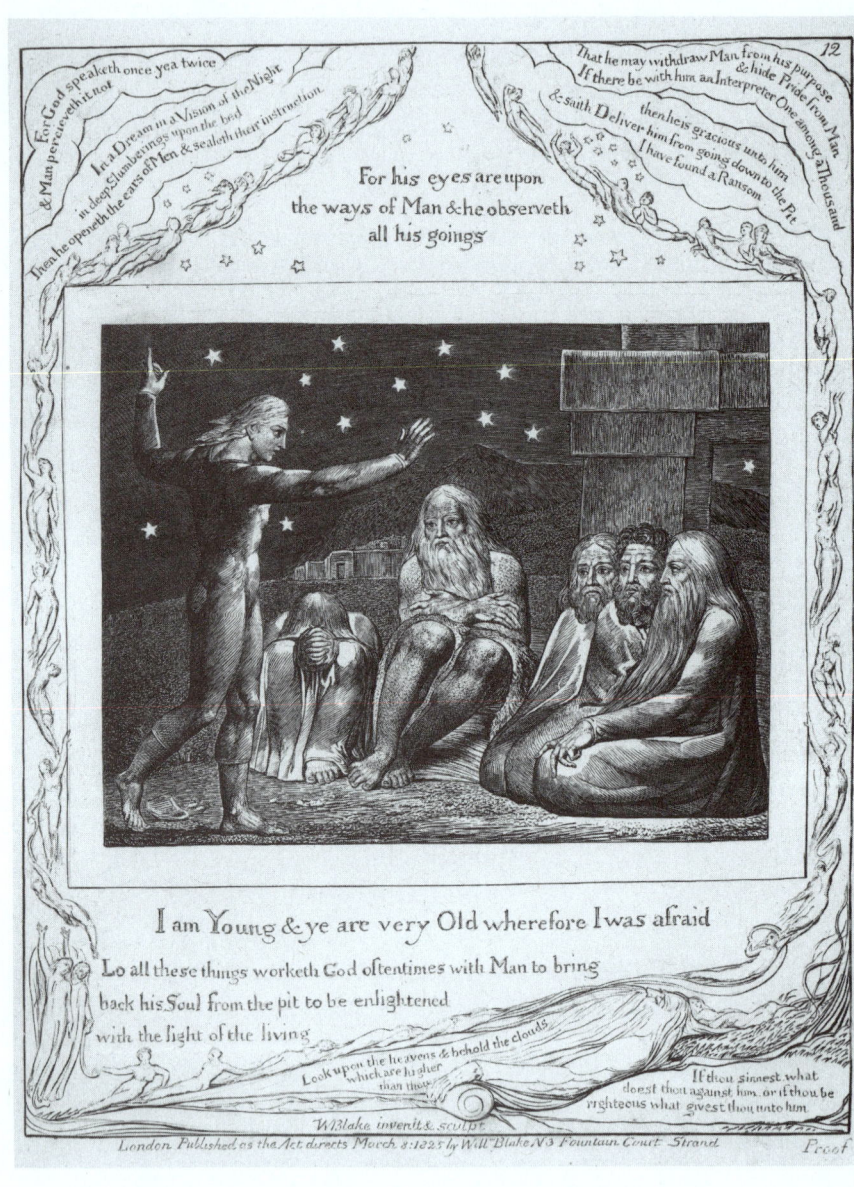

For God speaketh once yea twice
& Man perceiveth it not

In a Dream in a Vision of the Night
in deep Slumberings upon the bed
Then he openeth the ears of Men & sealeth their instruction.

That he may withdraw Man from his purpose
& hide Pride from Man
If there be with him an Interpreter One among A Thousand

then he is gracious unto him
& saith Deliver him from going down to the Pit
I have found a Ransom

For his eyes are upon
the ways of Man & he observeth
all his goings

I am Young & ye are very Old wherefore I was afraid

Lo all these things worketh God oftentimes with Man to bring
back his Soul from the pit to be enlightened
with the light of the living

Look upon the heavens & behold the clouds
which are higher
than thou

If thou sinnest what
doest thou against him. or if thou be
righteous what givest thou unto him

W Blake inventt & sculpt

London Published as the Act directs March 8: 1825 by Will Blake N3 Fountain Court Strand

Proof

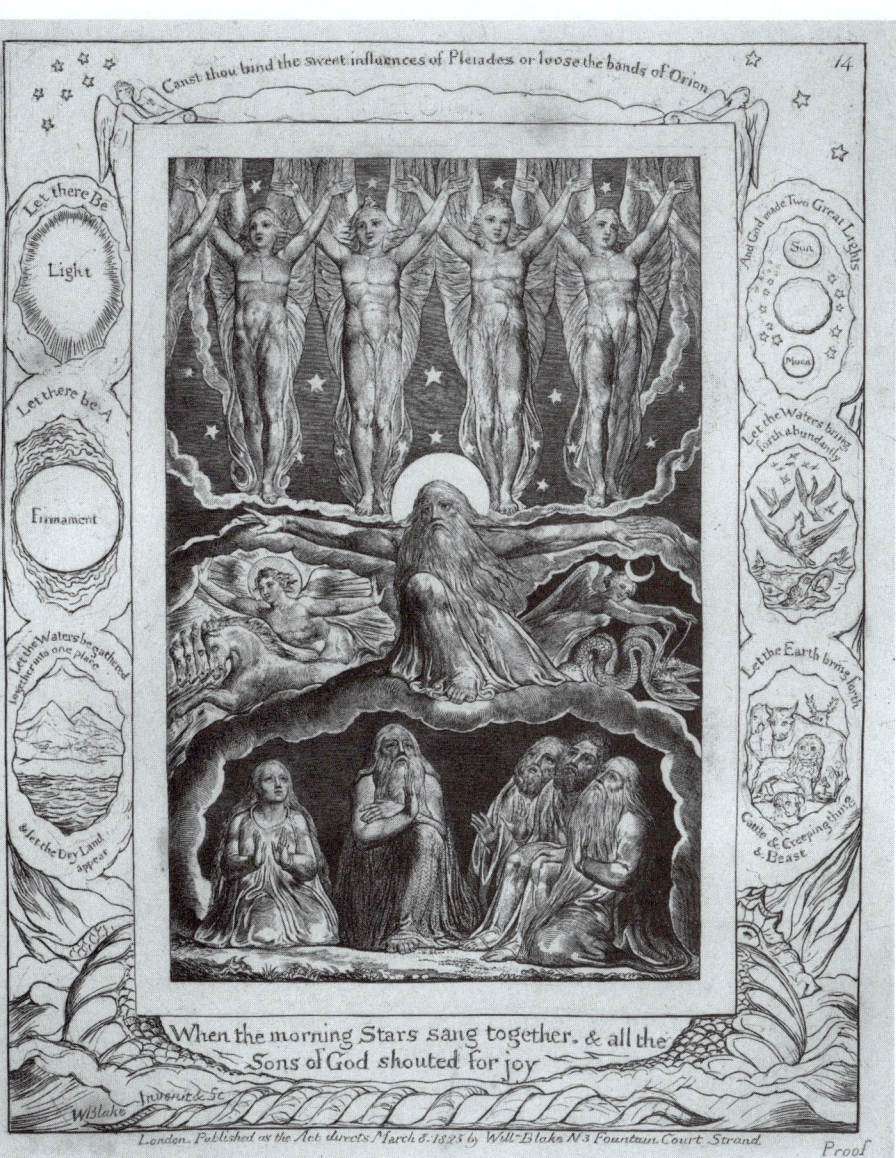

Canst thou bind the sweet influences of Pleiades or loose the bands of Orion

Let there Be

Light

Let there be A

Firmament

Let the Waters be gathered together into one place

& let the Dry Land appear

And God made Two Great Lights

Sun

Moon

Let the Waters bring forth abundantly

Let the Earth bring forth

Cattle & Creeping thing & Beast

When the morning Stars sang together, & all the Sons of God shouted for joy

W Blake Invenit & Sc

London. Published as the Act directs March 8. 1825 by Will.m Blake N.3 Fountain Court Strand

Proof

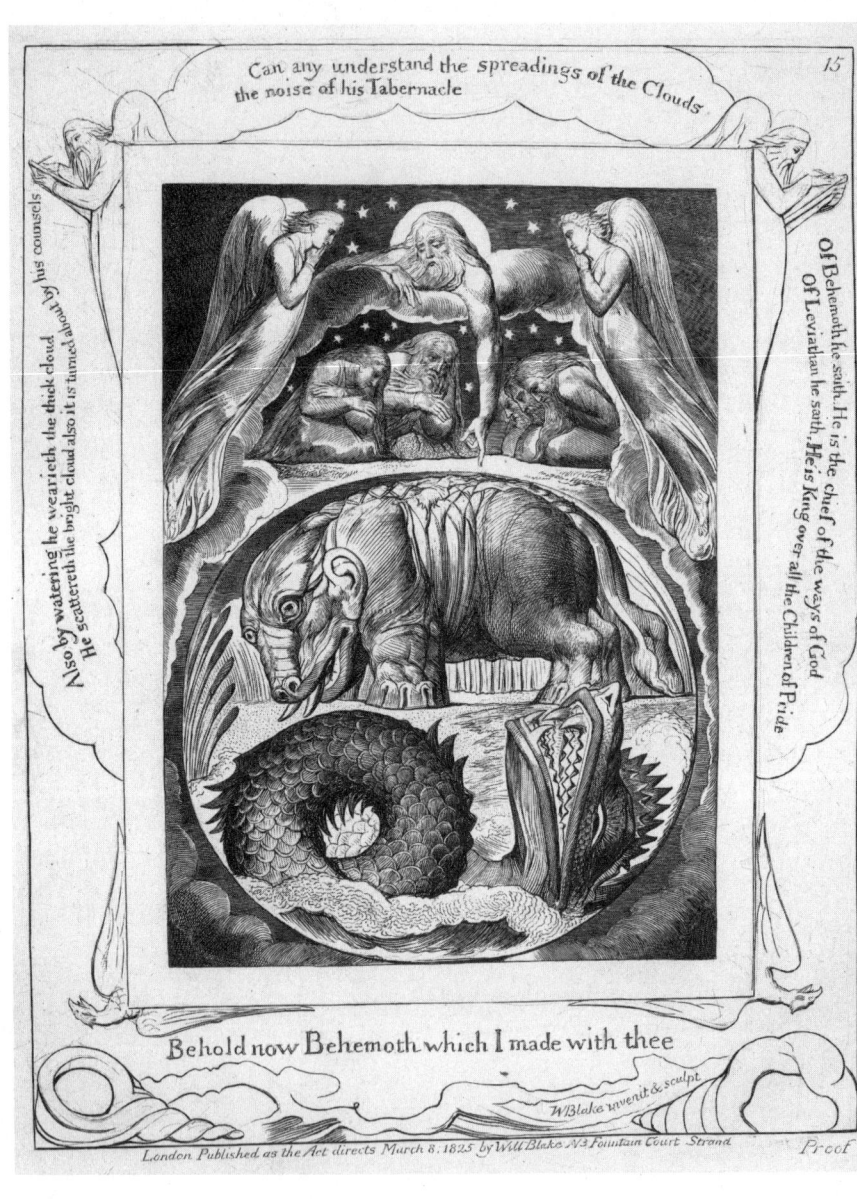

Can any understand the spreadings of the Clouds
the noise of his Tabernacle

15

Also by watering he wearieth the thick cloud
He scattereth the bright cloud also it is turned about by his counsels

Of Behemoth he saith. He is the chief of the ways of God
Of Leviathan he saith. He is King over all the Children of Pride

Behold now Behemoth which I made with thee

W Blake invenit & sculpt.

London Published as the Act directs March 8. 1825 by Will Blake N 3 Fountain Court Strand

Proof

And so it goes on, the interflow of the words and the images, as God creates the world; then shows it to Job. I wasn't expecting this in Providence, despite the city's name which might have come out of Milton. Suddenly there is Behemoth and there is Leviathan, battling it out on a different plane; seen through a telescope, a porthole into the past. The beginning of the world is happening even as God speaks and Job sees outside of their reality, the reality of God and Job. Their here and now is ours, and all the more terrifying for that.

Gilchrist saw those two beasts as evidences of Blake's Gothic feeling, presented like a medieval wood-carving. In the twenty-first century they're fantastical natural history: the Behemoth flayed, flapping their elephantine tail and rousing their walrus tusks. The Leviathan rising up, all purple and green in the lightning flashes that Blake draws to indicate the roar of it all. He makes everything elemental, out of two dimensions, into the fourth.

Hair flows, faces glow. Flesh reverberates. Thunder rolls. Blake preaches from his pulpit-prow. Ahab is Satan is God. These animals could go either way, like us, to freedom or captivity. Harold Bloom says the Leviathan and Behemoth were the forerunners of Blake's Tyger: two horrible beasts, as Bloom says, who represent the God-ordained tyranny of nature over man, two beasts whose final name is human death, for to Blake nature is death. And Jesus was Cetus, Leviathan, D.H. Lawrence declares. Likewise Bloom, the great Jewish critic who looked like a sad old whale himself, says that Melville's Moby Dick is closer to the beasts of Job, and to Blake's Tyger.

Who made them? Who made thee? Who can decide? A tyger like a whale like a poet. A fearful symmetry. It's all preordained. We get what we deserve.

In the autumn of 1849, twenty-two years after Blake died at Fountain Court, Herman Melville arrived on the Strand, staying in an upper room with the same narrow view of the river as Blake, where he experienced his vision of the white whale, which would end with the same quotation from Job,

& I only am escaped alone to tell thee.

His book was not well received. Some people thought he was crazy. A later note in the *Contemporary Review* agreed, declaring *Moby-Dick* to be like a drawing by William Blake, madly fantastic in places, full of extraordinary thoughts. Leviathan is not the biggest fish, Melville replied, I have heard of Krakens. He was increasingly drawn to Blake, telling friends how much he was touched by his work. When he bought Gilchrist's biography in 1870, as Michael N. Stanton noted, it included every plate from the Book of Job; it was also strewn with other images that seep into Melville's own last work, *Billy Budd*: it is possible that he saw the first American exhibition of Blake's art at Boston's new Museum of Fine Arts in 1880, prompted by loans from Anne Gilchrist. Its catalogue lists Blake's Body at the Bottom of the Sea being eaten by fishes, and the engraving of Glad Day, described as a personification of Morning.

   Billy Budd is a deeply Blakean book, with its many references to *Paradise Lost* and the innocence of the Handsome Sailor, who in the nude might have posed for a statue of a young Adam before the Fall; he has not been proffered the questionable apple of knowledge, ere the urbane Serpent wriggled himself into his company. Billy's significant personal beauty—his welkin blue eyes, the rose-tan on his cheeks, his yellow curls and shapely ears—could be composed of Blakean components; not to forget that his exemplar at the story's opening is a shapely Black sailor, a cynosure star to all his friends. Victim of conspiracy like Blake—his jealous nemesis, Mr Claggart, a Satanic master-at-arms, has the alien eyes of certain uncatalogued creatures of the deep—Billy, dumbfounded by evil he cannot understand or explain, goes willingly to his death, wearing his white jumper and white duck trousers as if already in his shroud. His besotted captain, Starry Vere, calls him an angel of God. Yet the angel must hang.

For a moment he seems to ascend, as through a vapory fleece hanging low in the East, shot through with a soft glory as of the fleece of the Lamb of God seen in mystical vision. Billy ascended; and, ascending, took the full rose of the dawn. And so he becomes Blake's Glad Day, an Albion rose, as he dangles there like a pearl drop. After his body is consigned to the deep, splinters from the yardarm from which he hung are circulated like relics of the true Cross.

When Melville died, forgotten, in Manhattan in 1891, the manuscript of *Billy Budd* still lay in his desk, waiting, like *Moby-Dick*, for the modern world to come along. In 1927, the ever sensible E.M. Forster, later to write the libretto for Britten's opera of *Billy Budd*, summed up the subtle connections for us in his *Aspects of the Novel*. Discussing the two books and their sense of prophecy, he said we need to set aside our single vision of literature and find a different set of tools to make our inquiry of such works. Is this right? Forster asks. Another prophet, Blake, had no doubt that it was, he replies, quoting the poet

May God us keep
From single vision and Newton's sleep,

and noting that Blake had painted that same Newton with a pair of compasses in his hand, describing a miserable mathematical triangle, and turning his back upon the gorgeous and immeasurable water growths of *Moby-Dick*.

Fifty years later, in 1976, in a film by Nicolas Roeg, Thomas Jerome Newton, an alien who has fallen to earth, rises to his feet in a New Mexico church as the pastor invites the congregation to sing an old English hymn for a new friend of ours.

Pale as cocaine would allow, hair red and gold like a comet,

Newton joins in with the words of Jerusalem, singing falteringly and almost bashfully from the sheet he holds in his hand, his girlfriend Mary-Lou by his side. It is an act. In fact he is dreaming of his planet far away, where he spins in watery space with his alien wife to the song of a humpback whale. The film is chaotic with collapse and defeat and doubt, with rising and falling bodies, prone and unknown, like a breaching whale, like a cloud. His names give him away. This Newton is a prophet in the wilderness come to sort this planet out, to warn us of environmental and nuclear catastrophe. You can see where this is going. No one takes any notice.

I'm not a scientist, he says, sitting in the desert under a deep blue sky, but I know all things begin and end in eternity. He is speaking in Blake's voice, as Roeg would acknowledge, echoing the artist's Last Judgment

Eternity exists, and all things in eternity.

All things begin and end here, in the desert, at the bottom of the sea, on Albion's shore. I know of no other film in which a figure is placed in such disconnected relationship to a landscape or a room, so strangely positioned in otherness: the duotone hair, the hooded head like a candle, the artificial way of walking or holding themselves, like a painting by Nash or a Blake print. Roeg sets Newton on a bench, in an examining chair, stumbling down a scree, crouching on the shore, standing at the end of a pier, to the sound of the wind or of nothing, the flick of his hair. Everything is doubly ordinary, as if nothing else really mattered and no one else was really there. He only dresses like us as a disguise: his suit is a little too black, his heels a little too high. He appears as a tradesman in overalls or an overcoat; he winces at human voices and has no genitals or corneas. He can see the future and past happening at the same time, all around him, like an Edwardian visitor seeing the ghosts of Versailles. Moving as in an oceanic dusk, unageing like Dorian

Gray as everyone else crumbles away, grounded by his own technology and under under surveillance, he watches his monitors as Billy Budd appears on one of them, his pale neck ready for the noose. The phone cord dangles provocatively. They had to pick on someone.

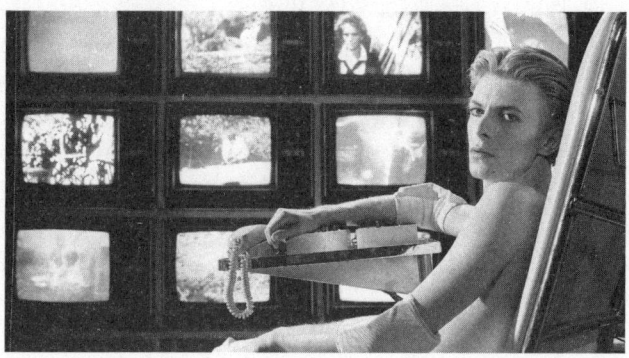

So he picked on me. I saw that film every day for a week at the local cinema when I was at college, secretly taping its soundtrack on a cassette recorder stashed in a bag at my feet. At church I pretended to sing hymns the same way, the way he lay in Mary-Lou's arms like a pietà, as if he weighed almost nothing at all. And I wondered what his bird-like bones would look like at the end, those cheekbones, those hips. Those eyes.

Five decades later, three years before he died, I was asked about his influence in an interview recorded in a museum where his costumes lay in a basement downstairs. I struggled to find a comparison for a person who had exerted so much power over me, someone I never met but saw from afar. I looked around, feeling out of my depth as always, and couldn't decide what to say. Then I remembered that argument with my friend, and I said, William Blake.

———

We lie on the beach late at night, Mary and I, on the damp sand, in the dark, watching the stars fall. The comet is a blur in the sky. I can't get enough of the dark water, of this beautiful mortal town and my friends. Watching the stars fall.

For five weeks I go without any other news. Candidates and sociopaths do not have my attention. They go about their business without the benefit of my eyes. The news here is what the beach cast up overnight. A dead gull, a merganser, a surf duck. A sea robin, bony with fins that act as legs and a horny brow like a cow. A scattering of dozens of drink cans, partly rusted, escapees from some recycling effort. Three huge cartilaginous fishes, slowly turning to jelly. Dory sniffs at them, liquefying versions of beautiful things they once were.

She carefully chooses the correct place to lower her hindquarters. I look away, to afford Dory her dignity. We go to check on the studio of an old friend. He has gone but left his pictures behind, all racked and ordered in the efficient, barn-like house he built; even the risers of his stairs are built-in drawers. Carefully numbered and labelled on their panels, his art, slowly disintegrating, being claimed by the sea air, the same sea he painted, again and again.

I feel like another person, only the same one. So cold I go to bed with my clothes on. I need blankets to protect me against the night. I eat and drink with the same knife and fork and spoon and cup and plate every day. I go down the lane every day. When she goes for her walk, Dory waits for her leash to be unclipped, to be released to the beach. I wait for the same thing. All dogs are visionaries, as I said, noses to the ground. They scent out the future and the past. Art and artists, saints and saints, books and books all pass them by, future compost to be sniffed at, as they pass on. I know Blake will heal me. Art isn't from the future. If it was, why would we bother? We'd just wait for it to catch up.

———

Back home, Lilian and Freddie find an old oyster shell on the beach. It has a rectangular slit in it. Carefully cut with precision, through the layers of growth. We wonder about it. Then we take command of a wrecked ship, wobbling on its deck as if it were still on the high seas. What cares these roarers for the name of king? Later I look up the shell on the internet. Others like it have been found on Roman sites. No one knows why these holes were cut in them. I hold it to my eye. It fits closely like a mask. This English shore is crumbling away, tumbling with the past.

The police officer standing in the precinct doorway tells me to get off my bike and walk. A chap passing by tells me not to bother and keep on riding if I were you. All the marine villas are peeling with paint. The sea rides up the cobbles of the beach with a rattle. It's high tide. It's a short train ride along the coast from where I live. I got on at my local station and next thing I knew I was here. Along the seafront there's Gypsy Lee in her booth, still ready, a fortune-teller, to tell you who you are. There's a poster on the town museum wall advertising the starman and his band in Bognor, playing through amplification, the choice of the young generation, it says, but I got here fifty years too late. I ride along the promenade, instructed to ring my bell by the signs. England always tells you what to do when you can't make up your mind. I do as I am told.

The town blurs into the village. I clamber down the shingle bank fit to tip me into the sea. Then I ride up his road to his cottage. It's been empty for years. Standing at right angles to the lane, its thatch holed like a scarecrow losing its stuffing. There's no one about on this weekday afternoon in spring.

Imagine the uproar when the Blakes arrived close to midnight with their sixteen boxes, suspicious portfolios and a strange machine. Millenarians or anarchists or, worse still, atheists. All the houses stand shoulder to shoulder. The pub is just across the street; it would have taken no time at all to march a soldier down to it, by his collar and the seat of his pants. Round the corner was the grand house of the man who kept Blake employed for the duration of his three years' slumber. All far too close together, I realise, for all the road ended in the sea.

Jonathan lets me in. Suddenly we're in their bedroom. Uninvited. It feels kind of rude. The steep eaves running down one side to the bare boards. The little square window looking out to the street. The garden in front. The stairs winding up one way and down the other, like a helter-skelter ride. Jonathan explains, in detail, how and why the place is falling apart. There was a dead squirrel in the bath when he first arrived. He makes his excuses and goes downstairs. There's a hole punched in the roof as though someone has reached down to pull William out. Or maybe the angels were too eager and forgot to brake. Straw falls to the floor. I fall to my knees and kiss the boards where his feet walked.

You can see the sea at the end of the lane from the window. A blue bar visible over the trees. This place is empty. He's long gone. There;s no reason to stay here. Within minutes I'm back there, in Neptune's embrace. No one asks if I was wearing swimming trunks. You can't stroll along this beach after a storm. Its cobbles roll under your feet. The roar must have been intense sometimes, running all the way back up the lane to his window, shaking the frame of the house. I pick up a handful of stones and put them in my pocket, then ride back down the promenade. The two windmills that stood on the little headland are long gone, too.

These Mills are oceans, clouds & waters ungovernable in their
    fury:
Here are the stars created & the seeds of all things planted,
And here the Sun & Moon recieve their fixed destinations.

Now there are no more mills, but modern blocks of apartments looking out to the still ungovernable sea. Along the tide-line is a row of markers with red caps like lampshades. Each one has been adopted as a perch by elegant cormorants, preening their black wings. As the tide recedes beneath them, it reveals the golden sands where Blake walked with great figures from the past. He also rode his pony, Bruno. Beloved Bruno, he called him. I imagine him giving rides to children on the beach, the man with the sky in his eyes. I bet Bruno loved him back, with his dark eyes.

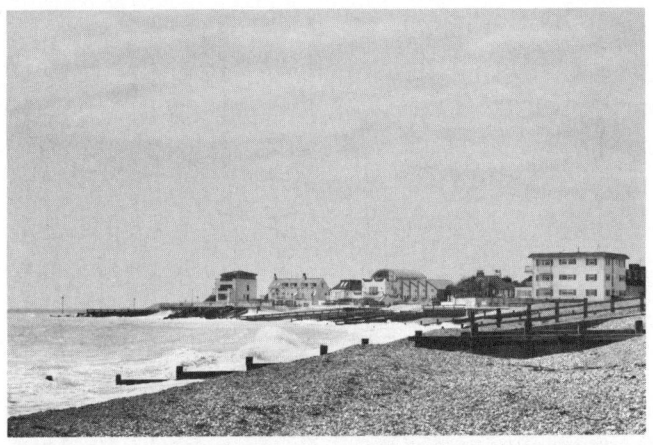

From here on the shore becomes ordinary seaside, kerbed in concrete, a hard promenade, bleak in the spring chill when the sun falls behind the clouds. On the road back to the station there's another plaque on a wall, the white-painted worn-out end of a Victorian terrace peeling gently away. An estate agent's sign says the flat is for sale.** The blue plaque says Joyce stayed here in 1923; he wrote *Finnegans Wake* upstairs. He was just round the corner from Blake's house. He took the initials of his anti-hero, H.C.E., Here Comes Everybody, from a nearby churchyard. On Sundays he took Nora's sister to Mass. He had no excuse; Our Lady of Sorrows was only a few doors down the road. His

** £119,000, since you ask.

face turned cinnabar in the sun. That summer Yeats asked him back to Dublin to meet some of his fans. Joyce turned him down. He bought a pair of suede shoes and a pair of white trousers for the summer heat wave. Nora made him take them off. They were transparent, she said.

So was he. There were tremendous storms sweeping in from the sea and the seagulls cried. He kept on writing. The book swelled like the tide. I'm now on the third floor, he told a friend. Over me, thank goodness, is the roof.

I ride round the corner. There's another plaque where Rossetti had his studio. He was lured here, too, by the sea. I imagine them all at the station. Blake, Rossetti and Joyce, standing next to me, peering up at the departure board, waiting for the delayed 14.56 to Victoria, asking the harried service provider what has happened to the train. The future makes us retrospectively stupid. How strange we will seem from then.

A long dark tunnel runs under the tracks, piss-stained and unlit. The kind of inner-city subway where you might find the ghost of a flea. The trains rumble overhead on time. Vans drive past. No one knows what goes on down there. Lurking in the shadows, set into the brick wall like alternative stations of the cross or advertisements on an escalator, are a series of mosaics depicting scenes from the life of Blake's art.

They glitter like discotheques. Newton, Nebuchadnezzar, Pity, following me; The Tyger and the Glad Day, rising and receding as they catch the eye. Lambeth boys are playing football in the middle of the street. At the other end of the tunnel, in the burst of steel-diesel light, there's a nineteen-thirties block of corporation flats. A small plaque is stuck on the wall. The cars pass by as fast as they can. There's no view across the river. But there's a tube station at the end of the road, and plenty of all-night convenience stores.

I've seen this street all my life, looking down from the train

as it took me in and out of the city. This is the first time I've
stood there. It is the closest I can get to Blake. Today, at least.
It is the nearest we have to a photograph of him, the empty-
eyed building about to be pulled down in 1913.

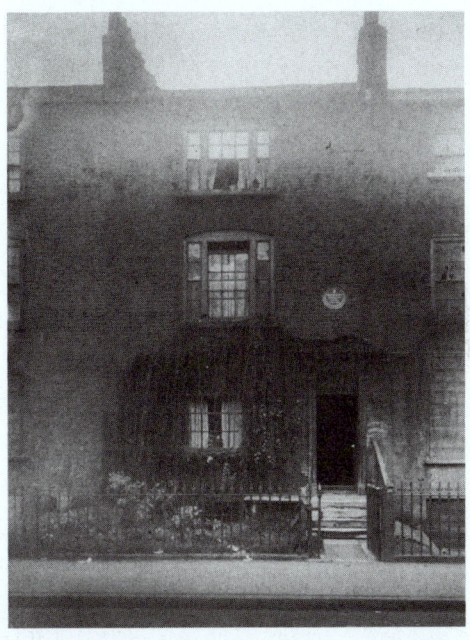

His house rendered in ghostly grey, the sort of place you'd
expect a poltergeist brick. Tattered with ivy and rusty railings,
as if it might yet be saved. As if it weren't too late. As if you
might see his face at the window. The little gate that squeaked.
The steps up to the door. The half-drawn blinds. The back
garden where they sat naked in their bower, safe from prying
eyes.

Steadily the places where he lingered were erased. Over the
river they'd already built a hotel on the site of his demise. It was
now a dank alleyway overlooked by the Savoy's laundry, busy
laundering Oscar Wilde's sheets and Lawrence of Arabia's underwear. The steam rises up in a cloud through the enclosed space
between the buildings; there's nothing to say this is where

England's greatest artist ascended to the sky. In the sixties they tore down the house in Soho where he was born and replaced it with a brutalist block. They named it William Blake House, and its ground floor was occupied by a health food café named Cranks. None of these things was a joke. They made a note of his birthday on a slab stuck over the stairway to nowhere like an escalator; you'd think his dreams had disappeared in the dust.

Where would his visions go now? Would his flea stalk through someone's front room while they were drying their socks on the radiator? Would the Ancient of Days hover over the fried chicken shop? The Lamb of God become a kebab? Where would the swallows roost? What would they eat?

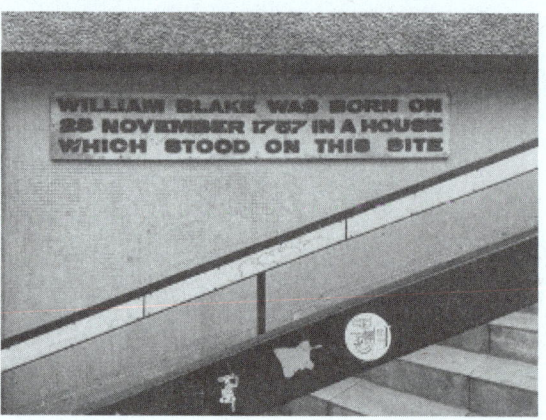

And yet: this is still the city he knew. He's still here, in its streets and alleyways. He's there with the protesters and the tourists and the down-and-outs and the friends that you meet.

I turn round on my bike, hesitating in the middle of the road like a lost delivery boy with a pizza cooling in my bag. Something might happen if I stick around. I might get run over. Or be transformed. That would really be something.

Someone shouts Robocop! at me, for reasons I cannot quite work out.

———

Summer falls away as I take the train out of the city, travelling east. The river is a shock after the sea. So still yet not still, trailing under the willows. A pair of geese sail by. I essay an elegant entry but I just fall in. Instantly out of my depth. The way I always feel in a college town. I founder in the cold, surprised. I make for a fallen tree, hauling myself out by a root. I crouch on the river bank. I'm naked and there's no one about. The sign says this place is called Paradise. I got lost on my way here. Afraid I'll be late. After all this time.

I run up marble stairs, passing dark galleries of things from the beginning of time, presided over by the museum's director. M. R. James. The discreet, half-glazed door might lead to a solictor's office, if it wasn't flanked by glossy Italian paintings from the Renaissance, full of classical nudes and fantastical fish. The archivist is waiting for me. I see her silhouette through the misty glass. The room is archaeological, narrow, with wooden shelves and a long table. On it, propped up on an easel, is Nash's painting, The Cliff to the North.

It's astonishing. So modern and so old, wholly composed of wash and cross-hatching, flooding the paper. You could fall into it or swim back to the shore. The surface is everything. The female figure leans into the scene. The shadow of her bobbed hair on the downs, melancholy as an angel. The moon is an after-image, scratched out of the black; the sea is irradi-ated, lit from below. Something Graham Robertson might have drawn. This room is named after him. It says so in gold letters over the door. Something else to be grateful for. He stands in the corner, a slight figure in a long coat. He looks a lot like me.

The picture is full of energy. The spark of a shooting star; the way the downs fall down. The fact that you can't see the shore makes it all the more eerie. The moonlight shines on the sea as a watery path. The sense of suspension and foreboding, a sensual nightmare. Who wants to be normal? Nash never lost that excitement, that awareness of the strangeness of the world, how we turn it into a strangeness of our own. Blake could be down there, just out of sight, walking with his spirits on the beach. I hold on to my breath. All this would be enough, worth the packed train and the air leaking out of my tyres and my knees muddy from the river's slithery sides, even if this was the only thing I saw in that room.

But it isn't.

Next to Nash's painting is what looks like a Tupperware box. I half expect to find Ellen's sandwiches in it.

Instead, nestling inside in a cloud of tissue, are Blake's spectacles. Quite nonchalantly, as though he'd laid them down for a moment. Two hundred years later—as if she were an optician and I was trying them on for size—Ellen holds them up to my eyes.

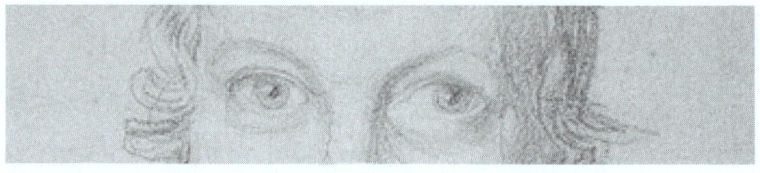

Everything suddenly turns half-size. The lenses, circled in steel, show how weak his long sight was. He needed science to make up for it. Their specification—left lens 3.50 dioptre, right lens, 3.25 dioptre—indicates that Blake needed them to see far away.

I'm looking through his eyes. It's like being inside his head. The sun bursts through the window. I see a tree magnified like a flea. I am seeing what he could see. The world according to him.

I shake inside. I want to phone a friend. I imagine all the words and visions coming up on the lenses. The spectacle of his life enabled by the technology of his spectacles. Refrigerators, cheap books.

How did they get here? Catherine Blake gave them to Samuel Palmer, whose son, Alfred, said they were much valued by his father. Maybe he even wore them, second-hand, to be granted his hero's second sight; his son remembers him using a pair of large, round, neutral-tint spectacles, carried specially for sunsets and the brightest effect on water. In 1908, Alfred, now living in Sennen Cove, having burnt twenty-four of his father's sketchbooks because they contained unmanly images, had sold Blake's spectacles to Lord Rothschild, who, because he could afford it, gave them to Geoffrey Keynes. Disliking relics (he'd burned Rupert Brooke's khaki tie that Eddie Marsh had slept with under his pillow every night), Keynes passed the spectacles on to this museum, whose director put them on Blake's life mask in an act of surrealism.

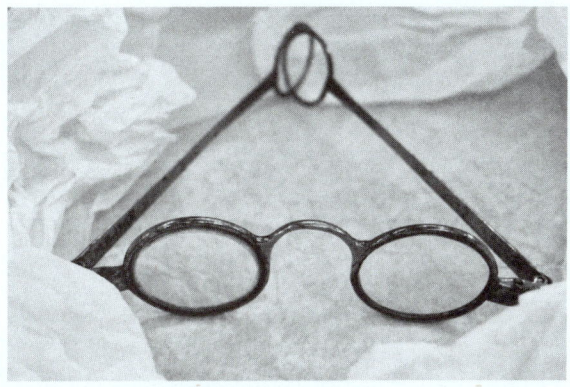

Here they lie, out of their pressed-cardboard, pull-apart case covered in shiny green-black paper embossed with rectangles and a tiny flower. In its shabbiness, the snug fit of the box, I see the way Blake handled this dainty, useful device. Something that was in his hands every day. No relic but a tool of his trade. The two halves of the case break open and William's chilly fingers find the familiar shapes inside. Carefully looping the arms over his ears, under his wide-brimmed hat, he climbs up the hill, to hear the voice of God.

It's cold on the heath. He rests at the top of the rise from his exertions. Listening to the birds. It is hard work entering paradise. He hums a song to himself.

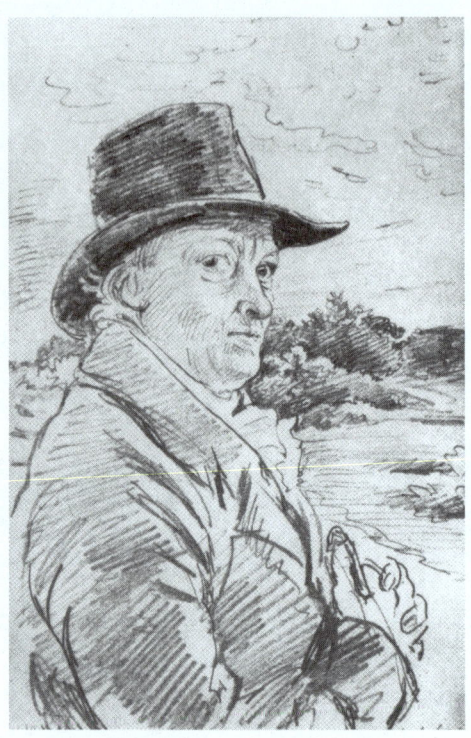

I see the window and the trees. Everything sharp, reduced to the size of the images in the books in front of me.

As I open them up, out they come, an album of glittering Christmas cards or votive icons. I realise the room is dim because of the brightness of the things inside it.

I hold my breath again. I can hear them, like a song on the radio before you go to sleep at night. *Songs of Innocence and Experience.* I have never seen anything like them in my life. How can something so small be so loud? I want to turn them up.

One set is Blake's personal copy, printed in Lambeth in 1795 and kept by him until 1819, when he sold it to John Linnell, for £1. 19s. 6d. The reference point for all the others that followed. On the cover page he has written, in his fine hand, registering his copyright to eternity, where all things begin and end.

Title Page

I shiver, and it's not from the river. I ask Ellen for a magnifying glass. Refrigerators, cheap books. Only then does their miracle become clear, like a good martini.

I try to get it right. That memory. Stuck on my eyes. I realise what I love about art. It is just playing around, like dressing up, but it makes people take you seriously, sometimes. It can be whatever you want it to be, whatever you need to be at the time.

In Blake's master copy, the outlines are printed in black. In the second copy, sold to John Linnell in 1825 for £5. 5s., they are orange-red. Both were coloured in by William and Catherine. In one the colour is delicate, almost translucent, like painting on an eggshell or porcelain. In the other, it is so vibrant and solid that the paper itself can't contain the colours and they leak out of their bounding line like a flood of Indian ink.

It's enough. But there's more.

I feel like a detective who's lost the plot. The wanting, the withholding. I can't contain myself. I whimper like a dog. With the evidence in front of me, I can see how it was done. The layers of meaning and love. The process is as clear as the ink is opaque. As clear it will ever be, or ever was. It's not an exercise, not a reproduction in a book of collected verse or an image on a screen.

It's the real thing.

I can see that Blake has drawn the sharpest and finest of black lines around the elements he wants to sharpen. Sometimes they thicken—around a tree trunk, for instance. At others they taper to the thinness of the leg of a spider, like the one that dangles from a corner of my bathroom like a spider chandelier. All his world is crammed in there. This is the natural world that surrounds Blake's fables.

His innocence, my experience, standing there, quivering, as I turn the pages.

Enough is never enough. They keep on coming, like fire-works, one after the other, bursting out of the paper they were painted on. I laugh to myself: at the lambs and oxen huddled together at the riverside with ducks and leaping frogs, at the trees that twine up to the sky. I'm excited and not about to apologise. I'm out for a walk with William on the heath, who's pointing out scenes with his cane. His proverbs come to life: the chimney sweeper in a snowy yard; the angel child carried on their father's head; the father he would never be.

Like many of Blake's humans, he appears to wear a kind of transparent sheath, a mock piece of modesty that only makes him more naked, oddly androgynous, turning his skin trans-parent; revealing, as my sister remarks, his innards underneath. The sheep bend their fleecy heads to feed. No one wears shoes in Blake's ancient time. They keep you from feeling the elec-tricity beneath your feet, the way my friend Pat walked the bay barefoot at the age of eighty-eight.

Then there at last. The Tyger, prowling, standing stock-still at the bottom of the page, under his verse, a semi-grin on his face. More Tigger than fearful beast in the night. The stars and their tears. The forests and the skies. That they are all high-lighted with flecks of shell gold, these images, like a lily or a rose or chalice, makes it seem a sacrilege to look at them. Only more so when I see Blake's careful numbering in the corner of each page, as if he were turning them for me, guiding me through them, standing by my side.

They sing his words, these images, while the lambs bleat and the lions purr and the tygers roar; I can hear them as I open each one like doors of perception, a symphony of Blake. They evade reproduction, even though Blake reproduced them. His intention is all. You feel his hand in the way that they float, barely on the page at all; in the sadness of the fact of how few people have ever seen or will see them. Later, eating my crisps on the train, stunned by what I just saw, I realise mid-bite that these pictures need to be seen at night by candlelight, in the dark or at dawn, preferably accompanied by solemn attendants and trumpet blasts. Or something of that sort. Not scrutinised by me, damp from the river, in my shorts, untutored, without an art book in the family home.

They all flutter in there as I close the book gently but firmly, to stop them from escaping out into the street; the way I saw a red admiral butterfly on the floor of the crowded station concourse and had to ask the young woman at the coffee stall for a paper cup to capture it before running across the road to find a front garden for its release. Someone said thank you, but it wasn't the butterfly.

Yes. There is more. Close by my elbow, on the table, are three other items, patiently awaiting my attention.

Catherine Blake's plaintive scene from *The Monk* is tiny and golden-brown on rough canvas: the pathetic figure of the mother is bent over her babe, who has already departed this life. The darkness of her cell goes on and on. It is the single most painful thing in this room. The what if, the what could have been.

Her only other known painting is even smaller, the size of an old-fashioned envelope. It came to her after William had gone. It is intense with abstract shapes. At its centre is the strange disembodied face that she saw in the flames and which, I now realise, has a grey wing at the side of its head like a god of sleep. It floats in a stormy nothingness, far from anything their contemporaries would have known. There's something spooky about it. The note on the back from Frederick Tatham says it was taken from something Mrs Blake saw in the Fire during her residence with him.

Pl VI

Curious as by her, he adds, patronisingly. I want to kneel down and pray.

Blake takes a lot of looking at. He makes your eyes ache. He takes a lot out of you. His demands. It's all those pictures and that mirror-writing. Each one a window into his head. I'm not sure I can take any more. Everything's a bit jittery. I don't

435

feel I have the right to be here. That I might be exposed as a fraud, here under false pretences, ready to be escorted out of the door. But Ellen, its keeper, affects not to notice. Her role here is as much therapist as anything else.

Lacking my own spectacles, which I do not wear, or the expertise of a connoisseur, which I do not possess, I ask for a magnifying glass so I can look at *The Gates of Paradise*, engraved for children in 1793. Barely bigger than a credit card, each image is pressed into the page. Minute dramas, like haiku or netsuke, they could be carved out of ivory, like scrimshaw. The drowning young man, his Shelleyan arm thrown in the air, is engulfed by waves that rock round him like mountains. The book was intended as a child's primer. The stuff of dreams or nightmares. Blake never patronises. You would never forget pictures like that.

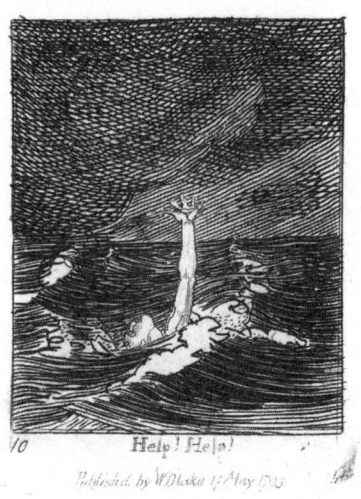

10   Help! Help!

Published by WBlake 17 May 1793

Then, out of a big red box, Ellen produces Mrs Blake's third work of art. The most astonishing thing to see, after all this time. Our flame-haired hero in his prime. Those big blue eyes, face flickering in the pencil line Kate used to outline her fantasy lover, at the age of twenty-eight. The picture measures just six by four inches and it hung on Marsh's wall. All his visitors admired it—Nash and Lawrence included—as Eddie sang in the bath. Blake: their guardian angel, incandescent, made of stardust, undiminished, fiery locks standing on end as if caught in a draught. His curls twirl into outer space, the universe reclines in his hair, the lightning flashes across his face. I want to hear him sing out loud, even if only for one day. Pl XVI

There's one last picture in the room. Like the best present, best left to the end. I've been ignoring it for fear of what it might or might not say. A page from his prophecy for America, 1793. Propped up in front of me.

Blake's hand, in all the words and figures picked out in his carefully inked line. His wyvern, an astro-whale, curly-tailed sea-or-air dragon clashing his scales and flaring red meteors. The plunging patriarch in his white robe wielding his vengeful harpoon. The Atlantic itself rearing up to overwhelm the American plains as the whole scenario hangs under those purple rain clouds split by a zigzag of lightning and a glittering smudge of shell gold. And down there, at the roots of the tree, as if on the seabed where three terrified figures cower, there it is: that grey shape, a great whalish thing.

The afternoon is already half over and the light is starting to slant outside the window. I tell Ellen that no one in the world could be closer to Blake than we are, at this moment. Standing in this room, half the size of a village hall, with his spectacles lying on the table as if he'd just stepped out for a comfort break, leaving his books and paintings behind.

For a few seconds, we don't speak. Everything is silent. The busy college street outside, the courtyard of the café across the road where I ate lunch, the person on reception downstairs with chipped black varnish on their nails. None of them stop being, but for that moment they do.

Then I pick up my pencil and notebook—what good are notebooks?—and leave as I arrived. Shaking down the road on my bike. Asking directions for the station. Another cyclist points out the way and follows behind me to make sure I take the right turning. Such kindness shown. The woman riding ahead of me alerts me to the potholes. This is not a lonely city at all, and I am not alone.

On the packed train home a tall youth in a tracksuit with Pitbull branding emblazoned on its arms and legs stuffs a chicken and bacon wrap in his mouth and eats profiteroles like a wolf, noisily, all the while scanning the feed on his phone which never leaves his hand, flashing up its hundred images a minute, each one demanding his attention. A pair of lads congratulating themselves on a joke, a news item from Lódź, a bronzed woman in a bikini, wrestlers in the ring; messages from his friends. I'm trying to read *Dorian Gray*.

Eventually I give up and make my excuses and make my move, pretending I'm getting off at the next stop. But as I stand up to ask him to let me by, he says, Oh, are you going? in the politest voice, as if he were personally disappointed.

It is the spectator, and not life, that art really mirrors, Wilde says.

I want something else, I realise.

There's nothing to stop the bitter wind blowing in from the plain. It's a winter's day, and England is flooded again. The ditch round the man-made hill has filled up like a moat, turning the vast green mound into an inundated pyramid. The stones start to appear through the rain. It's thirty years since I was last here. I have photographs of me and my parents, standing against the stones, wearing our coats, looking vaguely unhappy, wondering what would come next. The place is far bigger than I remember. The rings of the ramparts plunge steeply into the earth, more like giant trenches than anywhere safe for a boy to roll down. Defensive, as if what happened here required protection and secrecy.

The mud is grey and slippery as the slip on a potter's wheel. A dilution of chalk and earth. I'm shivering, and it's not from the sea. The water this morning felt warm compared to this bleak place. Miles inland on the southern uplands, the cold is so bitter, so pure, it's difficult even to look at what we have come here to see. The shadow of the sun seems very far away. My hands shake as I hold my camera, as I try to draw the stones which will not stand still.

They defy you in their individuality, like characters on a stage. Each with their own names. Divided, bony, pitted with holes, stuck in the grass. Gutted, guttered, rivered, run through with cracks and crevasses; sheered off, hacked about, disinterred, unquarried from unquiet graves. Some are caved with little grottoes, ready for a virgin to appear. Others look like elephants or whales, charismatic megafaunae, mid-century modern, masonic. Far more eccentric and abstract than I expected. Shocking. Sculpturally random and rare, unrefined, undressed, each one demanding inspection in the rain.

Each one holding your eye. Each one on the verge of collapse. Not growing out of the grass but screwed into chalk sockets as dental implants. Disturbingly unstable in this wind, this soaked earth. Naked, just stuck there, enigmatic and futile in their grand design. It's overwhelming, almost reclusive, the way they stand in your face but fall back into the landscape at the same time. Pevsner thought this place must be felt as much as known. No field is left untransformed. The site is sown with a stone crop. So scattered with monuments it resembles a stone age car-boot sale, or the aftermath of a shipwreck on the plain.

From no angle do they look probable, these deceiving stones. Because the weather is so brutal, because I'm hungry and cold, because the hood of my coat keeps blowing off, I can't even think about what they mean. I don't have the words and it's one big game, rings around the village, houses cowering inside, pretending they aren't there. That they are not slowly encroaching, seeking revenge on their burned brethren, shifting position every time I look away.

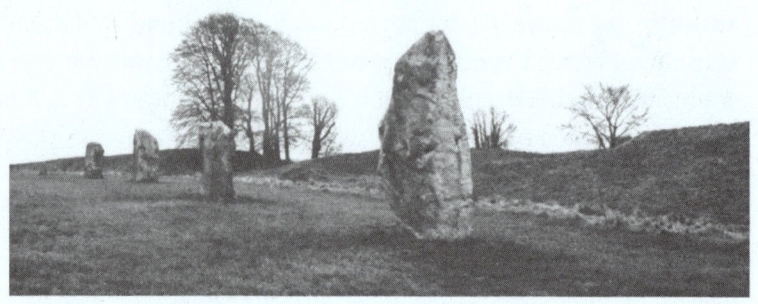

The same stones, everywhere, following me about. Rearranged Dragged out of the grass and set in concrete like bollards. A visitor centre and café, muddy feet on Jerusalem's mat. The whole place is a conspiracy of silence. Who lived here? What did they eat? People have tied coloured ribbons to the trees, inviting anyone to pray for their joy and despair.

No one apologises or explains. The rain never stops. I give up trying to draw them and seek shelter in the house of God. In the dark recesses of the church erected defiantly over all this pagan uproar—someone had to provide cover for priests and their miracles—is a huge font, designed for complete immersions. It's more like a bathtub; I could lift up the lid and jump right in. Carved elegantly into its side are a pair of wyverns, gently curling their tails round and round. They look as though they've just hatched out of the circles, biting their way through the turf to menace Michael the archangel. He wields his crozier of cosmic power like a harpoon. The monsters close in on either side, jaws open wide. There might be lightning in the sky. He's wearing a pleated skirt.

For a moment, I wonder who is going to win. But as I peer closer, I realise they're not ferocious at all.

They bear messages of love, and I've seen their like before.

———

Two o'clock in the morning, an ocean away. The lane takes me down to the shore. There's snow on the sand and the water's edge is scattered with bright-green glitter, the colour of a quetzal feather. The tiny bioluminescent creatures flash, then fade away. I wish there was a way to say all these things. All the people I love. I stand on the sand in the dark, held up by my bones for a sign.

A single star falls.

Yesterday afternoon it was impossible to get in again. A white wall of surf raced along the backshore. We watched from the sandy bluff as lithe black shapes moved in the foam: surfers, like another species, as if they'd just come from the sea rather than entering it, tall with their boards as they slid in the waves. A pair of seals bobbed in the distance, ready should they be needed.

Everything was silent. No shouting. No one asking, is it cold? No exclamation marks. No punctuation. No names. No bright lights in the sky. Just the sea and the snow coming on. Their bodies rising and falling. The water catching them like lions. Everything happening now. Running out of words.

I've been leaving and arriving in this place for years. It was waiting for me. The blue-green waters, the teal-coloured end of my days.

Overnight, the wind changed direction again. It is so cold I've stopped thinking. I feel punctured, animal. The stars spin round. The blackness of the ice, the sharpness of the sky. The lighthouse in the distance, flashing like an eye. The coldness of the water, the brightness of the night.

In the silver-grey morning, black shapes break the horizon. A series of triangles and islands, dark against the sky. They roll and dive, twisting and turning with elastic life, rising and falling, sending clouds in the air.

Ancient creatures, loving aliens.

Vast and silent, the first and last of their kind.

It's the hottest day of the year. Even before the library opens, the shadows of the city are too sharp to bear. He's up there, stranded on the piazza, crouched on a block, bold as brass, next to the station, bolted together like a locomotive. Paolozzi's robotic Newton, outrageously naked and blank-eyed, twelve foot high, a giant left over from an age when people believed we had once been as big as elephants or whales.

I sit nervously at his feet, waiting for him to stand up, clank across the quad, and unlock the doors

I'm shown to a private room at the top of the stairs. Catherine wheels in a kind of tea trolley on which lies a parcel roughly wrapped in wrinkled brown paper, tied up with string. A package from the post office with a note saying while you were out. Inside is a green leather-covered box, lined in brown velvet. And inside that, all cosy in its plush velvety bed, is Blake's Notebook.

His brain, bound together in fifty-eight pages. I feel like I've been writing the biography of a two-hundred-and-sixty-seven-year-old man still alive. As though I'd finally met him. Perhaps I should say, Good morning, Mr. Blake.

Dante Gabriel Rossetti bought the book for half a sovereign in 1847 (he borrowed the money from his brother), and had his neat, florid and inaccurate transcriptions of Blake's poems bound to the back of the book.

I really believe that is what ought to be done, he said.

He lent the book to Alexander Gilchrist to allow him to write his biography. Then it went on its travels to Manhattan and Brooklyn before ending up back here, in the care of this place, where it took a lot of form-filling and convincing to get me sitting here at this table at ten o'clock on a Tuesday morning.

The book slides out onto foam wedges to support it. It's the size of the one you are holding in your hands. One of the most powerful things I've ever held. My naked fingers open it up. It's like opening up his mind. I'm losing mine. I once held Shelley's notebook, pulled from the pocket of his corpse, its sodden pages of poems and monsters and obscene drawings having gone through the spin-cycle of the Mediterranean Sea. This survivor feels like some urchin picked Blake's pocket when he was browsing in the mall of the Exchange. Or perhaps it's Prospero's book drowned, deeper than did ever plummet sound.

Catherine taps away on her laptop in the corner, keeping her eye on me as I turn the pages he flicked with his hand as he searched for a quote he had written down, the beginnings of a verse or a picture or a prophecy, what he or Mrs Blake saw; all recorded here in ink and pencil, as they happened.

I'm diving in a sea of Blake. All those forms I filled in. It's a magical thing, the journal of a magician, containing all his spells; cryptic, arcane, conspiratorial, one long incantation, makes you want to sing. As if all his work were crammed in there, undiluted. Just add water and colour and we could reconstitute the whole of his artistic and spiritual being from these pages. The memoir he never wrote, a fractured book of hours, perpetually unfinished. A blueprint for Albion. Compressed, full of air and dead flowers. I expect to find the key to his life inside, the Blakean code to it all.

It was already second-hand when Blake inherited it. The book belonged to his brother, Robert; it still contains his sketches, strange eerie creatures, solemn and rudimentary, ghostly traces of William's apprentice, still waiting to become. The heady connection gives the notebook a collaborative, emotional charge; as if, like Blake's printing process, it is still haunted by Robert, a loving ghost; now no longer wracked and consumptive, dying in his brother's arms at nineteen, but living and encouraging, the bond between them unbroken, held together by this stitched book; keeping William young, too, true to the dreams of his youth. He used the book for forty years and he kept it close even when it was full, like a missal, a reference for himself, his own chapter and verse.

His scratchy, itchy hand races over every page, uncontained, like his mind, running in parallel lines, then down the sides, then upside down; sometimes round sketches at the centre of the page, sometimes wandering off on its own accord. When he got to the end he turned the book around and started writing again from the back. Paper was expensive, after all. His *Finnegans Wake*. There's no rhyme or reason to it, although it's full of both. It's a vortex of ideas, an anatomy lesson, and I can barely follow Blake's process, his neural networks firing like sparks in the dead of his night.

All those dreams in Lambeth and Soho, the raging sea on Felpham's shore; like the tide, it holds nothing back: it is what he was for. Continually overwritten and overdrawn, it lies in loving layers of meaning beyond any palimpsest, any ancient manuscript. It's action art in action, bespattered with intuition, accusation, assertion and even revenge, not least against his fellow artists and unfaithful friends.

As I open it up everything else fades away around me: the lights, the hush, the weight of a building laden with all the books in the world. I hope Catherine can't see how I tremble. I'd like to howl. I turn the pages, trying to follow his train of thought. His hand is almost illegible as it fights to catch up with himself.

He has observed the Golden Rule
Till he's become the Golden Fool

It's impossible to tell which came first, the pictures or the words; where one begins or the other ends. They merge into a single mass, a tense echo of the intensity of his visions. His whole design like a black hole outside our universe.

A woman's figure, lithe like a tree, reaches upwards, great sprays of ecstatic branches curving into the air out of her hands. She's Daphne, root-bound, energy made graphic, human-botanic-astro-real; part woman, part plant, part leaping dolphin. Everything is interchangable; it's all about how you feel. Dark angels and stray faces fly like insects, hovering over the proceedings as the mile-long verses of words slide into one another, alongside dates and aphorisms and new demands for attention. It is incredibly childlike, this sense of the unconstrained,

Ideas
of
Good & Evil

such an intimate thing I feel I should look away. Like finding someone's private stash of porn. Especially when I find myself peeking round the bedroom door, a dressing table and mirror to one side, Kate sitting on the edge of the bed, one gartered leg crossed elegantly over her knee, dainty foot held out like a dancer, curly head bent as she adjusts her stockings.

Behind her lies her forever lover, William, curled up on the pillow, head in the arch of his arm, dreaming in the morning light. There's a couplet underneath, a caption to the coupling that has just taken place:

When a Man has a Married Wife
he finds out whether
Her knees & elbows are only
glued together

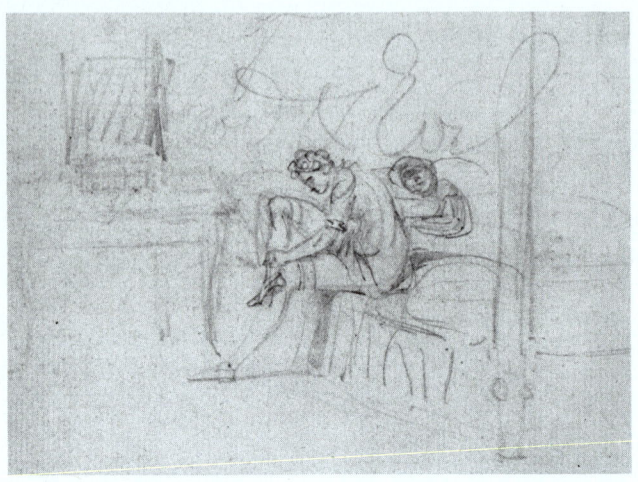

It's a scene from Rembrandt or *Don't Look Now* or *Ulysses* or a parody of a Gillray cartoon. But who cares who pays the rent when you're lying next to me?

I'm a voyeur and I'm getting all the clues at the last minute, just as I'm trying to finish this book. As though he's been playing tricks on me all along and I got it all wrong. His words collide like worlds, never-ending songs, always going on. This is literally, literally, how his mind worked, the engine room of his art. There are drafts for the *Songs of Innocence* and *The Gates of Paradise* in here, but it's hard to disentangle them from the briars of his breathless graffiti, to tell them apart. It's so entirely random, and therefore entirely of a piece, that when you're least expecting it, like love, suddenly there—under a note on the Virginity of the Virgin Mary & Joanna Southcott—is his crouching tyger, drawn in pencil, then exquisitely inked in. It was sketched for a scene in Hayley's *Ballads*; but it looks more like a page from Darwin's journal or a creature from Hokusai's *Great Picture Book of Everything*.

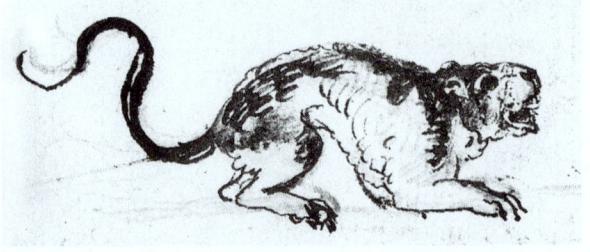

Tail curling in the air like a lash, forepaws and claws ready to leap, a loving snarl on their face, their velvet tears, indisputably a living animal to the life, drawn from the life. Did he who made him stand in front of the cage at the 'Change as the tyger posed for their immortality and potential clients? This is the artist's own drama, flicking through the pages of his life, switching backwards and forwards in time, filled with quivering moments of revelation, trauma and ecstasy.

Tuesday Jan^{ry} 20 1807 between Two & Seven in the Evening – Despair

> *I say I shant live five years*
> *And if I have one it will be a Wonder*
>
> June 1793.

Figures curve in the air as if in a ballet by Matisse. A man is seen from the rear, pissing. A demon careers in with streaming hair, a miniature human in their mouth. A baby sits in a cage like a pet budgie. And in one corner, a tiny figure looks down at a hound at their feet, the dog's head turned up longingly at their keeper. Such intense attachment in so few strokes.

Imagination is a matter of scale. A wing-wide drawing based on Michelangelo sees a gigantic eagle swooping down out of the cloud to feed on a naked female, her arms and thighs akimbo. Another minute sketch looks like a peach, but turns out to be a man's bare arse. Everything is rehearsed in this catalogue, an interior monologue, Blake's work-in-progress.

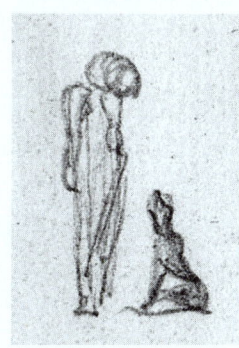

A pair of stick figures stand at the bottom of a ladder as a third climbs up to the crescent moon. A pencilled Nebuchadnezzar, the size of a matchbox, crawls like a defeated lion. And in quick clear lines—because, unlike eagles and tygers, he saw it on the pillow next to him every day—is Kate's face, open, clear-eyed, seeing into space; a clairvoyant stare so powerful it makes me scared.

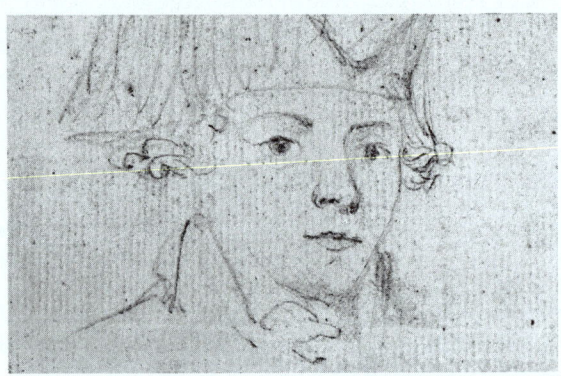

23 May 1810 – found the Word Golden.

The Nature of Visionary Fancy or Imagination is very little known

South Molton St

Sunday, August 1, 1807.

My Wife was told by a Spirit to look for her fortune by opening by chance a book which she had in her hand . . . I was so well pleased with her Luck that I thought I would try my Own . . .

I'm tempted to say that in Kate he'd found his happy medium. He often addresses himself in the third person as he imagines, for the Year 1810, Additions to Blake's Catalogue of Pictures, as if he might rerun that lost cause, his sole exhibition, of which no one took any notice. He is reduced to reviewing himself.

His own critical mass. No great work of art ever prospered without adversity. Blake became his own enemy and best friend by being so wild and untamed island of his own.

'Madman', I have been call'd, 'Fool' they call thee
I wonder which they Envy, Thee or Me?

And there is The Tyger, in words, written out, then crossed out again. Scored by their claws. Razored, roaring, revolutionary, ready to pounce. Pure energy. A happy sad thing.

I realise that if I'd seen all this before, I might have not written this same book. Perhaps I ought to turn it around, and start writing it again from the back.

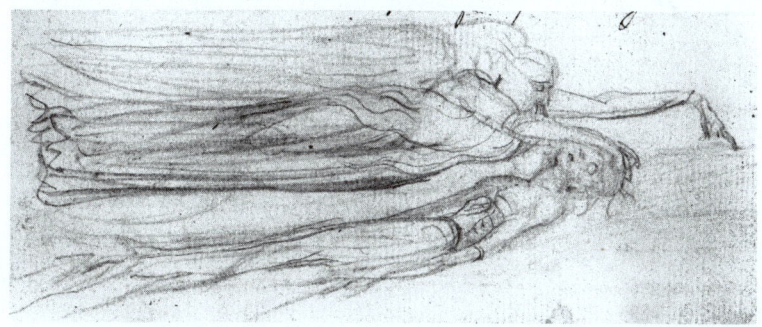

Then, as if this weren't enough, God arrives on the scene, out of the blue, zooming in over Adam's body; another Michelangelo performance, one hand on the forehead of the first human, the other touching the new-made earth. The speed of the drawing, swift as a deity's wings in an astral wind, presents the bare bones of the colour print it will become: its scaffolding, its skeleton, its layers stripped away, only to reveal something even more mysterious underneath. Naked, uncut. Art, someone said, is imagination acting on experience. His innocence. He was a man without a mask, said Samuel Palmer.

William Blake: Madman, Mental Prince, English Blake:
A New Kind of Man.

As though everything else, everything after this, was about colouring in. One endless cycle, a circuit completed, then started again. Rather like trying to write about him; he's always bringing you back to where he started. Back to where he began.

I still know nothing about him.

So I stopped writing this book, and went back to the sea.

Credits

Editor: Louise Haines, with thanks to Nicolas Pearson. *Co-ordination:* Victoria Pullen. *Production:* Alex Gingell. *Copy editor:* Tim Waller. *Proof reader:* Holly Kyte. *Book design:* Richard Marston. *Cover design:* Jo Thomson. *Publicity:* Patrick Hargadon. *Marketing:* Olivia Marsden. *Photography:* Jeroen Hoekendijk, James Mackay, Howard Sooley, Andrew Sutton, Martin Rosenbaum. *Representation:* Georgina Capel, Irene Boldini, Rachel Conway, Polly Halladay. *Pegasus Books USA:* Jessica Case, Claiborne Hancock, Meghan Jusczak, Maria Fernandez. *Website:* Krishna Stott, philiphoare.co.uk.

Thanks

United Kingdom: Adam Low, Neil Tennant, Michael Bracewell, George Shaw, Angela Cockayne, Olivia Laing, Richard Porter, James Mackay, Tilda Swinton, Keith Collins, Amanda Wilkinson, Laura Cumming, Iain Sinclair, James Norton, Gareth Evans, Andrew Logan, Tony Peake, Hugo Vickers, Robin Muir, Peter Conradi, Prophecy Coles, Edward Parnell, Martin Thomas, Jay Auborn, Dawn Melville, Anthony Caleshu, Woodrow Kernohan, Ros Carter and the John Hansard Gallery, Paul Flather, Katie Taylor, Katherine Anteney, Rachel Collingwood, Carole Burns and my colleagues at the University of Southampton.

Alex Farquharson, Alice Chasey, Aki Gurung, Jennifer Carding and Tate archives; Jonathan Mullard and The Blake Cottage Trust; Imogen Greenhalgh and the Royal Academy of Arts; the

Keith Collins Will Trust; LUMA Foundation; Diamuird MacCulloch, Peter Davidson and the Gerard Manley Hopkins archive, Campion Hall; Ellen Gage and Emma Darbyshire, The Fitzwilliam Museum; Matthew Waters and Catherine Angerson, The British Library; Jessica Sutcliffe and The Helen Muspratt Archive, The Bodleian Library; Lucy Bamfold, Derby Museums; Susan Pacitti, Glasgow Life.

Ireland: Adrian Le Harivel and the National Gallery of Ireland, Simon O'Connor and the Museum of Literature Ireland; Logan Sisley and the Hugh Lane Gallery; Fr Noel Barber, SJ; Margaret Doyle and Clongowes Wood College SJ; Catherine Nunes, Alan Gilsenan and the Shaking Bog Festival; Vanessa Daws, Michael Daly, Patricia and Marguerite Byrne, Angel Bruton, Peter Wilson, Clara Fuquen, Jim and Ann Wilson.

USA: John Waters, Dennis Minsky, Debbie Minsky and Dory, Mary Martin, James Balla, Albert Merola, Sal Del Deo; Martin Smick, Duane Slick, Andrew Raftery, Christin Fitzgerald and the Rhode Island School of Design; Ellen Gallagher, Marc Balet, Nejma Beard, Sara Atwood, Scott McVay; Sharon Polli and the Fine Arts Work Center, Provincetown; Stormy Mayo and the Center for Coastal Studies, Provincetown.

Home: Christina Moore, Nigel Larcombe-Williams, Oliver and Cyrus Larcombe Moore; Katherine Moore, Sam, Harriet, Jacob, Lydia and Max Goonetillake; Clare Goddard and Sheila Goddard; Michael Holden and Charlie Baker; Mark Ashurst, Lilian Ashurst and Freddie Ashurst.

Philip Hoare, Southampton/Provincetown, February 2025

Images

Front and back endpapers, Introduction, 12, 14 a, 205, 210, Pl IV, a, XII, a, Tate Images; 204 Tate/ Estate of Eileen Agar, 296, Tate/Estate of Humphrey Spender, 300, 320, Tate/Estate of John Banting; 303, Tate/Estate of Barbara Ker-Seymer; 8, 23, 74, 147, 155, 197, 199, 202, 214, 236, 302, 322, 332 a, Pl II a, IV a, b, c, VII, a, b, c, IX, a, b, X b, XII,b, c, d, XIV, a, Alamy; 10, courtesy Martin Thomas and the Keith Collins Will Trust; 14 b, Henry Grant Collection © London Museum; 16, William Stukeley, *Abury, A Temple of the British Druids*, 1742; 34, 35, 37, Algernon Blackwood, *Pan's Garden*, 1911; 48, 190, 190, Alexander Gilchrist, *The Life of William Blake*, 1863, 1880; 50, 120, 237, Metropolitan Museum of Art; 52, 61, 99, 143, Pl III a, Library of Congress; 68, 70, Morgan Library, 78, 79, 83; Conrad Gesner, *Historiae Animalium*, 1588; 81, 98 a,179, Pl I, Wikipedia; 92, courtesy of the Royal Society Library; 98 b, 100, 121, 136, 211, 225, 227, 384, 388, Pl II b, VIII b, XI, a, b, c, d, courtesy of Yale University Library; 109, National Gallery of Art, Washington; 118, 181, 194, Pl V b, VI, b, c, VIII, a, XV, a, XVI, The Fitzwilliam Museum, Cambridge; 121 b & c, *International Times* archive; 138, 189 A. St. John Adcock, *Famous London Houses*, Dent, 1927; 170, 298, 342, National Portrait Gallery, 176, 184, 186, 196, 217, 332 a, 446, 447, 448, 449, Pl III b, Bridgeman Images; 191, New York Public Library; 207, Estate of Helen Muspratt, Bodleian Library; 218, Thomas Hawkins, *The book of the great sea-dragons, Ichthyosauri and Plesiosaur, gedolim tanini, of Moses. Extinct monsters of the ancient earth*, 1840; 222, Estate of Eileen Agar/Bridgeman; 261, courtesy of James Mackay; 283, courtesy of Clongowes Wood College, SJ; 284, Marius Maxwell, *Stalking Big Game with a Camera in Equatorial Africa*, 1924; 285, Jeroen Hoekendijk; 290, Michel Soskine; 309, 311, 335, 345, 351, 353, 356, 427, Getty Images; 372, © Illustrated London News Ltd. / Mary Evans; 410-417, courtesy of Rhode Island School of Design Museum; 421, Studiocanal Films Ltd/Mary Evans; 428, Martin Rosenbaum; Pl III c, Derby

William Blake and the Sea Monsters of Love could not have been written without the pristine brilliance of the William Blake Archive, blakearchive.org

William Blake 28 November 1757 – 12 August 1827
Catherine Blake 25 April 1762 – 18 October 1831

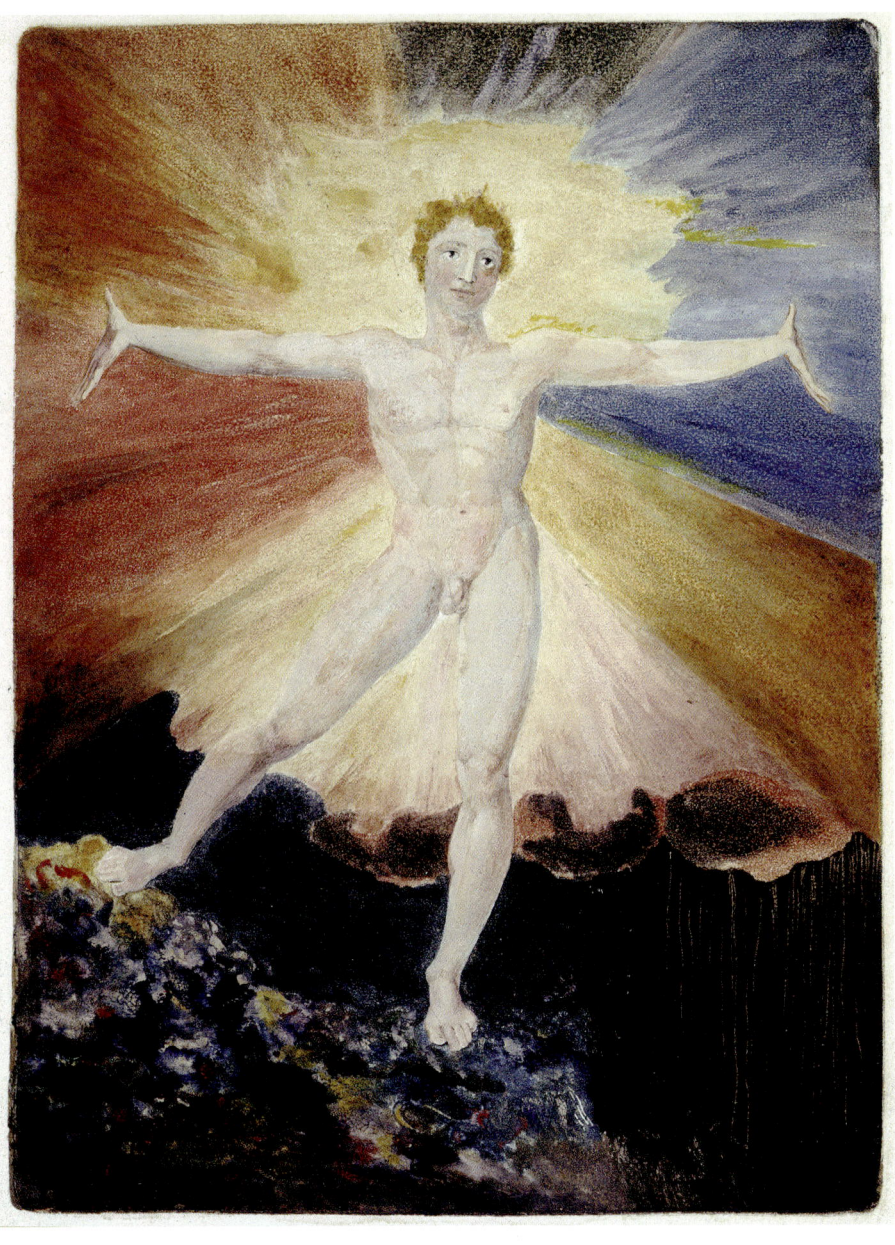

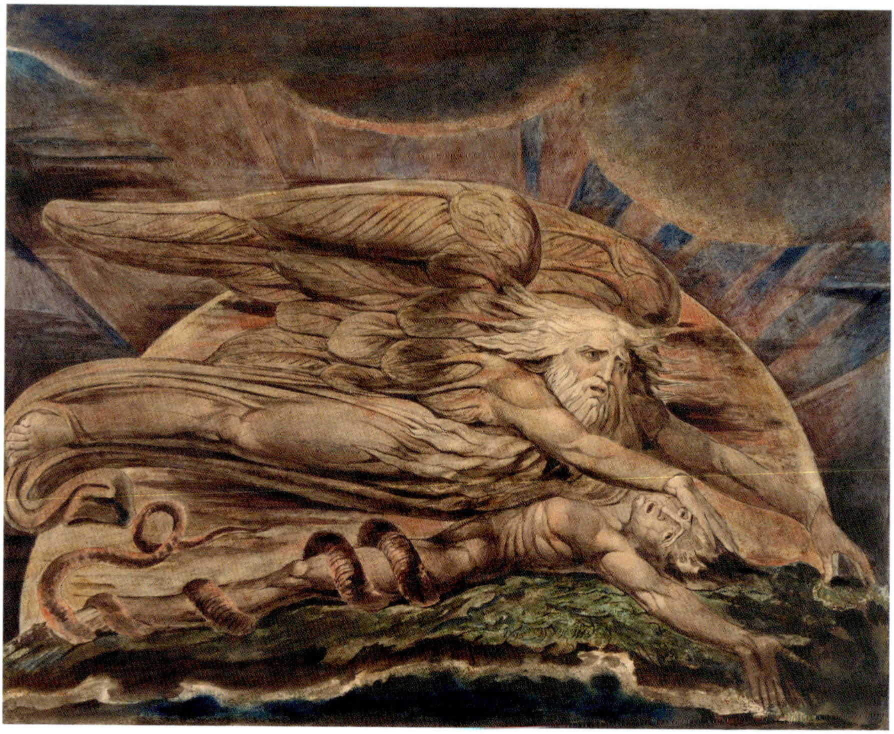

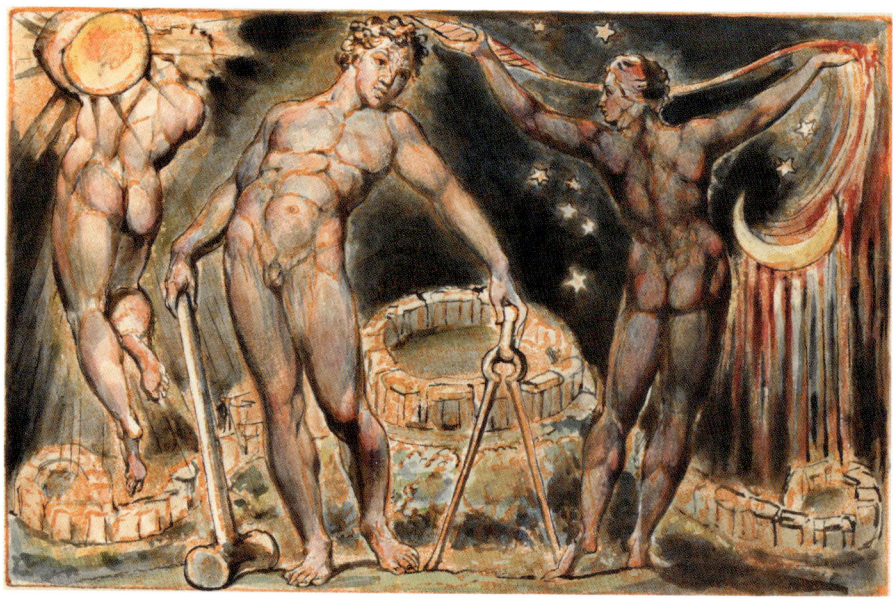

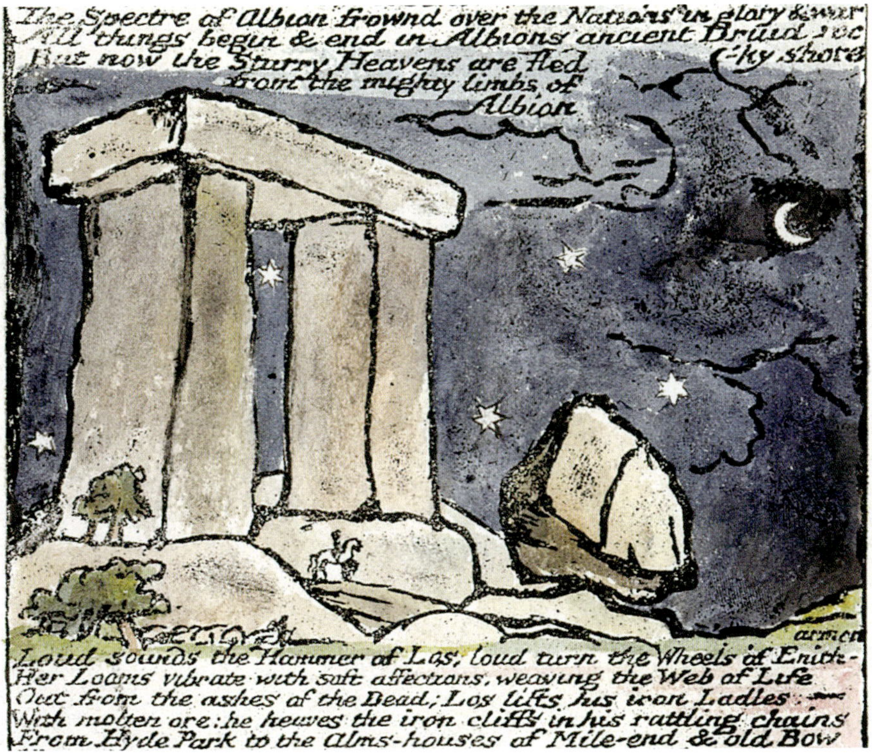

The Spectre of Albion frownd over the Nations in glory & in war
All things begin & end in Albions ancient Druid rocky shore
But now the Starry Heavens are fled from the mighty limbs of Albion

Loud sounds the Hammer of Los, loud turn the Wheels of Enitharmon
Her Looms vibrate with soft affections, weaving the Web of Life
Out from the ashes of the Dead; Los lifts his iron Ladles
With molten ore: he heaves the iron cliffs in his rattling chains
From Hyde Park to the Alms-houses of Mile-end & old Bow

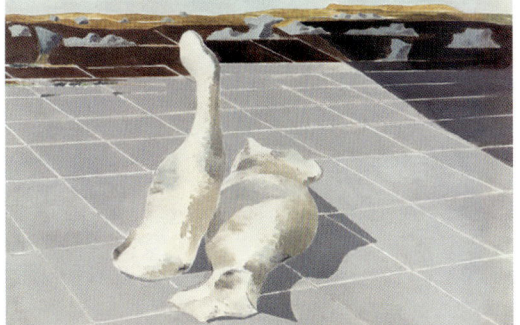

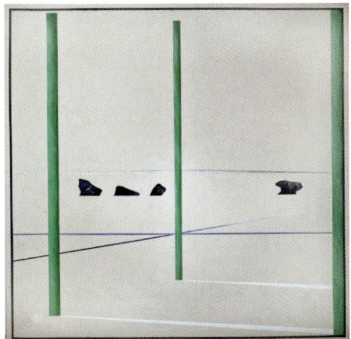

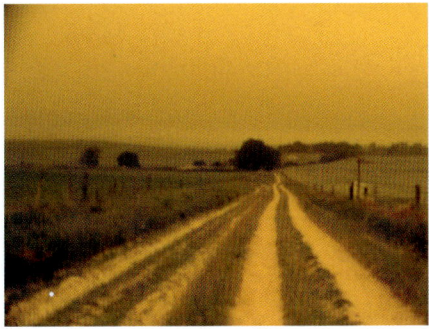

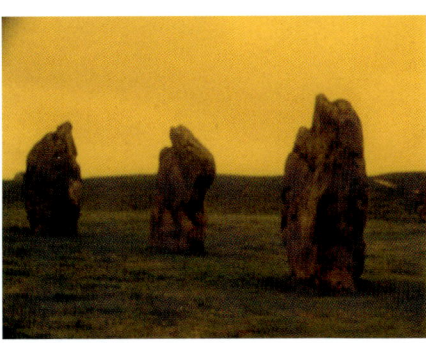

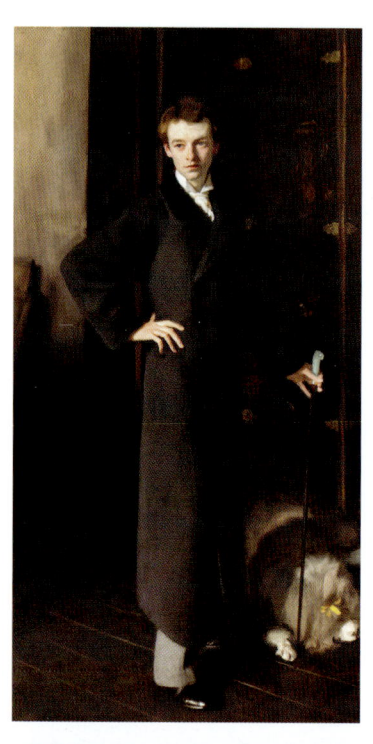
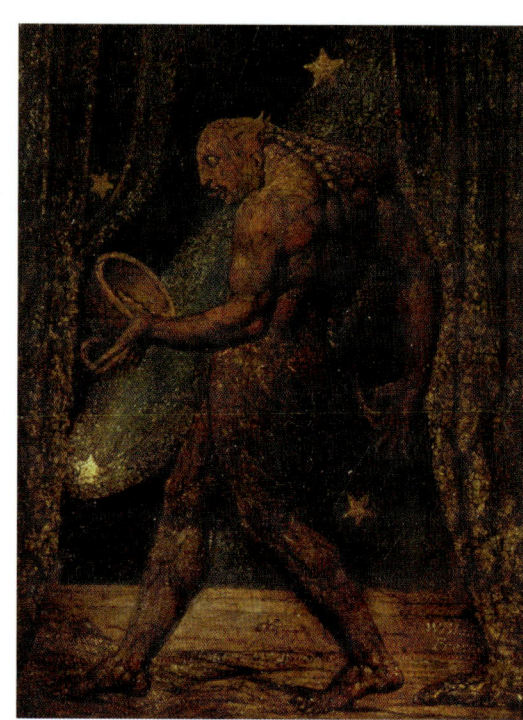
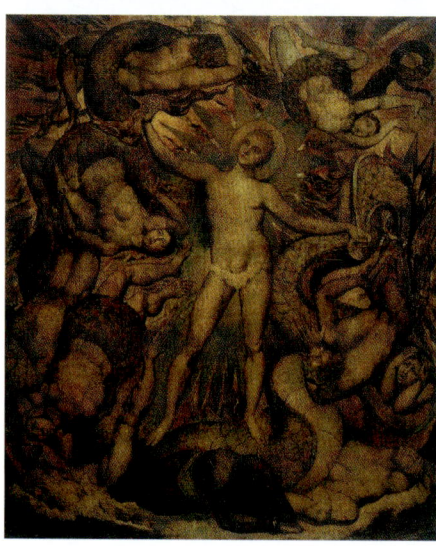
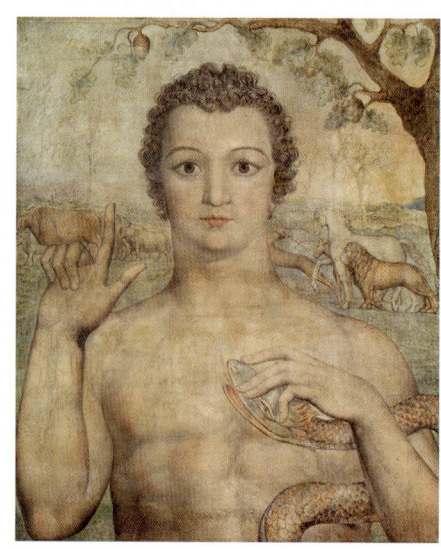

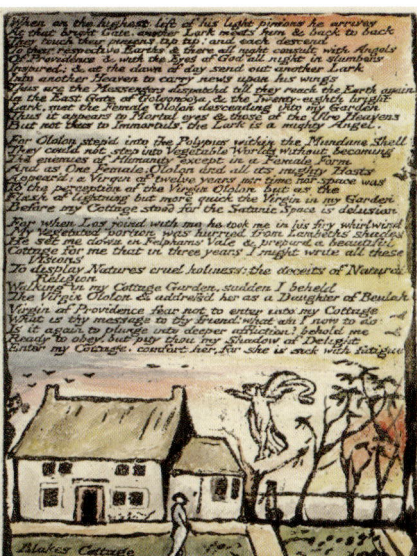

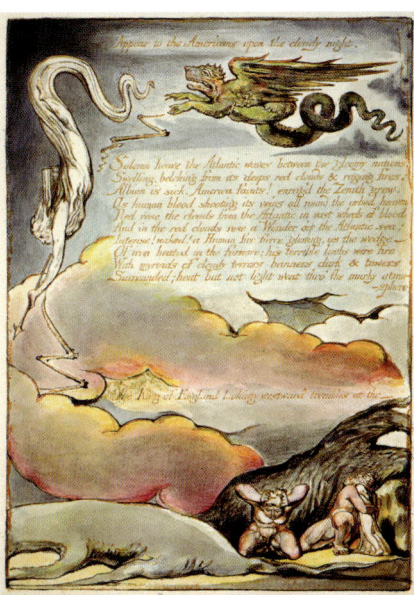

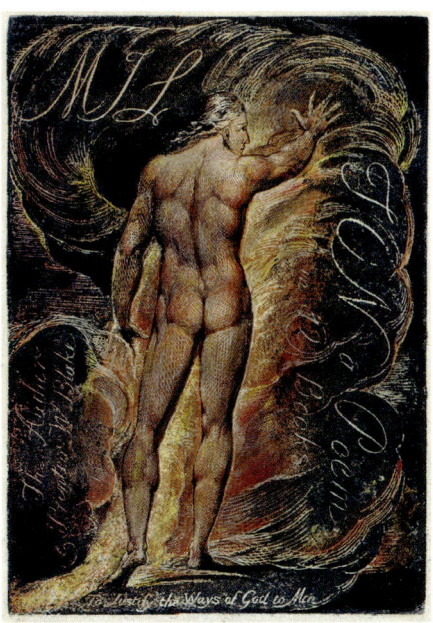

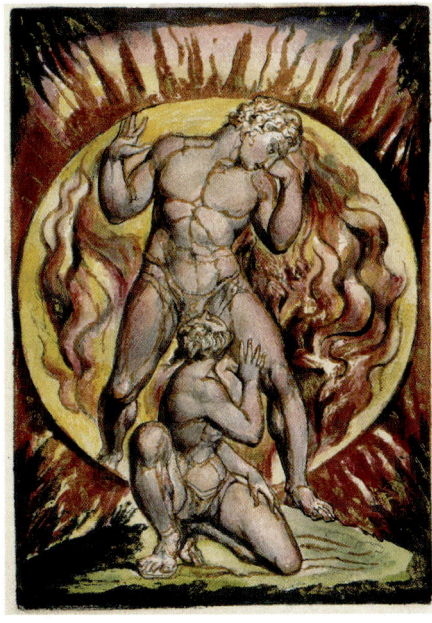

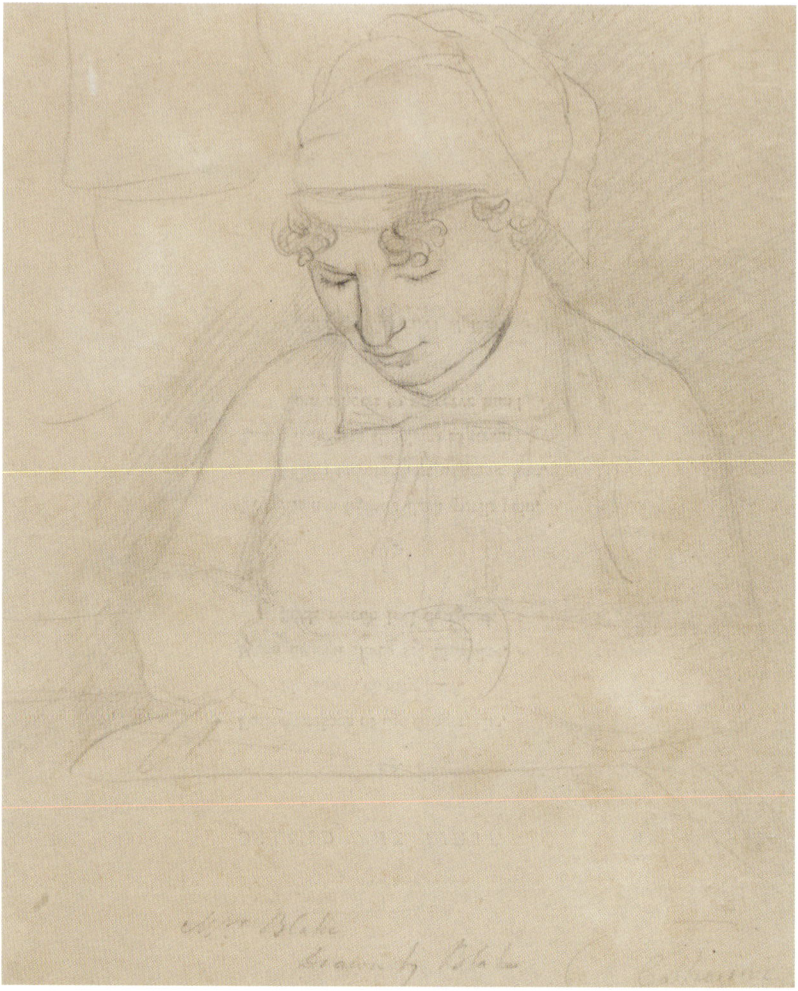

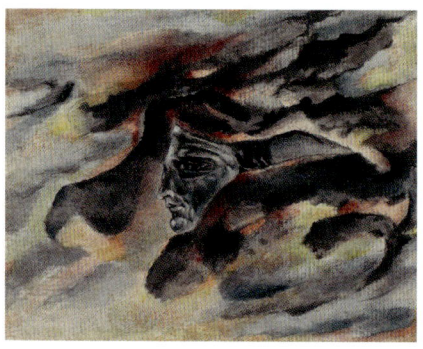
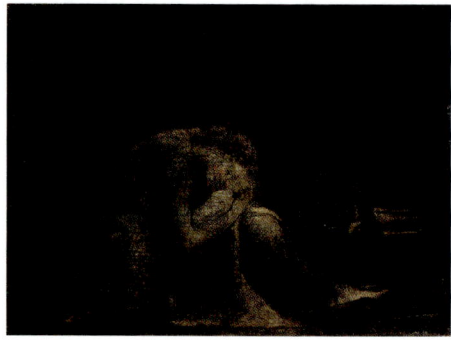

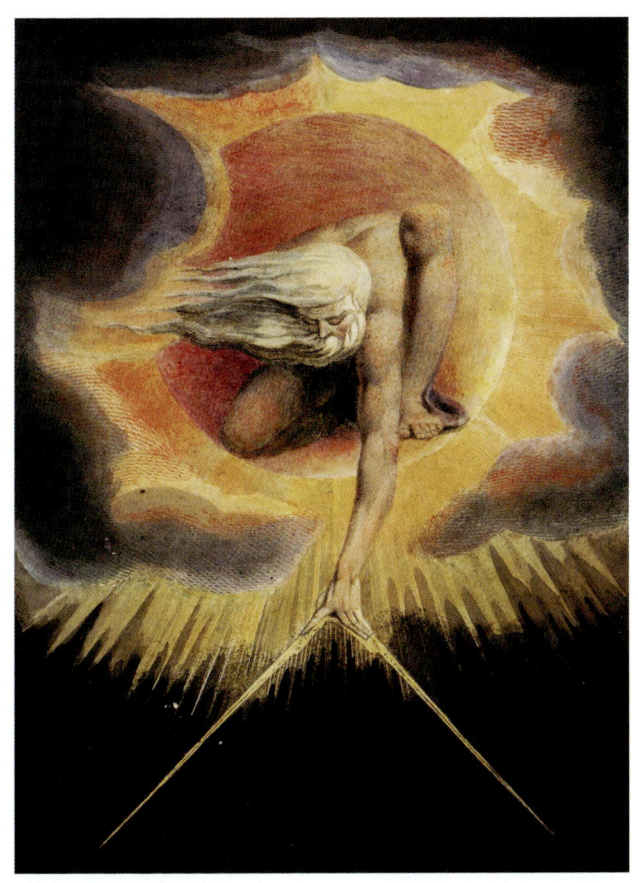

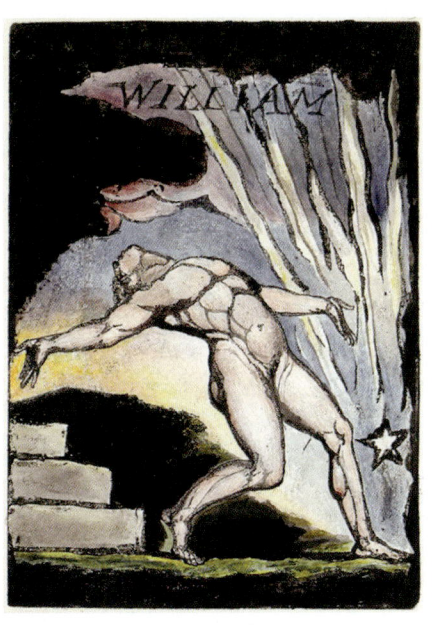

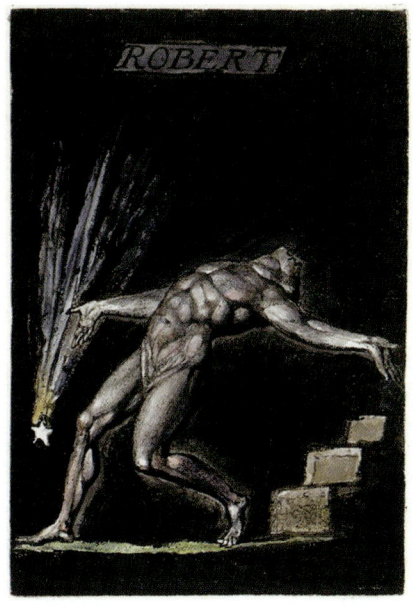

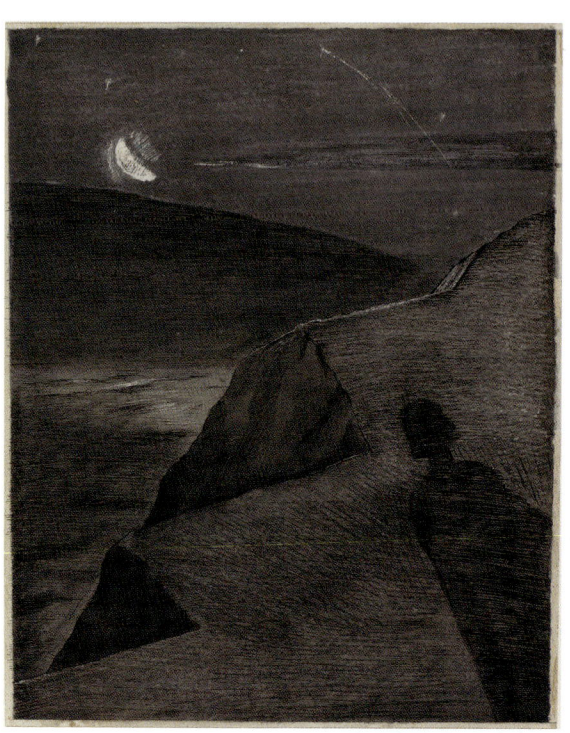

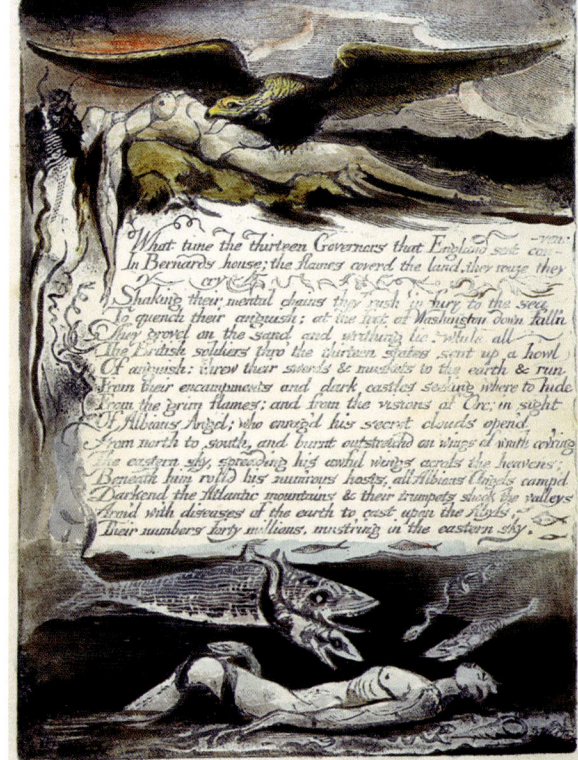

What time the thirteen Governors that England sent con--
In Bernards house; the flames coverd the land, they rouze they
cry
Shaking their mental chains they rush in fury to the sea
To quench their anguish: at the feet of Washington down falln
They grovel on the sand and writhing lie, while all
The British soldiers thro the thirteen states sent up a howl
Of anguish: threw their swords & muskets to the earth & run
From their encampments and dark castles seeking where to hide
From the grim flames; and from the visions of Orc; in sight
Of Albions Angel; who enraged his secret clouds opend
From north to south, and burnt outstretched on wings of wrath coving
The eastern sky, spreading his awful wings across the heavens;
Beneath him rolld his numrous hosts, all Albions Angels camped
Darkend the Atlantic mountains & their trumpets shook the valleys
Armd with diseases of the earth to cast upon the Abyss
Their numbers forty millions, mustring in the eastern sky.

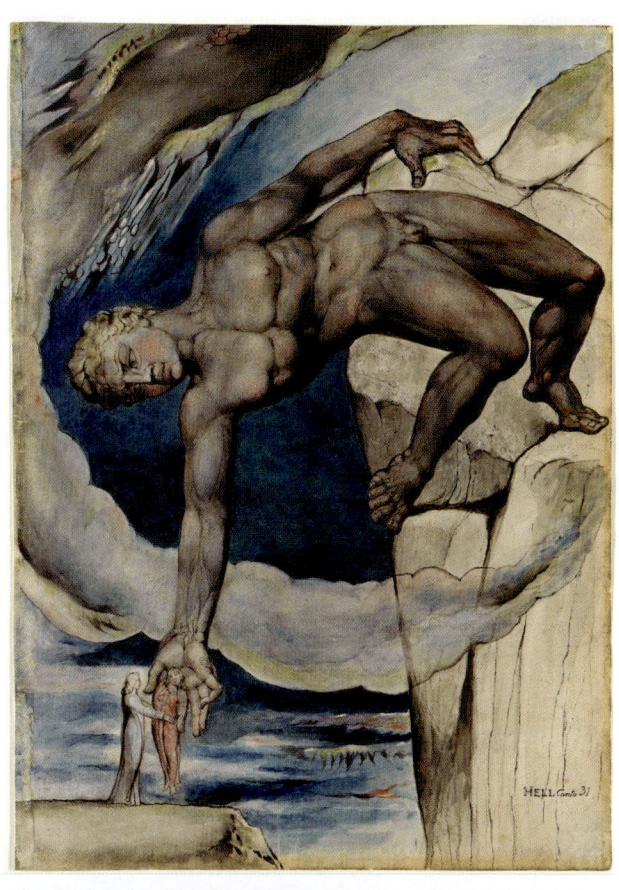

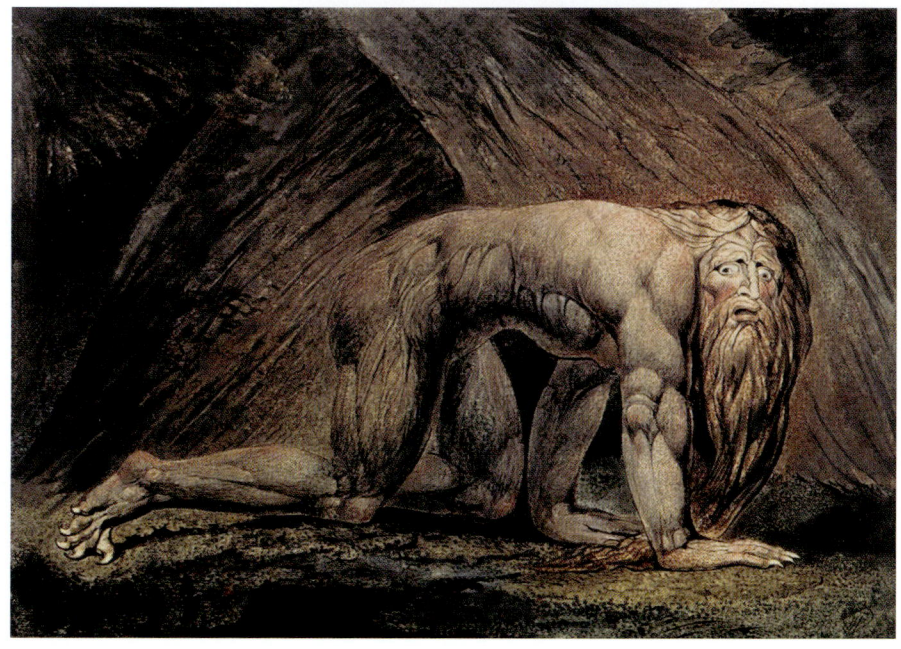

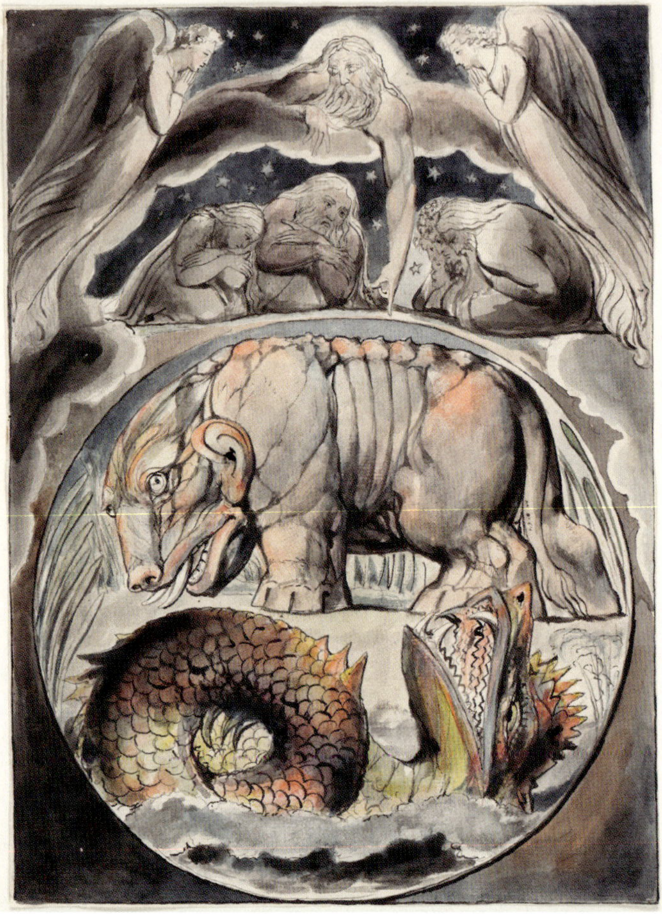

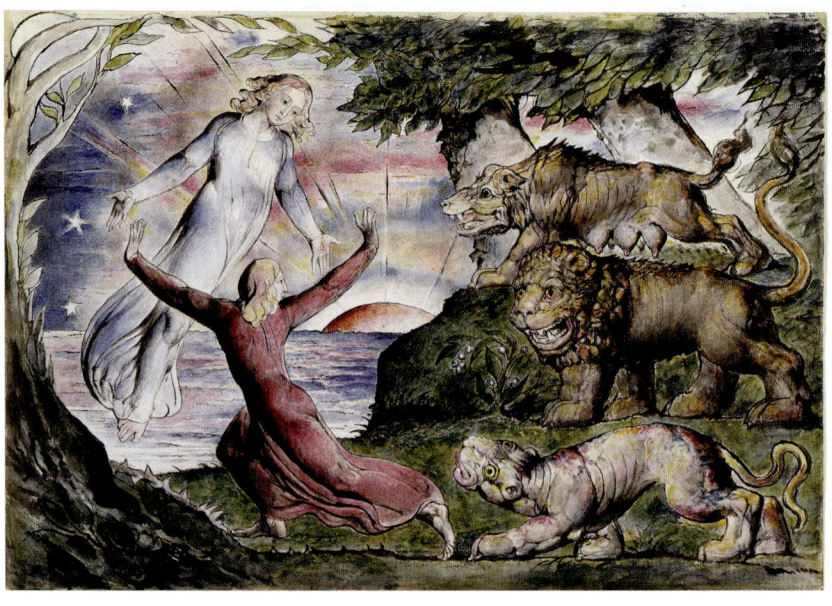

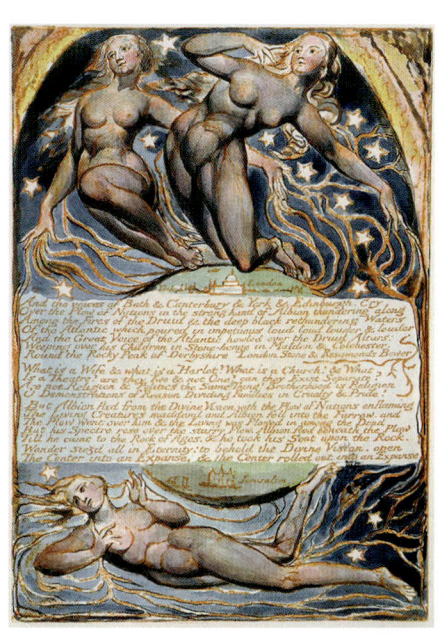
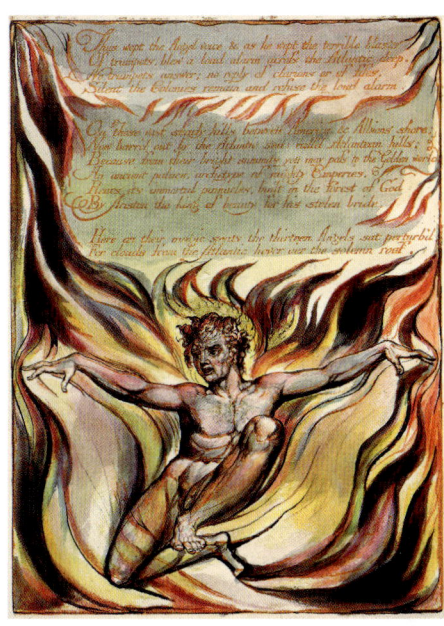
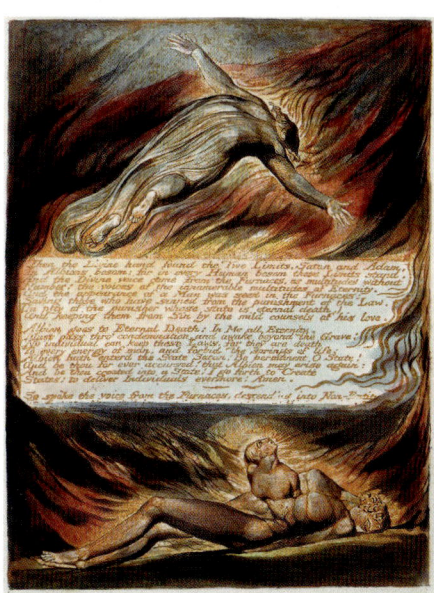
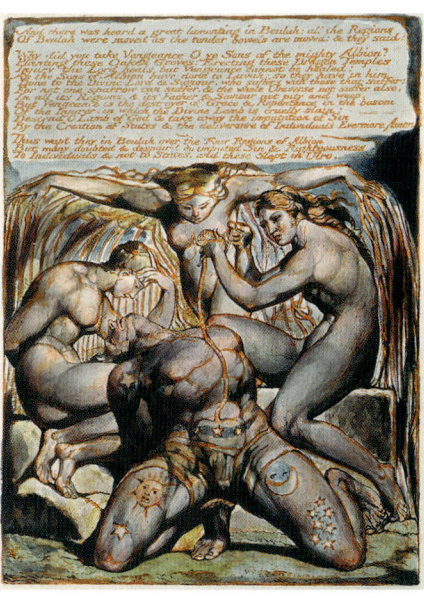

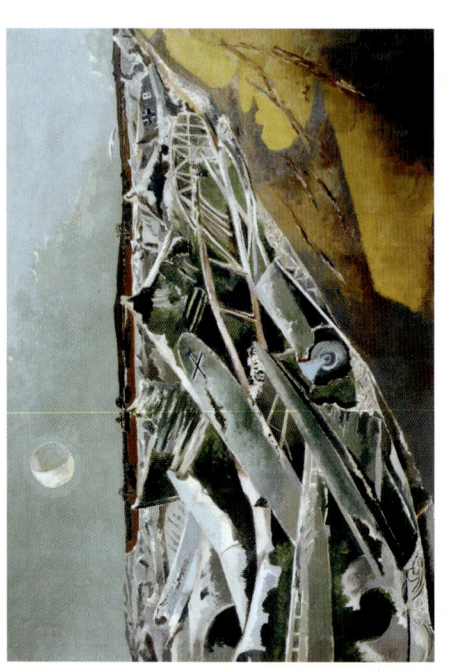
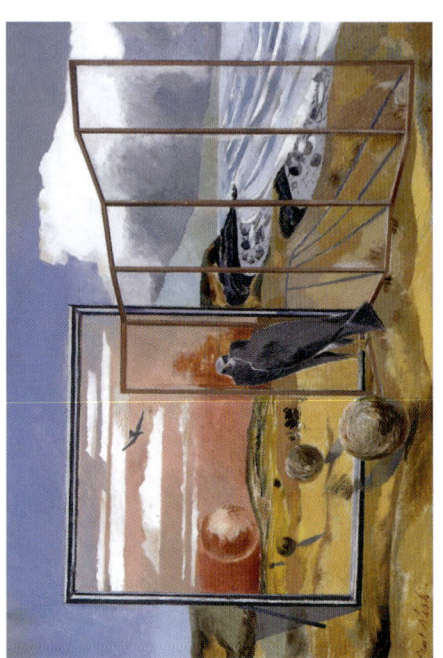
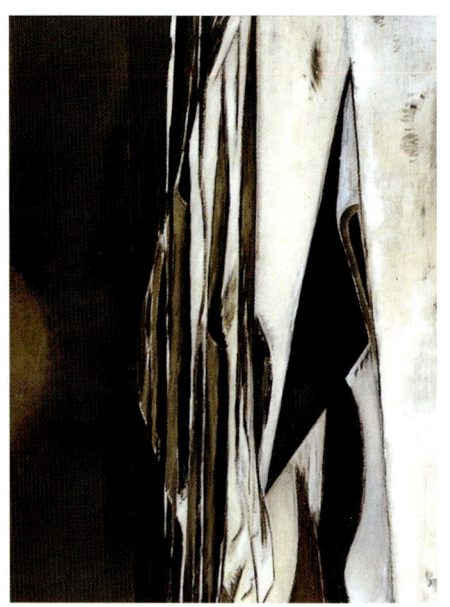
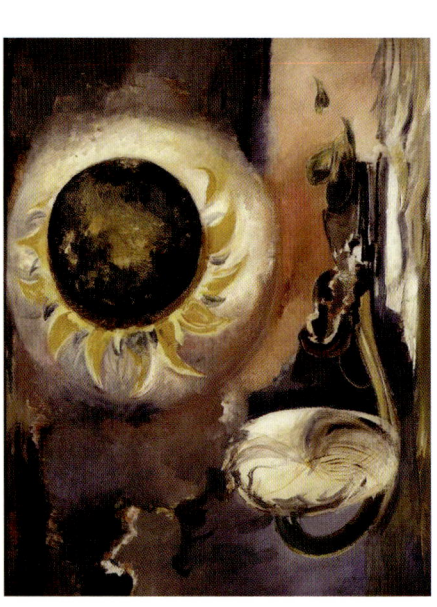

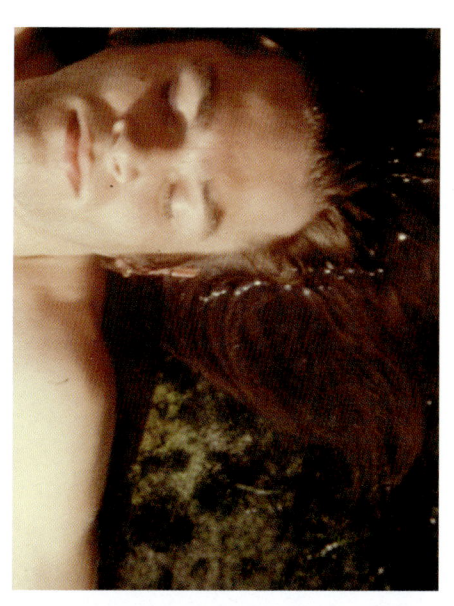
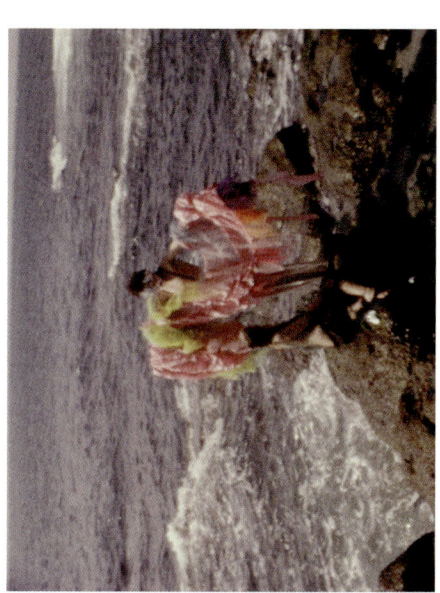
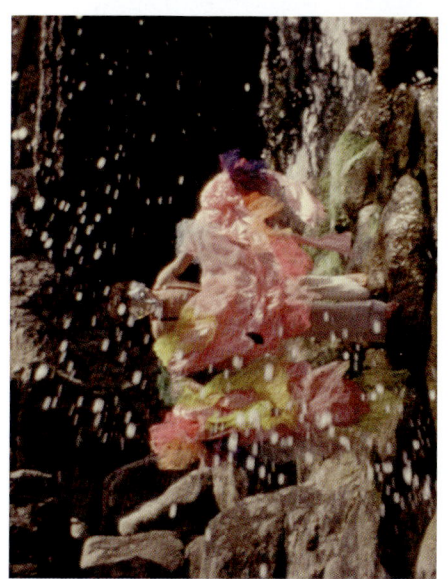
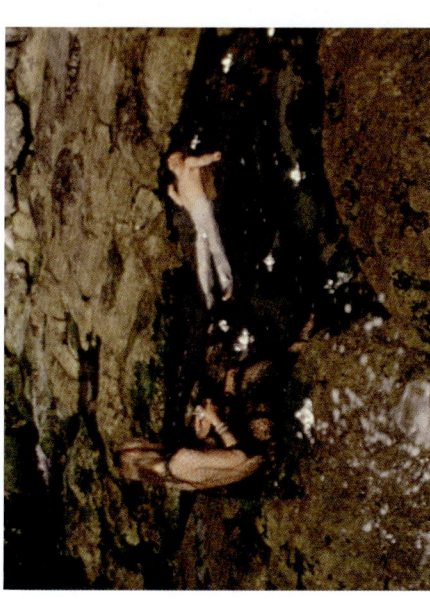

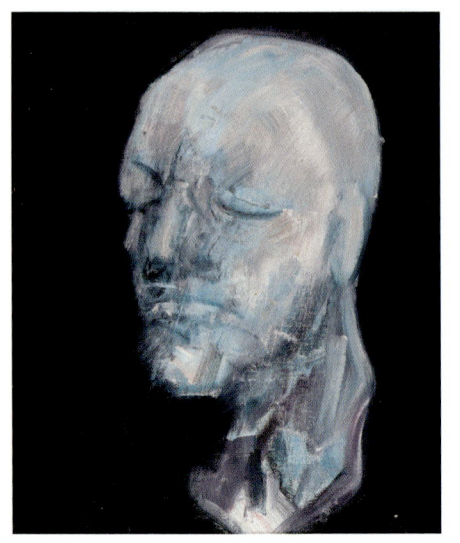

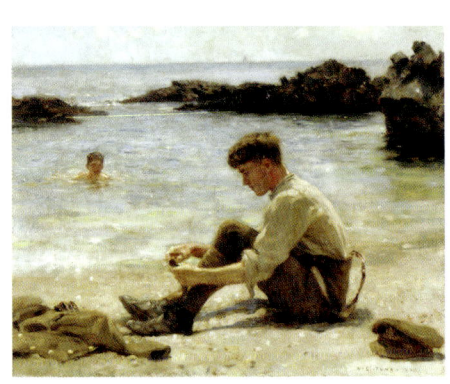

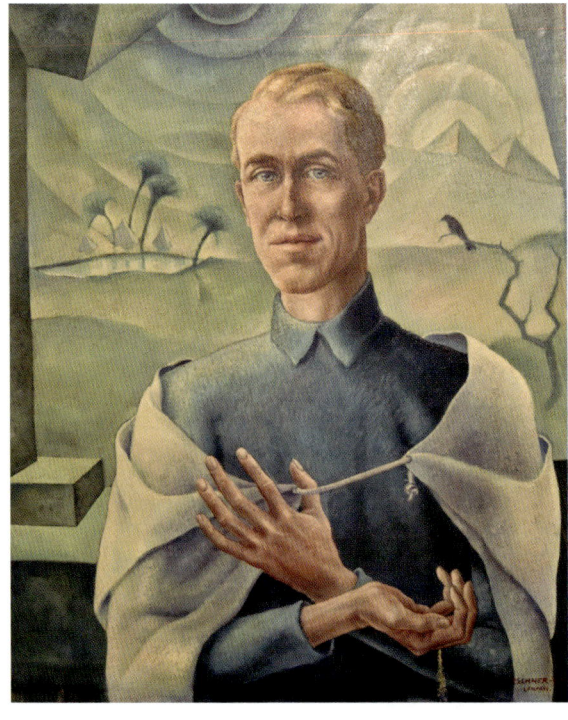

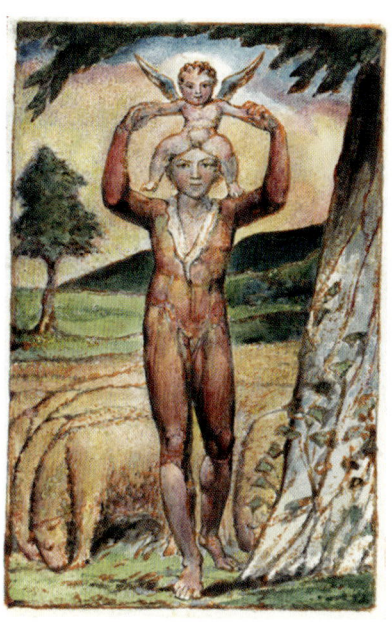

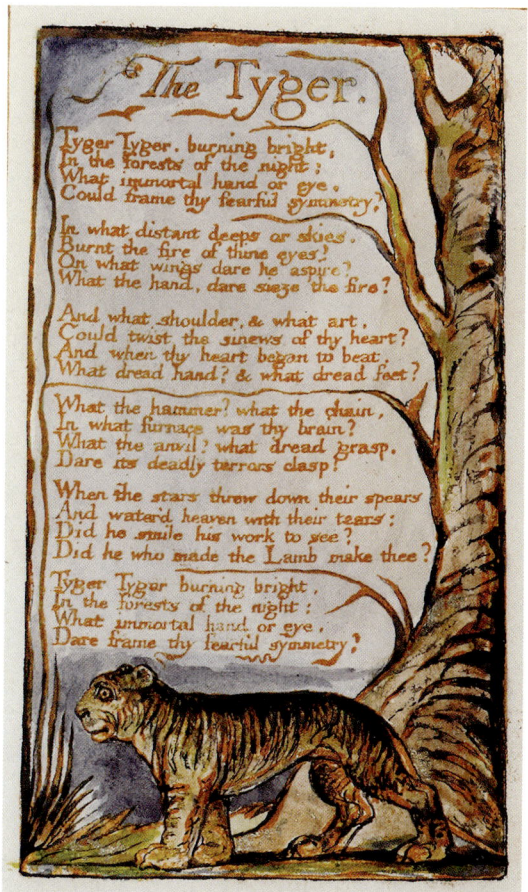

The Tyger.

Tyger Tyger. burning bright,
In the forests of the night;
What immortal hand or eye.
Could frame thy fearful symmetry?

In what distant deeps or skies.
Burnt the fire of thine eyes?
On what wings dare he aspire?
What the hand, dare sieze the fire?

And what shoulder, & what art,
Could twist the sinews of thy heart?
And when thy heart began to beat.
What dread hand? & what dread feet?

What the hammer? what the chain,
In what furnace was thy brain?
What the anvil? what dread grasp.
Dare its deadly terrors clasp?

When the stars threw down their spears
And water'd heaven with their tears:
Did he smile his work to see?
Did he who made the Lamb make thee?

Tyger Tyger burning bright.
In the forests of the night:
What immortal hand or eye.
Dare frame thy fearful symmetry?

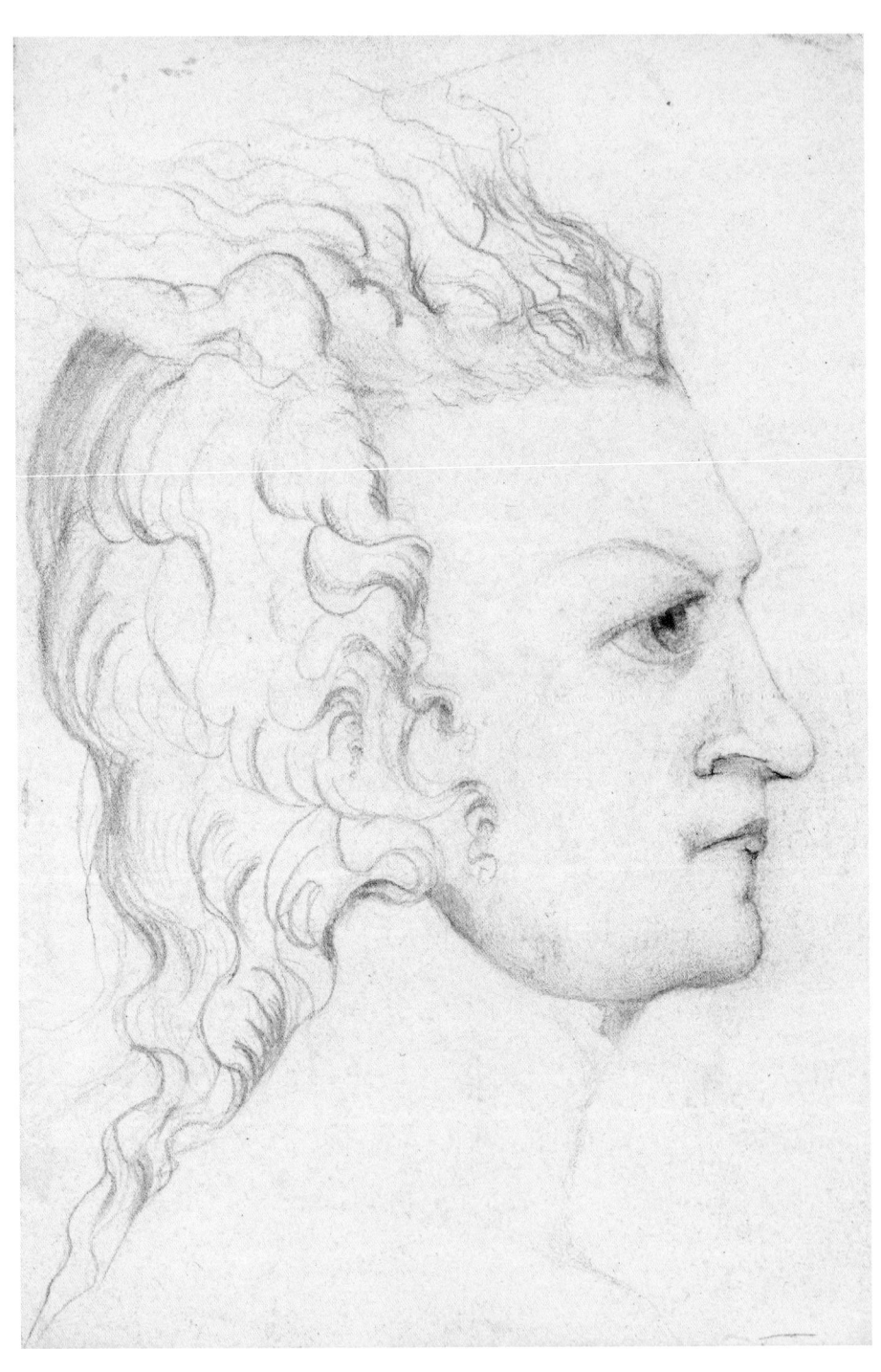

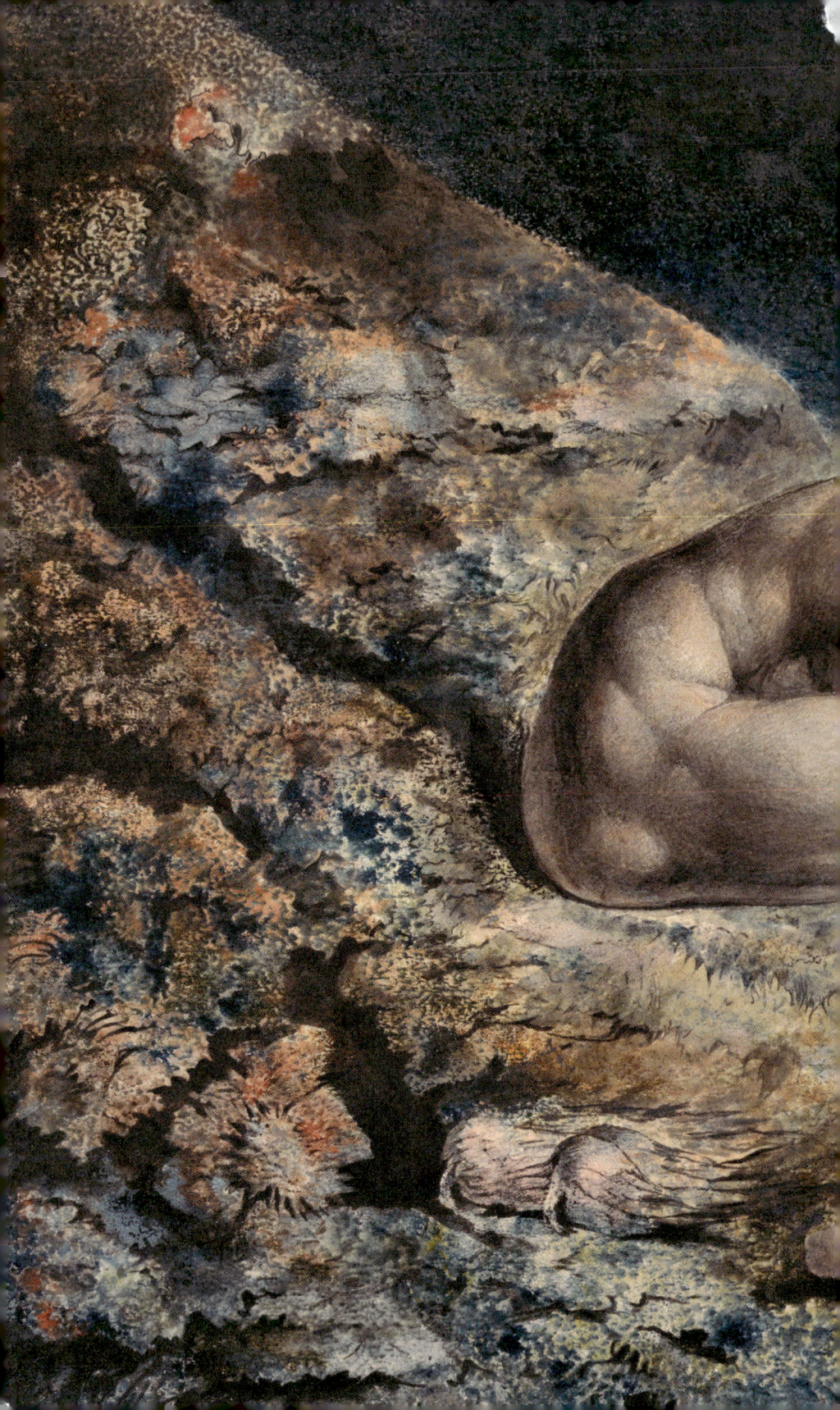